The Pope's Army

The Pope's Army

The Papacy in Diplomacy and War

John Carr

Pen & Sword
MILITARY

First published in Great Britain in 2019 by
Pen & Sword Military
An imprint of
Pen & Sword Books Ltd
Yorkshire – Philadelphia

Copyright © John Carr 2019

ISBN 978 1 52671 489 3

A CIP catalogue record for this book is
available from the British Library.

Printed and bound in the UK by TJ International Ltd,
Padstow, Cornwall.

Pen & Sword Books Limited incorporates the imprints of Atlas,
Archaeology, Aviation, Discovery, Family History, Fiction, History,
Maritime, Military, Military Classics, Politics, Select, Transport,
True Crime, Air World, Frontline Publishing, Leo Cooper, Remember
When, Seaforth Publishing, The Praetorian Press, Wharncliffe
Local History, Wharncliffe Transport, Wharncliffe True Crime
and White Owl.

For a complete list of Pen & Sword titles please contact

PEN & SWORD BOOKS LIMITED
47 Church Street, Barnsley, South Yorkshire, S70 2AS, England
E-mail: enquiries@pen-and-sword.co.uk
Website: www.pen-and-sword.co.uk

Or

PEN AND SWORD BOOKS
1950 Lawrence Rd, Havertown, PA 19083, USA
E-mail: Uspen-and-sword@casematepublishers.com
Website: www.penandswordbooks.com

Contents

List of Plates

Prologue

For God's providence constantly uses war to correct and chasten the corrupt morals of mankind, as it also uses such afflictions to train men in a righteous and laudable way of life.

Saint Augustine (early fifth century)

His holiness, Pope Leo X, therefore, has found the pontificate in a very powerful condition, from which it is hoped that as those Popes made it great by force of arms, so he through his goodness and infinite other virtues will make it both great and venerated.

Niccolò Machiavelli, The Prince (1513)

When Machiavelli jotted down his advice to statesmen that would become his acclaimed political analysis *The Prince* in the early sixteenth century, the Roman papacy was at the height of its powers. In the fourteen centuries since its beginnings with Saint Peter, the Roman Catholic Church had soared in spiritual stature, but at the same time had found it progressively more necessary to defend itself by force of arms against foes in Italy and elsewhere. Italy itself was in chaos. As long as it administered a political state based on Rome, the papacy was compelled to employ worldly and secular measures such as warfare to preserve its more important sacred and non-worldly inner nature. 'Without the Vatican state, we could not have done our worldwide job.'[1] That state could be likened to a walnut, whose tooth-breaking outer shell protects the delicate kernel inside. This is the story of that tough outer shell, as it were.

Anyone of a thoughtful cast of mind who picks up a book with the title of *The Pope's Army* may well wonder what organized religion, as typified by the Catholic or any other faith, really has to do with the organized violence for which armies have existed since the beginning of time. The above quotation from Saint Augustine (in his massive work *City of God*) offers one explanation of why wars occur, though it's doubtful if very many people from his time to ours have really learned the lesson. Christianity, it is argued, came into the world specifically to render superfluous the use of force in human affairs by transforming the person from within, from a warlike beast to a child of God. Then why, the argument goes, has it not succeeded? Why should even popes, who hold themselves (along with Protestant and Eastern Orthodox prelates) to be the personifiers of Christian charity, ever need armies?

This book will not pretend to philosophically dissect the issue, much less resolve it. However, there are two basic attitudes to take. The first is the atheist view that since religion is a fantasy anyway, there is really no issue to resolve; churches are just human organizations like all the others, with their interests and power plays and recourses to force to get their way. But that is a bleak vision indeed, and holds out little or no hope for the betterment of humanity. The second is what might be called a 'pragmatic Christian' view: that even though Christianity is anti-violence in creed and outlook, its institutions in a fallen world often need to employ a fallen world's instruments, including that form of deadly organized violence called war.

Could the Bible be a guide? Throughout the Old Testament we are regaled with fierce and bloody descriptions of the centuries-long battle of the Israelites against a variety of foes, with the writers leaving us with no doubt whose side they are on. Then the New Testament opens with a dramatic change in tone. In the description of Jesus' arrest in the Gospel of Matthew (26: 51–2), we read of a disciple drawing his sword and chopping off an ear of the high priest's servant. 'Put up again thy sword into his place,' Jesus admonishes the attacker, 'for all that take the sword shall perish with the sword.' The incident is retold in the gospels of Mark, Luke and John, with a few variations. Luke and John report that it was the servant's right ear that was cut off; Luke adds that Jesus at once touched the man's wound and healed it, while John names the servant as Malchus but mentions no instantaneous healing. However, John provides the vital detail that it was none other than the disciple Peter who attacked the servant in the belief that he was defending his master Christ. As the Apostle Peter is credited as the founder of what grew into the Roman Catholic Church, it can be argued that he was the original one-man papal army.

There is another passage in Luke's gospel that displays Jesus' realistic thinking about what will happen when the disciples are left alone in the world: 'He that hath no sword, let him sell his garment, and buy one.' (Luke 22: 36–8) The successors of Saint Peter felt compelled to pick up that sword and use it over the centuries – at least until 1870. At the risk of making a generalization, the combined biblical message might be: practice peace, but prepare for war in case it comes. If one were to ask any popes in past centuries why they led or employed armies, they would doubtless cite the above passage from Luke.

I had toyed with the vague idea for a military history of the papacy for several years, until Philip Sidnell, my commissioning editor at Pen & Sword, unexpectedly retrieved my original proposal from the vaults and gave me the go-ahead. At the time, I was hard at work on my previous work for Pen & Sword, *The Komnene Dynasty: Byzantium's Struggle for Survival*, and once that was completed, began to tackle this one with hardly a hiccup. Philip's constant encouragement and kindness via e-mails across the miles of continental Europe have been a great help. I can only hope that the result meets the expectations of Pen & Sword's demanding corpus of readers. Many thanks also to the indispensable Matt Jones at Pen & Sword and copy editor Ian Hughes, who steered me away from a few hazardous editorial shoals.

I would also like to thank my good friend and head of the Vatican Radio English-language service in Rome, Dr Sean Lovett, for opening doors for my research, as well as Monsignor Charles Burns, a former Vatican archivist and present canon of Saint Peter's, who most kindly and pleasantly gave me valuable insights into the principles underlying papal diplomacy through the ages and remains a staunch pillar of support.

And in case any reader at this point or later in the book might be wondering, I am not a Roman Catholic.

JCC
April 2018

Chapter 1

To Fight or Not to Fight?

Christianity came into the world as a decidedly pacifist creed. The abolition of violence among members of the human race was inbuilt into Christ's message. Turning the other cheek was a radical message indeed, seemingly going against basic human nature. However, as evidenced by Jesus' pessimistic observation about having to buy a sword to deal with the evils to come, human nature still had to be contended with. The early Christian communities were noted among the unbelievers for their honesty and peaceableness. Some, though, tended to think of the faith in power terms: the Acts of the Apostles opens with someone asking when Christ 'will restore the kingdom of Israel'. Wisely, an answer is not given. The emphasis, instead, is on personal healing and salvation; kings and kingdoms and armies, as symptoms of the ailing world, merit no particular regard except as pesky inconveniences that have to be put up with.

But human differences quickly clouded this idyllic picture. First, the Greeks and Jews of Jerusalem argued over widows' relief, then Saint Stephen was stoned to death by the Jewish high clergy anxious to prevent the new doctrine from spreading and undermining their ancient authority. Into Stephen's place stepped a man who had cheered on the execution; the Pharisee Saul was on his way to Damascus to nab more Christians when he was stopped in his tracks by the celebrated mystic encounter recounted in the Acts. Newly converted, and with his new name of Paul, he travelled with Peter throughout the Roman provinces of the East Mediterranean spreading the faith, but always under threat of arrest.

The first military man to appear in the Acts is one Cornelius, 'a centurion of the band called the Italian band,' and described as a devout man in every way. According to the text we have, Cornelius dreamed of being ordered to contact the Apostle Peter who was reported to be in the area. Peter ignored Jewish ethnic taboos and consented to enter Cornelius' home even though he was a non-Jew and a centurion, an officer of the occupying power. This incident, perhaps symbolically, marks the start of Christianity crossing over from the Jewish cultural boundaries into the European. The apostles and their helpers remained a thorn in the side of the local authorities, disrupting local politics and condemning corruption. Riots often broke out. At one point Paul was stoned and left for dead, but recovered. When he crossed into Macedonia he and Silas were thrown into jail for preaching 'customs which are not lawful' for Roman citizens. Back in Asia Minor Paul got into considerable trouble at Ephesos (now the Turkish town of Kuşadası) when he trashed the very lucrative worship of the pagan deity Diana and escaped thanks to his powers of persuasive speech. Paul was arrested in Jerusalem and tried, and as he was a Roman citizen he was put on a ship to Rome to go before the emperor himself. At first confined in the dismal Mamertine prison in Rome, he was beheaded under Nero sometime between AD 64 and 68. The point to be made here is that throughout his career and ordeals, right up to his martyr's end, Paul not once had recourse to violence or, from what we know, even incited any use of armed force against his oppressors.

The other apostle, Peter, was of a different stamp. The story that he was the one who sliced off the high priest's servant's ear in the Garden of Gethsemane conforms to what the scriptures describe elsewhere of his character: quick to wrath and prone to acting and speaking before thinking. The intriguing question arises of what Peter was doing with a weapon that night, in what was an hour of prayer and submission. Almost certainly he was carrying it for self-defence, but this does not sit well with the general image of Jesus' disciples as messengers of peace and holiness. This image, though, may be a historical exaggeration; too much may have been made (especially) in the West of 'the Prince of Peace'. The conditions of the Roman-occupied Middle East were not the conditions, say, of placid nineteenth-century Protestant England or prosperous North America, where highly sentimentalized liberal imaginations of Christ were prone to develop. Violence was a part of the era, and any sensible person would be expected to take precautions against it. Jesus, moreover, well knew that his message was so radical and all-encompassing that it would be a source of conflict for ages to come. There was no room for wimps in the great challenge ahead: 'I am come to bring not peace but a sword.'

There are plenty of other utterances that indicate Jesus' political realism. One of them appears in Mark 13:8: 'For nation shall rise against nation, and kingdom against kingdom… and there shall be famines and troubles: these are the beginnings of sorrows.' The implication was that the nascent faith needed to be aware of these inevitable evils, and the only way it could deal with them was by forming a worldly organization of its own, complete with a defence mechanism. In short, the faith needed a 'rock' to be built on, and Peter's very name, signifying rock in Greek (his real Jewish name was Simon bar-Jona), pointed to him being it. The gospel of Matthew reports that Peter was given this honour because he was the first disciple to recognize Christ as the Messiah. 'On this rock I will build my church,' Jesus said, in words that the Roman Catholic Church has ever since used to justify a primacy (albeit a strongly-contested one). The gospels of Mark and Luke echo the story. Peter himself made his way to Rome to join Paul in about AD 42, and built up the city's Christian community. Both were put to death under Nero, Peter by being crucified upside down on the site of what is now the Vatican. In the centuries to come, the papacy would fully recompense its foes for the crime done to its founder.

In an imperfect and often hostile world it was perhaps inevitable that the Christian injunction to turn the other cheek would eventually be challenged from inside the faith itself. The great majority of early converts were poor and underprivileged and often glad to remove themselves from the pressures and conflicts of the world. But as time wore on, sects began to fracture the church and strain the basic teachings. More important, Rome's emperors saw Christianity as a threat to their concept of themselves as embodying the state religion. The execution of Peter and Paul by Nero was the beginning of more than two centuries of intermittent persecutions; the worst were those of Domitian (94–96), Trajan (98–117), Marcus Aurelius (161–180), Septimius Severus (193–212), Decius (249–251) and especially Diocletian (285–305). Scores of thousands of believers perished in various brutal ways, such as being used as human torches to light up athletic contests or thrown to wild beasts.

When Domitian took power the Roman Empire had been in existence for more than 120 years, and strains had become apparent in how a multicultural empire could carry on the older, more parochial authority of the Roman Republic. It was no longer a matter for the Roman natives or the Italians, who would not have put up with absolutism. But authoritarian influences from the east made it relatively easy for the emperors, from Augustus onwards, to establish themselves as *divi*, or divine heroes, one step below living gods. It was the eastern part of the empire that went a step further and considered the emperor the *deus*, or fully-qualified divinity, a title that Domitian was the first to officially assume; and it was to be expected that this god-emperor would launch the first large-scale persecution against the one faith that expressly refuted that claim.

Despite the obstacles thrown in its path, the church in Rome held together. By the second century it had gradually organized itself under a *papa*, meaning father, a term applied to the bishop of the city (and origin of our word pope). There were frequent councils of bishops from Rome and the outlying regions, but as the importance and influence of Jerusalem waned, Rome became the Christian centre of gravity, as it were. Peter had preached to the Christian colony in Rome, and may actually have established it. At his death he left it in the hands of Linus (also known as Saint Linus of Volterra), whom tradition accepts as the second pope. The third pope, Anacletus, held office from 76 to 88, when the Gospels were being put together. His successor, Clement I, saw the faith through the persecution of Domitian (one of whose intended victims was Saint John the Evangelist who escaped to the remote Greek island of Patmos). According to a legend, Sisinnius, the Prefect of Rome, suspected his wife of being a secret Christian and came upon her attending a mass officiated by the pope in a catacomb. When Sisinnius tried to have Clement arrested, he and his arrest squad were struck blind; a twelfth-century fresco painted to commemorate the occasion describes them as 'sons of whores'.[1] We might take this as a very early sign of papal physical power over adversaries. That power by the second century had grown until the emperor Decius grumbled that he would rather have had a rival emperor than a pope to deal with.[2]

Not until Constantine I in 313 were the Christians of the empire able to finally breathe the air of religious freedom. A year earlier, Constantine had secured the throne by trouncing his opponent Maxentius at the momentous Battle of the Milvian Bridge outside Rome; he himself vowed that before the battle he had seen a shining cross in the sky with the words *By This Conquer* in Greek. True or not, this legend is the first instance of Christianity coming down on the side of official armed force against the foes of the faith. Constantine had, as it were, the stamp of divine approval for his army and its campaigns, in which he was invariably victorious. His army, almost to a man, had enthusiastically adopted a modified cruciform emblem, the *chi-rho* (from XP, the first two letters of the Greek *Christos*), on their shields and standards. The Christian army had come into being. In 313 the Edict of Milan removed the ban on Christians; seventeen years later Constantine completed the colossal task of moving the empire's capital from Rome to Constantinople, a far more strategically-situated centre. With him went the senior church hierarchy, leaving Rome itself in the hands of its bishop, who for the sake of tradition was still known as the pope.

For the purpose of holding a large empire together, Nova Roma (as Constantinople was originally meant to be called) was a far better strategic site than malaria-ridden Rome could ever be. Rome itself was close to Italy's west coast, whereas the great bulk of the empire's interests lay in the east; the old, time-consuming military route down the Appian Way to the heel of Italy, the rough crossing of the Strait of Otranto and the days-long tramp over the winding Via Egnatia through the rugged Balkan mountains had been the only way Roman arms could maintain control of the eastern provinces. With the renewed rise of the hostile Persian Empire under the Sasanids, a far quicker connection with the east was required. The location of Constantinople, at the chokepoint of Europe and Asia, removed all those obstacles at one go.

The dedicatory celebrations for the new capital on Monday, 11 May 330, gave the city officially to God and Christ. Gone for good was the emperor-worship of old. Constantine regarded himself – as the hundred-odd subsequent Late Roman and Byzantine sovereigns would regard themselves – as Christ's vicegerent on earth. The task of the emperor, the civil service and the military was to fight for the spread of the Christian faith among the pagans, and to defend it against attacks when necessary. In its 1,100 years of life the Byzantine Empire would unswervingly dedicate itself to that policy; in a specialization of labour, the emperor would handle secular and physical security, leaving the patriarch, or church head, to the equally important spiritual sphere. All Roman Byzantine armies were God's armies, in theory and fact. Even through the political turmoil after Constantine's death in 337, the basic principles of the Christian state were never in doubt.

No such stability existed in the West, where the bishops of Rome had no strong secular authority to buttress their own positions, especially against foreign invaders. Even at the height of Roman imperial power in the first century, some early popes felt they had to assert themselves in power terms. In 96 Clement I had written to the other Mediterranean dioceses claiming primacy in decision-making – the opening gun in the age-old papal claim for superiority in Christendom. The claim did not go unchallenged by the eastern regions, as well as the important seat of Carthage; the resulting dispute would plague the papacy for a couple of hundred more years. After 330 the church was led by the patriarchs in Constantinople, who had their hands full battling heresies and fixing the official Christian creed as solidly as possible in the service of the army and state. After the authority and decisiveness of Theodosius I finally brought about this result, the Eastern Church settled into a secure, if somewhat dull, routine.

In the West, however, the clergy could enjoy no such complacency. In the fourth century the barbarian invasions of Italy made the people of that peninsula, and outlying areas such as Gaul, look to the bishops of Rome as the sole authority that could be relied upon. 'The bishops of Rome felt responsible for feeding and defending their people.'[3] As the eastern empire gradually morphed into Byzantium, the bishops, or popes, of Rome were thrown upon their own resources. The emperors in Constantinople were too far away, and local political leadership too fragmented; the Church in Rome was the only symbolic power common to all the West European peoples, and by default was looked to for guidance in times of crisis, which was most of the time. Moreover, the prevailing Greek language and liturgy of the early Church had shifted eastwards, leaving Latin as the common medium of the Church in the West; the old empire was splitting, amoeba-like, into two distinct worlds, one Greek and one Latin. Widening the rift were the Latin Church fathers, Saints Ambrose, Jerome and Augustine, who developed a theology that underpinned the rise of the papacy to primacy in the West.

The bishops of Rome were quite conscious of their growing prestige. Ammianus Marcellinus, a pagan observer, noted as early as the fourth century that some of them had acquired an unreasonable measure of wealth and pomp. They were not all Italians: until Pope Damasus I (366–384), two Syrians, five Greeks, two Africans, one Dalmatian and one Spaniard (Damasus himself) had also occupied the throne of Saint Peter. Damasus' election was a bloodily-contested one, with rival gangs clashing inside a Roman church; when the affray ended, 137 bodies were carried out of the devastated building that was subsequently rebuilt to become what is now Santa Maria Maggiore.[4] Papal warfare, however disorganized, had begun.

In 402 Theodosius' son Honorius, who had been given the West to rule (with Theodosius' other son Arcadius ruling the East), moved his palace to Ravenna on the Adriatic coast in north Italy, a city more defensible than Rome. The popes followed Honorius and by some accounts were the real rulers in Ravenna. The organizing tradition of the old Roman Empire had given the Western Church a more political and worldly structure than was the case in the Greek East, where the emperor was in total control and the clergy thus freer to pursue its spiritual and metaphysical concerns. In the absence of a reliable single fount of political authority in the West, the Roman Church and its considerable resources stepped into the gap. In the words of Will Durant:

> The Roman Church followed in the footsteps of the Roman state: it conquered the provinces, beautified the capital, and established unity and discipline ... Rome died in giving birth to the Church; the Church matured by inheriting and accepting the responsibilities of Rome.[5]

This maturity came not a moment too soon. As early as the 370s a new and vigorous people had emerged from the tribal turmoil of north-east Europe to seriously threaten the southern European cradles of civilization. These were the Visigoths, who were able to take advantage of weak imperial leadership and cross the Danube en masse. In 378 Valens, the Constantinople-based emperor, rode out with an army to stop them at Adrianople (now Edirne in European Turkey); in the resulting battle Valens perished in a blazing cottage after losing two-thirds of his force. Valens' successor Theodosius I had stabilized the situation by enlisting Goths as *foederati*, or allies-in-reserve, giving them lands to cultivate in return for allegiance. But the weakness and incompetence of Theodosius' successors encouraged the commander of the emperor's Gothic auxiliaries, Alaric, to start his own freebooting expeditions, first in the Balkans and then down the Italian peninsula.

After sidelining the helpless Honorius at Ravenna, in 410 Alaric surged towards Rome. Honorius advised the Senate to buy off the Goth leader with gold, but Alaric wanted territory as well. The pope, Innocent I, appears to have favoured giving Alaric what he wanted, but the negotiations broke down. On 24 August the Goths burst into the Eternal City, looting and killing. Church after church was stripped of its treasures; only the basilicas of Saints Peter and Paul were untouched, to serve as refuges for thousands of terrified Romans. According to Saint Augustine, the Goths respected the Christian places of worship and all who sought refuge therein.[6] One legend relates that a Goth soldier burst into a house to find a young girl guarding valuable holy relics; the soldier was about the grab them, when he was halted by the girl's voice telling him that he could take what he liked, only that it all belonged to Saint Peter, who would most surely punish the soldier for what he had done. The intimidated Goth left the house to report the incident to Alaric, who ordered that the girl and the relics be taken to safety in Saint Peter's basilica.[7]

Some credit for Alaric's leniency to the clergy can be given to Innocent I, the fortieth pontiff and the first who definitely merits the title of *defensor urbis*, or defender of the city in an expressly political and military sense. As far as we know, Innocent employed no armed force against Alaric; but his defence of Rome in the political and social spheres may well have been just as effective. The sack of Rome lasted for two days, after which Alaric withdrew (taking with him Honorius' sister Galla Placidia as war booty) to let the city lick its wounds. Shortly afterwards, Alaric died of a fever, depriving the Visigoths of strong leadership. For the next thirty or so years, while the Goths staked out new conquests in Gaul and Spain, successive popes worked hard to rebuild the old splendours of Rome. But the old Rome itself was clearly on its way out. Constantinople was now the centre of the East Roman Empire, soon to become the Byzantine Empire, with the Italian rump fated to wither away. More barbarians appeared out of the European mists: the Vandals (whose name, perhaps unfairly, has become our synonym for senseless destruction) traversed Spain and ended up in North Africa, while the Franks and Burgundians took control of large parts of Gaul. Then out of the vastnesses of Asia came the most fearful horde of all, the Huns, who under Attila swept like a hurricane across Europe, hammering the eastern and western parts of the empire alike. In 453 Attila swooped over the Alps, aiming straight for Rome. But the pope, Leo I, kept a cool head.

Leo (440–461) brought the talents of statesmanship to the office of bishop of Rome, elevating it above what it had been so far. He had a willing ally in Valentinian III, the western emperor, whose wife Eudoxia Licinia donated to the papacy the chains that had bound Saint Peter during his imprisonments in Jerusalem and Rome. (According to legend, the two chains magically fused themselves into a single chain of 38 links that is preserved today in the basilica of San Pietro in Vincoli.)[8] As Valentinian fled inside the walls of Rome, Leo and a small delegation boldly travelled north to confront Attila. On the banks of the Mincio river (probably not far from present-day Verona) the pope stopped the Hun warlord in his tracks. Frustratingly, we have no real record of what was said at that epochal meeting. The bulk of historical opinion leans towards the theory that Leo offered Attila tribute and possibly the hand of Princess Honoria (daughter of Galla Placidia) in return for calling off his campaign. Honoria herself, banished to Constantinople after being accused of having an affair with a chamberlain, had found something attractive in what she had been told about this Hun chieftain, known far and wide as 'the scourge of God', and sent him her ring. Attila had quite reasonably interpreted the gesture as a marriage proposal, which he used as an excuse to claim half the western empire.

An alternative line of speculation is that the highly superstitious Attila took seriously the pope's warning that all invaders who dared to enter Rome were quickly punished for it by unexpected death – the latest example had been the Goth Alaric, carried off by a fever forty-three years before. We know that disease and a shortage of food afflicted the Hun ranks, and these may well have contributed to Attila's hesitation. There were also reports that imperial troops were on their way from Constantinople, sent by Marcian, the eastern emperor, in defence of the western portion of the empire. Perhaps it was a combination of these warnings that decided Attila to turn back over the Alps. He still wanted Honoria, and insisted that she should be sent him, but as temporary consolation took a young wife from Hungary. On his wedding night he ate and drank to excess, and then bedded his bride; the combined exertions proved too much for even his powers of endurance and in the morning he was found dead from a broken blood vessel in his throat. Back in Rome, Pope Leo could take credit single-handedly for delivering Rome from its latest deadly threat. A true *defensor urbis*, he was henceforth known as Leo the Great.

The contrast with the ineffectual Valentinian III was sharp. The western emperor himself, no doubt feeling himself outclassed in the ability stakes, personally murdered one of his most competent generals, Aëtius, who had done much to keep the Huns at bay. In revenge, the emperor himself was slain – 'murder had long since become the accepted substitute for election'[9] – to be replaced by the one who arranged his demise, Petronius Maximus. In response to Petronius' arbitrary rule, his opponents called on the leader of the Vandals of North Africa, Gaiseric, to come to Rome and topple him. In 455 Gaiseric sailed from Carthage with a large fleet and landed at Ostia, Rome's port. Leo the Great and his priests found themselves the sole defenders of the approaches to the city; meeting with Gaiseric, Leo gave him permission to enter Rome but was able to extract a promise from him to refrain from killing people and burning houses – and looting Christian churches. The Vandal leader kept his promise, but only just. He apparently felt free to allow his soldiers to strip Rome of all its pagan and ancient treasures, to loot the homes of the wealthy, and carry off thousands of civilians as slaves. Gaiseric could have felt it was payback time for the Punic Wars of old. 'Carthage,' notes Will Durant ruefully, 'had leniently revenged the Roman ruthlessness of 146 BC.'[10]

The 455 sack of Rome delivered the death blow to what remained of Italian Roman civilization. In a single century, Rome's population had shrunk from 1.5 million souls to one-fifth of that. What happened there mirrored what was happening all over Italy. Barbarian tribes without number – Heruli, Sciri and Rugi, to name just a few – were surging down from the Alps into the warm and pleasant peninsula. What remained of civic duty or public-spiritedness was eroded almost to nothing as morale plummeted among rich and poor alike. It was too bad to last, and the crowning debacle came in 476, when the last of the western Roman emperors, a mere boy ironically named Romulus Augustulus (little Augustus), was deposed and packed off to an unusually early retirement. The insignia of office reverted to the eastern emperor, Zeno, who in Constantinople could now rest in the knowledge that he was the true and unchallenged Roman emperor. Politically, Italy had become barbarian-ruled territory, where only the pontiff in Rome could exert a strong Christian authority, as Leo I had shown. The way was open for the popes, by necessity as much as by conviction, to begin to wield military as well as political and religious clout.

Chapter 2

Fortifying the Papacy

The man who officially terminated the West Roman Empire was a German-born general who commanded the Roman armies. Odovacar (or Odoacer), against all precedent, declined the imperial office and ruled Italy as a *de facto* republic, by force of ability alone, quite content to accept the emperor in Constantinople as the true sovereign. This way he freed himself from troublesome dynastic issues that would have interfered with the practicalities of his rule and probably spawned deadly intrigues. In 489, thirteen years into Odovacar's rule, the Ostrogoths (East Goths) appeared out of Eastern Europe to fall on Italy. Emperor Zeno had enlisted them as allied *foederati*, but distrusting them, had craftily sent them over to Italy to suppress Odovacar, whom Zeno saw as a usurper.

The Ostrogoth leader, Theodoric, met Odovacar in battle outside Ravenna and defeated him. For three years Odovacar remained holed up in Ravenna until, lured by a false promise of negotiations, he agreed to meet Theodoric, who promptly sliced him in two with his sword with such ease that Theodoric is said to have quipped afterwards that his victim 'must not have had a bone in his body'.[1] With skills such as this, Theodoric easily became the king of Italy. Though he made Ravenna his residence, he displayed a keen interest in the affairs of Rome and the papacy. By all accounts he never learned to read and write. But for a third of a century this expert Ostrogoth killer gave Italy a just and moderate government, presiding over a generation of security and prosperity. Even from distrustful Constantinople he received respect. Wrote the Byzantine historian Procopius:

> His manner of ruling over his subjects was worthy of a great emperor; for he maintained justice, made good laws, protected his country from invasion, and gave proof of extraordinary prudence and valour.[2]

A chastened Zeno made Theodoric a patrician and *magister militum* (army commander). Though the great majority of Italians welcomed this strong alien protector, the military remained the preserve of the Ostrogoth elite.

To Theodoric's credit, he made no attempt to impose the Arian Christianity of the Ostrogoths – declared a heinous heresy by the Church – on the faith of the Italian people, a fact for which the papacy was grateful and which undoubtedly smoothed his reign. On the other hand, however, the decline of the classical Greco-Roman spirit under Theodoric was swift. The philosopher and scholar Severinus Boëthius learned this the hard way after allegedly conspiring to topple the heretic Theodoric, supposedly with the backing of Constantinople; in 534 the gentle and thoughtful Boëthius was executed by a particularly ugly combination of strangling and clubbing. Theodoric himself repented of his decision. Legend has it that two years later, amid a raging fever, he imagined he saw the head of one of his execution victims in a large fish served at his table. Death surprised him, say ecclesiastical historians, as he was about to promulgate a decree making Arian Christianity the official creed. Despite his successful and effective reign, the heretic Theodoric was not mourned by the Church.

Succeeding Theodoric was his widow Amalasuntha, acting as regent for her underage son Athalaric. Eager to smooth over the ruling Goths' differences with the Roman populace and clergy, Amalasuntha cultivated relations with Pope Felix IV. But the papacy itself was weakened by rivalry between pro-Gothic and pro-Byzantine factions; Athalaric died at eighteen, and Amalasuntha married her cousin Theodahad who, though elevated to king of Rome as a result, had no great use for the Romans. The papacy could be little more than a helpless spectator as Theodahad deposed and jailed his wife, and then had her strangled. All this was relayed back to Constantinople, where Emperor Justinian I nursed plans to end the western chaos by clawing back all of Italy into the empire's fold. For too long the old home of the Roman Empire had been eaten away physically by barbarian incursions and morally by the Arian heresy. Theodahad's harsh ineptitude and the fate of Amalasuntha moved Justinian to act.

The emperor prepared his operation well. Lulling the Ostrogoths into a false sense of security, he sent his experienced general Belisarius to Tunisia, from where he crossed over to Sicily and then the Italian mainland. A couple of short-lived popes supported Theodahad, but the great mass of orthodox clergy were dead against him. Theodahad's Goth soldiery had no great faith in his ability to stem the Byzantine advance, so they assassinated him and elected Witigis, a more vigorous character, in his place. Witigis left a 4,000-man contingent in Rome to delay Belisarius and moved north to Ravenna to organize a more effective defence. Pope Silverius wisely advised the Senate not to resist the Byzantine advance and sent a message to Belisarius telling him the way was open. The Byzantine general entered Rome through the Porta Asinaria on the night of 9 December 536. In March 537 Witigis struck back with 150,000 men, surging towards Rome and besieging the city. The Romans began to grumble about shortages of food and water, but Belisarius and his contingent of a mere 5,000 men held out. After a futile year, Witigis withdrew.

The first victim of the popular discontent was Pope Silverius, deposed after being accused (probably unjustly) of having pro-Goth sympathies, and subsequently murdered by a member of Belisarius' wife's knife-carrying bodyguard. His successor, Pope Vigilius, was the papal nuncio in Constantinople and had the support of Justinian's wife Theodora. Uncomfortably for the official Church (not to mention her husband), Theodora was a feisty, worldly and strong-willed woman whose beliefs leaned towards the Monophysite heresy. This heresy taught – against the official creed – that Christ had only one nature, the divine one, and was not a mystic blend of human and divine, as the classic Christian dogma still holds. Such religious hair-splitting might seem incomprehensible to many in our secular era, but we must not forget that for many centuries such issues were as real as our own 'political' issues are to us today, and were quite capable of moving large armies and igniting great wars. Theodora helped Vigilius become pope on condition that he go easy on her fellow-Monophysites. Justinian, for his part, never quite trusted Vigilius to be a good bishop of Rome. Around 550 the emperor exiled him to a barren rock in the Sea of Marmara for refusing to toe the official ecclesiastical line; he died while returning to Rome. This outright imperial attempt to control the papacy left a bad taste in the mouths of the western clergy and contributed to the further estrangement of the Eastern and Western Churches.

Belisarius, believing he had Italy under Byzantine control, returned to Constantinople to don the wreath of victory. But the Ostrogoths were not ready to concede the struggle. Stepping into Witigis' shoes was Totila, who between 541 and 543 rallied his forces enough to defeat a Byzantine army at Faenza and recapture the peninsula, bottling up the Byzantine contingents in Ravenna, Rome and Naples. When Naples fell to Totila, Justinian bestirred himself enough to send Belisarius back to Italy to put matters right; but the general was given inadequate forces – perhaps because Justinian already suspected him of having designs on the throne. Aware that he was outnumbered, Belisarius decided to abandon Rome to its fate and concentrate on defending Ravenna. Totila's Goths surged into Rome on 17 December 546, tearing down the city walls and seizing wealthy families to carry off as hostages. Other sections of the population fled into the countryside, so that when Belisarius hurried back to Rome he found a deserted, ruined city. With his meagre force he dared not bring Totila to a set battle and asked to be relieved of his command. Justinian replaced him with the septuagenarian Narses (and thousands of extra troops), who defeated and killed the Goth leader at Gualdo Tadino in 552. A year later, Totila's successor Teia met the same fate in the shadow of Mount Vesuvius, and the threat from the Goths was ended.

Narses, despite his advanced age, gave Rome a sixteen-year breathing space in which it could grow back to some of its previous prosperity. The popes were brought into the picture on 13 August 554 by an edict of Justinian called the Pragmatic Sanction which essentially gave them administrative power to govern Rome and its region. The decree stipulated that 'fit and proper persons, able to administer the local government, be chosen as governors of the provinces by the bishops and chief persons of each province'.[3] In Rome the chief 'fit and proper person' was the bishop, or pope. The Byzantine imperial power in the city was restricted to the *cartulari*, ranking as dukes, residing on the Palatine Hill, their authority delegated by the Byzantine governor of Italy in Ravenna.[4] Thanks to the Pragmatic Sanction – a true stroke of political pragmatism – the way was clear for the Lateran Palace, the seat of the popes, to fill the power vacuum. Justinian, who had made a personal mission out of clawing back the Italian half of the empire, died in 565 (possibly from overwork), to be succeeded by his nephew Justin II, whose delicate mental condition quickly broke down under the strain of rule. At precisely this moment of imperial weakness, a new wave of barbarian invaders swept down into North Italy.

The Lombards had originated on the banks of the Elbe river in North Germany. Apparently in search of a warmer climate, they migrated south and east to the Danube, where they embraced the Arian form of Christianity. In 568 they veered westwards from the North Balkans and inundated the great plain between the Alps and the Apennines that is still called Lombardy. It was an easy conquest. But unlike the Ostrogoths before them, they confiscated the native Italians' lands and did not conceal their hostility to Constantinople. Five years later they ravaged the outskirts of Rome. A young Roman deacon named Gregory witnessed 'castles destroyed, churches burned, monasteries and convents razed to the ground, fields deserted and the whole countryside desolate'. Within thirty years of their first appearance, the Lombards controlled all the peninsula except the imperial enclaves of Ravenna, Rome, Naples and the toe of Italy. In 605 the brutal Byzantine emperor Phokas came to a shaky accommodation with the Lombards, but he was far away and out of touch. It was time for the papacy of Rome to come up with a seriously strong pontiff to fight the good fight in Italy. And Gregory proved to be the man.

Gregory was born about 540 into a wealthy Roman senatorial family and lived luxuriously in his youth in a villa built near Nero's palace on the Caelian Hill. While still young he inherited a considerable fortune and at thirty-three became the Prefect of Rome. By the end of his one-year term he had become quite disgusted with politics, and the apparently hopeless state of Italy in general, and eager to exchange the futilities of Mammon for the spiritual riches of God. His sudden transformation was astounding. He used his fortune to establish seven monasteries, and gave away what was left to the poor; he abandoned all social rank and turned his lavish home into the monastery of Saint Andrew, becoming its first inmate; he ate nothing but raw vegetables and fruit, fasted so often that he risked serious malnutrition, and in general lived three years of extreme privation that he called the happiest of his life.

About 577 Pope Benedict I noticed Gregory's intense piety, and perhaps a strength of character beneath it, and hired him as a Lateran deacon. Two years later Pope Pelagius II sent him as papal nuncio, or ambassador, to Constantinople. He spent six years there, his ascetic manner and appearance in sharp contrast to the splendours of the Byzantine court, returning to Rome to become the abbot of the monastery he had founded thirteen years before. In 590 a serious outbreak of bubonic plague in Rome carried off Pelagius. Clergy and people alike clamoured for Gregory to take his place, but the supreme power of the pontificate was the last thing this holy man wanted. He appealed to Emperor Maurikios away in Constantinople to nullify the Roman people's decision, but somehow the letter was intercepted and Gregory was seized and, we are reliably told, taken forcibly to be consecrated pope. Before the papal insignia of office could be put on him, he organized the population of Rome into seven groups, by age and social class, and had them merge into a giant procession, led by himself, to traverse the city and pray for deliverance from the epidemic. According to legend, when the procession was passing over Saint Peter's bridge across the Tiber, the form of the Archangel Michael wielding a flaming sword appeared in the sky, whereupon the plague ceased forthwith.[5] The angel is said have hovered over the circular Mausoleum of Hadrian, which was promptly renamed the Castel Sant'Angelo, or Castle of the Holy Angel.

Pope Gregory I had his work cut out for him. The Constantinople-based Eastern Church had the emperor to fight its political and military battles. But the bishops of Rome, representing the Western Church, could count on no such backing. Ironically, the eclipse of Byzantine power in Italy by the Lombards made Gregory's task easier, as he was now the sole potentate who had the power to confront them. At the time of his consecration he was about fifty, described as dark and bald, with a sparse red beard. He was gentle in speech and suffered constantly from a variety of ailments, including indigestion and low-grade fever. Even as pontiff he led the most austere life possible. He spent Church revenues not on himself but on feeding the poor and sick of Rome. Despite his ailments he ruled with military sternness.

With the imperial headquarters at Ravenna now cut off, and its troops unpaid and demoralized, Pope Gregory was the only Roman leader of any stature available. It was he who ably negotiated with the Lombards ringing the city like a noose, while maintaining public works and relieving the poor. Under him the papacy matured into a political power in its own right; the pope became, in essence, the king of Rome. Gregory also made sure that the Church's authority carried its writ to the farthest corners of Europe, including France and Saxon England, which began its conversion to Christianity under his guidance. As a scholar he was not outstanding – he knew no Greek and his Latin was less than perfect – but to make up for these intellectual failings he had a supreme talent for governing, earning him the enduring title of Gregory the Great.

Did Gregory have any knowledge of military matters? The question cannot be answered one way or the other. On one hand, his distaste for worldly power politics, and yearning for the simple devout life, marked his whole tenure. On the other, his sojourn in Constantinople would assuredly have familiarized him with Byzantine defence and military policy; his self-confidence in dealing with the Lombards indicates a talent for political negotiation. But as far as we know, at this point the Lateran had no armed force of its own. How, then, could Gregory or any pope have the confidence to be able to defend the city?

The advent of the seventh century found Italy governed by three powers: the Byzantine Empire, which at the time had its hands full with the Persians and later the Muslims, and was hence ruler of Italy in name only; the Lombards, who constituted *de facto* the main military and political power; and the Rome-based papacy which had overwhelming spiritual and moral stature but no actual army. The popes of the seventh century scored a coup by converting the Lombards to Catholicism, de-fanging them as potential foes. At the same time, relations with the Constantinople-based Eastern Church were worsening over doctrinal issues that need not concern us here. The popes after Gregory I were uncertain about how to deal with the widening rift, which of course had potential strategic consequences. Emperor Heraclius in Constantinople, a leading figure in ecclesiastical-military history thanks to his recapture of Jerusalem from the Persians, was eager to mend fences with Rome. But such was the dizzying succession of short-lived pontiffs (five of them in the fourteen years after Gregory), each of whom had a separate agenda, that all attempts at reconciliation fell through. The Byzantine authority based at Ravenna was simply too weak to give the Italians any sense of political and military security.

The popes, as the most prestigious of Italy's rulers, were compelled to take the reins whether they liked it or not. Pope Honorius I was concerned enough over the security of the papacy to write to Gothic king Chintila in Spain urging him to be 'more eager in wiping out the heresies of the unfaithful'.[6] The term 'wiping out' carried an unmistakable connotation of force.

The message to Chintila was an early sign of the papacy gradually turning its back on the East and looking to the West for its worldly support. Yet the popes insisted on having a say in who ruled at Constantinople. Though they owed allegiance to the emperor, they feared a kind of 'doctrinal infection' from various heretical views emanating from the East. In the 640s an intractable theological dispute moved Emperor Constans II to resolve the issue through strong-arm tactics; he ordered his exarch in Italy to arrest Pope Martin I (or assassinate him – the point is disputed) on the grounds that the pope was insisting on debating abstruse topics that the emperor had banned as destructive to ecclesiastical order. One evening in 653 the new Byzantine exarch sent men to abduct Martin in the middle of a June night, while he was celebrating Mass in the Lateran palace, and bundled him onto a ship moored in the Tiber to face trial in Constantinople. On the way his ship put in at the Aegean island of Naxos, where the pope stayed for a year – most likely to restore his failing health. When he and his captors arrived at Constantinople in September 654, he had to face the jeers and insults of the populace and then spend three months in a freezing jail cell with minimal nourishment.

Martin went before a Byzantine tribunal on a charge of having become pope without imperial consent; to this was added a probably false charge of conspiring against the throne. The tribunal found him guilty on both counts and sentenced him to death; when the sentence was pronounced he was taken into a courtyard and roughly stripped of his papal apparel, leaving him 'naked in several places,' as a large crowd looked on and cheered. With an iron chain around his neck, and the executioner's sword carried before him, Martin was led to death row, to keep company with hardened criminals and stain the cell floor with the blood from his tortures. To its credit, however, the Eastern Church leadership protested against this treatment of the bishop of Rome. Patriarch Paul, though himself on his deathbed, demanded that the pope's life be spared. Thus Martin was sent to Cherson in Crimea, to die peacefully in September 655.[7] Ever since, the Roman Catholic Church has honoured him as Saint Martin of Todi.

If the reactions of official Byzantium to some Roman popes seem especially harsh, it must be remembered that the empire was extremely jittery over incursions by the Muslim Arabs who, newly fired by the Prophet Muhammad, were beginning the first stage of their swift expansion in the south-east Mediterranean. By 654, at the time Pope Martin was facing his ordeals in Constantinople, Arab fleets had captured Cyprus and Rhodes, both vital for Byzantine trade. Small wonder that in the face of this deadly threat, the Eastern Church feared any split in the ranks of Christendom, whether coming from Rome or anywhere else. No doubt many in the East believed that 'heretics' such as Pope Martin deserved to be suppressed at all costs. But in Rome the view was that Constantinople was acting despotically by not allowing the Romans to freely choose the only ruler they trusted. Both sides were right in their ways, which of course only fuelled more mutual hostility.

For the time being, however, the papacy was cowed. Martin's successor Eugenius I managed a doctrinal compromise between Rome and Constantinople that preserved a peace of sorts but really satisfied no-one. In 663 Emperor Constans visited Rome, ostensibly to pay homage to Pope Vitalian (Saint Vitalian of Segni), but in reality (his enemies said) to seize whatever pagan treasures had remained in Rome.[8] On his way back Constans stopped in Syracuse, where he remained for several years. One day in 668, as he was lounging in his bath, one of his Greek attendants smashed his skull with a heavy soap dish. The purloined Roman treasures ended up in the hands of Arab pirates.

Succeeding Constans was his eldest son, who became Constantine IV. Almost from the outset of his reign, Constantine was overwhelmingly preoccupied by the Muslim incursions in the east of the empire and had little time for the problems of Italy. The Arab caliph Muawiyah, founder of the vigorous and expansionist Damascus-based Umayyad house, sent a fleet up to the very shores of Constantinople for five consecutive years; the fleet fell back in 678 after being decimated by the Byzantines' devastating secret weapon – Greek Fire, a mixture of sulphur, pitch, nitre, surface petroleum and pine resin, shot from flame-throwers. Muawiyah agreed to a humiliating peace with Constantine, who took back several Aegean islands which the Muslims had seized. The emperor then had to turn his attention to the Bulgars, a new enemy in the north-west. His first attempts to stall the Bulgars' advance failed, and he found himself having to buy them off in order to turn his attention to Rome.

At about the time that the last smouldering Arab ship was fleeing down the Sea of Marmara, Constantine wrote to Rome proposing an ecumenical council to resolve the doctrinal differences between the eastern and western halves of the Church. Such differences, as we have seen, could have serious political and military consequences, and at a time when Islam from the east and pagan tribes from the north were constantly jabbing at the empire, ecclesiastical unity was considered essential for imperial security. Pope Agatho (Saint Agatho of Palermo) fully agreed, and in late 680 more than 170 delegates poured into Constantinople from all points of the Christian compass. Over sessions lasting ten months, the Sixth Ecumenical Council forged a basic agreement – though Agatho had the embarrassing task of having to disown doctrines held by several of his predecessors. Cordial ties were thus resumed between Constantinople and Rome. But four years later Constantine IV died suddenly of dysentery while still young, to be succeeded by his sixteen-year-old son Justinian II – one of those rulers to whom the term monster may be applied without exaggeration.

Justinian's natural arrogance led him to call another ecumenical council, the Quinisextium, so-called because it was intended to clear up points left vague by the Fifth and Sixth Councils. It was a needless and rather ludicrous exercise in power; some of its decisions banned the giving of Christmas presents, playing dice, curling one's hair and going to the baths in the presence of a Jew. More importantly, the Quinisextium was entirely an affair of the Eastern Church. Rome had been left out, so when Justinian sent a copy of the Quinisextium decisions to Pope Sergius I, with an order that they be promptly enforced, the pope stoutly refused on the grounds that several of them went directly against time-honoured Roman practice. In 692 orders went out to the imperial garrisons in Ravenna and Rome to arrest Sergius, but they refused – perhaps the first concrete instance of an official armed force deployed to defend a pope. The whole population of Rome rallied around the pontiff; to escape the public wrath Zacharias, the imperial envoy sent to apprehend Sergius, hid under the papal bed, from which he emerged only when the pope promised him a safe-conduct.

Justinian raged, but ineffectually, as his cruelties had already thoroughly alienated his people; three years later he was toppled, and as punishment for his misrule, in what had become a standard Byzantine practice, his nose was cut off, earning him the sobriquet *Rhinotmetos*, or Noseless. Yet such was the diabolical energy of this man that in 705, ten years after his overthrow, he returned to seize power again. His disfigured face made him even more terrifying than before, as he instituted a reign of terror in revenge for the indignities he had suffered. He seems to have retained enough common sense to try and mend fences with Rome, inviting Pope Constantine to Constantinople in 710 for a courtesy visit. (More than 1,200 years would pass before another pope visited the seat of the Eastern Church, when in 1967 Pope Paul VI called on Patriarch Athenagoras.)

The papacy had now become too powerful and popular in its home city to accept terms from anyone. The trend, which had taken concrete form under Sergius I, was straining relations with the Byzantine authority in Ravenna. Justinian looked on this trend with alarm, fearing it could trigger another east-west rift. His reaction was typical, sending a fleet to Ravenna to arrest the local bigwigs who were shipped to Constantinople where Noseless promptly had them executed. When Pope Constantine arrived, Justinian treated him with elaborate courtesy, to the point of stooping to kiss the papal foot. Both leaders agreed to a compromise over the provisions of the Quinisextium. But if Noseless expected the Bishop of Rome to accept the suzerainty of Constantinople, even through flattering diplomacy, he would be disappointed. In a vain attempt to reassert Byzantine primacy John Rhizokopos, the imperial exarch of Ravenna, went to Rome to put to death several members of the papal Curia after a travesty of a trial.

Meanwhile, Justinian's days were numbered. After inflicting horrific atrocities on his rebellious subjects in Crimea he was toppled and replaced by one of his generals, Philippikos Bardanes. Rushing back to save his throne, Justinian was seized and beheaded. Legend has it that Noseless' head was sent to Ravenna and Rome for public exhibition; the rest of him, deemed unworthy of a Christian burial, was thrown into the sea. But as far as Rome was concerned, the change was for the worse. Philippikos Bardanes, an Armenian by origin, was determined to enforce the ecclesiastical rules by force, denying Rome any say in them. To Pope Constantine it was a crass betrayal of what Justinian had pledged. For months the imperial militia clashed with the Romans in the streets, ending the strife only when the pope led a procession, with standards flying, to separate the warring parties. But the new emperor himself lasted less than two years before he was rudely awakened from a midday siesta and taken away to be blinded on the grounds that he had usurped the Byzantine throne. Two insignificant emperors followed, until in 717 the capable Leo III was crowned. Though Leo's reign would revive the fortunes of Byzantium, it augured yet more problems for the papacy.

From early in his reign Leo was faced with a peculiar security problem. Edward Gibbon sums it up thus:

> Christians had wandered far away from the simplicity of the Gospel…
> The worship of images was inseparably blended, at least to a pious
> fancy, with the Cross, the Virgin, the saints and their relics… in the
> peace and luxury of the triumphant church, the more prudent bishops
> condescended to indulge a visible superstition for the benefit of the
> multitudes.[9]

Put plainly, the official Christian Church's elaborate use of icons and worship of the saints began to strike many as excessive. The universal public veneration of icons and other religious imagery was likened to pagan idolatry. In many quarters a kind of proto-puritanism sprang up; the movement was heavily influenced by the Jewish elements in the empire, who had never given up their old opposition to 'graven images' and even more by the newly-appeared Muslims who adhered to the same prohibition. As the clergy in parts of the Eastern empire were coming under the sway of this new Puritanism, Leo, partly for strategic reasons and partly out of conviction, decided to go along with the new trend – placing him on a direct collision course with the popes.

Iconoclasm, as the new policy was called, went against every instinct and practice of the Roman Church, not to mention the mass of simple believers in East and West alike. Starting in 726, the papacy looked on horrified as Leo smashed or dismantled as many of the holy mosaics and icons of Constantinople as he could; anyone, including clergy, caught hoarding or hiding icons risked the death penalty. At this, Byzantine troops in Ravenna rose in revolt and assassinated the emperor's exarch; backing them was Pope Gregory II as well as a good deal of the Eastern clergy. For the second time in a quarter of a century, a pope was able to count on the alliance of an imperial armed force that refused to obey its emperor. Gregory wrote a stern letter to Leo, robustly defending the use of icons and statues and advising him to keep his hands off them. The emperor's reply was to send officials to arrest Gregory, but the ship carrying them sank in the Adriatic. Gregory died shortly afterwards, to be succeeded by the equally resolute Gregory III. The cold war between pope and emperor intensified when Leo confiscated the revenues of the churches of Sicily and Calabria, and Gregory III decreed excommunication for anyone harming or destroying a sacred image.

The western world owes Leo III a great debt in that in 717 he repelled a year-long Muslim siege of Constantinople that, if it had succeeded, would have left south-east Europe open to Muslim penetration. That battle, plus the repulse of the Moors by Charles Martel at the battle of Tours in 732, saved Christian Europe. The usually cynical Gibbon admits that these two events 'rescued our ancestors of Britain, and our neighbours of Gaul, from the civil and religious yoke of the Koran'.[10] But at the time, the issue was not so clear-cut. Probably because militant Islam had yet to offer any serious threat to Italy, the bishops of Rome saw the iconoclastic emperor in Constantinople as a far more immediate problem to deal with. And in a domestic sense, Leo III was his own worst enemy. All that his fanatical iconoclasm managed to accomplish was to divide his subjects, east and west, into opposing doctrinal camps – and give the papacy a yet stronger justification for its independence.

The march of events was clearly favouring the papacy, which sought a stronger historical and documentary basis for claiming the powers of Christ's vicarage on Earth. Around 800 someone in the Roman Curia dreamed up one of the most audacious forgeries in history, the so-called 'Donation of Constantine'. This fraudulent document purported to prove that Constantine the Great in the fourth century had essentially left the western half of the empire to its own devices, granting Pope Sylvester and his successors the authority to crown anyone who could rule as emperor of the West. It was a total myth, but few at the time had the means of exploding it,[11] and Pope Leo III (not be confused with Emperor Leo III) milked the propaganda for all it was worth. Conditions in Constantinople, moreover, worked in his favour, as in 800 the Byzantine throne was occupied by Irene, the first empress in her own right. Besides being a woman, and hence considered unfit to rule as a monarch, she was widely believed to have murdered her own son. Leo saw a fantastic chance to achieve two aims at once: to remove Irene from the throne by marrying her to the man who now, in the West, had arisen as a unifying figure of Western Europe – Charlemagne.

On at least two occasions in the late seventh and early eighth centuries, the popes had enjoyed support from imperial armies that for one reason or another had refused to carry out unpopular orders from Constantinople. But these were only accidental lucky breaks; no pope could feel militarily secure as long as he had no armed force of his own, and as long as the Lombards were in control of most of Italy. It was to remedy this lack that the papacy began to look farther afield for a political and military power that could be more reliably called on when necessary. And by the close of the eighth century that power was the rising Frankish kingdom. The rise had begun when Charles Martel, the 'Hammer of the Franks,' halted the Muslim incursions at Tours and established his family as the rulers. In 751 Charles' son Pepin proclaimed himself Pepin III, King of the Franks and *rex Dei gratia*, as a papal representative anointed him with holy oil.

The tie between the papacy and the Frankish kingdom was almost complete, but lacked that historical documentary evidence that would have given it a stronger backing. Unfortunately, as in the case of the spurious 'Donation of Constantine,' another questionable document was produced, purporting to give the popes full sovereignty over the huge slice of Italy from Rome to Ravenna. Back in 754, when the Lombards still remained to be dealt with, Pope Stephen II and Pepin had joined forces to confront the Lombard king Aistulf, who holed himself up in Pavia promising to give up his holdings. Once Pepin and Stephen had withdrawn, Aistulf reneged on his pledge and led an army to Rome, burning and pillaging on the way. After a nine-week siege of Rome, Pepin – claiming to have been guided by a letter personally written by Saint Peter himself – appeared at Aistulf's rear and scattered the Lombards for good. In August 756 Pepin undertook a solemn pledge over the tomb of Saint Peter in the Vatican to donate whatever territory he had wrested from the Lombards to the Church. This included almost the whole of central Italy from Rome to Ravenna, an area that for the next 1,100 years would be known as the States of the Church.

Pepin had little or no authority to make such a gift. His 'pledge' over Saint Peter's tomb was legally as fraudulent as the saintly letter he used as an excuse to invade Italy. Technically, Italy was still under Byzantine rule, and the Constantinople emperors had always dreamed of restoring that rule in fact as well as in name. But as Byzantium lacked the military means to enforce their rule, Pepin *de facto* stepped in to fill the vacuum. It was Pepin's son Charlemagne who cemented the Church's spiritual and political authority into a durable structure that at last gave full military coverage to the legally shaky States of the Church and the popes who ruled them. By 800, when he had suppressed the Lombards in Italy and temporarily tamed the Saxons, he felt confident enough to travel to Rome where, on Christmas Day, Leo III crowned him head of the Carolingian Empire.

The road appeared open for Charlemagne to forge the European Union of his time. The only areas outside his influence were Anglo-Saxon England, the Byzantine Greek Empire based on Constantinople, and in the Middle East the Arab Muslim caliphate of the Abbasids. It would therefore have appeared natural to the popes, as the spiritual leaders of Western Europe, to lend their spiritual underpinning to this rising star. The papacy provided the region with a living link to the old Roman past: its language was Latin and its structure mimicked the old imperial one. The arrangement, in fact, was similar to that prevailing in Byzantium: while the emperor (in this case Charlemagne, the self-styled *patricius Romanorum*) exercised secular authority, he left spiritual authority to the popes in a system that worked for both sides. The papacy could now relax in the knowledge that Charlemagne's troops were there to protect it as a last resort, especially against the seditious riots that roiled Roman society every so often. 'France,' writes Will Durant, 'was now the richest possession of the Latin Church.'[12]

The Roman clergy for some time had represented the ablest and most educated elements in Western European society. In the early years of Charlemagne's rule Saint Agobard, the archbishop of Lyon, worked tirelessly to humanize the judicial system and eradicate superstition. Pope Leo IV renewed and rebuilt Saint Peter's basilica in a grander form than before. From Ireland to Istria the Church encouraged a new piety to offset the barbarous politics of the time. Inevitably, rivalry arose with the Greek side that was in the process of converting the eastern European Slavs to Christianity. The papacy of the ninth century could come to no agreement on how to handle the Slavs; in the end they were split down the middle, with the Czechs, Slovaks, Hungarians and Poles throwing in their lot with Rome, and the Bulgarians, Serbs and Russians adhering to Greek Constantinople – an arrangement that, amazingly, still holds, despite the intervening centuries of enormous political upheavals.

The birth of the States of the Church, even though by largely fraudulent means, introduced a new actor into the European family of nations. The popes were now state leaders, and inevitably departed from the Byzantine Greek practice of keeping church and state in separate compartments. In Rome the church now *was* the state. It would follow that as a state, it would need its own armed force for its defence. Yet that is the one thing we do not see happening. There were certainly people in the papacy (and outside it) who were prepared to use force to gain their ends. It is about this time, or somewhat earlier, that we hear of the pope's *defensores*, or armed bodyguard. We don't know how many *defensores* there were, or how they were armed. The popes could also count on forces employed by the Duchy of Rome, which acted when the Byzantine exarch tried to personally arrest Pope Sergius I; the duchy's army scared the exarch so much he hid under the pope's bed. We know that Pope Constantine's *defensores* accompanied him to Constantinople in 710 to answer charges of insistent disobedience, but little else is known about their duties, which seemed to mirror Byzantine imperial practice.[13]

The papacy's many-sided struggle to maintain its territory and prestige continued unabated through the eighth century. Paying an armed mercenary force was a vital part of that task. The Church had enough money thanks to revenues from extensive property assets and generous bequests from royal and noble families in Western Europe. The popes, in the words of Roger Collins, a modern historian of the papacy, 'had to act as secular sovereigns or face losing their authority to others'.[14] The issue of who was to occupy the throne of Saint Peter, then, was of the highest political and economic as well as spiritual importance, and as a consequence, the power struggles over the saint's sepulchre were often violent. For example, in 767 Toto, the duke of Nepi, plotted to replace the dying Pope Paul I with his own brother Constantine. Backed by the Lombard king Desiderius who jumped at this chance to disrupt the papacy, Constantine led an armed faction that on 28 July 768 battled in the streets with supporters of the legitimate papacy. Toto perished in the fighting, forcing Constantine and his band to take refuge in the Lateran palace, where he claimed to be pope.[15] A few days later he was seized and led around Rome on a horse, 'in a saddle designed for a woman' for maximum public humiliation, and with heavy weights on his feet, and then formally deposed. His punishment was completed by his eyes being put out – an imitation of standard Byzantine practice – after which he was shut up in a monastery. Stephen III was confirmed as Paul I's successor.

By now it had become apparent that the process of choosing a pope, which could happen many times in a single year, was fraught with political complexity. Unlike most of his predecessors, Stephen came from a humble background, adding a class dimension to the usual manoeuvrings, while the usurper anti-pope Constantine had been a layman. On 8 April 760 a council had been called at the Lateran to settle the issue of just who was entitled to be elected pope. The council ruled that henceforth no-one but a professional clergyman could aspire to the Church's highest office. Perhaps because of his non-aristocratic background Stephen III had found his powers limited by an upper-class cabal in the Curia and appealed to Desiderius for help. Again the Lombard king was only too glad to help the popes – thereby burnishing his own image – and in summer 771 infiltrated a Lombard detachment into the city. The way had been secretly prepared by a Lateran chamberlain, Paul Afiarta. The Romans, too, had had enough of the curial cabal, and cheered on Afiarta as the resistance crumbled. Stephen was allowed to emerge and be seen by his people, while Afiarta had the pope's chief foes blinded.

Stephen's death in January 772 encouraged the aristocratic faction to elect one of their number as Hadrian I, who besides being well-connected was also ruthless. Afiarta was arrested and executed in a jail in Rimini. The new pope handily blamed the Lombards for the recent chaos in Rome, and while Desiderius mobilized his forces for a march on Rome, Hadrian enlisted the aid of King Charles of the Franks who swept the Lombards from the Alpine passes and blockaded Desiderius at Pavia. Charles then moved on to Rome, where he met a grateful Hadrian. But in return for the king's help the pope wanted a *quid pro quo*. This was the fulfilment of the supposed twenty-year-old 'Donation of Pepin' that had promised the papacy a large chunk of Italy, including Ravenna and the Lombard duchies.[16] Spurious or not, this so-called 'Donation of Pepin' was accepted as fact by the popes, who from 753 onwards considered themselves the rulers of what became the Papal States. (The date has a curious significance in that according to tradition, Rome was founded in 753 BC).

The first result of the pope's new power was the surrender, deposition and exile of Desiderius. Charles named himself king of the Lombards as well as the Franks, thereby neutralizing what had been the popes' most formidable foe and adding muscle to the new papal domain. But the honeymoon between Hadrian and Charles soon cracked, as the Franks appeared to favour an iconoclastic version of Christianity that was gaining the upper hand in Byzantium but was deplored in Rome. In addition, it was becoming clear that the pope was becoming a political tool of the Frankish kings while theoretically at least owing allegiance to the emperors in Constantinople. While Hadrian never had any intention of becoming a king, neither did he want any king giving him orders. Scholars have been unable to shed much light on this murky state of affairs, but what seems clear enough is that from 750 onwards the papacy – now buttressed by a state extending far beyond the Rome city limits – made its gradual break from Constantinople, whose exarchate in Ravenna vanished at about the same time.[17]

So far, the popes had sought military aid wherever it could be found, either from the Lombards or the Franks, but it was always external aid. Violent clashes such as those in Rome in 768 and 771 were mere outbreaks of partisan thuggery rather than military operations. Though he had his squad of *defensores*, the pope was still a long way from becoming a general. And this raises the question: was there any serious thought about a pope becoming a general, about raising and maintaining a purely papal army without having to depend on outsiders?

If there were such thoughts in the early Church, they must have been well masked. The popes and senior clergy were men of the book, not the sword. Christian doctrine as expressed in the New Testament made it clear that the world of politics and the world of the spirit were two distinct entities; what was Caesar's was Caesar's and what was God's was God's, period. Every pope considered himself a man of peace, however cunning his diplomacy. In fact it may be argued that the development of papal diplomacy was a response to the need to avoid war, as the missions of Leo the Great demonstrated. Such an attitude could be maintained as long as the popes were protected by foreign armed forces. But could that protection be taken for granted? Some sought an answer in theology. Early on, it was obvious in a practical worldly sense that 'the Church [had] to perform certain functions and that consequently there must be people in the Church capable of carrying out these functions'.[18] Should these functions include military ones?

Church doctrine might have appeared to argue in that direction. In the Roman Catholic (and Greek Orthodox) view, the Church is an all-encompassing entity in which the spiritual and the earthly duties cannot really be separated, as both emanate from the supreme and timeless duty of standing in for Christ on earth. The one merges naturally into the other and comprises every aspect of human life. We need not delve too deeply into the theology of the issue – which indeed is outside the scope of this book – to conclude that theoretically at least, the popes could call on plenty of arguments to form and command their own fighting force if they wished. We have already seen how Christ's words about having to buy a sword for troubled times was a powerful argument in that direction. The popes could never feel physically quite secure. On 25 April 799 Leo III had been leaving the Lateran palace to bless the new spring crops when he was set upon by a gang that tried unsuccessfully to blind him. We don't know the motive for the attack; but we can make a shrewd guess, as Leo's twin sins in the eyes of the Roman nobles were that he was too much of a puppet of Charlemagne, and a commoner to boot. Leo had fled to the protection of Charlemagne, who had his heart set on being crowned 'Western Emperor' in Rome, which duly occurred on Christmas Day 800.

It may have been no accident that from that date the papacy began to decline dramatically in influence. One reason could have been complacency under Frankish overlordship. Another may have been the instincts of the Roman population, which now numbered 40,000. Never ones to be impressed by the trappings of power, the Romans were too close to the popes to be awed by them; they could see at first hand the inevitable corruption and abuses that seeped into the system. Too many pontiffs became the puppets of warring factions, and the character of the occupants of the throne of Saint Peter declined steeply. There were plenty of people in Rome who despised the popes' control by the Franks and had no hesitation in showing it. Charlemagne's son Louis the Pious and his successor Lothair attempted to recreate order, but Pope Paschal I chafed at this suzerainty, going so far as to order the murder of two senior papal officials seen to have been puppets of the Franks.

The autocratic Paschal, said to be dominated by his mother Theodora, was succeeded by Eugenius II, who gave back the laity their role in electing a pope but was helpless to prevent Frankish militias from raiding the Roman countryside. A more serious threat came from the Muslim Saracens, who by now had the run of the Mediterranean Sea. In 846 about 10,000 of them in seventy-five ships swept ashore at Ostia, brushing past the defences that Pope Gregory IV had hastily erected, and burst into the Borgo, the district adjacent to Saint Peter's, killing and looting. The paltry forces of Lothair, the supposed protector of the Holy City, could put up no resistance.[19] A devastating earthquake in early 847, accompanied by a serious fire in the Borgo, dealt further blows to Roman morale.

The Saracens, moving from their base in Sardinia, reappeared off the West Italian coast in 849. Pope Leo IV called for help from the west coast cities of Naples, Amalfi and Gaeta, which fitted out a fleet under Caesarius, a son of the Duke of Naples. Off Ostia, the port of Rome, Caesarius stopped the Saracens, aided by a timely squall that sent many of their hulls to the bottom. (Raphael much later commemorated the victory by a fresco in the Vatican.) Ostia was a lucky break for the popes, but that didn't mean they were out of danger. The initial defences of the Borgo were boosted over the next three years to grow into what became the Leonine City (*Civitas Leonina*), a walled-in enclosure stretching from the Sant'Angelo Castle around the Vatican hills and ending back at the Tiber downstream, named after the reigning pontiff. The walls, some twelve to fifteen feet high, were built of stone, brick and mortar and buttressed by two dozen round towers. Three gates, the *Posterula Angeli* near Sant'Angelo, the *Porta Sancti Peregrini* and the *Posterula Saxonum* (Saxon Gate) to the south allowed access. The finished complex was inaugurated on 27 June 852 with a solemn barefoot procession of bishops, priests and monks headed by the pope; the heads of all the clergy were stained with ashes, in a gesture of repentance for past sins that presumably had allowed the Saracens to directly threaten the Holy City. Leo stopped before each gate, invoking the blessings of Saints Peter and Paul on the Leonine City, the new rock of the Church. At the close of ceremonies the pope – hailed as the 'Restorer of Rome' – distributed gifts to the crowds.[20]

Some of the money to pay for the Leonine City project came from the Carolingian emperor Lothair, Rome's rather inadequate *defensor*. Evidently, Lothair felt he deserved a reward for putting his money where he had failed to put his soldiers. To be fair, he had to put up with incessant Norse raids on his own lands, plus opposition from his younger brothers Charles (the 'Bald') and Louis (the 'German') who wanted to carve out their own domains. Eventually, Lothair had to give way to those pressures, and by the 843 Treaty of Verdun gave Charles the western portion of the empire (which would become France) and Louis the eastern (which would become Germany), leaving Lothair with the middle section that included the northern half of Italy. In 855 Lothair became seriously ill, and despairing of his life, called in the papal debt by demanding that the pope crown his son as Louis II. Leo IV died that same year. The popes continued to depend politically and militarily on the Carolingian kingdom. Under this French umbrella Pope Nicholas I (858–867) made stalwart efforts to restore the prestige of the Church in the face of the Italian political factions that battled to control it. Street fighting erupted again as the pope shut himself in the Lateran in prayer.

Nicholas' successor Hadrian II (867–872) was a weak man completely under the thumb of Lothair. He was forced to give up the booty gained from the Saracens to the extortions of the Duke of Benevento. But the next pontiff, John VIII (872–882) was made of tougher material and asserted his authority over the Church and over his French 'protectors', ruled now by Charles II (the 'Bald') and sorely pressed by Norse depredations. At home, faced with a fresh Saracen threat, John ordered a fortress to be built around the basilica of Saint Paul and its immediate neighbourhood south of Rome, to guard the approach from Ostia. He also looked for actual military allies, and after generous payments gained the services of the dukes of Amalfi and Salerno. A request to Charles for help was not even answered. Thus John took a momentous step for a pope: after assembling a fleet he decided to command it himself. In 877 off Cape Circeo, midway between Rome and Naples, he personally vanquished a Saracen fleet, capturing eighteen ships and freeing about 600 Christian galley-slaves. For the first time in history a reigning pontiff had become a commander in the field.

The death of Charles the Bald that same year ignited a succession crisis that was reflected in Rome, where pro-French and pro-German factions battled for primacy. Charles' successor Carloman, who *ex officio* was essentially the king of Italy, attempted to reassert royal control over the popes. He had in tow a bishop named Formosus whom he aimed to make pope, but ill-health forced Carloman to leave Italy. Tiring of the constant turmoil in Rome, during which he had been briefly kidnapped by Duke Lambert of Spoleto and given no food until he endorsed Carloman, John quit the city for the calmer atmosphere of Troyes in France. There he hurled excommunications against Formosus and his handlers. The health of Carloman's successor Louis the Stammerer was even worse than his predecessor's and he lasted just a year. With the imperial house in such a weak state, John gave his support to Charles III (the 'Fat'), son of Louis the German, whom he crowned in Rome in 881. But if the pope thought he could call in the debt and secure the crown's support in return, he was mistaken. Charles stayed in the north, caring little about the fate of Rome or the papacy, which meanwhile had found it necessary to pay off the Saracens against any further attacks.

During this period the papacy resorted to yet another dubious piece of propaganda to shore up its shaky reputation. This was a text called the Pseudo-Isidoran Decretals, dreamed up to invest the popes with yet greater political and judicial power. Though we now know it to be false, like the 'Donations' of Constantine and Pepin, it carried great weight with the papal establishment, but at the same time spawned a whole new crop of disputes with the Frankish monarchs. None of this boded well for Rome. John VIII is reported to have come to a violent end: a disgruntled relative tried to poison him, but seeing that the poison didn't have much of an effect, brought a hammer down on the pontiff's head to finish the job. If the story is true it reflects a venomous political atmosphere in the papacy, which got no better under the brief pontificate of Marinus I (882–884), who was talked into revoking the excommunication of Formosus and allowing the latter's intrigues to continue. Popes became nothing more than the puppets of either the pro-French or pro-German factions or local potentates who wanted to control them, such as the dukes of Spoleto, who picked men of less than sterling character to be their papal servants. Of such men there was no lack: Pope Hadrian III (884–885), a puppet of the French faction, made his mark by having the leader of the pro-Germans blinded and his wife forced to walk naked through Rome while being beaten by croziers. The theatrics would have been unnecessary. Hadrian was succeeded by the pro-German Stephen V (885–891), who found himself on the receiving end of a new appearance by the Saracens. It was Guido, the duke of Spoleto, who dealt with the Muslims in a sea battle off the island of Liri as Stephen could only look on helplessly. In a mere ten years, since John VIII had commanded a papal fleet, the popes had relinquished their unofficial role and reputation as *defensores* of Rome.

Charles the Fat was deposed in 878, and died a year later. His sole achievement was the admittedly important one of reuniting the fragmented Carolingian states into what would in time become the Holy Roman Empire. His successor Odo chose Paris as his seat of government, while some (but not all) of the wild Norsemen who had been pillaging France gradually slowed to a settled Christian existence and gave their name to Normandy.

For Rome, the net result of these French developments was that the popes lost their chief foreign protectors and stood at the mercy of the Italian factions that never ceased in their efforts to control the throne of Saint Peter for their own purposes. There were four main factions, led by the dukes of Lombardy, Spoleto and Tuscany respectively, and a native Roman one under Theophylact, a high papal official (his Greek name, meaning 'protected of God,' raises speculation that he could have been of Byzantine Greek origin) all jostling for primacy against the prevailing pro-German establishment.

It was about this time that certain noble ladies of these factions, in an outburst of feminist ambition, pushed their way to positions of high influence over the popes. We are not sure why this happened at this particular time; perhaps one woman of determined character managed to set an example that was followed by others. The moral vacuum of the papacy and its structure had probably become so obvious that the whole male establishment had become discredited, and all it needed was for a few tough-minded women to step in and put matters right. The result was that in the late-ninth century Rome was as much governed by women as by the popes and their entourages. It was what some historians call 'the Rome of the female popes', though other less charitable descriptions are 'government of the countesses' or 'government of the prostitutes'. There seems little doubt that some, if not most, of these ladies earned their influence through careers as courtesans. Gregorovius paints a picture of a cabal of 'beautiful, ferocious and lascivious' women who based their power almost exclusively on their sexual control over men, and over the very papacy itself.[21]

We may confidently dismiss as a fairy tale the story of a supposed Pope Joan, an Englishwoman by birth who, disguised as a man, travelled to Athens to study theology and then moved to Rome, where she amassed enough influence to be elected successor to Leo IV, only to be unmasked when labour pains seized her and she gave birth to a child on the way from the Vatican to the Lateran.[22] Equally spurious is the story that in consequence, prospective claimants to Saint Peter's throne had to prove their masculinity by sitting on a chair with a hole in the seat through which the existence of the necessary genitalia could be manually confirmed. In 891 the pro-German Formosus became pope by dubious means. Despite his name (meaning well-shaped in Latin), he was an odd-looking man with a bulbous bald head and tufts of grey hair sticking out in front and at the sides. Early in his reign he earned the enmity of one of the 'virulent Venuses'. This was Angeltrude, the wife of Guido, Duke of Spoleto, who occupied a senior post in the Lateran. Angeltrude was tireless in her efforts to unseat Formosus and drive the pro-German faction from Rome, setting Spoletine armed gangs to fight the pro-Germans in the streets. Alarmed, Formosus appealed to the German king, Arnulf of Carinthia, to liberate the Church from the threat of what the pope called 'the tyranny of bad Christians' – a barely veiled reference to Angeltrude, who in his view should stay home and be a good noble housewife instead of meddling in male politics. Arnulf came as far as North Italy, but refused to proceed to Rome, fearful of the power of Angeltrude's husband, who it seems could muster a respectable military force as a deterrent.

Duke Guido's death in 895 didn't stop Angeltrude, who now aimed to place her son Lambert in her late husband's position. Formosus appealed anew to Arnulf, accompanying the appeal with a promise to make the German king ruler over all the Carolingian domains. Angeltrude sent her son to Spoleto to keep him out of danger and stirred up a street revolt in Rome. Formosus was seized and shut up in Sant'Angelo Castle, but this time Arnulf took the crisis seriously and marched into Rome, liberating Formosus almost without striking a blow. As Angeltrude retreated to Spoleto vowing revenge, Formosus kept his promise to Arnulf and in February 896 crowned him emperor in Saint Peter's. It was but a momentary triumph. Back in Germany, Arnulf cared little for papal affairs, which left the way open for Angeltrude to murder the pope by poison two months later.

Formosus was not allowed to rest even in the grave. Such was Angeltrude's visceral hatred of him that she talked the next pope but one, Stephen IV (Formosus' successor Boniface VI lasted a mere two weeks in office), to carry out one of the more gruesome acts in European history. By order of Stephen (or more accurately Angeltrude), the corpse of Formosus was dug up, re-robed in papal vestments and propped up in a hall in the Lateran Palace to be tried on charges of ecclesiastical irregularity in crowning Arnulf. Writes Gregorovius of what became known as 'the Cadaver's Trial':

> The attorney for Pope Stephen rose to his feet and addressing that horrendous mummy, at the side of which stood, trembling, a deacon acting as its defence lawyer, proclaimed the charges. Then the living

pope addressed the dead one harshly: 'How could you, with your foolish ambition, usurp the Apostolic See?'[23]

We are assured that the corpse was stripped of its bizarre vestments, and what remained of three fingers of the right hand (used by popes in the gesture of benediction) were hacked off. Then, accompanied by the supportive howls of the Roman mob, the mutilated dead pontiff was taken to the Tiber and thrown in. But a nemesis of sorts was at hand; the Lateran basilica in which the macabre trial took place was shortly felled by an earthquake, and that same year (897) Stephen IV was toppled by a pro-German counter-revolt and strangled in jail. To such a condition had the patrimony of Saint Peter sunk at the close of the ninth century. Could it ever recover?

Chapter 3

Who's the Boss in Europe?

Though the papacy might have presented a sorry picture, this was not the case with the Church itself, which throughout Western Europe had grown into the third great pillar of the feudal system, after the nobles and the commoners. Whatever the personal attributes (or lack of them) of the men under the papal mitre (or of the scheming women behind them), millions of people high and low continued to go to church, read the Bible, listen and confess to their priests and build churches and cathedrals of striking size and beauty – all concomitants of a living popular faith which, like a deep river, flowed on unaffected by the turbulence and pools of pollution on the visible surface.

The great economic strength of the Church lay in its land. Decade after decade, century after century, pious people in high places bequeathed their property to the Church hoping for reconciliation with God and forgiveness of sins in the next world. By the time of Charlemagne these holdings had mushroomed into extensive estates, administered by bishops and abbots; tracts of perhaps 100,000 acres or more were not uncommon, while 5,000 acres was considered poor by comparison. By the twelfth century about one-third of all the usable land in Europe would come to be controlled by the Church – and ultimately by the pope. This land, of course, was worked by peasants who had to be available for military service whenever the king or lord required it. But since churchmen were not supposed to fight (*pace* John VIII), a system was worked out whereby the bishops and abbots parcelled out part of their holdings to lay vassals who would in theory recruit the men. Once the Church acquired a piece of real estate it could not be sold or otherwise alienated. That gave senior clergy enormous power, as they ran no risk of losing any assets and thus could wield huge influence in royal courts, especially as they had at their disposal large reserves of military manpower.

There was little to distinguish senior clergy from their lay counterparts in lifestyle. Writes Wallace Ferguson:

Men who rose to influential positions in the church were not necessarily more religious in character or interests than the ordinary lay nobles … They loved hunting and fighting and took an active part in feudal politics. Many a lusty bishop led his mounted vassals into battle, light-heartedly swinging a mace in place of a sword and thus avoiding the sin of shedding blood.[1]

In such conditions it was hard to locate where the realm of the world ended and where the realm of God began. The majority of senior clergy, in fact, were involved in a gigantic conflict of interest, and many were acutely aware of that fact. Some may have been taken in by the fiction that crushing an enemy's skull was somehow 'less sinful' than stabbing him with a blade. Yet the Church in general did have a somewhat higher social conscience than the rest of society; this was demonstrated by what was called 'the Peace of God,' by which the nobles on the warpath pledged not to harm peasants, churchmen, merchants and other non-combatants or their property. Not surprisingly, this 'Peace' was observed far more often in the breach rather than the observance. But it set a precedent that would be followed.

The blurred area between what a senior churchman (including a pope) could or could not do in the political and military sphere gave rise to much confusion, which could only be cleared by drawing a bold line between the secular and sacred realms. In the case of the papacy, despite the sad condition of individual pontiffs, Rome stuck to its position as the spiritual fount of western Christendom, preferring diplomacy to the sword. But as the tenth century began, a new power coalescing in the north began to test that position. In Germany, with the death of the Carolingian Louis the Child in 911, the German dukes elected one of their number, Conrad of Franconia, as king. Though he reigned largely as a figurehead, Conrad I was able to arrange the succession for Henry I (the 'Fowler') who secured the eastern frontiers and established a measure of control over the aggressively-independent dukes. Henry's son Otto I (the 'Great'), who took the throne in 936, granted large tracts of land to the clergy on condition that he appoint them himself – in an ecclesiastical as well as a political sense. This way the 'Charlemagne of Germany' ensured that the German clergy was totally dependent on the king. What did this mean for the pope's authority in Rome?

Otto inevitably found himself drawn into the Italian cauldron, which in the middle of the tenth century was as malodorous as ever. To the north of the Papal States were four margraves, that is, virtually independent feudal domains: Friuli, Spoleto, Ivrea and Tuscany, all of which had an interest in preventing any expansion of the Papal States. In 904 Berengar of Friuli (who claimed the now rather meaningless title of King of Italy) had defeated Louis III of Provence in battle over who should control North and Central Italy, while a succession of weak popes could only look on impotently. Theophylact, whom we have met as a leader of a Roman faction, acquired a senior administrative position in the Lateran Palace as well as the titles of duke, commander of the Roman militia, consul and senator. In actuality he shared this power with his strong-minded wife Theodora, who insisted on also sharing his formal titles. Of course, she made enemies. One of them was the bishop and diplomat Liutprand of Cremona, who had no hesitation in branding Theodora a 'vile disgrace' and 'shameless meddler' and other epithets rather reminiscent of what was heaped on her fabled Byzantine namesake five hundred years before. Yet like that namesake, she had an incisive and thoroughly political brain, and even the livid Liutprand had to concede that for all her flaws, 'she ruled Rome with a firm hand.'

Yet Theodora was a rank amateur beside her daughter Maria, who by the age of fourteen was developed enough to be shepherded by her scheming mother into the bed of Pope Sergius III. If the aim was the cold-blooded one of getting Maria pregnant by a pope, with all the attendant privileges that would entail – not to mention the delicious possibilities of blackmailing Sergius – then it succeeded admirably. After the pope's death Maria married Alberic I, the Marquis of Camerino, ensuring his alliance. As their son, also named Alberic, was growing up, Maria matured to become the most formidable of female surrogate pontiffs, better known to history as Marozia (roughly 'Big Mary'). Later illustrations portray her as a large and shapely woman, with a smouldering dark Mediterranean attractiveness – qualities which by themselves would have given her an advantage in the Roman society of the time. Well might the austere Gregorovius write that in those years 'the Roman church had become a brothel'.[2] Marozia's marriage to Alberic I (the first of several husbands) enabled her to form a coalition that repulsed the Saracens when they established a foothold at the Garigliano river between Rome and Naples in 915. There Pope John X, at the head of an alliance of the duchies of Benevento, Naples and Salerno, decisively defeated the Saracens, who no longer would be able to threaten Central Italy. John took the field in person, along with contingents from Berengar, Theophylact and Alberic I, to blockade the Arabs for three months and eventually smash their base in August. John X was thus the second pope after John VIII to be credited with a military victory in the field.

Apart from such sparks of energy, the history of the papacy in the tenth century does not make for edifying reading. From 900 to 999 no fewer than twenty-two putative heirs of Saint Peter were put on the throne and toppled from it, in the majority of cases by foul methods. For a quarter of that century Marozia ruled the Roman roost. John X, who may have been one of Theodora's lovers, was thanks to his victory at Garigliano considered a capable man, hence to be done away with. The evidence strongly suggests that Theodora and Marozia arranged the death of Alberic, freeing Marozia to marry Guido, the Duke of Tuscany. Marozia and Guido gathered a military force that toppled John and locked him in Sant'Angelo Castle, where Guido himself, it was said, suffocated John with a cushion.

In 928, at the height of her power, Marozia was proclaimed *senatrix et patricia*, for all practical purposes the ruler of Rome, papal and secular. In the following year her husband Guido, holding the largely ceremonial title of Consul, conveniently passed away. By 931 Marozia's bastard son by Sergius III was, according to most accounts, old enough to be raised to the office of pope as John XI. The act raised Marozia's prestige yet further as the mother and mistress of popes, but it was not necessarily good for her son, as another son of hers – this one legitimate by Alberic I – captured John and jailed him in Sant'Angelo, where he was allowed to exercise his spiritual functions before his death in 935. Marozia, meanwhile, in 932 married the late Guido's brother Hugh of Provence, the king of Italy – officiated by her son the pope – making her queen and further cementing her power.

Marozia's downfall was startlingly sudden. Her marriage to Hugh was the last straw for her son Alberic, who had never accepted his half-brother John XI's legitimacy and distrusted Hugh. During a vigil in Sant'Angelo before the crowning ceremony the hot-tempered Alberic slapped Hugh in public for some affront. In the ensuing procession Marozia, now somewhat heavy but still remarkably good-looking, and her new spouse were disturbed by a commotion. It was a crowd of angry Romans stirred up by Alberic, who by now must have perceived the whole corrupt structure of his mother's rule and the papacy and wanted no part of it. Just twenty years old, he mobilized as many as he could of the Roman people to overthrow the whole rotten edifice. He ordered the gates of the city shut so that Hugh could not reach his soldiers outside the walls; the king escaped by lowering himself down the castle wall, and vanished from history. Alberic promptly deposed mother and stepfather, shutting up the former in a convent, where she died four years later, aged forty-four. Alberic II, as he now became, set himself up as *princeps atque omnium Romanorum senator*, or dictator of a virtual Roman republic. He would keep the popes in their place as mere priests and leave the running of Rome to what he considered more qualified people.

Alberic can be credited with the first serious attempt to clean up the Roman administration in centuries. Though he could easily have claimed or usurped the title of king in place of the discredited Hugh of Provence, he remained a republican at heart, content to rule as head of a government of *optimati*, or 'the best men,' all but ignoring the titular kings of Italy. Alberic's popes, needless to say, were completely under his thumb. Yet he was by no means anti-clerical. He rebuilt monasteries and convents, donating his own mansion on the Aventine Hill to the head of the Cluniac monastic order of France. Yet he could not have done all this without influential backing, and this came from Rome's landowning and business classes which for too long had been sidelined by the closed system surrounding the papal curia. Steeped in ancient Roman history, he named his son Octavian in an attempt – ultimately vain – to revive the imagined robust glories of the Augustan age.

For some twenty years Alberic's fair but austere rule earned the respect of other Italian and European potentates – all, that is, except Germany's Otto I, who had his eye on the figurehead royal house of Italy and planned to add it to his other realms. In 951 Otto had made an experimental foray into Italy, defeating forces loyal to King Berengar II and forcing Berengar to recognize him as overlord. On the basis of this, Otto proclaimed himself king of Italy as well as Germany and asked Pope Agapetus II to crown him emperor in Rome. Certainly not, replied Alberic through his mouthpiece Agapetus. But by the end of August 954 Alberic was dead, to be followed by Agapetus a year and a half later. Alberic may have been in poor health, as a few days before his death he made the leading clergy and nobles of Rome swear on the tomb of Saint Peter that his son Octavian would become the next pope. In December

955 Octavian, aged just eighteen, became Pope John XII, who seems to have inherited enough of his grandmother Marozia's infamy to become one of the most debased characters ever to occupy the throne of Saint Peter.

With Alberic gone, the papacy under John XII was able to claw back some of its former power. But the prestige of the institution certainly did not benefit. Almost all accounts of John XII portray him as a ruthless sexual predator. No-one of either sex or any age was safe from his obscene attentions in the Lateran Palace. Even Catholic historians blush at the stories of licentiousness told about his rule, where the Lateran, staffed with prostitutes and other decidedly un-Christian types, witnessed 'orgies of debauchery'.[3] The ridiculously young pontiff was reported as taking bribes for consecrating bishops, having sex with his father's widow, niece and mistress, and spending the rest of his time out hunting. Some cardinals wanted to impeach him, but he simply refused to attend any hearings or even answer the charges against him.

Otto in Germany heard about all this, of course, and saw his chance. His first move was to convene an ecclesiastical council at Saint Peter's in December 963 to try John on charges of gross immorality. The pope was tried *in absentia*, as in the meantime he had fled to Corsica. His prosecutors pursued him there, to read him a damning indictment:

> You know, therefore, that not a few, but everyone, lay and religious, have accused you of homicide, perjury, sacrilege and incest with your relations and two sisters ... that you have made a toast to the devil and, playing with dice, have invoked Zeus, Venus and other demons.[4]

Admittedly, the great bulk of what we know about John XII comes from implacably hostile sources. The result is that he has received an extraordinarily bad press in the history books. He has been accused, for example, of appointing a stable groom as a deacon while drunk, and making a ten-year-old boy a bishop in return for the boy's sexual availability. 'There was no woman, widow, girlfriend, virgin or married woman, who had not been compelled to submit to the pleasures of the pontiff,' wrote Bishop Liutprand of Cremona, who supported Otto and had an interest in blackening the pope as much as possible. Recent authorities such as Roger Collins assert that John, on the other hand, did much to regulate monastic life in his domains and that he may have been nowhere near the sexual ogre he was made out to be.[5] John replied defiantly to his accusers by excommunicating the lot of them, but in Rome in late 963 the assembled delegates from all the North and Central Italian duchies, and the Roman nobles and commons, deposed John as 'a monster that no virtue redeems from his vices' and replaced him with Otto's own candidate, Leo VIII. The new pope lasted a year before John overcame the leaders of the pro-German party, had their noses slashed and tongues cut out, and restored himself as pope. One day he decided to seduce a woman he fancied; it was a fatal decision. Two titillating accounts vie for acceptance: one, that he had a fatal stroke while exerting himself in bed, and two, that her husband arrived at an inopportune moment and threw the amorous pope out of the upper-floor window.

That dramatic moment in 965 more or less coincided with events in Central Europe that would have momentous consequences for Europe and the papacy. Two years before, John XII had crowned Otto the Great as emperor, inaugurating what has become known to history as the Holy Roman Empire. Not only Rome's own Alberic II, but also Otto had dreamed of reviving the glories of ancient Rome in a Europe-wide domain (though ignoring the contemporary Byzantine Empire, which considered itself the real inheritor of the Roman tradition). Public opinion in Western Europe seemed to be ready for such a development. Anarchy and aggressively independent nobles had ruled the region for far too long. Otto thought in terms of a divinely-ordained partnership, with the emperor providing the political and military muscle for western Christianity, and the popes the spiritual underpinning. That, at least, was the theory. Reality would prove rather more troublesome as the Holy Roman Empire, despite its grandiloquent title, was never anything more than Germany, the Alpine regions and North Italy; moreover, the popes would not be content with just prayer and ceremony. The stage was set for a titanic struggle that would dominate European affairs for the next three hundred years. The subtext of this struggle was that the papacy had to continue to develop the means of defending itself.

At first Otto had little trouble with the popes. After John XII's embarrassing demise, he wanted John's temporary replacement, Leo VIII, back, but the Romans ignored him and elected Benedict V. (The Roman Catholic Church regards Leo VIII as an anti-pope, and hence does not officially recognize his rule.) Otto rode down from Germany in 965 to topple Benedict, pack him off to exile at Hamburg and replace him with the pliant John XIII. The nobles and commons of Rome seethed. Were they going to be saddled with pontiffs owing their seats to an alien power? And what about the sorry image of the papacy itself, which tainted all of Rome and its 30,000 people? The very term 'Roman,' wrote the waspish Liutprand of Cremona, had degenerated into a common insult, 'encompassing everything ignoble, mendacious, luxury-loving, miserly, unpleasant and sinful that exists in the world'.[6] Much of the European clergy would endorse Liutprand's judgement. Arnulph, the Archbishop of Orléans, in 991 went so far as to issue a stinging public rebuke to the popes and their recent track record:

> Where is it written that the innumerable priests of God, scattered around the terrestrial globe and provided with doctrine and goodness, should be subject to such monsters lacking human and divine knowledge, the disgrace of mankind?[7]

Such a spirit of clerical rebellion suited Otto I down to the ground. It appeared to be ample justification for his heavy-handed military interventions in Rome, that did not exclude starving the people to impose his papal choices. Thanks partly to this German callousness, Otto's puppet John XIII lasted three months before a popular revolt in Rome ousted him from the city in 965. Leading this revolt was the noble Roman family of the Crescentii which, however, soon had a change of heart and the following year restored John to his position. Most likely the Crescentii perceived an advantage in allying themselves with Otto I, who returned to Rome after the Crescentii had executed the populist ringleaders. Other leading rebels were hanged or blinded – a punishment very likely imported from Byzantium. A former prefect of Rome was seized and suspended by his hair from a statue, and then paraded around Rome seated backwards on a donkey – another Byzantine import, it would seem – grasping the donkey's tail like a bridle; after that ignominy, having got off rather lightly in the circumstances, he was exiled to Germany.

This, then, was the beginning of a long and bitter conflict between the Holy Roman emperors and the papacy. Otto the Great, in a sense, may have wanted to imitate the Byzantine Empire in establishing himself as a secular emperor who, however, derived his power ultimately from God, while the popes attended to spiritual rather than political concerns. If the arrangement had worked admirably in the East for the past six hundred years – and showed every sign of continuing indefinitely – why could it not also work in the West that had been roiling in near-anarchy for too long? There were two main reasons why it could not. First, Otto and his successors Otto II and Otto III weakened themselves at home in Germany by obsessing with the 'revival' of Rome; and second, the papacy, having had experience of wielding political power, was most reluctant to let it go.

For Otto II (973–983) restoring the glories of ancient Rome could have had emotional significance in that he married the high-born Theophano of Byzantium, a niece of Emperor John I Tzimiskes. In fact, Otto and Pope John XIII had been under the mistaken impression that the sixteen-year-old Theophano was a genuine palace-born Greek princess, and when the more prosaic truth emerged, there were thoughts of packing her off back to Constantinople. In the end, to avoid needless controversy with Byzantium, the pope married the couple in Saint Peter's on 14 April 972. The marriage turned out to be a fulfilling one, and a period of reconciliation with Byzantium appeared to be on the cards.[8] But in Rome matters did not run so smoothly.

John XIII's successor, Benedict VI, held office for just a year before the Crescentii, those inveterate foes of German influence, toppled him and shut him up in that trusty papal jail, Sant'Angelo Castle, where for additional insurance he was put to death. Rome at this time resembled nothing more than a seething Mafia-type underworld, where popes appeared little more than gang bosses fighting for their turf with secular nobles. The Crescentii had their next pontiff ready to trundle out in the person of Boniface VII (considered an anti-pope by the Roman Catholic Church). Imperial officials – possibly with the aid of soldiers – did restore some measure of order in 974. Boniface fled to Byzantine territory, carrying with him the papal treasury on which he would live comfortably for the rest of his days. Otto's choice fell on Benedict VII, who kept the papal tiara on his head for no fewer than nine years, propped up by Otto, who intervened to mercilessly put down a Roman revolt in 980. According to Gregorovius, Otto invited all the leading Romans to a banquet on the steps of Saint Peter's basilica. During the event he had several of his main enemies beheaded – taking a another page perhaps from Byzantium – inviting the rest to go on enjoying their meal as if nothing had happened.[9]

Around 983 a fresh Saracen threat to South Italy drew Otto and his forces southwards, where he met defeat at Stilo in Calabria. His ship was sunk, but he swam to safety. Returning unfulfilled to Rome, he buttressed his claim to Italy by crowning his three-year-old son Otto king of Italy and Germany. It was as he started out on a new campaign against the Saracens in the south that Benedict VII died, forcing the emperor to turn back – he couldn't risk leaving the succession to be upset by the Crescentii – and supervise the election of his Italian arch-chancellor Pietro di Pavia, who became Pope John XIV. This was Otto's last act, as soon afterwards he sickened, perhaps weakened by his ordeal by shipwreck, and died. He was buried in Saint Peter's, leaving his throne to the infant Otto III. Theophano, compelled to return to Germany, ruled as regent for nine years. Inevitably, the Crescentii filled the power vacuum, recalling the anti-pope Boniface VII from his refuge in Constantinople to be their papal puppet, and consigning John XIV to starve to death (or be poisoned, according to some sources) in Sant'Angelo Castle. Boniface, however, made himself so unpopular with the Romans that less than a year later the Crescentii themselves ordered his murder; armed gangs mutilated his body and threw what was left at the feet of an equestrian statue of Emperor Marcus Aurelius that still stands in the Campidoglio (Capitol) in Rome.

In 989 Theophano called at Rome to restore some order out of the chaos, forcing the population to swear allegiance to her young son. Pope John XV, who had been elected four years before, stood firmly in the imperial camp. The Crescentii seem to have been temporarily subdued; the head of the clan, Giovanni Crescentius (or Crescenzo), agreed to handle the secular side of Roman affairs, which he did quite effectively, taking a page out of the authoritarian book of Alberic II. Reliable information about this period of Roman history is meagre, but somehow it is not surprising that within a few years the pope and Giovanni Crescentius found themselves at odds. In 996 the former appealed to Otto III, now fifteen, who rode with an army over the Alps, carrying the supposed Lance that had pierced Christ's side (Constantinople claimed to have the authentic one). He reached Ravenna, where he learned of the pope's death. Crescentius, to avoid violence, held off from pushing his own candidate for pope, allowing Otto to promote his cousin Bruno of Carinthia, whom the emperor crowned at Saint Peter's on 21 May as Gregory V.

At this point the reader might well wonder why so many Roman popes, even into our own day, have changed their names when elected. Why did Octavian, the son of Alberic II, become John XII? Why did a German named Bruno take the name Gregory V? The answer lies in the supremely exalted position which the head of the Church assumed in the West. It was not enough merely to administer the Church and safeguard the spiritual welfare of the people, as the patriarchs did in the Byzantine Empire. A pope somehow entered a higher state of being when he assumed the tiara; he was considered to have been reborn in Christ, and hence deserving of a whole new identity after shuffling off the old human one. How seriously this theological twist was taken in Rome and among the faithful is hard to gauge. Considering the poor stuff that too many pontiffs were made of, the Orthodox Byzantines certainly did not consider them 'reborn' in any way. And it may not be too much to suppose that Otto III, who combined the qualities of the Greeks and Saxons to an extraordinary degree and through his mother was strongly influenced by the Eastern Church, decided to take the papacy down a peg or two.

But if many hoped that 'Western Christendom was in safer hands than for many years past',[10] they would soon be disabused. Otto himself nursed a grand and valiant but utterly unrealistic vision of a mighty Christian empire combining the Latins with the Byzantine Greeks, the Germans and all the other Europeans, north and south, in a majestic recreation of the classic Roman Empire, this time owing allegiance to Christ instead of the emperors. This idealistic vision, of course, would come up against the harsh reality of differing political cultures and mentalities among the European peoples which, from that day to this, bedevil any attempt at union. But young Otto appeared to have excellent prospects ahead of him, were it not for the fatal Crescentii. For some reason not fully explained, but probably to keep the social peace, the pope revoked the sentence of banishment on Giovanni Crescentius II, the brother of the deceased Giovanni, who revealed his true gangland colours by re-seizing power and driving Gregory out of Rome on 29 September 996. In his shoes was placed the ambitious and pliant Archbishop of Piacenza, John Philagathus, who became anti-pope John XVI.

Otto at first hesitated to act, on the grounds that the Roman climate was too unhealthy for him. He turned his attention first to putting down a revolt of the Slavs. But such was the contempt that the Italian clergy had for the anti-pope, who hardly dared show himself in public, that Otto and his army returned to Rome in February 998. While Crescentius II barricaded himself in Sant'Angelo Castle, John XVI fled the city, only to be captured by Otto's troops who blinded him and cut off his ears, nose and hands as a reward for his treachery. The following month the mutilated anti-pope was tried and sentenced to the now-familiar undignified penalty of being placed facing backwards on a donkey and paraded through the streets.

A month later Crescentius was seized with a dozen of his henchmen. They were taken to the highest point of the castle, and in full public view beheaded, their bodies flung down into the moat. The bodies were taken and suspended upside down on the foothills of the Mons Gaudii behind the Vatican hill.[11] The sensitive Otto was filled with remorse about what he had authorized – or, by some accounts, he conceived a passion for Giovanni Crescentius' sister Stephania, who became his lover but gained her family revenge by poisoning him. The poison seems to have acted slowly, possibly made to a Byzantine formula, and Otto wasted away, to die at Viterbo in 1002 at the tragically young age of twenty-two.[12]

Before his death Otto had secured the election of his spiritual mentor, Gerbert d'Aurillac, as Pope Sylvester II. A profoundly learned man, Sylvester was accused by his enemies of dabbling in the occult. On 12 May 1003, after seeing Otto in Germany, he became ill in Rome's church of Santa Croce in Gerusalemme and died shortly afterwards. Of course, we can never be sure whether such a pontifical demise had natural or pathological causes or was the result of foul play. Pontiffs close to the empire were never popular in Rome. The Byzantines in the East had elevated the technique of slow and gradual poisoning to a high art, to resemble wasting illness, and not a few Byzantine rulers had been disposed of this way. Since much Byzantine influence had passed over to Rome, we may be reasonably certain that several popes were given similar treatment. Whatever the truth about Sylvester II, he would have been a marked man anyway, as the second millennium opened with the return to power of the Crescentii. For twelve years this family ruled Rome with an iron fist, seeing off three puppet popes in succession – John XVII, John XVIII and Sergius IV. In this budding cold war between the Holy Roman Empire and the papacy, round one can be said to have gone to the latter.

Succeeding Otto III was a distant cousin of his, Henry II, who worked hard to assert his authority over Germany and Italy, and had himself crowned king of Italy in 1004. Much of his support came from the local clergy, which gave him additional leverage over Rome. His task was made easier in 1012, when Niccoló Crescentius became head of the family and decided on a low profile in the interests of the papacy. The family may have run Rome along the lines of a gangland clan, but if it came to a choice between backing the popes and backing the Germans, elementary patriotism dictated that it had to be the popes. But by now the Crescentii had passed their prime of power; Niccoló seems to have had little taste for violent and confrontational politics, and shortly found himself faced by new noble rivals in the south of Rome.

These were the Counts of Tusculum, an offshoot of the Theophylact clan that had given the world the likes of Marozia and Theodora, who had bided their time during the Crescentii ascendancy. As their name suggests, the Counts of Tusculum claimed ancient roots going back perhaps as far as the Etruscans. More likely they took their name from the Via Tuscolana leading out of Rome to the southeast, as that road passes near Grottaferrata, where the clan had its stronghold. Thanks partly to their founding of the Grottaferrata Abbey, a religious and cultural centre, the Counts kept themselves in good stead with the Holy Roman Empire. Naturally, they felt important enough to meddle in the election of popes, and when Sergius IV passed away in 1012, they directly challenged the Crescentii on the issue. Armed gangs from both parties fought in the streets; the Counts' gang prevailed, and one of their number became pope as Benedict VIII. One of the new pope's first acts was to invite Henry II to Rome to be formally crowned along with his wife Kunigunde.

Benedict proved to be a capable pontiff, a pleasant change from the string of nonentities who had preceded him. As was considered normal in those days, he moved to consolidate his family rule by promoting his brother Romano to be 'consul and senator of the Romans' and his father Gregory as 'prefect of the navy.' As in the case of John VIII a century and a half before, the immediate enemy to be tackled were the Saracens, who had not ceased their intermittent raids on the South Italian coasts. And like his distant predecessor, Benedict took personal command of an army in the field which, along with forces from Pisa and Genoa, dislodged Saracen footholds in Tuscany; leading a fleet, he also cleared the Arabs out of Sardinia. Benedict, then, must have had military as well as administrative capabilities. The Counts of Tusculum seemed to have chosen well. But other foreign policy issues pressed from the south.

The heel and toe of Italy, from Naples southwards, was in Byzantine hands, but those hands were weakening under the onslaught of many Norman adventurers attracted by the warm climate. These Normans allied with the local Lombards to rebel against Byzantine rule, but in 1019 the Greek military governor, Basileios Boioannes, beat them on the old battlefield of Cannae. Constantinople was understandably hostile to all foreigners who tried to poke their fingers into the Byzantine Greek territories of Italy, which were seen as part of the true patrimony of the Roman Empire and hence to be hung onto at all costs, especially as Sicily had long since fallen to the Arabs. One of these foreigners was the man whom the Byzantines scorned as the 'fake' Roman emperor, Henry II. In 1022 Henry led a large expedition into Italy, but Boioannes stopped him in his tracks and sent him scurrying back over the Alps. When Byzantine forces invaded the Papal States, Benedict fled Rome and appealed for help to Henry II, whose forces stopped the Byzantines. The Byzantine emperor at the time was Basil II, known ominously as the 'Bulgar-slayer' for his bloody accomplishments against Bulgarian foes. Basil aimed to use Boioannes to recapture Sicily from the Saracens, but he died before it could happen, and thereafter Byzantine power began its long downhill course, allowing papal Italy to try and fill the vacuum.

Benedict initiated much-needed moral and financial reforms in the papacy, hut he didn't live to complete them. His brother Romano succeeded him as John XIX. We are told that Romano/John may not even have been an ordained priest, and that he was promoted from layman to bishop in a single day. We may assume that the Counts of Tusculum exerted their considerable influence in that direction. There was talk of submitting the Church to Constantinople; Basil the Bulgar-slayer proposed that the western pope and eastern patriarch keep their separate domains without one trying to lord it over the other. If accepted, the proposal could have ushered in a period of general Mediterranean peace. But the Italian clergy, unwilling to relinquish its huge perks, scotched that idea. It did not make for a peaceful situation when Henry II's successor Conrad II called at Rome in 1027 demanding that the pope formally crown him. John complied, but in doing so triggered bloody rioting in Rome. The populace appealed to Conrad to restore peace, and John XIX was allowed to rule for the next five years in relative calm.

But nothing could hide the uncomfortable fact that even though the States of the Church extended from just south of Venice down to just north of Naples – about one-quarter of the territory of present-day Italy – the Papacy's writ was valid only within the walls of Rome. The chronic conflict with the Holy Roman emperors had drained its Italian resources. In the rest of the popes' supposed domain local nobles ruled pretty much unhindered. And that rule was none too secure, as pilgrims proceeding down the Italian peninsula towards Rome often were robbed by bandits. In the East the Greek branch of the Church maintained its position that the Roman popes had no business claiming ecclesiastical primacy; in Greek eyes they were (and still are) nothing more than what they had originally been – local bishops of Rome with no authority to rule states or define doctrine. As by now no self-respecting pontiff would agree to this, a split between the eastern and western segments of the Church was inevitable.

On the death of John XIX in 1032 the Counts of Tusculum engineered the election of another of their men, Theophylact, who took the name Benedict IX. The term 'man' would be a stretch, as he was barely into his teens. True to long-established nepotistic tradition, his brother Gregory became a senator. It seems that only through such nexi of family power could peace return to Rome for any length of time. Unfortunately, Benedict did not live up to the holiness of his name; a later pope would lambaste him as a 'thief and assassin,' which by now should come as no surprise. It was widely believed that Benedict offered the papacy for sale to meet huge debts incurred in purchasing the office in the first place, and in fact sold it to Giovanni Graziano, a senior priest who became Gregory VI, and retired to the Counts' comfortable castle in Tusculum. It was also rumoured that Benedict disliked the celibate life and wanted to get married.[13]

At this the Crescentii saw their chance to regain power and secured the election of an Italian bishop as Sylvester III. The Counts, taking advantage of the quicksand of Roman politics where power came and went in giddy patterns of intrigue, struck back and restored Benedict; but he may have become thoroughly tired of this see-sawing, and abdicated on 1 May 1045. Sylvester, however, enjoyed the throne for just three weeks as it became apparent that the majority of Romans favoured Gregory VI. His popularity was not a result of his morals – his purchase of the papacy was almost taken for granted – but of a new spirit of reorganization he seemed to represent. For too long Rome's popes had been the stooges of the powerful, whether it was a noble Roman family or the emperor in Germany. The throne of Saint Peter, writes a recent Roman historian, 'had become a throne just like any other, lacking any sacredness'.[14] The apostle himself would hardly have recognized what the church he founded had morphed into. No fewer than three clergymen were now claiming to be the pope: Gregory, Sylvester and Benedict IX, who seems to have wanted to hang onto his throne anyway.

The sheer absurdity of the situation was too much for the next emperor, Henry III, the son of Conrad II. In 1046, seven years into his reign, he decided to drain the Roman swamp once and for all. To Henry's German mind, this chaos at the heart of what was supposed to be the centre of western Christendom could be allowed to go on no longer. It was bad enough having three popes; even with a single legitimate pope, too many of them didn't last long enough in office – some measuring their tenure in mere weeks or even days – to be able to formulate a coherent policy. The German and French clergy were already chafing at the bit. The trio of squabbling pontiffs was earning the ridicule of Europe, not to mention the Greek branch of the Church in Constantinople. Henry called a top-level council that convened at Sutri near Rome on 20 December 1046. With the emperor presiding, Sylvester was banished to a monastery, Benedict was deposed and Gregory sacked for gross simony. To the chagrin of the Italians, the council concluded that 'only a foreign pope, protected by the emperor, could terminate the debasement of the Church'.[15] Henry's choice of pope fell on the Bishop of Bamberg, who became Clement II; he lasted less than a year, a victim apparently of lead poisoning from the Roman water supply.[16] His successor Damasus II managed only twenty-three days, felled by the malaria that was the scourge of the swamps around Rome. The Counts of Tusculum, sensing another power shift, pushed Benedict IX back onto the throne, where he sat for three uneasy years before Henry III's troops marched into Rome and unseated him; though excommunicated, he continued to insist on his papal legitimacy until his death on the Counts' estate in 1055.

The council at Sutri triggered a paradigm shift in relations between the papacy and the Holy Roman Empire. For the first time an emperor claimed the right to depose a pope if the latter acted in such a way as to discredit the supremely holy office. It appeared to be a step in the right moral direction, but who could say if future emperors would not abuse this power against otherwise capable popes? The state was set, in fact, for an extension of a raw power struggle between Germany and Rome, as not every pope could be expected to consent to such a diminution of authority. At first, however, the relationship went well. The new pope, Leo IX, himself a German, proved to be a model of piety and probity. He arranged protection for the streams of pilgrims and put the Lateran administration into the capable hands of a twenty-five-year-old German monk named Hildebrand, who became a cardinal subdeacon. It was a move fraught with huge political consequences that would raise the papacy to a new pinnacle of power and prestige, but embroil Central Europe in its bitterest power struggle to date.

Leo's aim was to build the papacy into more than a purely local organization that so far had been unable to defend itself against the ambitions of the Roman noble houses. He wanted the image of the papacy restored to what it once was; a truly holy organization that did not need outward signs of wealth to earn respect. He forbade priests from bearing arms, as apparently many had done as a matter of course. In 1049 he began a tour of European cities to check on the morals of the clergy. His dignified bearing made a great impression; 'vice hid its head as he approached'.[17] He ordered bishops to publicly confess their sins and a French noble to be publicly flogged for destroying a church at Verdun; the noble later worked on the rebuilding with his own hands. No priest was free from Leo's stern judgement. They were ordered to dismiss their wives and girlfriends, return to the rule of celibacy, and refuse monetary favours; those who didn't comply were defrocked or excommunicated. By 1052 he had completed the exhausting task of European reform and returned to Rome to face a specifically military threat. These were the Normans under the ruthless adventurer Robert Guiscard, who during the papal chaos in Rome had driven the Byzantines out of South Italy and was eyeing the central portion.

In return for his exertions in putting the papal house in order, Leo received the Duchy of Benevento in South Italy as a reward from Henry. Benevento was a part of the States of the Church, but a rival duke, Pandolf of Capua, wanted Benevento for himself and seized it with Norman help. Conveniently forgetting his own injunction against clergy bearing arms, Leo gathered up a considerable force of Swabian Germans, Italians and Lombards, placed it under the command of Duke Gerard of Lorraine and went with it to fight for Benevento. The pope could have expected reinforcements from the Byzantines, who still technically ruled much of what the Normans now occupied, but in name only. If he had such expectations, he was disappointed. The Byzantines – correctly, it turned out – suspected Guiscard of eyeing the jewel of Constantinople itself. The Byzantine Emperor Constantine IX Monomachos was most reluctant to provoke the Norman lion and had little reason to support a heretic (from the Greek point of view) pope.

The opposing armies met near the town of Civitate on 18 June 1053. Leo himself took quarters in the town while his forces occupied a steep slope to the east. The papal left was held by Italian and Lombard infantry and cavalry, with the right flank held by the Swabian Germans. Opposite the papal left were Normans under Richard of Aversa, with the Count of Apulia commanding the centre and Robert Guiscard himself on the Norman left; we are told that Guiscard also had some 'Slavic' infantry, but their identity is unknown. Richard of Aversa opened the action with a charge against the pope's Italians and Lombards, sending them fleeing. The Norman centre initially failed to seize a height on its front, but with Richard's success on the right, the defenders in the centre fell back. On the Norman left Humphrey of Hauteville had some trouble with the Swabian Germans, but was reinforced by Guiscard coming up from the rear. As the Swabian Germans fell back, Richard's Normans moved left to attack them on their flanks. Cavalry charges completed the papal defeat.[18]

The pope was taken prisoner and, we are told, received the obeisance of the enemy who asked him to forgive them for killing so many of his soldiers! The scene may have impressed upon his mind the incongruity of a pope making war, as he spent the nine months of his imprisonment in prayer and repentance, wearing sackcloth and sleeping on a carpet with a stone for a pillow. The ordeal placed a huge strain on his health. When his captors realized that he was not going to live long, they freed him. Back in Rome, as he blessed the rejoicing people, he asked for a coffin to be placed in Saint Peter's; he sat beside it for a day, and died. His body was deemed so holy that lepers and disabled people came from all over Italy to touch it.

It was the second time in nearly two hundred years, since Pope John VIII in 877, that a pontiff had personally taken the field against an armed foe. But whereas John had taken on the Muslim Saracens, and successfully at that, Leo had not hesitated to fight fellow-Christians. Judging from the depth of his dismay after the Battle of Civitate, his conscience bothered him. Was it the Church's job to shed fellow Christian blood, even if directly threatened militarily? There was no easy answer to that question, and as long as the papacy saw itself as primarily a spiritual rather than a political power, the dilemma would continue to haunt it. The States of the Church had to be defended, but would it always have to be by means of foreign powers? The campaign cast a shadow over Leo IX's reputation. According to a contemporary Roman historian, 'for that military action conducted against faithful followers of Christ... his fame as a holy pope has been seriously stained'.[19] One wonders, however, what the historical verdict would have been if he had won.

Leo's death was followed by an interregnum of several months, during which the western and eastern churches sped towards their final rift. In 1054, in an unseemly scene in Constantinople's great Sancta Sophia cathedral, Cardinal Humbert of Silva Candida, the chief papal envoy, slapped a bull of excommunication on all Greek Christians. Both Humbert and Michael Keroularios, the Greek patriarch, were haughty and bad-tempered men, and Keroularios replied in kind. The Greeks especially despised the papal claim to Christian supremacy and the Roman rule of priestly celibacy.[20] What would henceforth be the Roman Catholic and the Greek (or Eastern) Orthodox churches went their separate ways, as they do to this day. The great schism was not only a theological tragedy; its effects determined the course of European and Middle Eastern affairs for centuries to come. In immediate strategic terms the schism meant that Rome and the West could no longer count on eastern Christian military aid. In fact, Leo IX's campaign against the Christian Normans served as a precedent for what would become clashes between rival Christian armies.

The German monk Hildebrand, learning the lesson of the broken Leo, engineered a politically-safe election of his successor, a relative of the emperor's named Gerbert of Dollstein-Hirschberg, as Pope Victor II. For Hildebrand by now had become the power behind the papal throne. Leo's enforced nine-month absence in a Norman jail cell had given a massive boost to Hildebrand's career, making him the only effective decision-maker in the Lateran Palace. Backed up by Hildebrand, Victor renewed Leo's drive to rid the Church of simony (the purchase of holy offices)[21] and the widespread habit of clergy maintaining mistresses in defiance of the celibacy rule, which technically meant not only staying single but adjuring all sexual relations. (The Greek Orthodox Church, on the contrary, requires its ordained priests to be married men.) Two years into his reign, however, Victor was called to Germany to be the regent for the infant emperor Henry IV. A year after that he was dead, to be succeeded by another Hildebrand pick, Stephen IX, who lasted just a year himself. These two short-lived and ineffectual popes encouraged the Counts of Tusculum to try and claw back some power; Henry IV was still far too young to be effective, and so in a show of force in April 1058 they secured the election of the bishop of Velletri as Pope Benedict X. This man was putty in the Counts' hands, earning from the Romans the demeaning nickname *Mincio*, or silly fool. The ridicule took violent form in the now-familiar street clashes between rival factions.

In Siena to the north, foes of the Counts of Tusculum – backed behind the scenes by Hildebrand – chose Bishop Gerard of Florence who took the name Nicholas II and descended on Rome in 1059, accompanied by Godfrey of Lorraine as imperial protector. Benedict was swiftly pushed aside, and Nicholas was confirmed as pontiff. Nicholas' reign was also brief – just two years – but in that time he engineered a key reform of how popes were to be elected. To eliminate the chaos of factionalism and usurpation (his own notwithstanding) he instituted the so-called *concilio lateranense*, which ruled that only serving cardinals would be eligible for the papal office. The supremely important corollary was that Holy Roman emperors would no longer have any say in the process. It was the ideal time to reassert papal authority, as Henry IV was still a minor. But Nicholas was well aware that the emperor would not be a minor for long, and as a form of insurance he approached Robert Guiscard, the Norman warlord, for an alliance.

And where was Hildebrand in all this?[22] A grateful Nicholas II elevated him to the post of papal chancellor. In fact, he is believed to have been the inspiration behind the *concilio lateranense* and the recruitment of the Normans of South Italy as military protectors. He bided his time as Nicholas II gave way to Alexander II, duly elected by the cardinals according to the new rule. But the feisty Roman nobility nominated its own candidate Honorius II as anti-pope; the usual violent street clashes failed to provide a solution, so the German clergy threw its decisive weight on the side of Alexander. The new pope vigorously prosecuted the reforms begun by Victor II. In foreign policy he made two supremely important moves for the course of European history: he gave the green light for Spain to begin to eject the Moors in what became the fabled *Reconquista*, and equally portentously, gave his blessings to Duke William of Normandy's invasion of England in 1066.

It all redounded to the prestige of Hildebrand, who seemed the natural successor to Victor II. In 1073 the cardinals, grateful for their renewed power, called on him to take the papal throne. Most accounts claim that he preferred to rule behind the papal stage rather than on it. He had served no fewer than eight popes over a quarter of a century, and was quite content to go on doing so. But he was simply too popular; cardinals, clergy and people cried out that 'Saint Peter wills Hildebrand to be pope!'[23] He wasn't even an ordained priest, but that obstacle was soon overcome by a simple ritual, and the capable German monk took the name Gregory VII. One of his early acts was to draw up a new list of papal rights called the *Dictatus papae*. In it he asserted among other things that all secular rulers, no matter how exalted, were obliged on meeting the pope to kiss his feet. On his accession Gregory was in his fifties, small-built and not overly handsome, but with a keen eye and an indomitable will. This will he employed towards a goal breathtaking in its scope: nothing less than to unify a morally cleansed Church which could assume the spiritual *and political* leadership of all Europe and lead the West in a crushing crusade to recover the Holy Land from the Muslims.

The new papal assertiveness had its roots in a reform movement centred on the Cluny monastery in Burgundy. Cluny had been exempt from the rule of the local bishop, owing allegiance solely to the Lateran. Under a series of saintly abbots it had acquired a reputation for holiness that spread to other cloisters in the empire. One of the Cluniac tenets was that the Church had tainted itself too much through overly close connections with feudal politics and the world of wealth and influence in general. In Hildebrand's view these stains could be removed only by restoring papal authority and preventing kings and nobles from meddling in Church affairs. In 1075, as pope, Gregory took the first step in that direction by issuing his first decree outlawing lay investiture. This was the process by which secular rulers and nobles could invest local clergy with their authority. To Gregory this was an unacceptable interference in a duty which essentially was God's, and hence could devolve only upon His representative on earth, the pope. And who was ultimately in charge of human affairs: mortal kings and princes and dukes, or God? 'As the soul is more important than the body', ran Gregory's analogy, 'so the spiritual is higher than the secular authority'. As Gregory himself put it in a letter to a German cleric:

> Who is ignorant that kings and princes had their origin in those who, ignorant of God and covering themselves with pride, violence and perfidy, in fact nearly every crime ... claimed to rule over their peers – i.e. men – in blind lust and intolerable arrogance?[24]

The pope may have been bluntly quite correct in his analysis of the origins of terrestrial political power, but his conviction that terrestrial power was far inferior to the divine power was uncompromising. His decree on lay investiture in the *Dictatus papae* said it all:

> Only [the pope] gives his foot to be kissed by princes. Only his name is invoked in the churches. His name, Pope, is unique in all the world. He has the right to depose emperors. He can absolve subjects from their allegiance to unjust leaders... His sentence is unappealable. He cannot be judged by anyone. The Roman Church has never been in error and will never be in error in the future.[25]

This was absolutism of a kind seen rarely even among the ancient priest-kings of the Middle East. Not surprisingly, the Eastern Orthodox Church wanted no part of it.

Not everyone, of course, agreed with this new ideological vigour. The pope's initial order to European clergy to dismiss their wives and mistresses, for example, met with understandable resistance from those so ordered; his response was to excommunicate even senior bishops who would not obey. In this way Gregory managed to range a whole layer of German and North Italian clergy against him. There were also rumblings of discontent in the Curia, some of whose members resented Gregory's high-handed manner. The Crescentii caught on to the sentiment, and on the night of Christmas 1075 the Prefect of Rome, Cencio Crescentius, led a band of nobles into the church of Santa Maria Maggiore where the pope was conducting mass, seized him by the hair, dragged him outside and beat him bloody. But Crescentius had not reckoned on the alert Roman mob; when the news of the Christmas night fracas spread the following morning, an angry crowd flocked to the Crescentii tower where the pope was being held. The mood was so ugly that Cencio feared for his own life; he agreed to freed Gregory, who calmed the people and went on to Santa Maria Maggiore to continue the mass from where it had been rudely interrupted the previous night. But the mob had the last word; it tore down the Crescentii tower and forced Cencio to flee the city for his life. He ended up in Germany under imperial protection.

At a time when Henry IV was preoccupied with putting down a revolt in Saxony, he felt too weak to wrestle with the pope. But after the revolt was put down Henry unleashed his scorn against Gregory, whom he would not even call a pope but a 'false monk'. Gregory hit back with a triple thunderbolt against the emperor, including excommunication, anathema and deposition all in one flaming package. As Europe looked on in growing horror, Gregory appeared to be winning the argument as the German nobility became jittery at all the metaphysical doom being flung about. Thoroughly cowed, the German nobles had no objection to getting rid of the excommunicated Henry if it meant saving their own souls. They and the pope agreed to host a diet at Augsburg on 2 February 1077 to work out a solution to a dispute that had got dangerously out of hand.

Finding that he had few friends left, Henry decided to eat humble pie and ask for absolution from the pope. Gregory replied, of course, that he was willing enough to forgive the emperor on the Almighty's behalf. But still not quite trusting Henry, who for all anyone knew might stir up an anti-papal revolt in Lombardy, Gregory broke his journey at Canossa near Reggio Emilia, the fortified home of the hugely wealthy Matilda of Tuscany, a key backer of the pope. In the middle of a severe winter, on 25 January, Henry turned up outside the castle walls with a small escort. Gregory later wrote:

> [Henry] presented himself at the gate of the castle, barefoot and clad only in wretched woollen garments, beseeching us with tears to grant him absolution and forgiveness. This he continued to do for three days … At length we removed the excommunication from him and received him again into the bosom of Holy Mother Church.[26]

The pope can be excused the tinge of gloating in his account of the epochal meeting. He had scored a signal victory for the Church by making one of

Europe's most powerful rulers eat dirt before him. But Henry also was a winner in that by this display of humility he retained his throne which otherwise would certainly have been wrested from him.

That was not the end of the issue. The German nobles, disappointed, proclaimed a rival king in the person of Rudolf of Swabia; Henry got together an army to stop him, triggering a two-year civil war. In Rome Gregory could not resist the temptation to back Rudolf and for good measure excommunicated Henry again. Anyone enrolling in Rudolf's force, he said, would have their sins forgiven. But he hadn't counted on the German clergy who almost solidly backed Henry and decreed the deposition of Gregory and the appointment of a new pope. The clash of words became the clash of arms. Henry met Rudolf in battle on the banks of the Saale river on 15 October 1080; though Henry's force was worsted, Rudolf was killed. Henry, with blood in his eye, stormed down through Italy in March 1084, gathering Lombard allies en route, to besiege Rome. As the imperial troops occupied Saint Peter's, Gregory fled to Sant'Angelo Castle. The emperor was able to do this because a few months before a group of pro-Henry clergymen had met at Brixen in North Italy and deposed Gregory, reviled as 'the pseudo-monk Hildebrand ... a necromancer and murderer' and a fan of 'obscene theatrical shows'.

The Germans were not the only sackers of Rome in 1084. A few months after Henry's withdrawal the Normans marched up from the south and burst through the San Lorenzo Gate on 27 May to add their own dose of destruction. A large part of the city went up in flames; the biggest conflagration, about a square mile in area, devoured the whole district between the Colosseum and the Lateran. When confronted by protests, Guiscard blamed the Romans for starting the mess by opening the gates to Henry IV a year before. On the third day of the sack the Romans got up the courage to hit back, and at one point Robert Guiscard was in danger of his life, but his cavalry stationed outside the walls beat back the rising. Guiscard's revenge was terrible indeed; anyone suspected of opposition to the Normans was hideously tortured or executed, and their womenfolk raped. Those parts of Rome that had escaped the initial fires were now torched. Romans of all ages and social classes were dragged by Guiscard's Muslim Arab mercenaries into the Norman camp as captives. Only after an appeal by Gregory was Guiscard's thirst for vengeance slaked.

But Gregory had lost what prestige he had. The people of Rome could stand only so much tribulation. In the end the pope had little choice but to move out with the retreating Normans towards the south, where he lived out the remaining year of his life. It took a year for the Curia to elect a successor, the abbot of the Monte Cassino monastery who took the name Victor III. But Gregory's supporters were still numerous; just four days after his election Victor fled from the mobs to the serenity of Monte Cassino, wanting nothing to do with papal duties. It took the warlike Countess Matilda of Tuscany, in whose castle Gregory had witnessed the three-day shivering repentance of Henry IV, and a Norman prince to occupy the district around Saint Peter's to make it safe enough for Victor to finally be consecrated on 9 May. It didn't make much difference in the end. Victor still preferred the meditative life at Monte Cassino, where he passed away four months later. An anti-pope called Clement III, backed by Henry, was still kicking about, and he appeared to enjoy an advantage. But in 1087 a French Benedictine monk, Eudes de Lagery, was elected at Terracina as the legitimate Pope Urban II. Clement stayed on as anti-pope, but he became an irrelevance. The great struggle with the Holy Roman Empire seemed to have reached a stalemate. Yet few would have had any inkling that the new pope would have an even greater impact on the course of world history.

Chapter 4

'Dieu li volt!'

Urban's pontificate got off to a very shaky start. To make sure that everyone knew who was supporting the new pope on the points of their swords, the Normans escorted him to Rome in November 1087 and set him up in temporary quarters on the Isola Tiberina, the small island in the Tiber where the river makes a bend near the Palatine Hill. There was a good reason he could not move to the Lateran, and the reason was anti-pope Clement III, still clinging to his pretended office. Clement had his numerous supporters, and Rome yet again was treated to the spectacle of rival papal gangs brawling in the streets. When Clement's lot briefly got the upper hand in 1090, Urban was forced to flee. Henry IV saw this opportunity to restore imperial influence at the expense of the Normans and their puppet Urban, and at the same time to extinguish the power of Matilda of Canossa, probably the most powerful backer of the papacy at the time. Matilda – wearing a full suit of armour, we are told – led her own force that overcame the imperial troops and reinstalled Urban. The pope meanwhile had found fresh allies in a newly-prominent Roman family, the Frangipani, who took over the role of the Crescentii in supplying muscle for the pope's defence. Clement was brushed aside, though he would futilely hang on to his travesty of an office for six more years.

Urban's buffeting at the hands of Henry IV made him more determined than ever to assert the power of the papacy over all secular European rulers. But he chose a different tactic from his predecessor Gregory VII. Rather than butt the German emperors head-on, Urban instead came up with a massive propaganda weapon designed to appeal to European public opinion and force the leaders to go along with his super-leadership. This was to cleverly craft a scary portrait of a terrible enemy outside Europe that had trodden down the Holy Land and the sites of Christ's life on earth and required a massive Christian military response to claw them back. There was no military or strategic sense in such a scheme. Europe's kings had enough on their plates without worrying about faraway lands where their writ could not run. And there was no logical reason why Western Europe should suddenly decide to own the Middle East. But mass popular emotion, carefully cultivated, overrides all. Thus did Urban issue the call for a great crusade to 'liberate' the Holy Land.

To be fair, the Eastern Mediterranean did represent a security risk of sorts. By the end of the eleventh century the Seljuk Turks had become the dominant power in the Muslim world. In Rome memories of the Saracen raids were still vivid. The Turks had wrested most of Asia Minor from the Byzantine Empire, while their co-religionists the Fatimids governed Egypt. Plenty of Europeans, high and low, made the arduous and potentially hazardous, often-dangerous, pilgrimage to Jerusalem, and until 1070 the Fatimid rulers had welcomed these early tourists. But that year the Turks took Jerusalem, and from then on the pilgrims' land journey inland from the Palestine coast had become definitely risky; many groups were robbed and even killed. There were also appeals from Byzantium. The first was issued by Emperor Michael VII about 1074, sowing the idea of a crusade in the mind of Gregory VII, who dreamed of leading one himself even if it should kill him. His continual tussles with Henry IV were so wearing that at one point he cried, 'I would rather expose my life in delivering the holy places than reign over the universe'.[1] He actually broached the idea to Henry, but nothing came of it. There was, however, another potential ally: the Byzantine Emperor Alexios I Komnenos (1081–1118) was a pragmatic man who brushed aside concerns over papal supremacy and appealed to the pope to help him defend Constantinople against the Turkish threat. In 1092 Seljuk Sultan Malikshah died, triggering a civil war. With Alexios' appeal before him, and the Muslims divided, Urban saw his chance to act.

The Crusades have been justly called 'a Two Hundred Years' War for the soul of man and the profits of trade'.[2] But that became apparent only much later. It is doubtful whether Urban II was moved by any commercial considerations when he decided to enrol European public opinion on his side in the constant tussle between secular power and the papacy. In an age long before mass media as we know it, the move was a stroke of political genius. Alexios' call for help was the detonator he was looking for, the means by which ecclesiastical power could be turned into military power. What better way to demonstrate the importance of the popes than to have them lead an apocalyptic fight against the Muslims?

The romantic idea of a crusade, in fact, had been bruited around Rome for nearly a century, and possibly more. About 1001 Sylvester II had inspired an abortive Christian raid on Syria. Urban II, on the other hand, however enthusiastic about the idea of a crusade, was realist enough to realize that a campaign in the Middle East would present unforeseen difficulties; if the campaign were to fail, all Christendom would be discredited. It was not a decision to be taken at all hastily or lightly. But dangling before him was the shiny vision of putting some order into the disorderly Frankish and Norman knights by shepherding them into the holiest and noblest of causes – not to mention the possibility of bringing the Eastern Orthodox Greeks back into the papal fold. From the Atlantic to the deserts of Syria, the popes would reign supreme. Rome once more would be the capital of the world.

Urban's first move was to sound out public opinion in North Italy and France. Crowds mobbed him wherever he went. The enthusiasm reached a climax at a grand council of nobles and clergy at Clermont in late November 1095, where in the local cathedral the pope made a show of force by excommunicating his fellow-Frenchman King Philip I for adultery (not that it made much difference to the king) and the Bishop of Cambrai for simony. But that was just official business. Urban needed a bigger stage for his grand project, and so on 27 November, the day before the conclusion of the council, he had his throne set up on a platform in the open fields outside the cathedral, where thousands of ordinary people, unable to fit in the cathedral, had gathered in tents braving the cold. They were fond of their French pope, and the words that came from his lips, in French, stirred them to a frenzy. 'O race of Franks! Race beloved and chosen by God!' he began flatteringly, going on to explain that 'an accursed race, wholly alienated from God,' had 'invaded the lands of the Christians' and was threatening the Greeks:

On whom, then, rests the labour of avenging these wrongs, and recovering the territory, if not upon you – you upon whom, above all others, God has conferred remarkable glory in arms, great bravery, and strength to humble the heads of those who resist you? Let the deeds of your ancestors encourage you – the glory and grandeur of Charlemagne and your other monarchs.

The speech was a masterful piece of propaganda, carefully crafted to appeal to mass emotion – the now-familiar technique of political and media establishments. Urban could well have been Europe's first spin doctor, and a highly capable one at that. His description of the French as 'beloved and chosen by God' was frank chauvinism, swallowed whole by his unsophisticated hearers. His later well-timed references to Charlemagne reinforced the message. Then came the craftiest appeal of all:

> For this land which you now inhabit, shut in on all sides by the sea and the mountain peaks, is too narrow for your large population; it scarcely furnishes food enough for its cultivators. Hence it is that you murder and devour one another, that you wage wars, and that many among you perish in civil strife … Jerusalem is a land fruitful above all others, a paradise of delights … Undertake this journey eagerly for the remission of your sins, and be assured of the reward of imperishable glory in the Kingdom of Heaven.

'Shut in on all sides', 'murder', 'a land fruitful above all others', 'remission of sins', 'reward' – Urban's speech contained all the buzz-phrases needed to galvanize struggling peasant and bored noble alike. It was a heady mixture of moralism and appeal to greed. Small wonder that his hearers roared '*Dieu li volt!* ' ('God wills it!'). It became Urban's battle-cry, repeated at similar mass meetings in Tours, Bordeaux, Toulouse, Montpellier and Nîmes, over the next nine months. It was two years before he returned to Rome, but his fame had preceded him and 'the least pious city in Christendom' cheered him to the rafters.[3]

Two questions arise here. First, did Urban II really believe his own propaganda? The answer is most likely 'Yes', as the minds of powerful and influential people are very prone to conflating fact with fiction. He was without doubt a man of powerful faith, yet paradoxically that is what tempted him, like Gregory VII, to elevate himself above kings and peoples. The mass support he received from the common people of North Italy and France gave him the illusion of infallibility. He started out on his preaching tour exhorting his hearers to get out of their humdrum life and fight the enemies of Christ. Somewhere along the way, as he saw the economic distress and crime prevalent in the French peasantry, his oratory took an economic turn;

by going on crusade you can save not only your souls but also take over 'fruitful' Jerusalem, the 'paradise of delights,' and seize its wealth for your own. Crass materialism combined with simple piety to provide the motive force for the First Crusade.

Second, did Urban intend to be the commander-in-chief of the Christian forces? Gregory VII had dreamed of being such a commander. But Urban was not a soldier, and as far as we know had no pretensions to being one. So far the papacy, with the rare exceptions of John VIII and Leo IX, had relied on secular emperors and dukes to do its fighting. Urban intended to continue this tradition, though with a more hands-on attitude. As official leader he appointed Adhemar de Monteil, bishop of Le Puy, a capable and respected noble with considerable diplomatic skill who, however, would prove unable to fully control the bumptious dukes under him. Urban decided upon 15 August 1096 – when the harvest was safely in and the peasants could march – as the start of the great campaign. But events soon got away from him, as two enthusiasts known as Peter the Hermit and Walter the Penniless felt they could not wait and led 12,000 gullible peasants across Europe. Few among them had any idea of the geography and at every bend in the Rhine and Danube the children among them would ask, 'Is this Jerusalem?' After killing Jews in Germany and plundering the outskirts of Constantinople, the violent mob – for that is what it had become – was massacred by the Turks near Nicaea (modern İznik). (Peter the Hermit had long since abandoned the campaign and was living comfortably with Greek Emperor Alexios I.)

The pope, in fact, could not count on the kings of Europe, for the simple reason that he and his predecessors had been too free with the excommunication weapon. At that time Philip I of France, William II of England and Henry IV of Germany were all under papal interdict for past sins. Therefore he had to rely on dukes and counts, overwhelmingly French. Chief among them were: Godfrey of Bouillion, brave but fanatic; Robert Guiscard's son Bohemond, a ruthless and less-than-pious adventurer; and Raymond of Toulouse, a capable veteran of the Spanish *Reconquista*, but haughty and greedy. The First Crusade of some 30,000 men marched across Europe and seriously rattled Alexios when it came within sight of Constantinople. Exercising astute diplomacy, the Greek emperor managed to steer them safely across to the Anatolian mainland. After a series of encounters with the Turks they probed all the way to Jerusalem, which the remaining 12,000 or so crusaders seized on 15 July 1099. Many no doubt noted the words of Psalm 122: 'Our feet shall stand within thy gates, O Jerusalem.' The reality was not so pious. Raymond of Agiles, a priest with the army, reported witnessing 'wonderful things', such as:

> Numbers of Saracens were beheaded... others were shot with arrows, or forced to jump from the towers; others were tortured for several days and then burned in the flames. In the streets were seen piles of heads and feet.

Other observers noted such marvels as babies being snatched from their mothers and hurled over the walls or dashed against pillars. Some 70,000 Muslims were slaughtered and Jerusalem's Jews were crammed into a synagogue and burned alive.

It is legitimate to ask where Urban was in all this. Is it correct to assign him military responsibility for the excesses of the First Crusade which he inspired and claimed to lead? We shall never know, because while his Crusaders were sacking the Holy City he was dying. He passed away without learning of what had happened. After issuing his epochal call at Clermont he had worked feverishly to organize the campaign. In July 1096 King Philip of France formally recanted for his alleged adultery and his excommunication was lifted. In Italy the pope demanded that no-one should set out on the crusade without the local priest's permission and that newly-married husbands could not leave without their wives' consent.[4] This last decree was a wise one, as it ensured that enough young and productive family men would remain at home to keep the economy going, and the population renewed, while getting rid of the unproductive and criminal elements. It also indicates that Urban feared that mass enthusiasm could get out of hand, as Peter the Hermit's venture dramatically demonstrated.[5]

Naively perhaps, Urban expected full cooperation from Emperor Alexios in Constantinople; after all, had not Alexios implored the pope's urgent aid? But the view from Constantinople was that of a vast and menacing alien army descending suddenly out of nowhere, demanding to be sheltered and fed while the empire had plenty of its own problems. Alexios felt he had no choice but to send the Crusaders on their way as soon as possible. Besides, he and every other Byzantine Greek bristled at the Crusaders' effrontery; if any power could claim to have been a consistent crusader, it was Byzantium, which had once ruled Jerusalem and ever since Emperor Heraclius in the seventh century had been waging a constant struggle to keep the Holy Places out of the hands first of the Persians and then the Muslims. With the Muslim seizure of Jerusalem in 1070 the cause had received a setback, but Alexios never gave up hope of redressing the balance. If anyone was going to recover Jerusalem, it would be the Orthodox East, not the Latin West. As the First Crusaders set up their Latin kingdom – dubbed Outremer (Beyond the Sea) – with Jerusalem as its capital, Alexios bided his time.

In Rome, meanwhile, there had been a shift of power. Two new families, the Pierleoni and the Frangipani, emerged to vie for influence in the city. They were part of a new rising moneyed class of merchants and financiers that hoped to replace the old landed nobility. Not surprisingly, both families ranged themselves on opposite sides of the papacy-empire rivalry, with the Pierleoni backing the popes and the Frangipani the German emperors. The former were closer to the action as they had headquarters in Sant'Angelo Castle, the Tiberina island and the nearby Theatre of Marcellus, while the latter held much of the countryside, plus a small enclave between the Colosseum and the Circus Maximus. The easily-defensible Tiberina, accessed by just two short bridges, had been the refuge of Pope Victor III at a time when anti-pope Clement held Saint Peter's, and then of Urban II. In 1099 the Pierleoni (who had Jewish origins) ensured the election of Paschal II and backed him up with ample funding, receiving the governorship of Rome in return. This way Paschal was finally able to neutralize the anti-pope Clement and three of his putative successors within the next dozen years.

In Germany the Holy Roman Emperor Henry V, who assumed the throne in 1106 after overthrowing his father Henry IV, was as determined as his predecessors to keep papal hands off his realm and clergy. Paschal dug in his heels and refused to crown Henry unless he renounced the right of lay investiture; Henry responded by leading an army to Rome, encamping at Monte Mario, north of the city in August 1110. The pope sent legates to negotiate with Henry, and on 9 February 1111, after months of haggling, the emperor agreed to renounce his right of lay investiture in return for a clipping of the bishops' civil powers. But the arrangement was not at all to the liking of the senior Roman clergy, and three days later, as Henry was about to be officially crowned in Saint Peter's basilica, they refused to do it.

An angry Henry then renounced his previous promise, which in turn caused the pope to follow his cardinals and refuse to crown him.

Saint Peter's basilica became a battleground, as Henry and his German cavalrymen, their lances levelled, invaded the church and surrounded the pope and his cardinals pinned against the high altar. It was evening, and in the gathering gloom it was hard to tell friend from foe as German troops assaulted the cardinals and snuffed out the candles, and cries and curses filled the hall. When night fell Henry and his horsemen emerged from the basilica towing Paschal and his cardinals in chains, and leaving behind him the bodies of murdered priests. Two cardinals escaped to urge the Roman populace to resist and sent word to the Normans for help. In the Borgo, the quarter abutting Saint Peter's to the north, Henry heard the mob coming as it crossed the Sant'Angelo bridge and mounted his horse to ride off, but before he could get very far the attackers caught up with him and knocked him off his saddle, wounding him. One of his nobles rushed up and gave the emperor his own mount, only to perish at the hands of the mob. Eventually Henry's troops rallied and drove the attackers back over the Sant'Angelo bridge; with the pope still captive Henry moved his forces to the Mammolo bridge northeast of Rome to meet the expected Norman attack.

For two months Paschal waited for the Normans to free him, but they didn't come. He may not have known it, but Robert Guiscard's vigorous son Bohemond had his hands full in the Middle East and battling the Byzantine Empire, and could spare no time for Italian affairs. Giving up hope of deliverance, Paschal gave in and on 11 April signed what became known as the Mammolo Bridge Accord, conceding the right of lay investiture to Henry. The emperor in return got rid of his last anti-pope puppet, Sylvester IV, and two days later finally was crowned in Saint Peter's. But that was not the end of the pope's troubles. After Henry V returned in triumph to Germany, having achieved in two months what his father had failed to do in many years, Paschal faced hostility from the senior clergy for knuckling under to Henry. Two Lateran councils, in 1112 and 1116, declared the Mommolo Bridge Accord null and void; but the pope blithely ignored the rulings, as his mind was on larger matters, namely, what was happening in the Crusader kingdoms of Outremer.

Did the soldiers of the First Crusade, or any of the crusades thereafter, really constitute a pope's army? Urban II, the prime instigator, certainly wanted them to be; he considered himself a sort of absentee commander-in-chief, while necessarily leaving tactics to the princes and dukes who led the actual armies. But once the Latin Kingdom of Jerusalem got going under its own steam Urban's successors seemed content to exercise moral supervision at a distance. Of course they were vitally interested in the fortunes of Christendom in the Middle East, but beginning with Paschal II they acted as cheerleaders rather than makers of strategy. Many fine books about the Crusades, some of them multi-volume, have been written from various viewpoints, and it would be pointless to summarize them here. Strictly speaking, they were not papal military campaigns *per se*. The popes generally limited themselves to spiritual leadership and were willing to leave the conduct of military affairs to the hard men. And if those hard men were responsible for atrocities such as the Jerusalem massacre, that was regrettable; but war was war and besides, the thinking went, the Muslims should never have been allowed to seize the Holy Land in the first place, so they merely got what was coming to them.

Paschal himself took a hand in militarizing the Christian presence in Jerusalem by endorsing an organization that had its beginnings around the middle of the previous century, when a group of merchants from the Italian trading city of Amalfi set up a hospice in Muslim-ruled Jerusalem for sick or indigent Christian pilgrims. A constant stream of pilgrims had been arriving in Jerusalem for centuries, braving the considerable dangers of the voyage which in the later eleventh century had worsened with Muslim raids on pilgrim caravans struggling inland to Jerusalem from ports such as Jaffa. When the First Crusaders took Jerusalem in 1099, great areas of the surrounding countryside still harboured Muslim bands. It was to combat these that someone in what had become the Hospice of Saint John – we are not sure who – had the idea of employing armed and mounted knights to protect the incoming pilgrim caravans. By 1113 these knights had earned enough recognition to be recognized by Paschal as the first Military Order of Saint John, or the Knights Hospitaller, as they would soon become known, through their association with the hospice.

The Order was largely the creation of a holy man named Gerard, of unknown surname and probably an Italian or Lombard. Gerard and his institution had somehow survived the Muslim occupation of Jerusalem, though Gerard would claim to have been brutally tortured. The Blessed

Gerard, as he became known, was far from military-minded. His task was care for all needy human beings, whether Christian, Muslim or Jew. The Latin Kingdom of Jerusalem, of course, gave effective protection to the Knights Hospitaller, generously endowing them with money and property; their fame spread back to Western Europe where the ideal of fighting for Christ fired many young upper-class men to abandon what in many cases must have been boring lives to throw themselves into adventure in the places to which the Bible had given a mystic status. These men, added to whom were members of Latin King Baldwin I's own corps of knights, formed the core of the knighthood of Saint John. No-one knows exactly when the Knights Hospitaller mutated from a charity into a military body, but the process was almost certainly a gradual one. There was probably some sign of it when Paschal formed them into an order in 1113. By the time of the Blessed Gerard's death five years later, the order's military character was more pronounced; its head was now called the Grand Master, the second of whom was Raymond du Puy. It was under du Puy that the Knights of Saint John were formally bound to dedicate themselves to 'chastity, obedience and the military protection of Christians'.[6]

These knights soon spawned imitators. About the time Raymond du Puy took the helm of the Hospitallers, two 'God-fearing' Frankish nobles, Hugh de Payens and Geoffrey de Saint Omer, approached King Baldwin II with a plan not only of forming another military corps to defend the Christian pilgrims on their way to Jerusalem but also to be part of the defence of Outremer itself. The king gave his permission, and about half a dozen knights living in the south wing of Baldwin's palace near the ruins of the ancient Jewish temple banded together to form the Mendicant Soldiers of the Temple of Solomon, or the Knights Templar, as they were more commonly called. As it was King Baldwin who approved the formation of this group, we may assume that the papacy in Rome played little, if any, part. In fact, within a short time the Hospitallers and Templars would become bitter rivals, and almost certainly the lack of papal sanction for the Templars played a part in Rome's ruthless suppression of the order two centuries later. Yet it is also true that the efforts of both military orders, bloody as they were in the never-ending fight against the Muslims, promoted Roman Catholic policies in the Middle East.

Rivalry between the Knights Hospitaller and Knights Templar was just one facet of disunity in Christian Outremer itself. The older inhabitants of West European origin who had acquired a measure of wisdom in dealing with the local people and culture were constantly upstaged by arrogant new arrivals, mostly French, whose sole desire was to do battle. The separate parts of Outremer, such as the Kingdom of Jerusalem and the principality of Edessa (now northern Syria), vied for control. The Italian merchant cities of Venice and Genoa grew rich from the trade with Outremer and earned the enmity of the Franks. The military orders themselves in short order had amassed huge estates, veering rather far afield from the original Christian principles of the Blessed Gerard. All this played into the hands of the Muslims, who in 1144 wrested Edessa from Frankish control. The news came as a great shock to the West; in France a monk named Bernard of Clairvaux took up the crusading cry half a century after Urban II. At Vézelay in 1146 it was Clermont all over again: the fiery speeches, the crass distortions of reality, the hysterical crowds, the frantic stitching of crosses onto garments, the impassioned crusading pledges from King Louis VII on down. Holy Roman Emperor Conrad III, the first of the Hohenstaufen rulers, joined the movement, and before long a Second Crusade was in the works. Bernard asked Pope Eugenius III to handle the formal call to arms, but the pope declined, as he had troubles in his own backyard.

For several years before the accession of Urban II the papal Curia had been growing in importance. This was made up of what a short time later became the College of Cardinals, essentially assuming the duties of the old Roman Senate. The term cardinal originally applied to six deacons serving in the Lateran palace under anti-pope Clement III, but Urban II extended the title to Rome's twelve regional deacons. The papal administration was becoming more efficient, with the creation of the office of chancellor, or chief of staff. The cardinals gained the right to add their own signatures to all documents issued in the name of the pope. By the time of Paschal II and the Mammolo Bridge Accord conceding the right of lay investiture, the cardinals were powerful enough to openly condemn it. Paschal was browbeaten into revoking the accord, but that didn't do much for his popularity in Rome. Furious mobs forced him to flee in 1116, returning only to die in Sant'Angelo Castle less than two years later.

Henry V, meanwhile, had returned to Italy to seize the lands of the late Countess Matilda. In 1118 Cardinal Giovanni Caetani was elected Pope Gelasius II on the shoulders of the Pierleoni. Taking refuge at Gaeta, he refused to meet Henry, who tried to set up his own pope. The attempt fizzled out. Hardly had Gelasius time to don the papal mitre than Cencio Frangipane burst into the church at the head of an armed gang and seizing Gelasius by the throat, threw him to the floor where he repeatedly kicked him with the metal spurs on his shoes, showering him with insults and curses. Frangipani dragged the pope into the street and locked him up in the family tower near the Colosseum. The Pierleoni got together with other noble families and managed to rescue Gelasius, who fled to France, where he died that same year. He was replaced by a French clergyman who became Calixtus II, but it wasn't until two years later that Calixtus could enter Rome with the help of a loyal force under Cardinal Giovanni di Crema.

This is the first time in papal annals that we hear of a specific armed force acting on behalf of a legitimate elected pope. Until now, rival papal candidates, and then popes and anti-popes had their loyal bands of Roman supporters, mostly young and male, but they had never been more than armed gangs. How Cardinal di Crema organized his force remains vague; perhaps by that time the official papal authorization of the Knights Hospitaller in Palestine had found imitators in Italy. Certainly there was no lack of adventurous young men who could be persuaded to fight for the pope on a mercenary basis nearer home. As a sop to the Frangipani, he appointed one of their number to command the papal militia, which appears in history for the first time. Perhaps it was the same body of men led by Cardinal di Crema, one of whose first acts was to arrest the latest anti-pope (Gregory VIII) and pack him off to a monastery. By this time, as the papacy sought to increase the outward signs of its prestige in response to the disputes with secular authorities, we hear of a squad of *adextratores*, who were a kind of mounted bodyguard with the privilege of dining with every newly-consecrated pope.

Calixtus turned out to be a strong character who finally put paid to the controversy over lay investiture by agreement with Henry V, who in 1122 gave in to Calixtus' insistence on the right to appoint Catholic clergy anywhere in Europe; it represented a compromise in that in Germany at least, the emperor could be present at the election of bishops and abbots, and even decide among disputing claimants. This was the result of the Concordat of

Worms, after the German city where the debates were held. Germany joined France and England in retaining a say over the clergy, while the papacy could be content with its overall authority in ecclesiastical matters. It was a triumph of diplomacy for Calixtus, who himself was French and presumably more open to the feelings of the non-Italian clergy. The following year the Ecumenical Lateran Council – the first-ever synod not held in the Orthodox East – reasserted the papal ban on simony, mistresses for supposedly celibate priests, and the employment of laymen in the church administration. At the same time Calixtus ordered a rebuilding of the run-down parts of Rome, which earned him some popularity with the Romans.

Yet the poison of political factionalism continued to seep into the patrimony of Saint Peter. On Calixtus' death in 1124, it erupted anew. The Pierleoni and Frangipani fielded opposing candidates for pope; the former pipped the latter at the post by electing Celestine II who, however, was soon forced aside by the aggressive tactics of the Frangipani, who placed their man on the papal throne as Honorius II. As Honorius had been one of the signers of the Concordat of Worms, there were some hopes that the fierce rivalries in Rome might calm down. For a few years that appeared to be the case, as Honorius settled his southern flank by an accommodation with Roger II, the Norman ruler of South Italy. But on Honorius' death in 1130 (these puppet-popes, being mostly elderly on their election, generally did not live long in office), the Frangipani and Pierleoni clashed again, each promoting their own new pope. The College of Cardinals was now split almost down the middle between the adherents of the two powerful clans.

Pietro Pierleoni stepped up to the throne as Anacletus II, but quite soon the fact that he had a Jewish grandfather began to tell against him. Even though the grandfather had converted to Christianity, his opponents had no compunction in ridiculing him as 'Judaeo-pontifex;' even Bernard of Clairvaux, who sixteen years later was to power up the Second Crusade, forgot himself so far as to consider it 'shameful' that 'a man of Jewish origin was come to occupy the chair of Saint Peter'. Slanderous stories circulated that Anacletus liked to rob Christian churches to enrich his Jewish friends.[7] But the Normans and Holy Roman emperor Lothair III (Henry V's successor and the last Franconian ruler) were solidly behind him, as were the Romans themselves, who largely disbelieved such propaganda and supported Anacletus faithfully through the eight years of his reign.

The Frangipani, however, mobilized an armed force to try and topple Anacletus, who had to spend much of his time behind the battlements of Sant'Angelo Castle to fend off attacks by adherents of rival pope Innocent II, who occupied the Lateran Palace. Bloody clashes stained large parts of Italy until Anacletus' death in 1138 decided the issue in favour of Innocent. The Pierleoni decided to abandon their fruitless opposition, and the pope was able to reassert his authority in a second Lateran Council in 1139. Four years later the Romans appeared to repent of the destructive effects of their street rivalries; in 1143, 'desirous of renewing the ancient honour of the city', the leading citizens resurrected the Senate and formed themselves into a municipality, the Comune di Roma, which took the ancient *Senatus Populusque Romanus (SPQR)* as its motto, which is still in use.[8]

The Comune was the first sign that the business and professional side of Rome was setting itself apart from the papal framework which until now had defined the city. Rome until 1143 was synonymous with the Church; after that date the popes realized that they were just one power base among several. The Pierleoni took the lead in the secular government, with Giordano Pierleoni assuming the unofficial title of 'prince,' which simply meant a kind of appointed mayor with expanded powers. He was careful to shun his clan's haughty and aristocratic habits and to gain the friendship of the Roman masses who could all too easily end the careers of popes and politicians. Thus fortified, Pierleoni took a dislike to the new pope, Lucius II, and had him deposed. Lucius, after vainly expecting help from the Normans of South Italy, put himself at the head of an armed force which attacked the Comune's headquarters on the Capitoline Hill (now the Campidoglio). During the fracas a stone hit Lucius in the head, fatally injuring him. Furious opponents of the papacy sacked cardinals' homes, forcing the new pope, Eugenius III, to move out of Rome and take up residence at Viterbo, sixty miles north-east of the city. There he learned of the fall of Edessa to the Muslims and agreed to the Second Crusade.

Nothing constructive can be said about that crusade, as it was an unmitigated disaster. As they had half a century before, the princes of Europe dismissed the sage advice of the Byzantines and proceeded on their reckless way through the wilds of Asia Minor without a semblance of a strategy. The Greeks, though amused by 'the baggage train of the French … heavy with trunks and boxes of apparel designed to ensure the beauty of [their] ladies against the vicissitudes of climate, war and time', were nonetheless rightly suspicious of the Crusaders' motives and declined to offer any substantial help.[9] In 1148 those Frenchmen who had reached Jerusalem were wiped out by the Turks. While Bernard of Clairvaux struggled to explain the collapse of the crusade he had so fervently preached, Eugenius III also took some of the opprobrium. A monk named Arnaldo of Brescia had appeared in Rome boldly preaching economic and social reform, and denying the right of popes to be secular rulers in their own right. He was backed by the Comune and naturally by Conrad III, ever eager for any excuse to clip the popes' wings.

In 1152 Frederick I Barbarossa succeeded to the throne of the Holy Roman Empire. Perhaps influenced by the unhappy outcome of the Second Crusade, he made a point of mending fences with the papacy; thanks to his military help, Eugenius was able to return to Rome from his 'exile' in Viterbo, but died shortly afterwards. His successor, Hadrian IV, was an Englishman named Nicholas Breakspear who began life in poverty and first entered a monastery as a beggar. By sheer ability he had raised himself to the position of abbot, then cardinal, then pope. Hadrian was an implacable champion of papal rights; by force of character he at one point compelled Frederick Barbarossa to kiss his feet. But in Rome he had problems. Thanks partly to the folly of the Second Crusade, and partly to the influence of the secular Comune, the majority of Romans were not in a clergy-loving mood. When a cardinal was murdered, Hadrian placed Rome under an interdict and asked (or perhaps ordered) Barbarossa to intervene. In June 1155 Frederick was officially crowned in Saint Peter's; the emperor in return delivered Arnaldo of Brescia to a Church court, which ordered him to be hanged and his body burnt at the stake as a heretic. The ashes were scattered to the winds.

None of this, of course, solved the problem of papal relations with the secular authority. On Hadrian's death after a five-year reign Frederick Barbarossa was called upon to decide between two rival candidates for pope; unfortunately, the rivals refused to cooperate, and once again Rome witnessed the sad spectacle of multiple popes, each one claiming Saint Peter's patrimony. While Barbarossa picked the man who would become Victor IV, most of the cardinals preferred his rival Alexander III. The Synod of Pavia of 1160 recognized Victor, but Alexander excommunicated the emperor. It was about this time that a pope re-entering Rome after an absence would make a flamboyant spectacle of it, based on the triumphal processions of the ancient Roman emperors. Bedecked in scarlet and jewelled robes, he would ride at the rear of the procession through all the major arches in the city (so that no district would feel neglected). In front of the pope rode the prior of the subdeacons, carrying a handkerchief in case the pope wanted to spit unobtrusively or wipe his nose; behind the pope rode the prefect of Rome who, for some reason unknown, wore one red sock and one golden one, the colours of the Papal States.[10]

Small wonder, then, that over the next twenty years no fewer than four papal pretenders (named as Victor V, Paschal III, Calixtus III and Innocent III) would try to usurp the throne with German help. Barbarossa constantly sought opportunities to topple Alexander. In 1167 he led a German army into Italy, defeating a Roman force at Monteporzio near Rome. As Barbarossa entered the city Alexander fled, but returned when malaria decimated the invaders and forced Barbarossa to withdraw. The pope, meanwhile, had not neglected to secure allies farther afield. One of them was the Lombard League of North Italy. In 1176 Barbarossa sent an army against the Lombard city of Alessandria, named after the pope, but after a six-month fruitless siege he was trounced at Legnano. In the so-called Peace of Venice, the Church won the right to stay independent of the empire. Barbarossa, humbled, had to kiss Alexander's feet for a second time.

Yet inside Rome, papal relations with the Comune and the nobles remained uneasy. The power struggle of the days of the Pierleoni and Frangipani had never really gone away. Though the papacy tried to live up to the motto of '*Ubi papa ibi Roma*' ('Rome is where the pope is'), three successive pontiffs, Lucius III, Urban III and Gregory VIII, spent more time holed up in places such as Velletri in the south and Verona in the north, terrified of the impulses of the anti-clerical mob. Well might they live in fear, as on 25 August 1183 a gang seized a number of priests in the Tuscolana district, blinded them all except one, seated them on donkeys, placed hats on their heads with the names of the cardinals on them, and ordered the single unblinded priest to lead the sorry procession to Pope Lucius as a grim sign of the public hostility to him.[11] A peace of sorts returned five years later, when Pope Clement III agreed with the 56-member Roman Senate on a division of powers; the papacy had the right to coin money, though one-third of its revenues went to the Comune as a guarantee of good behaviour. The pope also agreed to reimburse the Comune for damages sustained in the recent unrest. At the same time, by the Treaty of Strasbourg, Clement mended fences with the Holy Roman Empire.

Given the circumstances in Rome, the popes could hardly pay much attention to Outremer, where discord among the Latin principalities and atrocities committed by a few French nobles paved the way for a vigorous new Muslim leader, Salah ad-Din Yusuf – better known as Saladin – to destroy a Frankish army in the terrible Battle of Hattin and seize Jerusalem. This event sparked the Third Crusade. As with Urban II and Bernard of Clairvaux, it needed some emotional trigger, and this was supplied by William, the Catholic archbishop of Tyre, who toured Europe's royal courts with accounts of the Fall of Jerusalem. Blinded by fervour, Frederick Barbarossa, though in his mid-sixties, set out for the Holy Land in 1189, imagining himself 'a second Moses who would open the way to the Promised Land'. It proved to be his doom. Ignoring sage Byzantine advice like the previous crusaders, he and his army plunged recklessly into the same Asia Minor death-traps that had seen off his predecessors. Turkish raiders and hunger decimated Barbarossa's ranks; he himself drowned after tumbling from his horse crossing the stream of Salef in Cilicia (now south-east Turkey). A mere handful of Germans survived to join the Latin siege of the Turks in Acre.

Clement III died on 10 April 1191, the same day that King Richard I of England set out from Messina in Sicily to add himself to the great crusade. The next pope, Celestine III, 'a timorous, vacillating man',[12] proved a more pliable tool in Hohenstaufen hands than Clement had been and was quickly persuaded to crown the late Barbarossa's son Henry VI in Rome. But the aggressively-independent Comune had other ideas, and insisted that the German emperor raze the tower of the Counts of Tusculum which the Germans had used as a barracks but which had become a hated symbol of the misrule of the old Counts of Tusculum. Henry agreed, and he and his wife Constance were duly papally crowned on 15 April. Two days later the Romans gleefully attacked the tower, leaving not one stone on another, though in their fury they blinded and then murdered the few people they found inside. Celestine marked time for seven more years, until his death – along with the sudden demise of the young and promising Henry VI – brought to the fore another of those popes whose strong hand on the tiller of Saint Peter affected the course of European history.

'Seldom has history seen a more abrupt and thorough reversal of fortune' for the papacy with the accession of Innocent III in 1198.[13] In that year the papal domains were hemmed in by the Holy Roman Empire in the north and their allied Normans in the south. Henry VI planned to add the popes' lands to his own, and might well have succeeded if he had lived. For decades the papacy had been forced to battle opponents at home and abroad through a succession of weak and short-lived pontiffs, and many men forecast its demise as a political institution. But with the arrival of Innocent III, all bets were off. Born Lotario dei Conti into the prosperous Segni family, he was given every advantage to study philosophy, theology and law in Paris and Bologna. At the age of thirty he was expert enough in diplomacy and canon law to be appointed a cardinal deacon; during the following few years he penned four learned works on theology, and at thirty-seven was elected pope with no opposition.

Of small stature, like previous powerful popes such as Gregory VII, and with a pleasant personality, he made a point of being utterly incorruptible and living simply. More an administrator than a clergyman – he was hastily ordained a priest the day before his consecration – he used his political talents and ruthlessness over the next ten months to oust the Germans from their Italian holdings, reassert genuine papal control over the Papal States, become the guardian of the infant Emperor Frederick II and make himself 'master of Italy'.[14] At this time two main factions, dominating the politics of Germany and Italy, now took form: the Welfs, who were old foes of the Hohenstaufens and by extension had influence over those supporting the papacy and a degree of Italian independence; and the Ghibellines, who staunchly backed the empire. (The name Ghibelline derives from Weiblingen, one of the Hohenstaufen possessions.) Innocent became a magnet for the Welf faction; unrest and a disputed succession in Germany gave him the power to choose a new emperor, and his choice fell on Otto of Brunswick, an uncouth and violent man who as Otto IV renounced all imperial claims to the Papal States.

Relations between various segments of the Papal States were not always of the best. In 1202 the Duchy of Spoleto was disturbed by a nasty little war between the neighbouring cities of Perugia and Assisi. Fighting on the Assisian side was a well-born sensitive and handsome young man of twenty named Francesco. He had spent his youth living well and basking in social popularity, but after being taken prisoner by the Perugians and spending a year in captivity, he emerged a changed man. His thoughts turned more to affairs of the spirit than to the world; in 1204 he felt he could turn his military urges in that direction and volunteered for Innocent III's forces. He had not served long when, falling ill and in the throes of a fever, he heard a disembodied voice asking him why he wanted to fight for a mere pope when he could serve the Lord more directly. Francesco recovered, returned to Assisi and spurned a future that was opening up for him as the inheritor of his father's lucrative trading business. While at prayer in a country chapel, he dedicated himself to the spiritual life and gave away all the money he had on him as a first step. Thus began the remarkable career of Saint Francis of Assisi, who in future years would again make his mark in a Christian army.

On the importance of the papacy, Innocent was maximalist and uncompromising: 'The Lord left to Peter the government not only of all the Church, but of the whole world'.[15] That sort of policy admittedly left little room for diplomacy in the ordinary sense, though by sheer force of will he pushed it through. His armed force, of whom Francis of Assisi was temporarily a member, was kept in readiness, though we can cast some doubt on its efficacy, as in 1203 a republican popular revolt under Giovanni Capocci succeeded in driving him out of the city for a year. He returned on a promise to give administration posts to some of the leaders of the uprising. Farther afield the Italian states, intent on their own conflicts, practically ignored him. But in the rest of Europe, from Spain to Norway, his writ ran strong. England's King John was strong-armed into handing over his land to the papal fiefdoms. A Greek visitor to Rome considered that Innocent was a successor not so much of Saint Peter but of Constantine the Great, the founder of the East Roman Empire. Yet it was against the Greeks that Innocent made the most controversial move of his career.

One of the pope's first acts on his accession – probably with the intention of restoring battered papal prestige in Europe – was to call for another crusade after the Third Crusade had petered out in stalemate. Saladin had recently died, and fresh hopes sprouted of rolling back the Muslim conquests in the Middle East. Innocent's plan was to go in via Egypt, secure that land as a rich and fertile base and advance on Jerusalem from the south. The Italian maritime control of the Mediterranean would make it easy. After the pope agreed to pay Venice 85,000 silver marks (estimated at nearly $100m in today's values), that city pledged transports for 4,500 knights and horses,

9,000 'squires' and 20,000 soldiers, as well as fifty war galleys, plus all the necessary supplies. But the rulers of Venice secretly had other intentions: their trade with Egypt was hugely profitable, and they would be mad to endanger it by a hostile invasion. While letting Innocent think they were on his side, the Venetians signed a secret pact with Egypt – probably sweetened by a large bribe from Sultan al-Adil – to send the looming crusade anywhere but Palestine.

Directing the Venetians' devious policy was the Doge of Venice, Enrico Dandolo, an amazingly vigorous man who despite being almost ninety still had a taste for adventure that would have done credit to a man less than half his age. Dandolo had set his sights not on the Holy Land or Egypt but on Constantinople, the glittering seat of the Byzantine Empire. That's where the money was; seize Constantinople and Venetian traders and bankers would be able to monopolize the Eastern Mediterranean. As a good subject of the pope, Dandolo also figured that the seizure of Constantinople would bring the 'schismatic' Greek Orthodox under the papal thumb; if he could do that, he would presumably have the best of this world and the next. The immediate problem, however, was money. The 85,000 silver marks Dandolo had required would have to come out of the crusaders' own pockets, and in the end only a little over half that sum was raised. All right, the doge said, let the army sail across the Adriatic to grab Zara, a Hungarian-controlled port that had become Venice's chief local rival. And the crusading leaders agreed.

Innocent was horrified and threatened to excommunicate all who took part in this campaign. No-one heeded him; the French forces that made up the bulk of the force captured Zara after a five-day siege. They then sent envoys to the pope begging for his absolution; he gave it but demanded that the booty seized from Zara be given back. He was completely ignored; the Venetians kept the loot, laughed at their excommunication and prepared to become even richer by grabbing Constantinople. Writes Will Durant in one of his many memorable phrases: '[T]he greatest and most powerful of the popes could not make his voice heard above the clamour of gold.'[16] Dandolo also nursed personal grievances against the Byzantines. Thirty years before he had been battered in a brawl while on a diplomatic mission to Constantinople where the Greek emperor, Manuel I Komnenos, had arrested thousands of Venetians in the capital on charges of economic extortion. In 1202 a young pretender to the Byzantine throne named Alexios appeared before the Venetian Senate pleading for help in overthrowing what he considered to be an illegal emperor. Dandolo and the French nobles asked him for the princely sum of 100,000 silver marks and the submission of the Greek Orthodox Church to the pope. The youth agreed. The real commander of the Fourth Crusade was Boniface of Montferrat, a Frankish noble with family connections to the Outremer regimes, but especially dazzled by the prospect of Constantinople. In fact, he probably never intended to move on to the Holy Land to fight the Muslims in the first place.

By now Innocent had realized what Dandolo was up to and flatly forbade an attack on the fellow-Christian Byzantines. Some of the nobles paid heed and went home, but most of the crusaders were persuaded that they were on the verge of capturing the richest city in Europe, and perhaps of the world. Thus that tragic and scandalous affair called the Fourth Crusade set sail from Venice in 1 October 1202 – 480 ships with priests perched on the forecastles chanting Latin hymns. On 24 June the following year the fleet arrived at Constantinople; resistance proved to be weak, and the sprightly old Dandolo was the first to jump ashore. The pretender Alexios was installed as the puppet Alexios IV. The Greeks fought back, killed Alexios after a couple of weeks and prepared for a drawn-out fight. But they were outnumbered. Within a month the Latins, 'like consuming locusts', were within the walls. They laid waste the entire city in an orgy of flame and destruction; treasures hundreds of years old were looted and Orthodox churches desecrated. Such was the dreadful pillage and butchery that one Greek witness rightly observed that even the Saracens would not have gone that far.[17] Thus was established the Latin Kingdom of Constantinople, French in language and rulers, that would last until the successful reconquest by the Greeks in 1261 – and leave the terms 'Latin' and 'Frank' even today with a bad taste in Greek mouths.

And what was the reaction of Innocent III to all this? The evidence is contradictory. The prevailing narrative so far has painted Innocent III as the victim of circumstances. We note his dismay at the campaign against fellow-Christians, and how Dandolo bamboozled him. But how could such an able and astute diplomat have been so fooled? Given his power and resources, he must have known what the Venetians were up to. And given his earlier protestations and threats of excommunication against men who marched against fellow-Christians, why should he a short time later have exulted in the submission of the Orthodox Church to Rome by 'rejoicing in the Lord' and expressing joy that 'the seamless garment of Christ' was now whole? Perhaps it was because he realized that after encouraging the idea of a crusade, it had gone in a direction he was unable to control. He probably never expected the crusaders to behave so inhumanely, and was shocked at reports of the destruction, especially the rape of nuns. As a civilized man, he had wanted none of this, and fretted about the bad light it would cast on the papacy. In short, his putative subjects, led astray by the grasping Venetians, had completely ignored him to commit what Runciman calls one of the greatest crimes against humanity.[18] There was nothing he could do now but acquiesce in the *fait accompli*.

Political turmoil in Outremer constantly engaged Innocent's attention. He was called on to settle a disputed succession in the Principality of Antioch and make an ally out of King Leo II of Armenia. The Greek Orthodox Church, smarting under the Latin boot on Constantinople, was trying to maintain its influence in the region, complicating the political tussles. Many Christians in Antioch, especially the prosperous classes, remained firmly Orthodox and looked askance at papal power. The problem turned ugly in 1207 when the Latin patriarch of Antioch, backed by the pope, tried to seize power in that city; the civil authorities thwarted the attempt and threw the patriarch in jail where he was left to waste away from hunger and thirst, and finally gave himself an agonizing death by drinking the oil from his lamp.[19] Realizing the complexity of the situation in Antioch, Innocent became tired of the whole business, especially when the fickle Leo of Armenia threw in his lot with the Greeks.

This was not the end of Innocent's crusading worries. In 1212 he was suddenly confronted with the spectacle of great masses of German children and teenagers who had walked for hundreds of miles across Europe. They were mesmerized by a young man named Nicholas who claimed God had ordered him to lead a Children's Crusade to the Holy Land. Some 30,000 children, mostly boys averaging twelve years old, left their homes to follow him. (Perhaps this was the origin of the legend of the Pied Piper of Hamelin.) On the way some starved to death, some became food for wolves, others were robbed of all they had. Those who made it into Italy appealed to the pope for help, but all he could do was quietly tell them to go home. Barely was that over than a twelve-year-old French shepherd boy named Stephen went to King Philip Augustus claiming that Christ had told him to lead his own children's crusade. Some 12,000 youngsters followed Stephen to Marseilles, where they were assured the sea would part and allow them to walk to Palestine. When the waters did not oblige, a couple of ship owners offered to take the hymn-singing young crusaders in seven ships; two sank with all on board, while the rest and their passengers were transported straight to the slave markets of Tunisia and Egypt. Frederick II, the Holy Roman emperor, had the ship owners hanged.

We have met Frederick II briefly before as the infant son of Henry VI. In 1212 he was eighteen when he received Pope Innocent's endorsement as future Holy Roman emperor. From a young age he displayed signs of extraordinary ability and talents bordering on genius. In 1214 Otto IV was defeated by the French at Bouvines, and Frederick took the throne. Very soon, despite Innocent's endorsement, he began to show signs of independence from the papacy. He was his own man, comfortable in any linguistic or religious environment, be it German, Italian, Norman, Greek, Christian or Muslim. As he took none of these elements too seriously he was able to manipulate them all. Based in the warm climate of Sicily, Frederick – described by his fans as *Stupor Mundi* (Marvel of the World) – aimed to unify all Italy under his rule.

Here he faced firm opposition in Innocent III, who was not about to let another German king, marvel of the world or no, lord it over his homeland. At first, however, the emperor acquiesced in the pope's call for a 'corrective' crusade to undo the damage done by the Fourth and re-direct efforts towards Egypt. In 1215 the Fifth Crusade duly got underway, led by King Andrew of Hungary, and besieged Damietta, at the easternmost mouth of the Nile. But on 16 July 1216, worn out by the cares of office and possibly in poor health, Innocent III fell ill at Perugia, where he had gone to settle a feud between Genoa and Pisa, and died in his fifty-sixth year. One of the most outstanding of pontiffs, he nonetheless would have had a sense of failure in not being able to recover the Holy Land. But the crusading baton was taken up with fervour by his successor, the elderly and mild-mannered Cardinal Savelli, who took the name Honorius III.

If the new pope hoped for another enthusiastic response from Europe, he was disappointed. The crusading fashion was fast fading. Europe's rulers had more immediate concerns. The Europeans living in Outremer, meanwhile, 'led indolent, immoral and luxurious lives and [had become] completely oriental'.[20] The local Orthodox Christians quite frankly preferred Muslim rule to what they had experienced in the Latin camp. The two military orders, the Hospitallers and the Templars, maintained some military and moral integrity, but at the same time made it clear that though they owed their allegiance to the pope, he was not their boss. Honorius persisted with his plan, despite difficulties in getting armies and fleets together, and in the spring of 1218 King John of Jerusalem (John of Brienne, whose hectic career would include becoming the next-to-last Latin emperor of Constantinople) found himself in command of a motley force sailing from Acre in a fleet of Dutch ships heading for Egypt.

The first objective was Damietta, on the easternmost mouth of the Nile. There John's Crusaders dug in while al-Kamil, the viceroy of Egypt, prepared to hit back. Al-Kamil marched north from Cairo, but found that his force was outnumbered, so he encamped at al-Adiliyah a few miles south of Damietta. Honorius, meanwhile, had managed to get a papal fleet started out from Brindisi under Cardinal Pelagius; he arrived in early autumn after the Crusaders had scored an initial victory by taking the Damietta fortifications. Pelagius, however, seems to have considered himself the supreme commander of the expedition, irritating the French and English contingents. A tactless and overbearing Spaniard, Pelagius had considerable energy and organizational ability. King John took quite a dislike to him, but the cardinal assuaged ruffled feelings by promising that Frederick II would soon arrive and assume overall military command.

But Frederick never arrived. Instead, he thought it wiser to concentrate his efforts on securing Italy. Of course, the Crusaders had no way of knowing this, and for months they waited in vain while clinging to their beach-head on the Nile. The fortunes of the campaign went back and forth; in the unusually cold winter of 1219 one-sixth of the troops perished of plague. Pelagius tried to restore morale by resuming the southward attack, and he was lucky enough to capitalize on a brief security crisis in Cairo to seize al-Adiliyah. But as winter turned into spring, and spring wore into a burning summer, Pelagius butted against a brick wall, constantly losing men. Leading princes and knights were either killed or on some pretext or other returned to Europe. In August Pelagius and King John had a fierce argument; the cardinal favoured an immediate all-out assault on the Muslim positions, while John thought it too risky. But the frustrated soldiers took matters into their own hands and flung themselves at al-Kamil's forces. Pelagius' feeble effort to put some order into them was ignored, with the result that the Muslims rallied to inflict a crushing defeat on the Crusaders.

At this point the cardinal-general received a visit from a friar who had gone to Egypt to see what could be done to end the war. This was none other than Francis of Assisi, already famous in his homeland, who from his early years had nursed a constant desire to fight for God and had accompanied the Crusaders as an informal diplomat. Pelagius granted permission for Francis to call on al-Kamil; Francis made a striking impression on the sultan's Muslim guards who decided that 'anyone so simple, so gentle and so dirty must be mad and ... touched by God'.[21] Al-Kamil treated him courteously, but ruled out any peace with the rowdy Crusaders and sent him back to Pelagius. But the Egyptians were in difficulties, as the Nile was unusually low and food was scarce, and al-Kamil extended peace feelers of his own. Pelagius responded with a fresh offensive that swept the Muslims out of Damietta on 5 November 1219. But once that city was in Christian hands, a dispute arose over whose Christian hands it should remain in. Pelagius, with a singular lack of political and strategic realism, wanted to add it to the papal domains. But King John of Jerusalem, backed by the Hospitallers and Templars, rather more sensibly wanted it for himself. The resulting impasse stalled the Crusader campaign.

It could be argued that the Fifth Crusade suffered from the absence of Frederick II. The 'Marvel of the World' wanted to be crowned in Saint Peter's more than anything else, and if he was interested in the East, it was through ambition rather than piety. Pope Honorius naively messaged Pelagius that Frederick's troops could be expected in Egypt any day; Pelagius accordingly stayed where he was, even though al-Kamil's forces were weakened by famine and the Crusaders could have gone all the way to Cairo with little hindrance. In February 1220 King John, who had never been on civil terms with Pelagius, left Egypt on the pretext of having to deal with a dynastic problem. With John gone, morale in the army plummeted; the soldiers sullenly ignored the cardinal's urgings to action. The papacy was also running out of money to finance this expensive crusade. But when Frederick finally realized his life's ambition and was crowned by the pope, he promised to personally sail for Egypt with an army in the spring of 1221.

Honorius had meanwhile advised Pelagius to give a hearing to any peace terms al-Kamil might offer, but when the cardinal heard of the imminent arrival of Duke Louis of Bavaria he took heart anew. Though Frederick was still nowhere to be seen, Pelagius urged a fresh offensive before the Nile waters could rise. On 6 July King John returned – though distrustful of the whole business – and 630 ships sailed up the Nile, accompanied by 5,000 knights, 5,000 archers and 40,000 foot soldiers. The Muslims lined up to stop them behind a tributary called the Bahr as-Saghir. John was uneasy; the Nile floods could be expected any day, threatening to maroon the Crusaders, and moreover, a Syrian army was reported on its way to help al-Kamil. But Pelagius was not to be stopped. Believing a false rumour that al-Kamil had pulled back to Cairo, he instead found him on the opposite bank of the Bahr es-Saghir.

The Egyptians had not been inactive. While the Nile was rising al-Kamil had sent detachments across the Bahr es-Saghir to cut off the Crusaders' link with Damietta; soon the water was high enough to enable the Muslim fleet to sail down the canal to block the Crusader fleet. Pelagius, whose lack of strategic sense had got his army into this predicament, wondered how he could get out of it. As the army had food for just three weeks, the Bavarian contingent persuaded the cardinal to order a withdrawal. After nightfall on 26 August the retreat began. Pelagius seems to have lost all control over his demoralized troops, and error compounded error. The army had accumulated a large store of wine and many soldiers guzzled it all down rather than leave it behind; thus inebriated, they could hardly walk. The Teutonic Knights, with Teutonic stolidity, burned their own stores, not realizing that the smoke signalled to the Egyptians the intention to retreat. With the Crusaders lumbering northwards, the Muslim commanders opened the sluice gates on the right bank of the Nile. The onrushing water caught the Crusaders on low ground, turning it into a vast quagmire, while al-Kamil's cavalry harassed them from the rear. King John managed to beat back the attacking horsemen, but thousands of foot-soldiers and accompanying pilgrims met their deaths in the mud.

Pelagius himself remained on board his ship, which thanks to the swift Nile current managed to evade the Muslim ships, but most of his vessels were captured along with his food and medical supplies. On 28 August he decided the game was up and extended peace feelers to al-Kamil. The cardinal may have had some faint hope in the reinforcements that Frederick II was believed to be sending. But the sultan clearly had the upper hand and was able to dictate his terms: the Crusaders would give up Damietta and observe a truce of eight years, the Muslims would give up the True Cross which they allegedly possessed, and all prisoners would be exchanged. As a guarantee, the sultan demanded that Pelagius, King John, the chiefs of the Military Orders and nineteen other European nobles stay with him as hostages.

The Crusader garrison in Damietta rebelled against the truce, especially as forty ships under Count Henry of Malta had just arrived. But thoughts of resistance evaporated under a shortage of food. Al-Kamil, meanwhile, rendered splendid hospitality to his high-level Christian hostages and made available to the Crusaders all the food and supplies they needed, as long as they got out of Egypt. This they did on 8 September 1221, after Pelagius and the other hostages were freed, while al-Kamil entered Damietta in triumph. One thing the Crusaders failed to take with them was the True Cross; the Muslim promise to hand it over seems to have been genuine enough, but when the time came, it was nowhere to be found.[22]

Cardinal Pelagius went on to serve as a papal emissary to try and settle awkward dynastic affairs at Antioch and neighbouring Armenia. From there he went to serve as a legate in Cyprus, and in 1223 set out from Acre together with King John and the heads of the Military Orders to sail to Rome to see if some papal order could be put into the turbulent affairs of Outremer. To avoid disasters such as Damietta, John asked that any further conquests by crusaders be placed under the jurisdiction of his own Kingdom of Jerusalem. The pope agreed, overruling the distrustful Pelagius, and began making plans for a dynastic union between Outremer and Latin-controlled Byzantium.

In Europe, meanwhile, someone had to be found as a scapegoat for the failure of the Fifth Crusade, and blame was duly pinned on Frederick II, who had reneged on his repeated promise to go to Egypt, and for whom the Crusaders had waited in vain for six years. Pope Honorius III, his patience exhausted, excommunicated him. Though hugely talented, Frederick was easy to dislike –'cruel, selfish and sly, unreliable as a friend and unforgiving as an enemy'.[23] The Church condemned him as a scandalous pleasure-seeker and to many clergy he was an outright heretic. To redeem himself Frederick finally set out for the Holy Land in 1228, on what became the Sixth Crusade. His notoriety preceded him; the Christians of Palestine wanted nothing to do with an excommunicant. But the emperor's multicultural background, linguistic and diplomatic talents and knowledge of the Middle East and its ways enabled him to achieve what legions of less sophisticated warriors could never do: meeting al-Kamil at Nablus, he charmed the sultan into giving up a considerable amount of Muslim-held territory including the cities of Acre, Jaffa, Sidon, Nazareth and Bethlehem and almost all of Jerusalem except the Dome of the Rock that was and is sacred to Muslims. It was a remarkable treaty by any standards. Christian and Muslim agreed to respect each others' holy places. 'Two cultures, brought together for a moment in mutual understanding and respect, had found it possible to be friends.'[24]

Sadly, the effect did not last. The great majority of Muslims in the region bitterly condemned what they saw as a great betrayal by al-Kamil, whose own imams insulted him to his face. In Jerusalem they were not impressed by Frederick's appearance, even though he went out of his way to accommodate them. His pink beardless face and weak eyes caused some to mutter that he 'would not be worth two hundred dirhams in the slave market'.[25] Many Muslims also were disturbed that Frederick appeared to disparage his own Christian religion; they would have respected a firmer Christian leader far more. In the Christian camp, too, there was a sense of anticlimax in that Jerusalem had been won not by force of arms but by the kind of secret diplomacy that any true soldier detested. Some resented the fact that the Muslim shrines in Jerusalem had been preserved; the Knights Templar especially were incensed that their original temple headquarters remained in Muslim hands. And if Frederick expected that by winning Jerusalem he would get his excommunication lifted, he was mistaken. He was not liked in the Holy City, especially after he had himself proclaimed King of Jerusalem, shunting aside his father-in-law John of Brienne. In the almost total absence of support from the two main Military Orders, his only real allies were the Teutonic Knights.

Not surprisingly, he found Christian support rapidly ebbing away. On 19 March 1229 Archbishop Peter of Caesarea placed Jerusalem under an interdict. Frederick replied by leading his forces first to Jaffa and then to Acre, where he expected to find support but came upon fanatical enmity. While considering desperate measures to keep himself in power, including plans to kidnap his chief opponents, he received news that Pope Gregory IX had mobilized an army against his estates in Italy. It was time for Frederick to leave Outremer, and fast. He planned to leave Acre secretly, at the crack of dawn on 1 May, but the secret was ill-kept and he found angry crowds lining the Street of Butchers pelting him and his entourage with animal entrails and excrement.[26] Humiliated and shaken, he landed at Brindisi on 10 June. The Sixth Crusade was over. There would be other futile attempts to march against the East bearing the name of crusade, but with Frederick's exit the crusading era was well and truly finished.

Chapter 5

'The Fair Land of France'

Pope Gregory IX was one of those pontiffs determined to put some backbone back into the papacy to enable it to deal with the Hohenstaufen emperors as well as political opposition in Rome itself. Born Ugolino dei Conti di Segni, as a cardinal he cemented ties with the English and Spanish monarchies; as pope he sought to follow in the firm footsteps of Innocent III, and soon found himself at loggerheads with the Ghibelline faction in the Comune in the form of the Poli and Frangipane families. The heads of these families had ceded their estates to Frederick II in return for membership in a noble class of Holy Roman Empire knights called paladins, so honoured for supposed feats in defence of the faith. This status appears to have enhanced their local prestige to quite overshadow the pope's, at which point Gregory deemed it prudent to move to Viterbo and then even farther north to Rieti and Perugia.

When Frederick II was still in Outremer the pope had sent an army into Sicily, but Frederick had little trouble defeating it in the field. Just how this army was constituted remains vague. So far the popes had appeared content to let secular powers do their fighting. The papal militia was probably only used locally, and only in exceptional cases, such as with John VIII in 877 and Leo IX at Civitate in 1053, did a pope command an army in person. These early papal armies were almost certainly mercenary outfits, fighting for pay rather than out of any religious fervour, though most of the personnel probably came from the communities and towns of the Papal States. They would have been led by professional officers of varying degrees of competence. The papal army that moved against Frederick's Italian domains would probably have been outnumbered by what the emperor could field against it. In February 1230 Providence stepped in to help the self-exiled Gregory by means of a severe flooding of the Tiber; this emergency, plus the resulting epidemic that could only be adequately handled by the papal Curia, moved the Comune to invite the pope back to Rome. Frederick, too, was in a conciliatory mood, and cemented his peace with the pope in the Treaty of San Germano in July.

Believing he had the papacy now under his thumb, in late 1231 Frederick instructed Gregory to send a new army out to defend Jerusalem. The emperor himself despatched about 5,000 soldiers, including 600 knights, to the East under Marshal Riccardo Filangieri. The force had a mixed reception as the Military Orders of the Hospitallers and Templars were still unsure of the pope's own intentions. There followed a confused campaign, with battles between rival Christian forces in Outremer and Cyprus as Filangieri tried to enforce Frederick's writ, with varying success. Gregory was unhappy with Filangieri's strong-arm methods, yet remained uneasily in favour of Frederick's policy. The result was chronic anarchy in Outremer that redounded to the prestige neither of emperor nor pope, while the Muslim potentates marshalled their forces anew.

The Treaty of San Germano temporarily set back the cause of the pro-imperial Ghibelline faction in Rome. But disturbances were renewed in 1234 when Luca Savelli, a nephew of the late Honorius III, staged a popular revolt 'for the liberation of the Church', supposedly from imperial influence. It soon became apparent that Savelli was little more than a tool of the Roman commercial and business class, backed up by many ordinary people. Mobs sacked the Lateran palace while Gregory again fled to Rieti to find an unexpected ally in Frederick, who through some astute diplomacy helped the pope return to Rome.

Politics in the Eternal City were extraordinarily fluid, with the pro-papal Welf and pro-imperial Ghibelline factions alternating in revolving-door power. It would have taken a remarkably strong-willed and powerful pontiff to steer a way through those twin thickets. Gregory IX appeared to possess this will; he had set up the Inquisition to stamp out heretics all over Europe, and included Jews and black cats among his pet hates, but local Roman intrigues defeated him. The year 1238 found him on the run again for three months. What followed was a vicious propaganda war. Hounded by the Ghibellines, he hurled a second excommunication against Frederick. The emperor responded by excoriating the pontiff as 'insane, an infidel prophet, profaner of the Church'. Gregory shot back with 'heretic beast of the Apocalypse'. The heretic beast had gained an advantage by defeating the Lombard League, and there was a serious risk that he might swallow the Papal States.

Frederick became a menace on the seas, where he tried to sink and capture ships carrying prelates to Rome to vote for the papal excommunication. In early 1241 he got his forces together and encircled Rome, taking prisoner two cardinals and several bishops. Encamped at Grottaferrata in the south, he was about to move on the city in the spring of 1241 when Gregory died. Two years before, in an apparent attempt to restore the international prestige of the papacy, Gregory had sent agents to France and England to call for yet another crusade. The kings of both countries had more immediate concerns and politely declined the call, but a band of French nobles donned their armour and saddled their horses and set out, only to be massacred by Muslim forces under the emir Rukn ad-Din at Gaza. Crusader incompetence reaped its harvest on 11 July 1244 when the Khwarizmian Turks captured Jerusalem,

Back in Italy there was a pause in Frederick's siege of Rome while Gregory's successor, the elderly and ailing Celestine IV, reigned for a little more than two weeks before himself dying, to be replaced by the capable and experienced Innocent IV. The emperor lifted the siege to give his Ghibelline faction some time to reassert itself, which it did by forcing Innocent into exile in Lyon in France. Frederick became the occupier of the papal domains except for Viterbo, which resisted his advance. From Lyon the pope declared Frederick deposed, a major propaganda blow for the emperor, whose Ghibelline allies in Rome began to falter. Disheartened, Frederick forgot all about Rome and moved to South Italy, where he died in December 1250. Yet the way was not clear for the pope to return to Rome. Ghibelline influence was still strong, mainly among the business class and the masses who controlled the Comune and distrusted the nobles and the cardinals.

Only Frederick's death in 1250 enabled Innocent to return to Italy; setting up his military headquarters in Naples, the pope is said to have exclaimed, 'Let the heavens rejoice and the earth be glad!'[1] Yet he appears not to have reckoned on two brothers in North Italy, Ezzelino and Alberigo Pallavicino, who had no use for papal control of their domains; they were, in fact, irreligious and cruel despots. Innocent died before he could come to grips with them, but in 1259 his successor Alexander IV sent an army that captured Ezzelino, who starved himself to death in jail, unrepentant. An even worse fate was in store for Alberigo, whose flesh was slowly ripped from him, after which he was dragged behind a horse until he died. There was nothing particularly exceptional in such barbarism; a papal state, like every other, had to play the hardball the times demanded, and few mourned the brutal Pallavicino brothers when the pope gave them a taste of their own medicine.

The passing of Frederick ignited papal hopes that the Hohenstaufen house could finally be tamed. The emperor's son and heir, Conrad IV, was the titular king of Italy, but Innocent was determined to change that. He toyed with the idea of recruiting Richard of Cornwall, the younger brother of King Henry III of England, as Holy Roman Emperor. Entering suddenly from the wings was Frederick's illegitimate son Manfred, whose claim to be regent of Italy sparked revolts up and down the peninsula. Pope Innocent eagerly threw in his lot with Manfred's opponents, but Innocent was already seriously ill when his papal army was routed by Manfred's forces near Foggia; the news probably hastened his end. Six years after Foggia, Manfred inflicted a second defeat on the pope's forces at Montaperto. Alexander IV, a nephew of the late Gregory IX, had little of his uncle's ability. The previous papal reign had seen a Roman senator, Brancaleone degli Andalò, set up a semi-dictatorship to free the rising business classes from domination by the nobles, but Brancaleone was soon toppled by the nobles he had tried to rein in.

Alexander felt safe enough to return to Rome, but factional unrest never stopped, driving him to Viterbo in 1257. Brancaleone in turn returned to power; his harsh vengeance caused the pope to excommunicate him, but on his death the following year the people venerated him almost as a secular saint. All this unrest was hardly calculated to make the popes feel politically secure, with the result that Alexander's successor Urban IV sought a strong protector, and believed he found one in Charles of Anjou, a brother of King Louis IX of France. It appears that the mercenary armies periodically employed by the popes to fight their secular battles had proved inadequate, either in numbers or quality or both. In papal eyes Frederick II's successors were nothing but a 'viper brood', so no help could be expected from them. If the papacy were to have any guarantor at all, it would have to be the French.

Louis IX of France, however, wanted to reconcile Innocent with the Holy Roman Empire, and by way of example had embarked on the Seventh Crusade in 1248. The king and his army spent six miserable years in Egypt and Palestine; ill and humiliated, he tried to recruit a Christian army against a new and fearsome force that had charged out of the eastern horizon, the Mongols, but failed in that also. Twenty years later, incredibly, Louis attempted another crusade – the Eighth – only to die of a gastro-intestinal ailment as soon as he set foot in Africa; his purported last dying word was 'Jerusalem'. The balance of power was changing in the East. In 1261 the Greeks took back Constantinople after a fifty-seven-year Latin occupation that did nothing for the papal reputation in the Orthodox world, and the legitimate Byzantine Empire received a new lease on life. More than ever before, the popes had to look westward for support.

It was Innocent's successor Urban IV who actually extended the invitation to Charles of Anjou to help him return to Rome and regain some semblance of political power. Urban also nursed hopes of re-taking Constantinople. But that could wait until he got rid of Frederick's stepson Manfred, who had set himself up as King of Sicily. And Charles of Anjou was seen as an essential tool for this. But as happened distressingly often to thirteenth-century popes, Urban just didn't live long enough; when he died after a three years' reign he was replaced by another Frenchman, Clement IV, who was an even bigger fan of Charles. In the spring of 1265 Charles, whom the pope had made ruler of the kingdom of Naples and Sicily (the 'Two Sicilies'), arrived in Rome and at once proclaimed his ambition to command the Papal States by installing himself in the pope's former quarters in the Lateran palace. He did not have the diplomacy to conceal his true nature, which was that of a cold-blooded, greedy tyrant, the very antithesis of his saintly brother, the king of France. 'He was a natural autocrat, with an unshakeable belief in himself as the chosen instrument of the Almighty.'[2] He also had his hard eye on Constantinople.

With the blessings of Clement, Charles from his capital at Naples led 30,000 men into South Italy to measure swords with Manfred; the pope was enthusiastic – or partisan – enough to call it a 'crusade'. The opposing forces clashed on 26 February 1266 at Benevento. Manfred's army was crushed and Manfred himself killed; when his body was discovered it was thrown from the bridge at Benevento, stoned by the passing French and papal soldiery, and denied a Christian burial. The only obstacle now to papal power was eighteen-year-old Conradin, the son of Conrad IV and last legitimate Hohenstaufen. Conradin rode into Rome in 1268, to a hearty welcome from the Romans, only to be defeated by Charles' forces near Tagliacozzo. Clement raised no protest as Charles had young Conradin beheaded; to him the only good Hohenstaufen was a dead Hohenstaufen. But there would have been plenty of Romans prepared to argue that the pope's own death that same year was just deserts for the crime against Conradin.

Heartened by this success, Clement was in the process of plotting a new Latin attack on Constantinople, when he, too, passed from this world in November. This was a welcome development for Charles, who kept the papal seat vacant, personally dominating the Curia for three years as he drew up his schedule of planned Mediterranean conquests. Shipyards along the coast of the Papal States were kept busy building ships for Charles' hoped-for drive against Byzantium. Byzantine Emperor Michael VIII pleaded with Louis IX for help. Louis appeared willing, but got himself involved in his final crusade in Tunis, where he died. Charles' fleet sailed for Tunis on the first leg of the expedition, but he was too late to see his brother alive. He finished the crusade that his brother had begun, defeating the emir of Tunis, and returned to Trapani in Sicily to winter in late 1270. On 22 November a ferocious storm hit the fleet, smashing Charles' biggest warships and drowning thousands of men and horses. Byzantium was saved, again. But what about the papacy?

For most of the previous dozen years the popes, from their refuge at Viterbo, had the almost superhuman task of trying to put some order in what remained of the Latin presence in the Middle East, supporting ill-conceived crusades such as those which finished Louis IX, asserting doctrinal authority over the rest of Europe and trying to keep the Papal States intact – all while plotting to somehow claw back the Orthodox Greeks of Byzantium into the papal fold. Not surprisingly, given the advanced age of the pontiffs at their accession, and their brief reigns, they proved unable to shoulder such a multifarious task. Tellingly, the three popeless years between 1268 and 1271 did not alter the political situation in Italy, which was dissolving into chaos. For those three years the cardinals, shut into the episcopal palace in Viterbo, haggled over who would be the next pontiff; they were forced into a decision only when the exasperated town authorities took the roof off where they were assembled, exposing them to the elements. The next pope, Gregory X, had to be recalled from Syria. Having been on the scene, as it were, Gregory keenly desired the crusading spirit to continue. 'A Christian as well as a pope', as Durant wryly notes, he commissioned a report on the progress so far, the *Collectio de Scandalis Ecclesiae*, which proved to be scathing in its criticisms: incompetence and corruption on the part of Western nobles and clergy alike had eroded the Latin principalities. Writes Runciman:

> While prelates spent their money on fine horses and pet monkeys, their agents raised money by the wholesale redemption of Crusading vows. None of the clergy would contribute to the taxes levied to pay for the Crusades ... Meanwhile the general public was taxed again and again for Crusades that never took place.[3]

One of the contributors to the report sadly noted that 'laziness, avarice and cowardice' kept men from sailing to the East, and more tellingly, 'few now believed in the spiritual merit' that crusading was supposed to earn its adherents.[4] The Military Orders were having recruitment problems, which eroded their ability to protect the Franks of Outremer, while the Italian merchants of Venice and Genoa were most reluctant to endanger their web of trade deals with the Muslims.

Armed with these adverse reports, Gregory summoned a church council to meet at Lyon in May 1274. It found few takers; the kings of France and England, though invited, pleaded excuses. The council in the end came to nothing. Gregory lived for two more years, to be succeeded by Innocent V, Hadrian V and John XXII, none of whom lasted more than a few weeks. It fell to Nicholas III to abolish the right of monarchs such as Charles of Anjou to serve as Roman senators. He also received recognition from the first of the Habsburg emperors, Rudolf of Habsburg, who confirmed the papacy as sovereign in the Papal States.

Meanwhile, the end was nigh for Charles of Anjou. So autocratic was his misrule in Sicily that on Easter Monday of 1282 the people of Palermo rose up and massacred every French soldier in the city; it is said that the bellies of Sicilian women made pregnant by French soldiers were ripped open and the foetuses trampled to death.[5] The revolt soon spread to the rest of Sicily; in a nightmare known ever since as the Sicilian Vespers, at least 3,000 Frenchmen were murdered. There was some suspicion that the papacy had secretly urged the uprising, but most informed opinion discounts that theory. Pope Martin IV, awed by Charles, in fact issued a formal protest at the massacres.

Interestingly, at the time Charles was preparing to lead a fleet against Constantinople, and for the second time in a dozen years he had been thwarted by a cataclysmic event. Blind with fury, Charles swore he would blast Sicily into 'a barren, uninhabited rock'. The timid Martin seconded that aim, but before Charles could act the Sicilians called in King Pedro III of Aragon, who arrived with an army and fleet and took Sicily under the Spanish wing. The strain of all this proved too much for the exhausted Charles, who died three years later. One result of these developments was that the papacy could stop worrying about South Italy and Sicily, now held firmly by the French and Spanish respectively. It had far more trouble in the centre and north, where several powerful mercantile states were ostentatiously asserting their independence of both pope and emperor. Milan, for example, was beginning to prosper under the Visconti clan. Siena, Florence, Venice and Genoa all developed their own independent administrations, and would not hesitate to fight the pope if he tried to extend his influence, as Siena did in 1270. The Papal States, now underwritten by the Habsburgs, ran in an irregularly-shaped ribbon from Bologna and Ravenna to south of Rome. Thus was set a pattern of powers and mutual antagonisms that would endure for centuries.

Meanwhile, the Muslim powers were on a roll in the Middle East. What Latin authority remained in Outremer was fast evaporating. An extremely competent, if ruthless, Kipchak Turk by the name of Rukn ad-Din Baybars Bundukdari – known to history more simply as Baybars – was fending off both the advancing Mongols in the east and rival Muslim potentates in Syria. A veteran also of battles with the forces of the Seventh Crusade, and based in Egypt, Baybars mastered Palestine, wiping out Christian communities in the process. Regent Hugh of Acre managed to hold out, thanks to the efforts of the Hospitallers and Templars. But with cold and steady efficiency Baybars knocked out one Latin domain after the other; Antioch fell to him in 1268, with great slaughter, and thousands of Western survivors were sold in the glutted Muslim slave markets. Regent Hugh became King Hugh III of Cyprus with authority over what scraps of Outremer remained, and the papacy for a while took new heart.

But Baybars knew how to be patient. Of candidate crusaders there was no lack. Prince Edward of England, the son of Henry III, gathered up about 1,000 men and sailed to Outremer in the hope of engineering a concerted attack on the Muslims with the help of the Mongols. Edward had some success at first, but Baybars' force was just too big to dent. The prince himself narrowly escaped death from an assailant's poisoned dagger and disheartened, returned to England in the autumn of 1272, to find himself already King Edward I. Three years later Baybars overran Anatolia (modern Turkey). In July 1277, while continuing his campaign in Anatolia, he died unexpectedly. The cause of his death remains unknown; perhaps it was wounds, perhaps too much drink. According to a most widespread rumour, he accidentally tossed off a poisoned cup of *kumiz*, or fermented mare's milk, that he had prepared for someone who had angered him.

The Franks of Outremer rejoiced at the news of Baybars' demise. But infighting in the province continued as the leaders appeared to be unable to take advantage of the temporary Muslim setback. Appeals for peace by Pope Martin fell on deaf ears. The new Egyptian leader, Qalawun, attempted to make peace with the threatening Mongols, but under Mangu Timur they advanced nonetheless and clashed with Qalawun at Homs on 30 October 1281. The battle, a standoff, gave a breathing space to Timur's Christian allies. Still, the Frankish leaders engaged in unceasing intrigues and quarrels. On 25 May 1285 Qalawun marched into the Hospitaller castle of Marqab. Honorius IV, another brief pope (1285–87), apparently never bothered to reply to a Mongol suggestion of common action against the Muslims; however, his successor Nicholas IV made a great show of receiving a Mongol ambassador in February 1288, but shrank from pledging any military action.

Uncertainty continued, with the Outremer nobility behaving with the utmost irresponsibility in the face of approaching annihilation; in 1289 Tripoli fell to Qalawun's forces. Nicholas nevertheless tried to recruit more crusaders, and found a few thousand among the rabble and peasantry of North Italy. These needed little prodding to carry out a drunken massacre of Muslims in Acre. All that it accomplished was to stoke the fury of Qalawun's determined son al-Ashraf. Leaving his harem at Damascus, al-Ashraf loomed before Acre with many thousands of infantry and cavalry on 5 April 1291. During a month-long siege the defenders of Acre received reinforcements from Europe, but they were too few to make a real difference. On 16 May the Muslim attack began; despite gallant resistance by the Hospitallers and Templars, the defenders were gradually forced back. Two days later al-Ashraf ordered his major assault on all points of the walls of Acre. It wasn't until 28 May that the city was finally in his hands, after a fearful slaughter of non-combatants in the streets. A lucky few escaped by boats. Never again, vowed the sultan, would Acre 'be a spearhead for Christian aggression in Syria'.[6] At about the same time, Tyre fell to the Muslims without a struggle, and the curtain closed on the 192-year history of Frankish Outremer. An outpost of Templars struggled on for a few more years until forced out in 1303.

As a West European outpost in the Middle East, Outremer was a complex and costly failure. The reasons for its failure are many, but a basic one was that it had failed to outgrow the crusading spirit that most of Europe had already forgotten about. No matter how many popes would, often fervently and sincerely, try to rekindle the flame of holy war against the Muslim, an increasingly weary Europe was unwilling to listen. It was not only Muslim determination that crushed the life out of the Frankish domains; the merchants and financiers of Italian maritime cities such as Venice and Genoa needed peace and stability in the Eastern Mediterranean, and frankly cared little about who was in charge there, as long as trade could flourish. Most moderate Muslims, who were among the beneficiaries of that trade, would heartily endorse that position. It may have been partly to give his subjects a chance at a lasting peace that Sultan al-Ashraf decided to eliminate the running sore of Outremer and close that troublesome chapter for good.

The fall of Acre gave Nicholas IV little time for hand-wringing as he was engaged in the perennial tussle between the papacy and the leading Roman families. Soon after his elevation Nicholas had to flee to Rieti in central Italy. Two powerful families, the Orsini and the Colonna, now dominated Roman affairs, and the pope backed the latter; after some confusion the Colonna came out on top. The Orsini stirred up a libellous campaign against Nicholas that was ended only by a compromise that enabled both clans to share power in the Senate. Following Nicholas was the saintly Celestine V, a retiring monk who originally didn't want the office and abdicated after just five months.[7]

The opening of the fourteenth century found the throne of Saint Peter occupied by Boniface VIII, the papal name of Benedetto Caetani, whose rising family had begun to rival the older-established Colonna. Boniface took his role seriously enough to make determined attempts to build up his world image and that of the papacy, which at the time was judged to be 'the strongest government in Europe, the best organized, the best administered

[and] the richest in revenue'.[8] No more would the realm of Peter be kicked about by every secular ruler who could field an army, or be blown about by the whims of the Roman nobility. He tried but failed to keep Sicily out of foreign hands by excommunicating the Spanish king of Aragon who claimed it after the Sicilian Vespers. When he ordered Venice and Genoa to stop squabbling and get together for a respectable crusade, they ignored him. When two cardinals of the Colonna family fell out, he flung excommunications at them; when they thumbed their noses at him, he mustered his papal troops and razed their castles in Palestrina, strewing salt over the rubble so that nothing would grow.

As a massive public relations exercise Boniface proclaimed the first Holy Year, a kind of jubilee, in 1300. Its purpose was ostensibly to better organize facilities for the stream of pilgrims that never ceased to flow to the Eternal City from all parts of Italy and farther afield to see the tombs of Saints Peter and Paul. But in the absence of any concrete evidence for that, the real purpose of the Jubilee year was certainly financial: Boniface needed money to bankroll his plans to conquer Sicily and Tuscany, and generally to maintain himself as the leading figure in Christendom, the man to whom the rest of the globe, religious or secular, should bow. Believers were told they could earn divine indulgence for their sins by simply visiting Rome and worshipping at Saint Peter's (the early basilica, not the present grand structure completed in 1626). The call electrified Europe. In 1300 alone some two million visitors – the precursors of the latter-day tourist hordes – surged into Rome; their modest offerings to the Church piled up into such wealth that 'two priests, with rakes in their hands, were kept busy night and day collecting the coins'.[9] This, the mother and father of all fund-raising drives, would set a lucrative example for centuries to come.

The money pouring into the papacy watered the mouths of West European kings such as Philip IV (the Fair) of France and Edward I of England, both of whom saw the Church as a convenient source of funds for their perennial rivalry, soon to explode in the Hundred Years' War. Their taxation of Church property to raise war chests angered Boniface, whose bull *Clericis laicos*, issued in February 1296, two years after his accession, asserted that only the pope could tax the Church. Philip the Fair had replied by halting the transfer of funds to Rome, while Edward I prosecuted any English clergy who actually forked over the tax. Boniface at the time had to back down.

Papal relations with France went from bad to worse. Exiles from the Colonna family were filling Philip's ears with tales of what a horrid pontiff Boniface was – greedy, ruthless, and even a closet heretic. A papal legate was arrested and jailed. In the closing days of 1301 Boniface penned an angry letter to the French king which history knows as the *Ausculta fili* (literally, 'Listen, son') whose title well describes its condescending tone. The letter was uncompromising, ending in a vague threat that the pope would take measures 'for the reformation of the kingdom [France] and the amendment of the king'. Just what those measures were to be was not spelled out; but as soon as the *Ausculta fili* was read to Philip, a furious noble snatched it from the hands of the papal envoy and flung it into the fire. A copy of it was consigned to the flames more officially, in front of the king and a crowd of Parisians, on 11 February 1302.

The event triggered one of the more significant developments in the history of European government. To bolster his position Philip the Fair called the first-ever States-General, an unprecedented meeting of the nobles, clergy and commons, starting a trend that half a millennium later would erupt into the French Revolution. All three classes backed the king, though a few dozen French priests preferred to throw in their lot with the pope. These and others attended a council in Rome in October 1302. Boniface used the occasion to reiterate his hard line; on 18 November 1302 he issued the bull *Unam sanctam*, in which he reiterated the old papal principle of the 'two swords' – one wielded by the pope and the other by whichever secular power the pope backed, both in the battle for Christendom:

> Within the power of the Church are distinguished two swords, the spiritual and the temporal; the first is wielded by the Church, the second for the Church, the one in the hand of the priest, the other in the hand of the king but by the priest's indication [because] the spiritual power must order and judge the temporal power.[10]

The encyclical went even further than the *Dictatus papae* of Gregory VII. It concluded by asserting the right of the 'bishop of Rome' (i.e. the pope) not only to overrule any secular ruler but also to determine the spiritual salvation of every human being on earth; any disagreement was tantamount to opposing God Himself.

Philip the Fair was having none of this; in June 1303 his clergy gleefully lambasted the pope in scurrilous terms such as 'sorcerer, murderer, embezzler, adulterer, sodomite and idolater'. Correctly assuming that Boniface would hit back with a heavy-duty excommunication, on 7 September 1303 the king sent Guillaume de Nogaret, his chief justice, and Sciarra Colonna, a leading member of the prominent Roman noble family, with some 2,000 armed men to burst into the pope's summer quarters at Anagni south-east of Rome and order him to cancel the planned excommunication and abdicate, threatening him with death if he did not. The seventy-five-year-old pontiff refused; Sciarra Colonna is said to have slapped his face and would have done worse if not held back by Nogaret. A few days later, the people of Anagni joined 400 horsemen enlisted by the Orsini to storm the villa, disperse the Colonna gang and free the pope before he could come to any immediate harm. It is said that Boniface had been given no food for three days, and when he passed by a marketplace he begged for some bread and wine in return for 'God's blessing and mine'.[11] The shock must have been a severe blow to his health, as he died two weeks later. 'With him,' writes Wallace Ferguson, 'died the mediaeval papacy.'[12]

Philip the Fair was now intent on turning the papacy into a French instrument. Boniface's successor Benedict XI excommunicated the ringleaders of what was called the Outrage of Anagni, but after less than a year he passed away – poisoned, it was said. With the help of the Colonna, Philip engineered the election of the Archbishop of Bordeaux, Bertrand de Got, as Pope Clement V. If the king wanted a puppet pope, he certainly got one. As Rome was in its usual state of partisan chaos, Clement gladly agreed to Philip's suggestion that pope and Curia move their establishment to Comtat-Venaissin, a papal-held province in South-east France. Its main town, Avignon, provided an impressive castle for the pope to live in while remaining technically in papal territory, as Avignon was just outside the border of the French kingdom. For the first time in its 1,200-year history, the papacy abandoned its traditional home; it entered nearly seven decades of what has been called the Church's 'Babylonian Captivity'. The term is apposite, as during that time the papacy, in believing it had escaped German control, placed itself totally under French domination, and not surprisingly, the seven so-called 'Avignon Popes' were all Frenchmen. The nationalist state was beginning to overshadow the ideal of the universal Church.

Western Europe, as a result, was beginning to fracture along ethnic lines. No more would Christian armies unite under a pope to battle the Muslim in the Middle East. There would be plenty of causes of war far closer to home.

Clement V wandered around France for four years before settling on Avignon as the papal headquarters. No doubt he and his successors felt safer there than in turbulent Rome, but France's rulers subtly made sure that they stayed there to promote French interests. It was at Philip's instigation that Clement agreed to eradicate the Order of the Templars, the military order that had originated in Jerusalem in the twelfth century along with the Knights Hospitaller, but in the meantime had become embroiled in accusations of financial wrongdoing. On 13 October 1307 Philip the Fair ordered the arrest of some 15,000 Templar knights and associated people in the kingdom. Charges of crime and heresy were flung at them indiscriminately. Many confessed falsely under torture; fifty-nine of them were burned at the stake, including Templar Grand Master Jacques de Molay, whose incineration was personally witnessed by Philip himself. In 1312 Clement abolished the Templars as a military order, turning over its assets to the Hospitallers.

One reason why France wanted to keep the popes pliant was the hope that it might expand its realm into the Rhône and Rhine valleys. This policy put the next pope, John XXII, at loggerheads with the Germans, who were struggling through a dynastic war. This only made the Holy Roman Empire yet more determined to defy the pope, who soon discovered opposition from other quarters. Around Europe political thinkers were arising who cast serious doubt on papal claims of absolute spiritual and temporal authority. One was the Italian Marsiglio of Padua, whose tract *Defensor pacis* (Defender of Peace) in 1324 asserted flatly that a pope could only serve as an administrator, a president of the Christian community, real authority for which should lie with general councils of the faithful, and hence he had no right to 'coercive jurisdiction'. It therefore followed that spiritual leaders such as popes should be subject to the secular authority, king or emperor, who would be the real *defensor pacis*. The unspoken corollary was that popes should cease fielding their own armies and limit themselves to spiritual duties alone.

John XXII, of course, ignored these ideas, admittedly radical for the time, and acted as any ordinary ruler would, raising taxes in order to build up Avignon into a capital worthy of the papacy and selling ecclesiastical offices for large profits. According to one modern ex-Catholic commentator, he 'felt that he could serve God best by winning Mammon to his side'.[13] In England, however, there was huge resentment at seeing English money flowing to a French pope. King Edward III quipped pointedly that 'the successor of the Apostles was commissioned to lead the Lord's sheep to pasture, not to fleece them.' Edward managed to limit the outflow somewhat, and by his Statute of Praemunire stripped local church courts of the right of appeal to the pope. To the outside world the Avignon papacy appeared intent on making itself as unpopular as possible, not hesitating to victimize the Franciscan monastic order, even burning some monks at the stake. John himself came under clerical suspicion when several sermons which he delivered in 1132 were deemed heretical. On his death in 1334 he was succeeded by a hardened Inquisitor, Benedict XII, who turned his energies to trying to end the Hundred Years' War between England and France. He also toyed with the idea of moving back to Italy, but continuing hostility there deterred him and he decided to remodel his lavish Avignon residence with the masses of money flowing in.

Benedict's successor, Clement VI, is remembered mostly for turning the Avignon papacy into a great money-making enterprise. This did not meet the approval of some in the Curia; one of them was the celebrated poet Petrarch, who denounced the French city as 'the temple of heresy, once Rome, now the false guilt-laden Babylon, the sink of vice, the sewer of the world' among other choice epithets, and longed to return to the imagined purity of Rome. Clement, too, spared a few thoughts for the Eternal City, and as a sop to his critics planned to proclaim 1350 as the second jubilee Holy Year in order to divert some revenues there. The Black Death plague had just devastated Europe, killing up to half the inhabitants of Avignon and triggering dark thoughts that perhaps the city might be paying for papal sins.

The plague had caused similar devastation in Rome, where street battles between clan gangs had been the order of the day ever since the popes had fled; there was no Curia there to tame political passions. A serious outbreak of fighting had occurred in May and June 1312 when Holy Roman emperor Henry VII had called at Rome to be crowned at the Lateran. Clement VI in Avignon had given his consent, as long as the coronation took place in the Vatican basilica and not the Lateran, which was in the hands of the pro-German Colonna clan. The Vatican, on the other side of Rome, was in pro-papal Orsini territory. For at least six weeks Henry and his Colonna allies tried to cross the Tiber, only to be stopped by the Orsini at the Sant'Angelo Castle. Unable to overcome the resistance, Henry withdrew to the Lateran to be crowned by cardinals who were thus forced to disobey a papal order. The ceremony was a dismal one, with reluctant cardinals performing their offices in a basilica half-destroyed by neglect and street fighting. Henry grimly left the city intending to gather a force strong enough to return and impose his will, but he died before he could do it.

Unrest continued in Rome. A commoner named Giovanni Arlotti briefly took control of the city by a popular revolt that was soon quashed by the senatorial nobility. The German emperors had made another attempt on Rome in 1328 in the person of Ludwig the Bavarian, a claimant to the Holy Roman throne who hoped to gain legitimacy by being crowned at Rome. Sciarra Colonna, probably the one who had manhandled Boniface VIII in the nasty business at Anagni a quarter of a century before, actually crowned Ludwig 'in the name of the Roman people', an act which earned him an excommunication from John XXII. The Colonna thus seemed to be ranging themselves on the populist side against the popes. Ludwig responded by backing an anti-pope known as Nicholas V, who re-crowned him with all the requisite ecclesiastical ritual; but such was Ludwig's unpopularity that he fled Rome in November 1329.

One more incident had to occur before Rome could have its Holy Year of 1350. For some years previously, Petrarch and others had petitioned Pope Clement VI to return to Rome; frequent embassies consisting of nobles and commoners had regularly traipsed to Avignon with the same appeal. One of them, in 1342, was headed by Cola di Rienzo, a notary and effective orator who had risen from a plebeian background by his own ability. The pope listened to him carefully and appointed him to a senior financial post in Rome. The job gave him influence and a platform for airing popular grievances against the merchant class. Rienzo spent the night of 19 May 1347 in prayer; in the morning he led a band that occupied the senatorial palace by force. Once in power, he decreed laws on equal rights, ignored upper-class protests, and began to lay plans for a grand empire based on Rome as of old. All, of course, without the popes or any kind of monarchical rule. Inevitably he had recourse to unpopular measures to enforce his vision of justice, with the result that on 15 December the mob attacked the senatorial palace on the

Capitol hill (now the Campidoglio), driving Cola di Rienzo to seek safety in Sant'Angelo Castle and eventually to exile in the country.

It was as Rome was shaking off this latest disturbance that the 1350 jubilee got underway, with elaborate rituals in the Lateran and the Vatican. As it had been fifty years earlier, petitioners crowded into Rome from all over Europe, hoping for forgiveness of sins and expecting that if they paid enough into the Roman coffers, they might return home in a state of grace. Overseeing this lucrative process was Cardinal Annibaldo Caetani, of a noble Roman family, whose brusque and authoritative manner alienated many people. One day someone shot an arrow at him; it missed, but his reaction was furious, having several people arrested and tortured and placing all Rome under a week-long interdict. Caetani sensibly left Rome for Naples, but on the way he fell ill and died – poisoned, it was said, by a glass of wine.[14]

At this point who should reappear but Cola di Rienzo, who professed a desire to reform the Church with the help of Holy Roman Emperor Charles IV of Luxembourg. On a mission to Prague he was arrested and sent to Avignon, but Pope Innocent VI saw that he could be put to good use and sent him back to Rome as a senator, along with an energetic and devout Spaniard, Gil Álvarez Carillo de Albornoz, the archbishop of Toledo, as a cardinal to reconstitute the papal authority. As soon as Rienzo arrived, on 1 August 1354, he set up an unwisely despotic rule that soon turned nobles and commoners alike against him. On 8 October he was assassinated on the steps of the senatorial palace; according to an anonymous chronicler of the period, his body was burned and the ashes pulverized so that 'not a mote remained'.

Cardinal Albornoz, on the contrary, employed his considerable political and military talents to shore up the tottering Papal States. There were four main states, counting from south to north: Latium (comprising Rome, Ostia, Anagni, Viterbo, Subiaco, Civita Castellana and Tivoli), Umbria (Narni, Spoleto, Foligno, Assisi, Perugia and Gubbio), the Marches (Ascoli, Loreto, Ancona, Senigallia, Urbino, Camerino, Fabriano and Pesaro) and the Romagna (Rimini, Cesena, Forlì, Faenza, Ravenna, Imola, Bologna and Ferrara). All these cities and towns fielded their own troops under the control of whichever powerful families ruled, and did not hesitate to use them against one another on any pretext. For the papacy proper, Albornoz set up the corps of Arbalestiers and Standard-bearers (*Balestrieri e Pavesati*) of about 3,000 men – remarkably, all commoners – who also had political duties, meaning that they were not restricted merely to keeping order and defending the papacy but also probably had security and intelligence functions.

Albornoz' blueprint for the state structure, the *Constitutiones Aegidianae*, set up an arrangement that would serve the Papal States well for five more centuries. During this time Innocent VI displayed a case of devastatingly-bad judgement by accepting a bribe from the Visconti, the ruling house of Milan, to sack the Spanish cardinal, who found himself out of office for about a year until the pope reversed his decision and reinstated him. In 1360 Albornoz and his new papal corps defeated the Milanese in battle and recovered Bologna for the papacy. Like other emperors before him, Charles IV had his heart set on being crowned in Rome, which had taken place in 1355. Many Italians hoped that the long stand-off between pope and emperor could finally peter out. Moreover, the way appeared to be clear for the popes to quit Avignon and return to the city of their origin.

Urban V, consecrated in 1362, leaned heavily in favour of a return. He received encouraging messages from Byzantine Emperor John V Paleologos suggesting a possible reunion of the Catholic and Orthodox churches, and even a crusade, as the Ottoman Turks were encircling Constantinople and had secured a hold in South-east Europe. Personages such as Petrarch and the Swedish nun and visionary Birgida Birgersdotter, known as Saint Bridget, were constantly urging him to make the move. Urban himself asked Albornoz to clear the Roman domains of widespread banditry; when that was done, Urban and the Curia made the trip by sea, disembarking at Corneto on 3 June 1367. Rome itself was finally prepared for his triumphal re-entry on 16 October. Unfortunately, Albornoz was not there to see his ambition fulfilled, as he had succumbed to an epidemic during the summer.

Urban found a Rome in the stages of sad neglect; everywhere he saw 'pools of mud and heaps of ruins ... shattered towers and homes consumed by flames and every kind of devastation'.[15] The pope's return, of course, signalled the end of what most Romans considered a 'democratic' government, that is, not one ruled by the Church or the noble families; but any dissatisfaction took second place to relief that Rome again was the seat of the papacy, and therefore important again in the eyes of the world. Even the Greek emperor John V deigned to visit. But Urban, a kindly yet irresolute character, was spooked by populist revolts in Viterbo and Perugia, key towns in the Papal States and, his nerve failing him, fled back to Avignon in September 1370. In vain did Saint Bridget warn him that abandoning Rome would mean his own death; her prediction came true three months later.

For the next few years Urban's successor Gregory XI remained attached to the comforts and relative security of Avignon. But he found his administration plagued with security problems, as the French prelates appointed to govern the Papal States in Italy had made themselves thoroughly despised by the mass of people. One Catholic voice of conscience was that of Saint Catherine of Siena, who complained bitterly to Gregory of 'the evil pastors who poison and devastate the garden of the Church'. By 1375 Florence and scores of other Italian cities were in open revolt against the French legates; the Florentines had gone so far as to create a red flag with the word *Libertas* emblazoned on it. Gregory struck back by excommunicating and essentially outlawing all Florentines, wherever they were to be found. It was an eye for an eye – in Florence the rebels strung up several priests and tore down Inquisition buildings. The city appealed to Rome to join the revolt and end papal rule once and for all. But the Romans hesitated, warned by Gregory's promise that he would return only if the city remained loyal.

But secretly the pope readied a terrible revenge. To douse the Italian revolt he sent a corps of Breton mercenaries under Cardinal Robert of Geneva, who did not hesitate to commit the worst of war crimes. After promising amnesty to the people of Cesena in the Romagna, he slew every man, woman and child in the community. Another papal commander, the English mercenary captain Sir John Hawkwood, slaughtered 4,000 people in Faenza, a feat for which a grateful pope awarded him control of two towns. A shocked Saint Catherine volunteered to travel to Avignon to canvass for a halt to such atrocities; though she almost got herself arrested through the vehemence of her denunciations, Gregory acceded to her request that he return the papacy to Rome, at the least to stop Rome from going over to the rebels. Convinced, Gregory sailed up the Tiber to Rome on 17 January 1377, but once there felt so insecure that he retired to Anagni. His diplomacy, however, pacified the rebellious cities. But his health was not of the best, and on 19 March 1378 he made arrangements for a successor; a week later he died longing for 'the fair land of France'.

The 'Babylonian Captivity' of the Church was over, and the Italians among the cardinals, not to mention almost all Italians, determined that there should be no more foreign interludes. The papacy was Roman and Italian, and must always remain so. The conclave of 7 April was an anxious one; the Roman mob burst into the deliberation hall shouting: 'We want him Roman or Italian!' The French popes had proved just too unpopular. The following day a Neapolitan was hastily chosen under the name Urban VI. But the French cardinals, considering themselves to have been intimidated, claimed that Urban had treated them with brutal contempt, refused to recognize the result and retired in a body to Anagni, where they proclaimed the election of Urban illegal. The dispute echoed in the courts of Europe; Charles VI of France and Queen Joan of Naples threw their weight behind the French faction, which elected as anti-pope none other than the butcher of Cesena, Robert of Geneva, as Clement VII. The rivalry came to blows on 28 April 1379, when Alberico da Barbiano, commanding the papal forces, defeated the French at Marino, in the Alban Hills south of Rome. Clement and his men fled to Avignon.

The victorious Urban turned his attention to Joan of Naples, whom he considered treacherous, as the Church had always considered the kingdom of Naples as it own. The hapless Joan, a French Angevin, was deposed and strangled and replaced by Charles III of Durazzo. But when Urban visited Naples he realized Charles' true colours and remained a virtual prisoner for some months. Rome meanwhile had stumbled into yet another bout of republican rule, so Urban moved to Nocera, where he flung an excommunication against Charles. The Neapolitan king sent troops to besiege the pope, who was saved only through the intervention of a squad of Breton mercenaries who had to be heavily bribed so as not to cart him off to their anti-pope boss in Avignon. Hardening his stand, Urban ordered the execution of six dissenting cardinals – 'foolish chatterers', he called them – and returned to a cool reception in Rome, where he sought to raise his standing by proclaiming a Holy Year for 1390.

Urban did not live to see what he had planned. His successor Boniface IX marked the jubilee by recognizing Charles' son Ladislas as king of Naples, neutralizing any threat from the south. The Holy Year brought in its due share of profits, mollifying the Roman merchant class in particular, and such was its success that another one was planned for the more logical date of

1400. But Boniface did not reckon on the Colonna, who one night in January of that year led an armed band through the Porta del Popolo into the city, shouting, 'Death to the tyrant Boniface!' But few rallied to the banner, and the ringleader, Nicola Colonna, slunk away to Palestrina. The pope's revenge was sweeping: after his forces clashed with Colonna east of the city, more than thirty of the Colonna family were arrested, condemned to death for sedition and beheaded, and the entire clan excommunicated. For the rest of his reign Boniface governed the Papal States with a rod of iron. His jubilee year was marked by the torture of revenue collectors whom he accused of siphoning off some of the pilgrims' contributions; other collectors were torn limb from limb by the mob for not diverting enough money to the people.[16] On his death in 1404 he was succeeded by Innocent VII, who received the support of Ladislas of Naples and his army.

But a serious schism was in full swing, as the anti-popes in Avignon remained adamant that they constituted the real papal authority. The states of Europe lined up behind one or the other; France, Spain, Scotland and some German princes supported the anti-popes, while Italy, England, Flanders, Portugal and most of the Holy Roman Empire backed Urban VI. Devout and conscientious people everywhere were sorely troubled by the spectacle of rival papacies thundering against each other. Reform movements emerged in England and Bohemia, further lowering the prestige of the wounded Church. Finally in 1409 conscientious churchmen from both sides met at Pisa to see if the disastrous schism could be healed. For five more years all efforts foundered on the stubbornness of the two rival popes, to whom a third was presently added. It took the resolve of Holy Roman emperor Sigismund of Luxembourg to resolve this *reductio ad absurdum*, take a page out of the book of Constantine the Great and call a general ecclesiastical council that convened at Constance in 1414. If it required a secular emperor to knock clerical heads together, so be it. The council eventually elected Oddo Colonna, a member of the famous (or notorious) Roman family that seems to have emerged from its excommunication, as the undisputed Martin V. Once more the papacy was one.

Throughout the fourteenth century the Papal States had found themselves compelled to follow the general trend among Italian city-states of employing private armies for their defence. The campaigns of that century were fought by the ruling families of each city who employed professional soldiers known as *condottieri* (from the *condotta*, or contract, they signed with the city authorities). The term *condottiere*, in fact, applied not only to the commander but also to any ordinary soldier who signed up as a mercenary.[17] Most of the fighting men would have been young, between their late-teens and late-thirties, and probably well enough off to afford their own weapons and armour, and in a few cases, a horse. Most were also probably from the city they served or its environs, and hence had a patriotic motive for taking up arms. A devout Catholic from the region of Rome, for example, would be expected to fight more stoutly for the pope than, say, a French mercenary. The tradition of male military service was not new, having been introduced by the Lombards in the eighth century. The pike came into common use along with the bow and crossbow, and shields became heavier, sometimes carried by a special shield-bearer. Armour, as well as horse-armour, became heavier as well, as military operations were conducted with a view more to deterrence than to actual fighting, which was employed as a last resort.

The system was fraught with risk. Men skilled in the use of arms, if unemployed, could become a menace to their own governments. Too many mercenaries found interludes of peace too placid for their liking and became brigands and robbers. Some units formed themselves into 'companies' of several hundred men who would hire themselves out to any paymaster anywhere in Italy. The command structure of these units was surprisingly democratic; commanders were elected by the troopers, who also had a say in the decisions. Booty from campaigns was divided fairly by rank and length of service.[18] The number of men engaged in such military service in Italy must have been in the scores of thousands. Besides Italians, there were a great many Germans, French, English and Catalans, many of them unemployed veterans of the Hundred Years' War. Around 1352 the so-called Grand Company under Werner von Ürslingen numbered some 10,000 men, including 7,000 horsemen and double that number of camp followers. Sir John Hawkwood's papal outfit became known – and feared – as the White Company.[19]

The practice of *condottiere* warfare outgrew its usefulness after about 1410. The chief reason was that the *condottieri* and their growing armies were increasingly expensive to hire; the fourteenth-century popes, by one estimate, found themselves spending nearly two-thirds of their state revenues on paying them.[20] Governments accordingly sought cheaper and more efficient ways of guarding security; states such as Milan, Florence and Venice began to prefer loyal militias. Military commanders continued to follow the *condottiere* model of campaigning, but a degree of political culture can be said to have 'civilized' them; the Malatesta brothers, originally serving Milan but moving over to Venice, typified the new breed. In the south the kingdom of Naples was being fought over by the French Angevin house and the Spanish Aragonese, while the Papal States maintained a constant struggle against being sandwiched by Naples and the restless states of North Italy. It all made for plenty of gainful military employment.

Chapter 6

The Papacy Unleashed: Alexander and Julius

W hen Martin V entered Rome in triumph on 30 September 1420, the Church was badly bruised by more than a hundred years of purgatory in the form of the Avignon 'Captivity' and the subsequent schism that had driven the prestige of the papacy to new lows. To raise urgent funds for a city which he found little more than a desert of mud and crumbling buildings plagued by hunger and disease and reeking of refuse and excrement, he organized an emergency Holy Year for 1423. It was in that period that regional allegiances – the precursors of nationalism – were beginning to stir the minds of thinking men all over Europe and push out of fashion the ideal of a Church-led global flock. The new pope at first trod warily, as the price for his accession was to consent to the terms of the Council of Constance that established the superiority of a general council over a pope in major decisions. Martin was able to maintain stability inside Rome and out by driving brigands from the outskirts and beheading those whom he could capture. But he encountered problems bringing to heel the militant rulers of the other Papal States who had been used to decades of aggressive independence.

Martin's successor, the Venetian Eugenius IV, who became pope in 1431, clashed head-on with the Council of Basel, lost the confrontation, and for ten years had to put up with an anti-pope named Felix V claiming to rule from the Swiss city. It seemed as if the Church was slipping back into its old bad habits. And indeed, at first Eugenius appeared more intent on penalizing the Colonna than anything else. He wanted some fortresses that his Colonna predecessor had given the family but which were strategically placed against a threat from Naples. To thwart the planned seizure the Colonna attacked Rome in April 1431; Queen Joan II of Naples sent a force to help the pope but the Colonna bribed its commander to fight for them instead. It took enormous expense in purchasing the services of *condottieri*, plus Queen Joan's cooperation, for Eugenius to seize the Colonna castles.[1] But in exercising his hard line (partly attributed to acute discomfort from gout), Eugenius had weakened his own position. The Colonna took advantage of a popular discontent that grew so menacing that on the night of 4 June 1434 the pope fled on a boat down the Tiber, dodging stones and arrows hurled at him, to Ostia, where he boarded a ship for Pisa; ending up in Florence, he made his residence in the convent of Santa Maria Novella.

In the meantime Eugenius had cemented solid diplomatic ties with the main powers of Europe and the fake anti-papacy of Basel collapsed from its own incompetence. But though Martin and Eugenius had clawed back some papal powers, the heady days of Boniface VIII were over. The French were especially resistant to papal power; in 1438 King Charles VII issued what is called the Pragmatic Sanction of Bourges, which in effect, deprived the pope of control over the French church, which became a throne-controlled state institution. Not long afterwards, the king of Spain took a similar measure, while the spirit of ecclesiastical independence was taking root in England and Germany as well. It was therefore some consolation to Eugenius that his reputation as a European peacemaker – his albeit temporary reconciliation with the Greek Orthodox Church was a signal achievement – enabled him to return to Rome in 1443 and in so doing prepare the papacy for one of its most powerful and prestigious periods.

Eugenius' successor Nicholas V (Tommaso Parentucelli) began his reign having to contend with the persistence of the old Roman families; to the old-established Colonna and Orsini were added Johnny-come-latelies such as the Porcari. Nicholas courted popularity by reforming tax collection and beginning an urban renewal programme to prepare for the next Holy Year of 1450 – including the start of work on what is now the Trevi Fountain. City walls, Tiber bridges and aqueducts were strengthened and Sant'Angelo Castle given new ramparts. The walls of the Leonine City, comprising what is now the Vatican and adjacent district, were reinforced, and plans were made to rebuild the entire pontifical area where most of the population of Rome, numbering at most some 20,000 souls, were huddled. Holy Roman emperor Frederick III Habsburg received his desired coronation at the pope's hands in 1452, though he would be the last secular ruler ever to enjoy that privilege, as the German emperors had by now abandoned their perceived duty as protectors of the papacy.

In the remaining three years of his reign Nicholas hardened his rule, seeing off an abortive popular revolt led by Stefano Porcari who plotted to kidnap the pope and the cardinals while they were celebrating High Mass in Saint Peter's and proclaim (another) Roman republic. The plot misfired; Porcari hid in a trunk in his sister's house, from where the papal guards dragged him to the gallows on 9 January 1453. A wry couplet made the rounds of Rome:

Since Nicholas became pope and assassin,/ Blood in Rome runs freer than wine.[2]

Western Christendom received a profound shock when on 29 May 1453 the 1,100-year-old Byzantine Empire, the light of the East and genuine remnant of the ancient Roman Empire, was snuffed out when the Muslim Ottoman Turks seized and sacked Constantinople. Thoughts of a crusade to repel the Turks and reclaim Constantinople revived. Two years later the new pope, the Spanish cardinal Alfonso de Borja who became Calixtus III partly on a promise to organize a crusade, halted his predecessor's public works to raise money for an eastbound campaign. Calixtus reportedly could think of little else. The anti-Turkish crusade was formally proclaimed on 15 May 1455, with a starting date for the campaign set for 1 March the following year. Calixtus ordered a crash shipbuilding programme at Ostia and sent legates to Europe's rulers requesting their cooperation in the great cause. Pedro de Urrea, the archbishop of Tarragona, was assigned to lead a fleet into the Aegean Sea to tackle the Turks. Such was the pope's fervour that an Italian diplomat got the distinct impression that 'anyone who gets in his way is guilty of a great sin.'[3]

Calixtus' idealism received a rude shock when, in the middle of feverish preparations for readying the fleet, news reached him that de Urrea, far from attacking the Turks, had chosen to attack Christian Genoa in collaboration with King Alfonso V of Aragon (who became also Alfonso I of Naples). This was treachery of the first order. The papacy had always feared being sandwiched between hostile powers, and now Naples and Milan were forging a marriage-buttressed alliance, hence the attack on rival Genoa. Swallowing his disappointment, the pope appointed Cardinal Ludovico Trevisan as grand admiral, with the authority to administer a huge chunk of territory including Sicily, Dalmatia, Macedonia, Greece, Crete and Rhodes in case his force was successful. But no pope could ever be sure of any secular leader's sincere support, and he had reason to distrust Alfonso. Therefore it was an unexpected piece of good news in 1456 when he heard that General John Hunyadi of Hungary had halted the Turks besieging Belgrade, thanks partly to the funds Calixtus had raised. The following year Cardinal Trevisan from his base on Rhodes trounced a Turkish fleet off Lesbos.

Meanwhile, many Romans complained that the city was being positively inundated by hordes of Calixtus' Spanish and Catalan hangers-on in the form of papal staffers and mere adventurers. Among them were three of the pope's nephews: Luis Juan, Rodrigo Lanzol and Pedro Luis de Borja, who Italianized their surname to Borgia and made clear they were in Italy to stay. Pedro Luis was named Prefect of Rome with his headquarters in Sant'Angelo Castle; Rodrigo was made a cardinal and vice-chancellor of the Church; while Luis Juan was also made a cardinal and sent as papal legate to Bologna. All these moves were the early cementing process for the future dominance of the Borgias in papal and Italian politics.

One of the new cardinals named by Calixtus in 1457 was a Sienese lawyer, diplomat and secret agent named Aeneas Sylvius Piccolomini who had risen in the Church hierarchy to become bishop of Trieste. On Calixtus' death in 1458 Piccolomini was elected as a compromise candidate as the Colonna and Orsini cardinals were about evenly split; moreover, nobody wanted the French cardinal who had initially entered the papal race with an advantage, and so after an especially acrimonious conclave Piccolomini became pope under the name Pius II. There had not been a Pius on Saint Peter's throne for 1,300 years, and he justified his choice of name by a scholarly reference to 'pious Aeneas' (a pun on his own name) in Virgil's *Aeneid*. Once consecrated, Pius made peace with the Spaniards and Naples as a preparation for a planned anti-Turkish crusade. At first he tried honeyed words with the Muslims. With more unctuous flattery than sincerity he wrote to Mehmet II, the Ottoman Turkish sultan who was settling himself in newly-conquered Constantinople:

Were you to embrace Christianity there is no prince on earth who would surpass you in glory or equal you in power. We would acknowledge you as emperor of the Greeks and the East ... Oh, what a fullness of peace it would be! The golden age of Augustus, sung by the poets, would return.[4]

Mehmet, if he received the message at all, must have ignored it. His mother may have been a Christian Greek, but this Turkish potentate had no intention of abandoning Islam. Receiving no response to this patently transparent piece of ingratiation, Pius called a congress to meet at Mantua (Mantova), which was notable only for the absence of the European leaders he had invited. The congress deliberated uselessly for about a year, but Pius was nothing if not determined; as pope he was a hard-liner who didn't believe in restrictive councils and was prepared to lead his crusade in person if necessary. But he had never been in the best of health and was quite advanced in years; he was on the point of embarking at Ancona – itself in the midst of a plague – when he died and the fictive crusade itself evaporated.

Before his death Pius had been hearing questionable accounts of the behaviour of young Cardinal Rodrigo Borgia and had written a stern letter to him about what he had been doing with 'several Sienese ladies' during a garden party:

> From what has been said, there was much dancing and flirting ... Decency forbids a complete account of what is said to have taken place ... you have become a laughing-stock.[5]

Rodrigo hotly (but probably disingenuously) denied engaging in anything improper, but as he was still in his twenties, Pius may have had him in mind when he drew up a list of new requirements for becoming a cardinal, including the rules that a candidate must be at least thirty and 'of blameless morals'. The latter condition would be observed far more in the breach than the observance. But for the moment the next pope, Paul II (another case of reaching back for old prestige names), was concerned more with internal power balances than with foreign policy – though he made sure he acquired a new papal tiara that cost a solid fortune, paid for in part by contributions from Europe's unwitting faithful. As if symbolizing his greed, Paul died unexpectedly after binge-eating melons.

The next pope, Sixtus IV, didn't trust the cardinals as much as his own family, the della Rovere, members of whom he appointed to senior security positions. For them specifically he created the rank of captain general of the papal army, seconded by the gonfalonier, or standard-bearer, a post harking back to the Knights Hospitaller of the crusader era. Other relatives were made prefect of Rome and commandant of Sant'Angelo Castle. It was well that security was on his mind, as there is some evidence that Sixtus approved of a plot to overthrow the powerful Medici family of Florence and install in that city a regime favourable to the papacy. The plot in 1478 flopped, dragging the Papal States into an inconclusive two-year struggle with Florence, which in revenge allied itself with Louis XI of France, a signal defeat for papal foreign policy. The pope was also drawn into a dispute with Venice which consumed so many resources of the Papal States that overtaxed citizens in several cities rioted in the streets.

In the summer of 1480 all Christendom was heartened by the news that the Knights Hospitaller of Saint John on Rhodes had fended off a determined Ottoman attack. The fighting had been bitter, an epic in itself.[6] The Turks in revenge struck at South Italy, seizing the port of Otranto and massacring half its inhabitants. Terror seized Rome. Sixtus issued a stern call to arms:

> If the Italians desire to safeguard their homes, wives and children …
> to remain in the faith to which all have been baptized and all will be
> reborn … they must prepare to go to war.[7]

As preparations for a counter-stroke against the Turks proceeded, Sultan Mehmet II died, triggering night-long rejoicing in Rome. At the end of June 1481 the pope and his cardinals accompanied a fleet of galleys down the Tiber and out to Ostia, as artillery boomed in celebration. After a brief campaign the Turks were expelled from Otranto, and the Papal States, not to mention the rest of Italy, could breathe again.

During the brief scare of the Turkish seizure of Otranto in 1481, Rodrigo Borgia had fathered his third child, a girl named Lucrezia. His family-mindedness didn't stop there; the following year he made his son Cesare, a mere six years old, into an apostolic protonotary – a largely formal office that represented the first rung on the ladder to an ecclesiastical career. At the same time he held in his arms a fourth child (a son) from his fertile mistress. But the papacy could not rest easy, as Ferrante of Naples turned against the pope and allied with Milan and Florence to squeeze the Papal States in a vice. The pope's sole allies were the Venetians, who were after Ferrara. The *condottieri* and their cohorts found plenty of employment. And of course those inveterate feuders, the Colonna and the Orsini, had to join the scrap, the former alongside Milan and Florence, the latter with the pope. In April 1482 Ferrante's troops invaded the papal state of Latium (now Lazio) and burst into Rome the following month, only to be ejected by papal troops aided by the Orsini.

But all was not well in the Vatican. While Sixtus waited for his Venetian allies to show up he had to deal with a college full of brawling cardinals by locking up Cardinal Giovanni Colonna in Sant'Angelo Castle. The Venetians under Roberto Malatesta duly arrived on 23 July and trounced the Neapolitans west of Rome at the Campo Morto, or Field of Death, so named after its malaria-ridden marshes. Five months later the pope signed a peace with Milan, Naples and Florence. Early in 1484 an outbreak of Colonna-Orsini gang warfare terrorized Rome shortly before Sixtus' death in August. On the news of his demise an exultant Roman mob destroyed much of his property; the cause of their ire was the onerous papal taxation that had enabled Sixtus and the cardinals to maintain a lavish lifestyle. And this brought to the fore the issue of papal revenues.

To raise money for a papacy that needed ever more of it, the practice of 'the extra-sacramental remission of the temporal punishment due, in God's justice, to sin that has been forgiven, which remission is granted by the Church in the exercise of the power of the keys' was taken from an old theological tome and dusted off for new use.[8] The ponderous verbiage was simply code for saying that if you had enough money, by forking some over to the Church you could have your sins forgiven. Elaborate theological reasons were concocted to justify such 'indulgences,' as the exchanges became known. The 'treasure' often mentioned in the New Testament, meaning spiritual treasure, was cynically interpreted to mean physical gold. And plenty of it duly poured in, donated by rich and poor alike to alleviate their guilt and metaphysical terrors. Much of the wealth went to build up Rome into something worthy of its glorious past, including the creation of the Sistine Chapel, but also to personally enrich pope and cardinals and their cohorts of hangers-on.

The scrappy nobles of Rome were ever eager to bloodily feud among themselves and drag the popes into the mess. Will Durant paints an inimitable prose picture of one such underworld-type war:

It was one of the polite customs of Rome to plunder the palace of a cardinal just elected to the papacy. In so handling the palace of one of the della Rovere cardinals, a young aristocrat, Francesco di Santa Croce, had been wounded by a member of the della Valle family. The youth revenged himself by cutting the tendon of della Valle's heel; della Valle's relatives revenged him by cleaving Francesco's head; Prospero di Santa Croce revenged Francesco by killing Piero Margani. The feud spread through the city, the Orsini and the papal forces supporting the Santa Croce, the Colonna defending the Valle … Violence, thievery, rape, bribery, conspiracy, revenge were the order of the day.[9]

Following Sixtus IV was the Neapolitan Cardinal Giovanni Battista Cybo, who was picked as a compromise during the usual intrigue-ridden conclave, which for the first time was held in the Sistine Chapel. Just over fifty, amiable and considered a pushover by the more aggressive cardinals, Innocent VIII (as Cybo became), had had seven children by various mistresses, but he only officially recognized one, Franceschetto, who turned out to be an utter scoundrel. Innocent disliked the headaches and guile attendant on forging foreign policy and left that task to his secretary of state, Cardinal della Rovere and the leading Florentine of the day, Lorenzo de' Medici.

Not long into his reign, however, Innocent was confronted by a curious foreign policy conundrum. In 1481 the Ottoman sultan Mehmet II had died, leaving his sons Bayezid and Cem wrestling for the succession. Cem (pronounced Jem) was defeated in battle and fled to the island of Rhodes, run by the Knights of Saint John. Bayezid II, as he had now become, agreed to pay the Knights a handsome annual stipend to keep Cem out of mischief. The Hospitaller Grand Master, Pierre d'Aubusson, felt he lacked the resources to keep the Ottoman prince fully safe, and sent him on to France. Several powers wanted to host Cem, but Innocent won; it was said that he offered d'Aubusson a cardinal's hat in return. Thus on 13 March 1489 Prince Cem, the 'Grand Turk', was escorted through Rome to the Vatican in an elaborate procession. Bayezid was glad to keep him in Rome and paid the pope handsomely for his upkeep; among the payment was the purported point of the lance that had pierced Christ's side on the cross. After a long illness, Innocent VIII died in 1492. And at long last, the cardinal who had been preparing diligently over the years to achieve the highest Church office was now about to strike.

Anyone meeting Cardinal Rodrigo Borgia in the late-fifteenth century might have been forgiven for wondering what exactly he had to do with the Church. His lifestyle was no different from any high-born secular ruler: he lived in palaces and had every material benefit he wanted, including his choice of women, who bore him three illegitimate children. Puritanism, however, had yet to percolate into Europe, and Borgia's image was not necessarily considered a bad one even in Church circles. His case conformed to the prevailing literal interpretation of the 'treasures' that God would shower on His faithful workers.

As early as 1471, when he turned forty, Rodrigo Borgia had been instrumental in securing the election of Pope Sixtus IV, who rewarded him with the post of chamberlain of the College of Cardinals and sent him to his native Spain as papal legate. His task in Spain was first, to raise contributions for the pope's planned crusade, and second, to end the war between the kingdoms of Castile and Aragon by arranging the marriage of Princess Isabella of Castile and Prince Ferdinand of Aragon – the same royal couple who twenty years later, as king and queen of Spain, would give the green light for Christopher Columbus to set out to discover a New World. On his way back to Italy in September 1473, Rodrigo's two galleys were hit by a violent storm; the cardinal's made it through, but the other sank with all on board, including three bishops and a couple of hundred members of his household, plus a lot of Spanish money.

Back in Rome, Rodrigo resumed his high-living ways, starting an affair with a much younger woman, Vanozza de' Cataneis. Sixtus' Holy Year of 1475 gave Rome another opportunity to enrich itself from waves of pilgrims and give Rodrigo a boy from his latest amour, named Cesare (Caesar), who by his name alone signalled that he was to be groomed for something important. That was the year that King Ferrante of Naples, the largest single territorial unit of Italy, made his formal entry in Rome to receive the pope's blessings. In November, however, the Tiber overflowed, filling the streets with mud and triggering a plague. The epidemic broke out anew the following spring; it became so bad that the pope and his cardinals, Rodrigo among them, had to flee the city. They were able to return only five months later, during which Rodrigo's erotic energies had given him another boy from his mistress. Another outbreak of plague forced Sixtus out of Rome yet again for a few months.

By the time of Sixtus' death in 1484, Rodrigo had been promoted from cardinal-deacon to cardinal-bishop, putting him in the front rank of *papabili*, or potential future pontiffs. He canvassed vigorously for the man who became Innocent VIII, bribing heavily where necessary, and was offered the post of archbishop of Seville; diplomatically, he declined the offer, as it would have put him in conflict with Ferdinand II of Spain, and the last thing he needed was a foreign policy problem of that kind. Besides, he preferred to be in Rome where the papal action was. By now his long and fruitful affair with Vanozza de' Cataneis was history, but he had compensated her with considerable wealth and a new husband who worked in the Curia. In 1488 Rodrigo's twenty-four-year-old eldest son Pedro Luis died, and three years later he arranged the marriage of his eleven-year-old daughter Lucrezia to a Spanish nobleman. Cesare, his son of sixteen, was sent to study law at Pisa, where he made himself quite objectionable.

The year 1492 opened with good news from Spain, where Ferdinand and Isabella drove the last Moors out of Granada; in Rome the pope celebrated the event with a special thanksgiving mass and spectacular entertainments. In March the Spanish kingdom expelled its Jews, many of whom resettled in more tolerant Rome. Innocent VIII died just three weeks before Christopher Columbus set sail on his epochal transatlantic voyage; three days after that date the cardinals' conclave met, and after five days of the usual horse-trading and backroom dealing in the Sistine Chapel, Rodrigo Borgia was transformed by near-unanimous vote into Pope Alexander VI. The reaction in the Catholic world was mixed, with praise for his diplomatic and social talents vying for prominence with condemnation of his lack of morals and scruples, plus a streak of cruelty; there was also some prejudiced sniffing at his Spanish background. He was now sixty-one and in good health, 'majestically straight and tall', but such was the heat on 26 August, the whole of which was spent in outdoor ceremonial, that he briefly swooned.

Alexander VI threw himself into his task with characteristic energy. He was no spiritual heavyweight, but that didn't matter much in the Rome of the time, as long as he got tough on crime, among other things. Murders in Rome were occurring at the rate of about seven a day; the pope not only hanged the first murderer caught, but also strung up the victim's brother and razed his house to the ground. The streets became a lot safer after that.[10] To boost Vatican defence he had a covered passage built between the Vatican and Sant'Angelo Castle – a construction that would soon save his life – and remodelled the castle itself with comfortable cells for the prominent opponents whom he planned to give a home there. For the first two years he balanced the papal budget which had been burdened with a deficit under Innocent VIII and gave Rome its headiest freedom ever. Inevitably, he crumpled some red hats, and one red hat decided to strike back.

Giuliano della Rovere was a cardinal who had been used to running the papal show behind the back of weak popes, and when he suddenly found himself powerless under Pope Alexander, he fled to France to talk King Charles VIII into invading Italy and deposing Alexander on a charge that he had bribed his way into office. Meanwhile Alexander sent his ruthless son Cesare Borgia to subdue the individual rulers of the Papal States who had become virtual local dictators. Borgia's harshness was praised by Machiavelli who opined that 'a prince ... must not mind incurring the charge of cruelty for the purpose of keeping his subjects united and faithful', and scorned those who, 'from an excess of tenderness, allow disorders to arise, from which spring bloodshed and rapine'.[11] Here is the first appearance of the modern notion of *raison d'état*, literally 'reason of state', which assumes that ordinary private morality and goodness cannot apply in matters of state, where the safety and prosperity of a nation are paramount, and often require a degree of ruthlessness to preserve; the collective here is more important than the individual. Alexander thus had no compunctions in acting as any secular ruler would, not hesitating to apply force where it was needed, to preserve a state that was still seen, even in Machiavelli's eyes, as being 'exalted and maintained by God'.[12]

Machiavelli's ideas on how to run an ecclesiastical state deserve some attention here, as they provided the intellectual foundation for a strong papacy. First, an ecclesiastical state is presumed to have originated by 'higher causes' than mere human ambition, and hence 'it would be the work of a presumptuous and foolish man to discuss them'. Second, he deplored that secular rulers such as the leaders of the Venetians and the French kings could use the bumptious Colonna and Orsini to control the popes.

Then arose Alexander VI who, of all the pontiffs who have ever reigned, best showed how a pope might prevail both by money and by force.

Alexander's first use of diplomacy was to ally himself with Venice, Milan, Ferrara and Siena to dislodge two strategic fortresses that Naples maintained in papal territory. Eventually Ferrante was pacified by the marriage of his daughter to the pope's son Giofre. Playing a key role in that reconciliation was Ferdinand II of Spain, whom the pope rewarded by giving him title to the newly-discovered American continent. Portugal was soon afterwards mollified by receiving title to the eastern portions of the new discoveries; the present division of Latin America into Spanish-speaking and Portuguese-speaking sections is a direct result of Alexander VI's happy belief that he had the power to give away a continent.

But the real enemies were on his doorstep. Ferrante of Naples died unexpectedly in 1494, causing the French king to plot an invasion of Italy to draw the Neapolitan throne into the French orbit and squeeze the Papal States in a pincers. Alexander was concerned enough to make a radical, and so far unthinkable diplomatic chess move: he sent an emissary to Ottoman Sultan Bayezid II in Constantinople, suggesting that the French sought to replace him with the pliant Prince Cem and proposing an outright alliance with the papacy and Venice. Here was the leader of Christendom suggesting a common cause with the pre-eminent Muslim power! The sultan showed some interest, but the returning papal emissary and the letters he carried were intercepted by Cardinal della Rovere; one letter promised the pope a huge amount of money in return for disposing of Cem and sending the body to Constantinople as proof. Modern scholarship disputes the existence of such a letter, but what is certain is that Alexander did make an overture to the Turks, supported by Venice and Naples.

Charles VIII, meanwhile, marched over the Alps, helped by the Milanese, and appeared in front of Rome in December. All those cardinals who detested the pope, plus the Colonna and Orsini who this time buried their enmity in a common cause with the French king, were ready to help Charles depose Alexander. The pope, sheltering in Sant'Angelo Castle, had recourse to desperate diplomacy; the next thing anyone knew, Charles was bowing before Alexander in the Vatican in return for being allowed to move his army through papal territory to Naples. The French took with them Cem, who two months later died of bronchitis (of course, there were the inevitable unsubstantiated rumours that he had been poisoned). The French army was a daunting sight to the Romans, who marvelled at new lightweight bronze artillery pieces, but otherwise the Romans had to endure the indignity of French soldiers breaking into and looting houses, while pope and king haggled over terms.

Alexander had been forced to make a tactical diplomatic withdrawal in the face of French numerical superiority, and still feared Charles. In May 1495 Charles left Naples and headed with his army back to Rome. To avoid meeting him a second time the pope left the city in the hands of his *chargé d'affaires*, Cardinal John Morton, the archbishop of Canterbury; this time the French soldiery were on good behaviour. Meanwhile, however, Alexander had been quietly forging an alliance with Spain, the Holy Roman Empire, Venice and Milan. Ostensibly formed as a front against the Ottoman Empire, in reality it was designed to eject the French from Italy. On 6 July, as Charles was on his way home, it was blocked by a Holy Alliance force at Fornovo, between Bologna and Milan.

The 10,000-strong French army had already been harassed during its laborious retreat over the Apennine passes, but at Fornovo it came on twice its number under the able *condottiere* Francesco Gonzaga, the Venetian captain general. Gonzaga's force was made up of 11,000 heavy cavalry, 2,000 mostly Albanian light mercenary infantry, 8,000 professional infantry and some Venetian militia. The opposing forces faced each other on opposite sides of the mostly dry Taro river, the French on the north-west side and the Italians on the south-east. While the French expected a frontal attack, Gonzaga planned a strong thrust on the French centre-left held by the Swiss contingent. This thrust was entrusted to the Milanese of the Count of Caiazzo, who would move while Gonzaga himself threw his own sector onto the French centre where Charles VIII was. On the Italian left, Bernardino Fortebraccio would lead his Venetian cavalry against the French right under Gaston de Foix. At least half the Italian force was kept back as a reserve, while the fierce Albanian auxiliaries were poised to sweep down at the right moment on the French rear.

The action opened in the afternoon of 6 July with an artillery duel that proved ineffectual. It had been raining, and the damp had made some guns unserviceable; moreover, the ordinarily dry Taro river had become a torrent. When Gonzaga gave the order to advance across the swollen river, Caiazzo found his way blocked by the unyielding Swiss; the most he could accomplish was to keep the French front occupied while the Albanians attacked the French left. But such was the Albanians' indiscipline that as soon as two of their commanders fell, the rest gave up fighting to loot the French baggage train, conveniently placed behind the centre. It ought to have been plain to Gonzaga by now that the swollen Taro had seriously upset his original battle plan of advancing straight across the river beds. The plan had been predicated on the assumption that the watercourse would remain dry and provide a straight run for his attacking troops. Now it had become a formidable obstacle.

Yet Gonzaga insisted on pressing the battle, veering leftwards to seek a convenient fording-place, only to get his troops mixed up with Fortebraccio's units. Moreover, he exposed his right flank to the French centre. The field of battle had become a sea of mud, sucking at man and horse alike. The French fought back with great courage and skill, making bloody use of their swords and daggers at close quarters. After two hours of slaughter, and with the onset of evening, both sides broke off the fight, exhausted. Gonzaga mourned some 4,000 Italian dead, including his uncle Ridolfo Gonzaga, who had inspired the original battle plan. The French suffered far less, losing at most 600 men thanks to their superior discipline and tenacity. On the strength of this result, Charles claimed victory, but as his army withdrew while the Italians stayed on the field – having captured all the French baggage to boot – Gonzaga could make an equal claim at having won.[13]

The battle of Fornovo found Alexander in Perugia, where he had gone to escape the danger of capture by the French. Back in Rome he applied all his energies to reorganizing and strengthening the Papal States. He promoted members of his wider family, many of them Spaniards, to top positions – in those days a wise precaution that would ensure loyalty more often than not – but one such appointment proved to be a disappointment; this was his eldest surviving son Juan, who was placed at the head of the papal army and ordered to reduce the Orsini fortresses near Rome. One of these was the castle overlooking Bracciano Lake. On 15 January 1497 a papal attack on the castle was hurled back by the Orsini, who had raised troops financed by French money. After Juan Borgia had withdrawn to Anguillara near the lake, he lost another battle at Soriano and was wounded.[14] Alexander had to pay heavy compensation to the Orsini, but in consolation he managed to boot the French out of the port of Ostia.

*   *   *

Five months later Juan's body, bearing multiple stab wounds, was found floating in the Tiber. Alexander went frantic with grief, but apparently never suspected what historians including Machiavelli have since claimed – that Cesare Borgia was behind the murder. Juan, however, had been an inveterate womanizer, 'made for Eros, not for Mars', and any number of jealous husbands or lovers could have been implicated, so the jury must remain out. The crime remains one of history's most enduring murder mysteries. But the pope himself recovered to turn over a new leaf: nepotism was abandoned and a Church reform commission set to work. The trouble was, though, that only the practice of mass simony, the sale of ecclesiastical offices, could give the papacy enough revenues to operate. He soon had to abandon his utopian dream. Merely to keep the papal state alive, every pope had to be in some degree a simoniac.

If tabloid newspapers and social media had been available in Rome at the turn of the sixteenth century, Pope Alexander VI would have figured hugely in the daily news feed. The more devout he professed himself – and there is little doubt that he was sincere in his faith – the more worldly and unscrupulous he appeared to become. Many of his actions, as we have seen, were necessary to build up and maintain a strong state that would protect all the people under the pope's protection. But his morals were not what stuffy northerners would approve of; he had no hesitation in taking a pretty blonde married woman, Giulia Farnese, as a mistress in order to give him yet more children to widen the Borgia power base, and her husband seems to have had no objection as long as he stood to benefit from the connection. The pope's enemies claimed that he even used tender-aged Lucrezia for sexual diplomacy. As Will Durant writes with his usual eloquence:

> There is no question that Alexander was a sensual man, full-blooded to a degree painfully uncongenial to celibacy. When he gave a public festival in the Vatican, at which a comedy was performed (February, 1503), he rumbled with amusement, and was pleased to have fair women crowd about him … He was a man. He seems to have felt, like many clergymen of his time, that clerical celibacy was a mistake … and that even a cardinal should be permitted the pleasures and tribulations of female company.[15]

It was in this atmosphere that the Holy Year of 1500 was celebrated. Again, the money-bearing tourist-pilgrims poured into Rome. At Easter the pope blessed a crowd of some 200,000 at Saint Peter's. He himself rode from church to church on a richly caparisoned horse. But there was also a hard side to the jubilee year: to give the pilgrims a sense of security, Alexander had eighteen street gang members hanged for mugging visitors. A severe flooding of the Tiber in November put a premature end to the festivities. Those entrusted with collecting the pilgrims' pence wanted the money to be set aside for a new crusade. But the pope, who knew better, diverted some of it to use for his planned campaigns to recover those Papal States over which he still had no *de facto* authority. In the north the French were becoming aggressive again, with King Louis XII having invaded and controlled Milan.

Then in 1503 the Romans suddenly found an outlet for their own sentiments about public and papal affairs, and they were by no means complimentary. It took the form of a Hellenistic-era statue discovered during road works in the Piazza Navona and set up as a curiosity. Some local wit named it Pasquino, perhaps after a nearby innkeeper, barber, tailor or schoolteacher. This early precursor of Twitter, and four other similar statues in Rome, quickly became bulletin-boards for anonymous wits and commentators, replete with the equivalent of what we now would call 'likes' and 're-tweets' – what became known as pasquinades. One of the earliest anonymous notes stuck on Pasquino was one attacking Alexander for 'selling Christ' along with Church offices for huge sums of money.[16] Pasquino had his own special day each 25 April, when supporters of the pope would attach their own propaganda messages; but at night those messages would be taken down and replaced by other far less respectful ones. (Pasquino's role as an alternative media platform, in fact, would continue until 1870.)

If anyone was acting as a papal general during the pontificate of Alexander Borgia, it was his son Cesare Borgia, who had inherited the determination and ruthlessness of the Borgia clan, but little of any of its culture or spiritual faith. The Romans watched in disbelief when on 2 January 1502 he decapitated a bull with a single stroke during a new year event in a city square. In addition to being handsome and physically powerful, Cesare walked and rode with the air of owning the world. For a while he was employed as his father's shuttle diplomat to settle troublesome dynastic problems involving the thrones of France and Naples – mostly in favour of the former. Cesare's next job was to be his father's instrument for restoring order in the Papal States which were in danger of disintegrating under the covetous eyes of their neighbours.

Bearing a sword etched with scenes from the life of his near-namesake Julius Caesar, Cesare set out to enforce the papal law in papal provinces such as Imola, Forlì, Faenza and Urbino that in the pope's view were in the hands of hostile parties. Starting in January 1500, Imola surrendered at once without a fight. But the tyrannical Caterina Sforza, who ruled Forlì, refused to capitulate; it was a wrong move to make against Cesare, who slaughtered the defendants and captured Caterina, who because of her continued obstinacy was eventually packed off to a convent. But money was short in his army, and it was only through a timely French injection of funds that Cesare was able to take Milan and put a smile on his father's face. Back in Rome he bought the allegiance of the Orsini, who swelled his ranks and enabled him to snatch the castles of the Colonna and Savelli.

Cesare's next campaign, in October 1500, was aimed at Rimini and Pesaro, whose feudal rulers – usurpers, in the pope's view – fled at his approach. It took a few months for Faenza to cave in; here Cesare was on his best behaviour, treating the losers with consideration and dignity. Next on the list was Urbino, which in hostile hands blocked a key route to the Adriatic Sea outlets. With his genius of a military engineer, Leonardo da Vinci, in tow, Cesare appeared to be heading for nearby Camerino, but suddenly switched course for Urbino which, taken by utter surprise, fell easily. Machiavelli was ecstatic at the feat, daring to hope (vainly) that the papal campaigns might presage the political union of all Italy. Camerino surrendered in July 1501. A year later Cesare made a quick march across Italy to thwart an attempt to turn Louis XII of France against him.

Naturally, those who feared a strong papal state conspired against Cesare. Venice and Florence seethed with plotters, as did Urbino, Perugia and Bologna, all in the papal fold but never quite securely so. The Colonna and Savelli, and to a lesser extent the Orsini, were perennially ready to join in any anti-papal movement. The Orsini were prepared ordinarily to ally with the papacy, but only as long as they could at least share control; a man with the bulldozing power of Cesare Borgia was not at all to their liking. The standard of revolt was raised at La Magione on Trasimene lake in September 1502. At first the conspirators enjoyed a remarkable success: the papal garrisons in Camerino and Urbino were expelled, and morale in Cesare's own army began to plummet. The pope quickly sent him a large sum of money left by a cardinal who had the good timing to die at this point, and helped him raise 6,000 rather more reliable troops.

Alexander himself displayed his talents in diplomacy and bribery, but Urbino and Senigallia still held out. As Cesare surrounded the latter city, an important Adriatic port, its commander offered to surrender. Cesare treated him well at first, but that same night, New Year's Eve 1502, he had him and three others strangled; two of the leading Orsini shared the same fate a few weeks later. An ecstatic Machiavelli rated Cesare's recapture of Senigallia 'the loveliest ruse' of all, while Louis XII saw in the campaign 'a deed worthy of the great days of Rome'.[17] The pope now hit back hard at the roots of the revolt; Cardinal Orsini was arrested and his property and goods confiscated, a shock that probably contributed to his death in prison in February. Cesare's next objective was the great fortress of Ceri held by the Orsini. Here Leonardo da Vinci's talents were brought into play; he devised a massive tower-lift capable of lifting three hundred men to the top of the castle walls. The defenders surrendered, promising to give up all the other fortifications to the Church. As the brief Orsini revolt against the popes sputtered out, the pope's daughter Lucrezia Borgia was installed as duchess of Ferrara.

After almost single-handedly restoring papal power in the Papal States, Cesare Borgia relaxed for a while in Rome. He was still only twenty-eight, and by all accounts the most powerful and feared man in all Italy. He stayed out of public view as much as he could, preferring to work at night to hold the Papal States' administration together – no mean task in an environment fraught with unseen menace. He was quick to see threats before others could, and deal with them in time, largely through skilful bribery. He was a stern, at time savage, disciplinarian, but his soldiers ruefully appreciated him all the more for it. His enemies accused him of fleecing rich clergymen on trumped-up charges, and doing the same to rich Jews; with his father he has been accused (mostly, admittedly, by Protestant historians) of resorting to poisoning when other means of pressure failed, but the historical record fails to support such allegations. One story which made the rounds for centuries afterwards told of a Vatican banquet hosted by Cesare that featured naked courtesans chasing chestnuts scattered over the floor.[18] As much ink was later spilled by hostile commentators to blacken the Borgias, there is no way of knowing whether this titillating tale is true. But the pope's soldiers would certainly have appreciated it.

In the summer of 1503 a heatwave hit Rome, along with an outbreak of malaria. Hundreds perished in the streets, either of disease or heat stroke or both; half the papal household fell ill and many died. On 5 August the pope's nephew Cardinal Juan Borgia passed away suddenly; Alexander, watching the funeral cortège pass, commented sadly on the intolerable heat. Other than that, observed a Venetian diplomat, 'nothing worries him'. A week later both the pope and Cesare complained of a fever; for a couple more weeks the pope suffered through various forms of treatment, including repeated bleeding. Alexander VI Borgia died on 18 August, aged seventy-two. It is reported that his illness had bloated him, and the papal undertakers had a hard time, 'joking and swearing', cramming him into his casket. Others swore 'that a little devil had been seen, at the moment of death, carrying Alexander's soul to hell'.[19]

For all Alexander VI's prowess in maintaining and governing the Papal States, he was not mourned in Rome. In fact, the news of his demise touched off widespread rejoicing; the Romans had never taken to a Spaniard defiling the throne of Saint Peter, and much less to the cabal of haughty Catalans who at times appeared to run the city. Even Machiavelli professed himself satisfied with the departure of the man who 'did nothing but deceive, and thought of nothing else during the whole of his life'. Catholic historians, without ignoring the defects, have tried to even out the historical legacy of Alexander; even Protestants such as William Roscoe aver that 'the vices of Alexander were accompanied ... by many great qualities which ... ought not to be passed over in silence'.[20] Whatever the moral and political judgements, however, Alexander VI Borgia undoubtedly strengthened the Patrimony of Saint Peter from the military and security standpoint, and to that end he no doubt felt himself justified in employing the timeless tactics of war, fair or foul.

As for Cesare Borgia, he appeared to recover slowly from the malaria, but remained helpless as the sudden vacuum of power in the Vatican had set off the usual mob violence in Rome, and the Colonna and Orsini moved to snatch back their fortified places. To pay his army Cesare seized control of the papal treasury by sending men to threaten the treasurer cardinal at the point of a sword. There was also the Borgias' most implacable foe, the della Rovere family, whose own cardinal Giuliano was known to be heading to Rome to run for the pontificate; Cesare ordered ships and men to intercept him, but the majority of cardinals put their slippered feet down against any disturbance. The weakened Cesare, the Colonna and the Orsini all agreed to pull all their armed men out of Rome to enable an unruffled conclave to proceed. Giuliano della Rovere was able to put together an anti-Borgia coalition which elected Cardinal Francesco Piccolomini, sixty-four, a nephew of Pius II, who took the name Pius III in his uncle's honour. Death cut short Pius' reign after less than a month, which was highly convenient for della Rovere who was easily elected Pope Julius II with Cesare's agreement.

But foreign affairs would not wait. The Venetians were making serious inroads into papal territory and the new pope sent Cesare to Imola to raise a new army. Cesare decided to sail to Pisa and march overland from there, but as he was about to board ship at Ostia a message arrived from the pope ordering him to give up his own fortresses in the Romagna. Julius obviously wanted as few rivals as possible holding significant strategic assets. At first the proud Cesare refused, only to receive a peremptory order to return to Rome. He found himself under house arrest, and having to suffer the indignity of handing over title to the Borgia fortresses to a personal foe, Guidobaldo of Urbino, who had now become head of the papal army. Whereupon Cesare was set free; he sought refuge in Naples, where he soon began plotting to stir up the provinces against Julius. But the pope was too quick for him – he notified King Ferdinand of Spain of what was afoot, the king had Cesare arrested, and the once-invincible son of a pope languished in a Spanish jail at Chinchilla near Valencia for two years. After a failed escape attempt in the summer of 1505 he was transferred to a prison at Medina del Campo. Thanks to the help of his brother-in-law, King Jean d'Albret of Navarre, and a priest, he finally escaped in November 1506 and joined the service of the king on campaign against rebellious vassals.[21] On 12 March 1507, during a stiff battle, Cesare – still only thirty-one – and one of his soldiers were surrounded and cut down.

Pope Julius II was proof that lightning sometimes does strike twice in the same place. The painter Raphael has left us with an unforgettable portrait of 'a massive head bent with exhaustion and tardy humility ... grave, deep-set, penetrating eyes, lips tight with resolution ... face sombre with the disillusionment of power'. His character matched the portrait: determined and violent-tempered to a degree uncommon even in the climate of the time, he waged war with the same enthusiasm as he built the grand new Saint Peter's, which we still marvel at today, and assigned Michelangelo to adorn the Sistine Chapel ceiling, along with other artistic masterpieces that give Rome its present timeless quality.

Like Alexander Borgia, Julius lived the carnal life to the full without feeling that it at all disqualified him from holding the supreme holy office. There is some evidence that in his thirty-three years as a cardinal he contacted a venereal disease that disfigured his foot so that he would never allow it to be kissed in the usual papal custom. Once wearing the papal tiara, Julius displayed his true avocation, which was nothing less than going to war. One feels he would have made a far better general than pontiff. But somehow he managed to combine the two roles into a seamless whole, breaking with precedent by assuming command in the field wherever he could. He was no diplomat; like any soldier, he could wield a blistering and foul tongue when the occasion demanded.

One of Julius' first acts was to set up a personal Vatican guard. Here Michelangelo came to his assistance by designing a special colourful uniform for a force of Swiss mercenaries who had proved especially reliable. The first 150 recruits presented themselves for service under Kaspar von Silenen, to be duly decked out with wide red-lined yellow and blue pantaloons and showy Spanish-type clamshell helmets surmounted by red ostrich plumes and ruffled collars, and toting six-foot-long pikes weighing six kilos each. On 21 January 1506 the Swiss Guard was officially established as the Vatican's elite military unit. The Guard's banner was a white cross on a gold, red and blue background, bearing the coat of arms of Julius II, to which would later be added that of every subsequent reigning pontiff. Taking with him the Swiss Guard and a modest 400 papal cavalry, the pope headed north to lay down the law in the troublesome papal domains. For the first time in half a millennium, Italians were treated to the sight of their Holy Father in person riding at the front of an army (though Guidobaldo was still technically the papal army commander). Naples, Mantua, Urbino, Ferrara and Florence all pledged contingents, while France agreed to send 8,000 men in return for three French clergymen being made cardinals.

Perugia was the first to submit; Machiavelli, who witnessed the events and didn't think military popes were a good idea, thought that the city's defender Gianpaolo Baglioni had been too hasty in submitting and could well have captured the pope if he wanted. Julius moved on to Bologna, veering round the city for a surprise attack from the east while the French moved in from the west. Bologna was in the hands of the Bentivoglio clan; after excommunicating them, Julius promised a full indulgence to anyone who could kill any one of them. This was enough to put the wind up the Bentivogli, who fled. On 11 November the pope rode through rejoicing Bologna in a chair borne on men's shoulders. Returning to Rome, he was lionized as a new conquering Caesar.

But Julius could not rest as long as Venice defied him. Venice had become the richest state in Italy, thanks to its pioneering banking and shipping practices that had earned it colonies all over the East Mediterranean. The pope might have consented to that arrangement if Venice had not been in illegal possession of Faenza, Ravenna and Rimini, which nominally belonged to the Papal States. These cities had to be clawed back; Venice was too strong to be taken on alone, so in 1509 Julius hitched his wagon to a coalition of European powers that also sought to bring Venice down a peg or two. The previous year, Louis XII of France and Holy Roman Emperor Maximilian I Habsburg had joined in the League of Cambrai that was ostensibly formed to stem Ottoman advances in Eastern Europe but actually was aimed at curbing Venetian power. The Papal States, plus Mantua and Ferrara, joined the lineup. On 20 April the pope appointed Alfonso I, the duke of Ferrara and husband of Lucrezia Borgia, as captain general of the papal forces.

For all his intelligence, Julius may not have fully realized at first that the real French intention was not just to humble Venice but to dismember Italy completely so that no unified power could form on France's southeast frontier. But he did come to realize it later, after Venice succumbed to a concerted attack and was forced to hand back the pope's cities to him. Immediately afterwards, Julius decided to boot the French out of Italy for one more time. Before that could happen he needed to stiffen his control over Ferrara. But Duke Alfonso, his captain general, called in the French in defiance of his boss's plans – Ferrara was his own town, and he, not the pope, would govern it with Lucrezia. Julius moved north and seized Modena; at Bologna he received the unexpected news that a French army was before

Ferrara, ready to seize the city for Alfonso. The pope, incapacitated by a fever, was about to accept this French *fait accompli* when the French retreated before the pope's Spanish and Venetian reinforcements.

The war with Ferrara dragged on through the winter of 1511. Armies since ancient times had generally avoided campaigning in the depth of winter, but Julius, now sixty-eight, trudged through the snow with his men to besiege the outpost of Mirandola, north of Ferrara. He exulted in being a soldier; while minutely directing all aspects of the operation he lived and drank and swore with the rest of his army while displaying admirable courage under fire. When men fell next to him he merely shrugged.[22] Mirandola capitulated after a two-week siege. Julius ordered all French troops found there to be executed, but by then they had probably escaped. The pope attempted to rest at Bologna, but the French drove him to Rimini and melted down a large bronze statue of Julius that was re-forged into cannon for Duke Alfonso. At the same time, the French re-took Mirandola. The Curia, thoroughly alarmed, decided to meet at Pisa on 1 September 1511 to judge the pope's conduct which, having started out well enough, seemed to have hit a fatal snag. Was *il papa terribile* (the terrible pope) on the ropes?

The Pisa council never got anywhere. It elected someone who called himself a pope but was never recognized by any secular power. Julius felt he could safely ignore it and asserted his authority in the Fifth Lateran Council, which overruled the Pragmatic Sanction of Bourges by which the French had claimed a certain independence in ecclesiastical affairs. Perhaps because of his exertions he fell seriously ill and for three days was on the verge of death; expecting the worst, the cardinals began to call together a conclave. But, horrifying his doctors, the pope took a stiff drink of wine and recovered as if by magic. Two months later he formed a Holy League of the Papal States, Venice and Spain, to be joined six weeks later by King Henry VIII of England. Thus restored in spirit (if not completely in health), Julius resumed his wars.

As the French retained a shaky hold on Milan and Florence, Julius engineered a Swiss alliance; the Swiss attacked the French at Milan but were repulsed and went home. On 12 April 1512, Easter Sunday, the French under Gaston de Foix (who had commanded a division at Fornovo seventeen years before) smashed the Holy League forces at Ravenna. Undaunted, Julius got the German emperor on side and paid the Swiss to rejoin the fight.

The Swiss poured into Italy through the Tyrol and caught the French by surprise, helping the pope drive them out of not only Ravenna and Bologna, but Milan as well. Duke Alfonso of Ferrara, finding himself outgunned, travelled to Rome to make peace overtures to Julius; the talks broke down after Alfonso refused to give up Ferrara. The duke returned to the city to boost its defences.

It was one crisis too much for Julius. In January 1513 he fell ill again. The diagnoses ranged from overeating to syphilis. He had his foes, and not only in the politico-military sphere. Machiavelli and the contemporary historian Francesco Guicciardini, for example, strongly disapproved of a religious leader going to war and killing people. Guicciardini lambasted him for 'bringing empire to the Apostolic See by arms and the shedding of Christian blood, rather than troubling himself to set an example of the holy life'.[23] A satirical pamphlet of the time portrayed Julius confronting Saint Peter to boast of his achievements:

> If you could catch a glimpse of the supreme pontiff, carried aloft in a golden chair on the shoulders of his men ... if you could hear the thunder of cannon, the blare of the trumpets, the blasting of horns, see the flashes of the guns, and hear the applause of the people ... if you could see and hear all of this, what would you say?

To which an unimpressed Saint Peter replies:

> That I was looking at a tyrant worse than any in the world, the enemy of Christ, the bane of the church.[24]

Whatever the pope himself thought of his impending meeting with Saint Peter, we are assured that he accepted death calmly, admitted that his sins were many, said formal goodbyes to his cardinals and planned his funeral with care. When the Terrible Pope passed away on 20 February, the people of Rome, ignoring the intellectuals, sincerely mourned him.

For all his faults, Pope Julius II strengthened the Papal States and ensured their survival in an ever-turbulent Italy for the next three centuries and a half. He made his share of strategic errors, such as inviting the French to meddle in Italian affairs, as it was common knowledge that whenever the French came, the French were unlikely to leave quietly. But he had the vigour to see off the French when they became untrustworthy. Some historians have seen in the Terrible Pope a war-lover with delusions of grandeur, nursing ambitions of becoming the master of Europe, but having precious little administrative ability to undergird those ambitions.[25] It may indeed have been that Julius was in the wrong job, by inclination a far better soldier than a priest. But as he was the head of a state, he would have been remiss if he had not employed all his talents, especially the military ones, to uphold its security. And in this, history has judged him to be a success.

Chapter 7

'Quare de vulva eduxisti me?'

One of the papal officials accompanying the army to Ravenna in 1511 was a young Florentine of thirty-six recently appointed by Julius II as papal legate to Bologna and the Romagna. Though not a soldier and hence unarmed, Giovanni de' Medici shared the actual soldiers' dangers on the battlefield, encouraging them. In one encounter he stayed perhaps too long – a Greek unit in French service captured him and took him to Milan. There many ordinary French soldiers, unknowing and uncaring of politics, came to him for a blessing and absolution. In such circumstances it was easy to escape and take part in the recapture of Florence by the Medici clan. When called to Rome for the conclave to elect a successor to Julius II, he was ill with a fistula and had to be carried on a litter. He was probably more surprised than anyone when he was elected and took the name Leo X; moreover, no money this time appears to have changed hands.

Leo was already well-liked, and hopes were high that the wars and intrigues of Alexander VI and Julius II would become things of the past. Even Duke Alfonso of Ferrara forgot his enmity to the Vatican and came to Rome to hold the new pope's horse in the lavish coronation procession. 'Poets, sculptors, painters, goldsmiths rejoiced; humanists promised themselves a revival of the Augustan Age.'[1] Leo was portly and tall, short-sighted and with soft hands that apparently had never done any manual labour. He began his reign with an undisputed disposition to do good and be a friend to everyone (except the Protestants, whom he professed never to understand). His fistula, though, always tormented him but he managed to hide his pain under a smiling and tolerant mask. Money flowed in from Catholic Europe like a waterfall; several cardinals became hugely wealthy, living in palaces and employing hundreds of servants. Almost every history of his times contains the phrase Leo supposedly uttered after his coronation: 'God has given us the papacy; let us enjoy it.' Writes Gregorovius:

All of Rome was a vast theatre where the pope seemed to be the Romans' *tribunus voluptatum*, with the Vatican teeming with a swirl of musicians, actors, charlatans, poets, artists, courtesans and parasites.[2]

Under Leo's pontificate Rome, whose population had soared to some 85,000, lived through the giddy height of the Renaissance. But what was such a pleasure-loving pontiff like in the political and military sphere?

Affairs of state were largely left in the hands of Leo's cousin, Cardinal Giulio de' Medici. It may have been he who thought of uniting Florence, Milan, Ferrara, Urbino and a handful of other cities into a single Church-ruled power under the Medici clan. There was good cause for this scheme as France to the north-west and Naples to the south were ever looking for ways to squeeze the papal domains. As always, the plan was dressed up as a preliminary for another anti-Turkish crusade, but Machiavelli among others hoped it would presage the political and military unification of Italy. Leo himself, when he could find the time for it, was as wily a diplomat as they come. Thanks to a combination of patronage and bribery, he secured Modena in 1514. In response the new French king, Francis I, planned another invasion of Italy. Leo readied his own army, but the Duke of Urbino, Francesco Maria della Rovere – possibly secretly in league with the French – refused to join him. The pope excommunicated and deposed della Rovere, but it took eight months for Leo to impose his will on Urbino.

Those months of conflict came close to exhausting the papal treasury as well as the general goodwill Leo had generated. On the plus side, Francis I decided to mend fences with the pope through a marriage alliance – expecting that someone like Leo would be a pushover in contrast to the tough Julius II. But no alliance could ultimately contend with the sudden eruptions of aggressive independence of states ordinarily considered safe in the papal fold. We know of at least two plots to assassinate Leo, probably involving one of his generals in Perugia, Gianpaolo Baglioni, who was found out, called to Rome and executed. These were signs of a mounting dissatisfaction with his rule, during which huge sums were spent on building the magnificent church of Saint Peter's as we know it today. What is not generally known is that much, if not most, of the money was pretty much extorted from the European faithful. Leo had no compunctions about selling cardinalates to the highest bidder. But in Central and North Europe the resentment was building up until in 1517 an obscure German priest named Martin Luther nailed his objections to Church practice to the door of Wittenberg Cathedral and began a movement that would burgeon into the papacy's biggest European adversary – Protestantism. Ever in need of funds, Leo borrowed money from banking houses at an eye-gouging forty percent, pledging his silver plate and jewellery as collateral. Leo also was obsessed with trying to recover Ferrara from Duke Alfonso, which he never could quite manage.

Worrying about Alfonso of Ferrara, the newly-emerging Protestant movement and the aggressive Ottoman Sultan Süleyman the Magnificent, and what to do about them, placed a serious strain on Leo's already questionable health. He sickened in August 1521 and recovered, but fell ill again in October. The following month it seemed as if he would recover; resting at his villa at Magliana, he learned that a papal army had ejected the French from Milan one more time. The news revived his spirits enough for him to return to Rome to wild public rejoicing. He walked a lot that day, and sweated a lot in the process. The next morning the fever attacked him again, but even the news that Piacenza and Parma had fallen to the papal forces failed to revive him, and he died at midnight on 1 December. The usual rumours of poisoning were bruited about, and surely there was no lack of suspects, Alfonso of Ferrara among them, but the historical consensus is that he succumbed to malaria.

Alfonso rejoiced at Leo's death and to mark the event coined a special medallion featuring a pun in the pope's name in the motto EX ORE LEONIS – 'From the Jaws of the Lion.' Italy's banks and some cardinals were left being owed huge sums, which triggered one of the biggest mass lootings in Vatican history. But artists and intellectuals mourned him as the city's greatest artistic and cultural benefactor. In the diplomatic field, however, whatever he had achieved rapidly became undone as his many foes around Europe took advantage of the sudden vacuum of power in Rome to press their claims. In North Europe the Protestant movement gained traction. What is more, the Holy Roman Empire was nearing the point of its greatest influence as Emperor Charles V took the throne. For all his greatness of character, Leo X in the end had not been able to see beyond the perennially warring states of Italy.

On 2 January 1522 the conclave elected a humble-born Dutchman, Adriaan Florensz, as Pope Hadrian VI. A young prodigy as a scholar, he was given high ecclesiastical office in Spain. His reputation for holiness and orthodoxy reached Rome, where Leo X gave him a red hat. Charles V may have subtly influenced the proceedings of the conclave, as Hadrian was the first non-Italian pontiff to be elected in more than one hundred and fifty years – and the last for some four hundred and fifty years more. Few Romans had even heard of him. But his name was soon on everyone's lips as he began a root-and-branch reform of the Vatican administration and morals, sacking hordes of papal hangers-on – he maintained just two servants of his own – and stanching the excessive outflow of funds for transforming the face of Rome. The licentious Mediterranean culture of Rome, and its new love of pagan art and culture, horrified him. The Pasquino statue flowered with all manner of bitterly satirical notes aimed at the pope, to which he replied by threatening to drown 'the whole tribe of satirists' in the Tiber. In short, Hadrian strove to bring Christ back to the Church, and thus de-fang the new Protestant movement.

Needless to say, he had a tough time. On at least one occasion he lamented to an old friend 'how much better it went with us when we were living quietly in Louvain!'[3] His reforms struck holy terror into the majority of churchmen who, if not actually corrupt themselves, had allowed corruption to exist and had benefited from it. A sort of financial panic seized Rome, and we know of at least one assassination plot against Hadrian. The pope's strenuous efforts at clearing the Roman political swamp led him to neglect foreign affairs, and so he left Alfonso in control at Ferrara while petty tyrants took power in Perugia and Rimini. In 1522 papal prestige suffered another blow when Ottoman Sultan Süleyman I (the Magnificent) seized the ethnically-Greek island of Rhodes after a furious and determined siege. For the past two hundred years or so the island had been ruled by the Knights Hospitaller (Knights of Saint John) as one of the few Christian outposts in the Aegean area. The Turks had failed to dislodge the Knights in their first siege in 1480, but this time Süleyman's sheer persistence paid off. The sultan was uncharacteristically magnanimous; out of respect for the fighting qualities of the Knights of Saint John, he allowed them to depart Rhodes and settle temporarily in Cyprus, after which they would find a new home in Malta.

The Turkish seizure of Rhodes threw a tremor of nervousness into Rome. There were reports that Turkish spies in the city had been caught and rumours that the Ottomans were planning to land in South Italy. But no–one except the papacy seemed to care much. Charles V and Henry VIII of England had just signed the Treaty of Windsor binding them to a joint attack on France. Even in the Curia, Hadrian's own chief minister, Cardinal Francesco Soderini, was unmasked secretly plotting with the French to seize Sicily. The pope could see no alternative but to join Charles V as insurance against a looming French advance on Italy. It was all too much for the quiet Dutchman, who quite bitterly regretted ever donning the papal mitre. On 14 September 1523, after less than two years on the throne, heartsick and ill, he died, leaving his possessions to the poor. Even so Rome, temporarily deprived of its freebooting finance, erupted in unholy joy. 'The Renaissance,' concludes Durant dryly, 'could not tolerate a Christian pope.'[4]

The good old days returned with the election of Giulio de' Medici, a nephew of the late Leo X, as Pope Clement VII. Aged forty-five, tall and good-looking, he was well-respected as a learned, cultured and more or less moral man. The Vatican again was filled with well-paid functionaries, its halls again resounded to feasting and entertainment, cardinals again went about with full purses and stomachs. There was every reason for the internal administration of the papacy to feel good. But in foreign and military affairs Clement was, quite simply, a disaster. This was not so much his fault as that of the flow of history. Two great monarchies had come to dominate Europe: the Holy Roman Empire and France. Charles V Habsburg found himself in control of huge chunks of European territory including all of Spain, all of South Italy and Sicily, the Netherlands and parts of present-day Croatia in addition to his own German domains. Small wonder that France's Francis I felt hemmed in and was obsessed with having Milan as a buffer zone. The Papal States were themselves sandwiched between French and imperial holdings, and inevitably, when the two European titans clashed the papacy suffered.

Understandably, the popes of this period were uncertain on which side to place their trust. Leo X had switched sides at least twice. Hadrian VI had been a Habsburg supporter but Clement VII vacillated according to which adviser had his ear at any particular time; after the French defeat at Pavia in 1525 he cosied up to Charles, but soon changed his mind as he sensed that the emperor was preoccupied with Ottoman Turkish advances in Central Europe right up to the walls of Vienna. By now one-third of Europe was in revolt against the Church. To Charles, the pope's shift towards his

French foe must have appeared treacherous, and he resolved to teach the unreliable Romans a lesson. Charles' predecessor Maximilian I had set up a new corps of pikemen called the *Landsknechte* (roughly translatable as yeomen) on the model of the renowned Swiss pikemen who had proved their worth in earlier battles against the French and were the best close-order fighters of their time. The first warning was sounded on 20 September 1526 when about 5,000 armed men under the pro-Habsburg Vespasiano Scanio and Pompeo Colonna burst into Rome shouting, 'Empire, Colonna, liberty!' and proceeded to thoroughly plunder Saint Peter's. One soldier donned the pope's white robe and red cap and went round performing mock benedictions.[5] Much worse was to follow.

Clement raised 7,000 fresh papal soldiers and in October sent them to punish the Colonna in their strongholds. He appealed to Francis I and England's Henry VIII, but neither responded. (Durant quips that the latter was 'absorbed in the difficult task of begetting a son'.) A second papal force was kept in the north to guard against a resurgence of Urbino. But Charles had a much grander scheme up his sleeve. He approached a Tyrolean *condottiere* named Georg von Frundsberg, who had a good reputation for commanding *Landsknechte*, to raise a punitive force. Von Frundsberg pawned everything he had, including his castle and his wife's jewellery, to recruit some 15,000 mercenaries 'not averse to breaking a lance over a papal head'. It was said that some soldiers carried a noose with which to string up the pope. Alfonso of Ferrara pitched in with four cannon.

Von Frundsberg's mostly Lutheran rabble crossed the Alps in November 1526 and advanced on Brescia, where a papal force under Giovanni de'Medici was overrun. Medici, known as Giovanni delle Bande Nere (Giovanni of the Black Bands) as his troops had worn them on the death of Leo X, was mortally wounded in the skirmish. Crossing the Po river and entering Lombardy, von Frundsberg ravaged that fertile province so thoroughly that it would not recover for many years. The governor of Milan, Duke Charles of Bourbon, added his own troops to the invasion force after taxing the Milanese people with insane brutality. Bourbon and von Frundsberg joined forces near Piacenza in February 1527, steamrollering down the Via Emilia and ravaging everything in their path.

At this critical juncture Clement and the Colonna had the good sense to make peace; at the same time Naples brokered a deal by which Bourbon and von Frundsberg agreed to spare the Papal States. The pope also bribed the latter with 60,000 ducats. Believing that he had averted disaster, Clement reduced his army to a mere three hundred or so men. It was one of the worst strategic decisions ever made by a pontiff. Bourbon and von Frundsberg most probably intended to stick to the deal, but his army shrieked with fury when it became known.

For four months they had endured a thousand hardships only in the hope of plundering Rome; most of them were now in rags, many were shoeless, all were hungry, none was paid… they refused to be bought off with a miserable 60,000 ducats.[6]

Bourbon didn't know where to hide to escape his raging troops who plundered his tent. Von Frundsberg was at his wits' end trying vainly to calm the men, but the strain triggered a stroke that ejected him from command and would ultimately prove fatal. Bourbon had in the end no choice but to lead his brigands on to Rome.

A curious and sinister episode prefigured what was to come. On 8 April, the Thursday of Holy Week, when about 10,000 people massed before Saint Peter's to receive the papal blessing, a wild-looking vagrant called Brandano (Bartolommeo Carosi) climbed up the statue of Saint Paul and yelled out to the pope: 'Thou bastard of Sodom! For thy sins Rome shall be destroyed. Repent and turn thee! If thou wilt not believe me, in fourteen days thou shalt see!' Two days later Brandano was seen wandering the streets crying out that God would soon deal with sinful Rome as He 'dealt with Sodom and Gomorrah'.[7] The instrument of this looming divine wrath, Charles of Bourbon, was on his way. He demanded that Clement buy off the attack with 240,000 ducats, four times the original bribe. Clement said it was impossible. Bourbon advanced to Florence, where he found his way blocked by local troops, and turned south towards Rome. It wasn't long before, looking out of the window, the pope could see the first ranks of the hungry 25,000-strong rabble swarming across the fields. To oppose them he could muster just 4,000 men.

On 6 May Bourbon made his first attempt on the walls of Rome under cover of fog. The defenders fired back, killing Bourbon, but the invaders burst through a weakly-defended spot and fanned out through Rome, killing and raping and looting at will. The 189-strong Swiss Guard and Roman militia were almost annihilated. Brandano's wild prophecy came dreadfully true. The slaughter in the city was beyond belief. Entire families were extirpated; not even children, old people or hospital patients were spared. Anti-papal fanaticism, especially among the Germans, far surpassed the point of criminal insanity. Some of the very wealthy were able to pay for their lives and those of their families. Tons of works of art and valuables were looted and destroyed; priests and cardinals were humiliated and then tortured, sometimes to death, and women were violated by the hundreds.

For eight days this hell continued, as Clement could only watch terrified from his refuge in Sant'Angelo Castle. Quoting from the Old Testament book of Job, he is reported to have called on the Almighty in despair: 'Why didst Thou take me out of the womb?' ('*Quare de vulva eduxisti me?*')[8] He stopped shaving, and spent the next seven months holed up in the castle, hoping vainly that some European king, or even Urbino, might march to his rescue. Nothing of a similar magnitude of disaster had been seen since the Latin sack of Constantinople in 1204, the result of similar satanic hatreds.

No sooner had the initial blow spent itself than a fresh epidemic broke out. The bodies of Roman and invader alike rotted in heaps on the streets. Then the Tiber flooded, spreading the plague and killing yet more. Clement remained a prisoner in Sant'Angelo. At this point Henry VIII of England hatched a crafty plan to improve relations with the papacy, which he needed to approve his planned divorce from Catherine of Aragon. He and Francis I offered to pay Charles two million ducats in return for the freeing of Clement and restoration of the Papal States, but the emperor declined. However, under military pressure from France, Venice and Florence, Charles reconsidered. Clement was finally allowed to leave his confinement on 7 December, after paying another large ransom to pay what was left of the imperial troops in Rome; he fled disguised as an itinerant pedlar, guarded by forty-two men of the Swiss Guard, scurrying over the Passetto di Borgo, the raised causeway that still connects the castle and Saint Peter's. It wasn't until mid–February 1528 that the last of the *Landsknechte* withdrew from the city. By some estimates half of all Romans had already perished; a Spanish soldier claimed he oversaw the burial of 10,000 corpses along the Tiber.[9] In years to come the Sack of 1527 by the '*Lanzichenecchi*' (which is how the Italians referred to the *Landsknechte*), attributed in large part to Protestant fanaticism, would not soon be forgotten.

A broken Clement travelled to Orvieto, where he had to lodge in a draughty old broken-down palace. That's where ambassadors from England, eager to get his blessing for Henry VIII's marital plans, found him, 'huddled in bed, his pale and emaciated face half lost in a long and unkempt beard'. After learning that the last of the *Landsknechte* had quit Rome he moved to more congenial quarters in Viterbo and allowed himself to hope again. But the European balance of power was no more favourable to him than it had been before the Sack of Rome. In late August 1528 he bowed to the inevitable and endured the humiliation of signing over three other papal cities and four castles – including Sant'Angelo – to the emperor. In return for that he was allowed to return to Rome some weeks later. He saw a city almost unrecognizable; some eighty per cent of its buildings were in ruins and the surviving Romans walking around in a daze of despair. The very papacy itself seemed to be on the verge of extinction.

The pope's rivals in Italy, meanwhile, were having a field day; Alfonso of Ferrara grabbed Reggio Emilia and Modena, while Venice seized Ravenna. Florence booted out its Medici clan. The French tried to talk Clement into pulling up papal stakes and moving to Avignon once more, but he resisted the suggestion. Though demoralized as few leaders have ever been, he still hoped that the papacy could remain a force in the world. And here Charles stepped in. He saw that in his epic struggle for supremacy in Europe, and to keep his Catholic subjects (especially in Spain) happy, it would be to his advantage to have the papacy on his side. By the 1529 Treaty of Barcelona the emperor handed most of the Papal States back to the pope in return for control of the kingdom of Naples. A formal reconciliation between France and the empire soon followed.

Charles and Clement met for the first time at Bologna on 5 November. The emperor knelt before the pope and kissed his foot – a mere two years after the horrifying Sack of Rome and the pope's utter humiliation at Charles' hands – but the gesture was plainly a surface one. Both leaders knew who was the boss in Europe. Months of diplomacy culminated in the formal coronation of Charles V in Perugia on 22 February 1530. Three years later Clement's great-niece married Francis' son, the eventual Henry II of France. It was the closest Italy ever came to unification until 1870, albeit under an alien monarch. The pope approved an attack on Florence designed to restore his own Medici clan to power there; an eight-month siege forced the Florentines to eat cats and rats while Michelangelo worked on the ramparts in between sculpting the Medici tombs. The Medici triumphed and drove out their rivals with severe reprisals.

Clement VII, worn out by his ordeals, died on 25 September 1534, a month before the demise of his arch-rival Alfonso of Ferrara. He did not die contented. Three years earlier his dispute with Henry VIII of England had cost him that whole kingdom. Alarmed by the spread of Protestantism, Charles had urged the pope to convene a general council to try and reconcile the doctrinal differences and remove a potential major cause of war in Europe. But the pope saw no advantage in it. Moreover, Italy lay under Spanish cultural domination that discouraged any reconciliation with heretics. It is no exaggeration to say that the Romans erupted in joy at the news of the death of the pope they had, rightly or wrongly, associated with the recent horrors. Mobs defiled his tomb. Some thoughtful people may have stopped to realize that the late Clement had been more a victim of history than a failure as pope; the great tectonic plates of history were moving on, as the idea of a universal Church began to crumble under the new ideal of the secular nation-state, and it fell to Clement to suffer the first severe shocks of this process.

The conclave of 1534 was hardly in a position to play the usual political games under Michelangelo's ceiling in the Sistine Chapel. The cardinals, only too well aware that nearly half of Europe was falling away from the pope's Catholicism, elected a mild-mannered man of sixty-six, Alessandro Farnese, as Paul III. Paul from the outset was determined to work with the ultra-powerful Charles, who finally visited Rome two years later. For the occasion Paul had part of the ancient Roman Forum district razed to make a straight road for the emperor and his 4,000 troops, 500 horsemen, Spanish grandees and fifty noble youths dressed in purple silk. These last walked before Charles who rode a white horse while two cardinals on foot held the bridle. At Saint Peter's the emperor conspicuously paid homage to the pope, to cultivate his own image as defender of the Church.[10]

Paul, meanwhile, saw no other way to raise the prestige of the papacy from its present low position than by a programme of house-cleaning. A commission under cardinals Gasparo Contarini and Gian Petro Carafa was assigned to investigate the present state of the Church; their report, the *Consilium de Emendenda Ecclesia* (Advice on Church Reform), was so damning that it was suppressed in case the Protestants got hold of it and leaked it to the world. The report, however, was the spark that ignited the creation of the Congregation of the Roman Inquisition whose purpose was to enforce religious orthodoxy and hopefully remove causes of dissent, conflict and war. It was the beginning of the Counter-reformation, a drive to improve the morals and holiness of the Roman Church in order to thwart any more breakaway tendencies at a time when the Muslim Ottomans were still the masters of much of Eastern Europe. Contarini, for one, hoped that the Protestants could eventually be reconciled, and had the agreement of Charles V, but all efforts to come to an agreement foundered on deep doctrinal differences.

This was the signal for the conservative Cardinal Carafa to concentrate on reform in the Church itself, ignoring what was happening north of the Alps. He had an unexpected ally in the person of a Spanish soldier in his forties named Don Iñigo Lopez de Recalde de Loyola, who had already decided to switch his service from that of the king of Spain to that of Christ. He had plenty of battle experience; a French cannonball broke both his legs while he was helping defend Pampeluna from a French attack in 1521, and he almost died during agonizing medical treatment. Recuperating in his ancestral castle, Loyola had access to just two books, both of them dealing with the lives of Christ and the saints. So far he had little or no interest in religion, and the books at first bored him. But they grew on him:

> [T]he legends of the saints proved as wonderful as the epics of courtly love and war; these cavaliers of Christ were every bit as heroic as the *caballeros* of Castile. Gradually the thought formed in his mind that the noblest war of all was that of Christianity against Islam.[11]

One night, we are told, he had a vivid vision of the Virgin Mary carrying the Christ child, and from that moment forswore all women – of which he had enjoyed many – to devote himself to the spiritual life. When he recovered, like the fictional Don Quixote he set out penniless, with only a mule to ride on, and arrived at the Benedictine Abbey of Montserrat. He had half-hoped to spend his life as a knight-errant, fighting for the good wherever he was needed. But he had a permanent limp, and moreover, 'the saints he had read about had no weapons, no armour ...'. For three years he lived simply as a monastic hermit. Then on 25 March 1522 he set out on foot – for Jerusalem.

At Barcelona, the nearest port, Loyola sheltered in a cave, begging for his food and never washing, flogging himself twice a day; he may well have died had not a kindly woman taken him in to treat him. For a year he was tormented with the memory of his many sins, often considered suicide, but he ultimately found a level of peace and spiritual understanding that enabled him to get back his health, both of body and mind. He sailed from Barcelona in February 1523. He stayed in Rome for a couple of weeks, but found its pagan flavour unsettling; in July he sailed from Venice to Jaffa, and after a hazardous voyage set foot in the Holy Land. In Jerusalem itself he was disappointed: the Ottoman authorities permitted no Christian preaching, and the local papal representative could only timidly suggest that he return to Europe.

Back in Barcelona he realized that he had been done a favour, that he had been extremely naive to believe that he was intellectually equipped to convert unbelievers. He had very little formal education and apparently knew no Latin. Realizing that he would need to broaden his attainments, especially in theology, before he could credibly become a religious man, he took courses and preached redemption among prostitutes and other underprivileged women. The Inquisition took note of his unorthodox methods and banned him from teaching. Taking just a donkey loaded with books, and dressed in his simple pilgrim's cloak, he set out for higher education in Paris. Enrolled in the city's university, he begged for his food and lived in squalid quarters. He wasn't much to look at, with his emaciated body, ragged beard and poor clothes. But he had a talent for seeing into the spiritual problems of others, and with his roommate Francis Xavier worked out the spiritual exercises by which the will could control the body.

In 1534 Loyola set out for the Holy Land along with six companions for missionary work among the Muslims. In an earlier age Loyola might well have joined the Knights Hospitaller or Templar. They walked through France and over the Alps to Venice hoping to catch a ship, but Venice at the time was at war with the Turks and nothing was sailing to the Middle East. They decided to go to Rome instead and offer their services to the pope, walking all the way and singing psalms. Loyola was ordained a priest in 1538 after the requisite minimum four years of study that the Inquisition prescribed for anyone to be allowed to preach. A year later, aged forty-seven, he founded the Society of Jesus (*Compañia de Jesú*), which according to H.G. Wells was 'the most direct attempt to bring the generous tradition of military organization and discipline to the service of religion'.[12] The Society, which quickly became known as the Jesuits, was recognized by Paul III in his bull of 1840, *Regimini militantis ecclesiae*. The title said it all: the Jesuits were to become a tightly-disciplined body just like any ordinary army, but to fight the never-ending war against unbelief with spiritual rather than physical weapons.

Loyola's spiritual exercises were an almost military-style manual of how a soldier of Christ should cultivate knowledge – especially self-knowledge – and the discipline to apply it. They were not for the faint-hearted. A Jesuit was supposed to undergo the most painful inner searching, even if it entailed periods of terror and despair. Only thus could he attain the psychological strength to enable him to help others. With military precision the Society of Jesus, whose constitution defined it as 'founded to employ itself entirely in the defence of the holy Catholic faith,' went forth to fight stoutly. There were four stages in its work: first, to educate young people in religiously orthodox schools; second, to win over doubters through the use of the confessional; third, to do missionary service in heretical (Protestant) and heathen (Muslim) lands; and fourth – and perhaps most important – to acquire diplomatic experience and influence by serving in the courts of nobles and princes. Writes one authority on European history:

> The spirit of the Jesuits was the spirit of their founder, and Loyola was a Spaniard and a soldier. As a Spaniard he was unshakably loyal to the orthodox faith and to the traditional practices and authority of the organized church, whose head was the pope. As a soldier he never questioned the orders or policies of his superior officer, in this case the pope, and he expected equally unquestioning obedience from those under his command.[13]

Ignatius Loyola was elected the first general of the Jesuit order on 17 April 1541. He was now fifty years old, but spent the first few days of his generalship washing dishes and doing the duties of the humblest orderly. In the following years, with Rome now its headquarters, the Jesuits worked out

Plate 1. Pope John VIII *[Catholic Encyclopedia]*

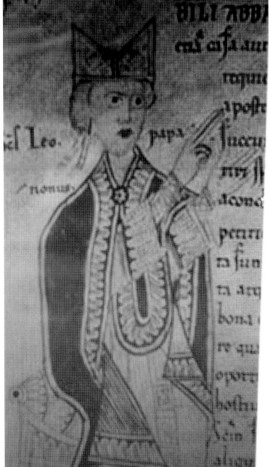

Plate 2. Pope Leo IX *[www.catholicireland.net]*

Plate 3. The Normans eject Pope Gregory VII from Rome, 1084 *[Chronicle of Otto, 12th century]*

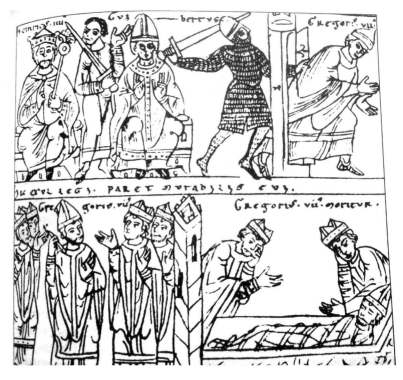

Plate 4. Pope Boniface VIII arrests Pope Celestine V, 1295 *[15th century print, Newton & Compton]*

Plate 5. Cardinal Albornoz enters Rome with papal guard, August 1354 [*Msgr. Charles Burns*]

Plate 6. French troops in occupied Rome, c. 1799 [*Paris: Vues des edifices de Rome antique dans l'intérieur*]

Plate 7. Soldier of the Noble Guard, c. 1801
[Newton & Compton]

Plate 8. Pope Pius VII *[Basilica of San Paolo]*

Plate 9. Pope Pius IX *[Basilica of San Paolo]*

Plate 10. Major Myles O'Reilly *[O'Connell family, online]*

Plate 11. The Battle of Castelfidardo, 1860 *[O'Connell family, online]*

Plate 12. A Zouave of the papal forces *[Catholic Encyclopedia]*

Plate 13. Nationalist *bersaglieri* breach Rome's Porta Pia, 1870, by Carlo Ademollo [*www.italiano-milano.org*]

Plate 14. Pope Pius XI, who negotiated the Lateran Treaty of 1929 [*Ferguson & Bruun*]

LA SCOMUNICA AI COMUNISTI

1. NON È LECITO
iscriversi a partiti comunisti o dare ad essi appoggio.

2. NON È LECITO
pubblicare, diffondere o leggere libri, periodici, giornali o fogli volanti, che sostengono la dottrina o la prassi del comunismo, o collaborare in essi con degli scritti.

3. NON SONO AMMESSI AI SACRAMENTI
i fedeli, che compiono consapevolmente e liberamente gli atti di cui sopra.

4. SONO SCOMUNICATI COME APOSTATI
i fedeli, che professano la dottrina del comunismo materialista ed anti-cristiano, ed anzitutto coloro che la difendono e se ne fanno propagandisti.

LA SCOMUNICA è una pena medicinale per la quale uno viene escluso dalla Comunione dei fedeli con gli effetti sanciti dal Diritto Canonico.

L'APOSTASIA è l'abbandono della fede cattolica.

Dovere dei fedeli è dare la più ampia diffusione al relativo Decreto del Santo Uffizio.

Plate 15. Pope Pius XII's condemnation of communism [*official poster reprint*]

Plate 16. Military-run aid centre in St. Peter's Square, 1944 *[Order of Malta]*

Plate 17. Order of St. John aircrew and attendants on pilgrim mission to Lourdes, 1951 *[Order of Malta]*

Plate 18. A striking image of three Savoia–Marchetti SM82 ex-bombers in St. John's markings over the Vatican, early 1950s *[Order of Malta]*

Plate 19. A Swiss Guard ceremonial line-up *[Order of Malta]*

Plate 20. Col. Mario Fine, commander of the Corpo Militare *[Order of Malta]*

a system of administration by which regional branches of the order would elect the General Congregation to act as a senior council. The Congregation would keep a wary eye on the general, who had an 'admonitor' and four staffers to look out for any serious faults in his rule and, if the general did not heed repeated warnings, could recommend to the Congregation that he be ousted.

Recruits for the order were selected along military lines. They had to be of pleasing appearance and good character, educated and of good social standing. The rookie Jesuit then underwent a long and rigorous period of further education and spiritual training during which he could be dismissed at any time. Upon 'graduation' he was assigned to a sector best suited for his particular talents and took the triple vow of chastity, poverty and obedience similar to that of the Knights of Saint John in Malta. The Society had an inner circle of experienced members who took a fourth vow, that of unswerving obedience to the papacy, and from whom the senior officers were picked. The general of the order held office for life, with essentially unlimited power over his subordinates. Any soldier might find himself sent to a crisis location at a moment's notice; to enable flexibility of action and movement the members were freed from dress code and duty-hours restrictions.

For Rome the era of artistic exuberance and free-thinking was over. The Inquisition imposed its rules on almost all human conduct, not hesitating to establish the death penalty by burning at the stake anyone convicted of occultism, homosexuality and deprecating sacred images. Press censorship descended with a bang through the Index of Prohibited Books in 1559. The theory behind it was that as religious divisions were the greatest single cause of political disunity and strife, they ought to be discouraged with the utmost severity. In 1549 Paul III succumbed to a heart attack and was succeeded by the easy-living Julius III, who brought back some of the lush and nepotistic lifestyle of the Medici popes. In fact he adopted a disreputable Neapolitan street delinquent named Innocenzio and made him a cardinal at eighteen, ignoring the boy's stunning incompetence to a degree that suggested to more than one observer that Innocenzio could have been Julius' illegitimate son. Under Pius IV Innocenzio (jokingly referred to as 'Cardinal Montino' possibly from his habit of sexual 'mounting') was accused of two murders and two rapes and was locked up in Sant'Angelo Castle for sixteen months. Pius V sent him to the Monte Cassino monastery with just enough money to keep him fed.[14] Julius lasted six years, to be succeeded by Marcellus II, who lived just twenty-two days and was followed by Cardinal Carafa as Paul IV.

Already seventy-nine when he took office, Paul was nonetheless described as 'a man of iron … the very stones over which he walks emit sparks'.[15] In short order he managed to alienate nearly everyone in Europe, including the most zealous Catholic king of all, Philip II of Spain. The king ordered the Duke of Alva to take 10,000 Neapolitan troops into the Papal States; in November 1556 Alva threatened Rome. Paul had no compunction in appealing to the Ottoman Turks to attack South Italy and Sicily to draw Alva away, but when that help was not forthcoming, and fearing a repeat of the terrible sack of 1527, the pope made his peace with Alva in return for accepting Spanish domination of the papacy. Paul IV had taken office in the midst of an intermittent eighteen-year conference held in the imperial city of Trent (now Trento in North Italy) that laboured to forge Catholic doctrine into a unified whole that could combat Protestant ideas. Several popes came and went during this uncertain period. Pius IV (1560–65), Pius V (1566–72), Gregory XIII (1572–85) and Sixtus V (1585–90) all upheld clerical morality and rigid orthodoxy. During this period Loyola (later canonized as Saint Ignatius Loyola) and his Jesuits consolidated their influence across Catholic Europe and sent missionaries as far as India. In 1568, five years after the conclusion of the Council of Trent, work began on the stunningly-adorned church of the Gesù at the order's headquarters in central Rome.

The Inquisition, known also as the Holy Office, never quite managed to take root among the Roman people, who at least once, in 1559, pulled down its headquarters in rage against its severity. Many Italians instinctively rebelled against the new austere Spanish fashion in clothing – all black, and not much different from the North European Puritans. Yet clerical morals definitely improved compared with the dissolute Borgia and Medici popes. Paul III beautified Rome with wide streets and new *piazze*; one of the new straight thoroughfares, the Via del Corso, remains one of the city's main shopping streets. Paul IV and Pius IV saw the raising of the great cupola of Saint Peter's, a marvel of engineering thanks mainly to the genius of Michelangelo, who was also responsible for much of the monumental Rome of today. On the other side of the ledger, Gregory XIII saw fit to release the wretched 'Cardinal Montino' from his confinement in Monte Cassino and allow him to return to Rome, where he died destitute and shunned by all.[16]

Ignatius Loyola died in 1556 at the age of sixty-five, perhaps worn out by the constant asceticism he practised. Though he bore no arms and neither did his army of Jesuits, he was a general in the true sense of the word, running the approximately 1,000-strong Society from his austere little room in Rome. The task was a heavy one, and did not benefit his often harsh disposition. Many of his meals were simply a handful of nuts, a chunk of bread and a cup of water. His death may have been unexpected, as it threw the Society of Jesus into two years of confusion. Only in 1558 was Diego Laynez chosen as general – over the objections of some Spanish nobles upset about his Jewish ancestry. Laynez triggered the suspicions of Paul IV, who was afraid he might grow into a rival pope. The concern grew when Francisco Borgia, a great-grandson of Alexander VI Borgia, joined the order, placing his considerable personal wealth at its disposal. Laynez, nicknamed the Black Pope after his unvarying black cassock, ruled until 1565, when Francisco Borgia became the third general of the Jesuits, who by then numbered some 3,500 members in Italy, Europe, the Far East and the New World, where they devoted themselves to preaching, educating and farming.

The year 1565 was notable for one of the signal Christian military successes against the Muslim Ottomans. We have seen how in 1556 Paul IV had been so desperate as to suggest that Ottoman Sultan Süleyman I attack the southern half of his own homeland of Italy to divert the attention of the Neapolitans under the Spanish Duke of Alva who were besieging Rome. Though not taken up at the time, the suggestion seems to have convinced the powerful sultan that western Christendom, already split between Catholics and Protestants, was demoralized and militarily weak as well, and that it might be worthwhile to make a show of strength in the Mediterranean. There was certainly no lack of Muslim imams and strategists who pictured Italy as the weak spot for an eventual attack on the European mainland. But before Süleyman could begin that, he had to eliminate a tiny but resolute outpost of military Christendom standing guard to the south of Sicily – and that was the island of Malta.

When back in 1522 the Ottomans had driven the Knights Hospitaller of Saint John out of Rhodes, there seemed to be nowhere safe to move to in the Turk-controlled East Mediterranean. Pope Hadrian VI, appreciative of what the Hospitallers had been doing in defence of Christendom for four centuries, offered them temporary refuge at Viterbo; the order's grand master, Philippe Villiers de l'Isle Adam, was named Defender of the Faith. Yet neither was Viterbo very secure; though close to Rome and well inside the Papal States, it was too vulnerable as the papacy dithered between the bone-crushing forces of France and the Holy Roman Empire. Morale in the Knights at this time was very low, but de l'Isle Adam resisted an attempt by Clement VII to turn them into an exclusive papal guard along the lines of the Swiss Guard. It was just as well, as the latter was about to be all but annihilated in the Sack of Rome.

At this juncture Charles V, who wanted to keep his Catholic options open, suggested that the Knights settle in Malta. True, it was a more or less barren speck in the Mediterranean, a chunk of ochre sandstone in the middle of nowhere, but boasting some good natural harbours. Out of alternatives, in 1530 de l'Isle Adam accepted the emperor's offer; Malta would be a Rhodes in miniature, a Christian stronghold in a Muslim-threatened and pirate-ridden sea. Over the years the Knights worked hard to turn Malta – the abode of about 12,000 Arabic-speaking peasants and craftsmen ruled by a haughty local French and Catalan nobility that did nothing to make the order feel welcome – into a going concern. The island's main harbour, Birgu, was built up along with the beginnings of a navy that would henceforth be the prime military arm of the Knights of Saint John. Early naval efforts were directed against the ruthless Tunis-based Muslim pirates and these operations inevitably led the Knights to copy the pirates' efforts. The experience thus gained enabled a Saint John's squadron to join several papal galleys in a Spanish-Genoese fleet that swept down on Tunis in May 1535 and ejected the forces of Ottoman Admiral Hayreddin Barbarossa.

In 1557 Jean Parisot de la Valette was elected grand master of the Knights Hospitaller. His election was a classic case of the right man appearing at the right time. His experience included serving as a slave on a Turkish galley, which gave him valuable knowledge of Ottoman naval tactics. A stern moralist, de la Valette banned gambling and prostitutes and recruited engineers to fortify the main harbour with San Michele Castle and Fort Saint Elmo. When in 1564 one of his commanders captured an Ottoman galley with the chief eunuch of Sultan Süleyman on it, the sultan fumed. For years he'd watched those 'pirates bearing crosses' attack Muslim targets in the Mediterranean and decided he'd had enough. Accordingly a large fleet set out from Constantinople in the spring of 1565 with orders from Süleyman to wipe Malta and its Knights off the map.

It looked like being a very one-sided contest. The sultan could command the manpower and resources of half of Eastern Europe, all of Asia Minor, the most productive regions of the Middle East and the whole South Mediterranean basin as far as the Atlantic. Some 180 galleys flying the half-moon standard bore down on perhaps 60 ships and 16,000 men defending Malta. Reinforcing the Knights were about 16,000 men raised by Philip II of Spain and that was all. The strategic significance of Malta, that would loom large in subsequent European history, was now obvious. Whoever controlled the island would control the sea lanes of the Mediterranean. In Muslim hands it would be a priceless jumping-off point for an invasion of the underbelly of Europe. As Pope Pius IV gave his blessing – which was about all he could reasonably do – Don Garcia de Toledo, a nephew of Philip II, helped organize the defence of Malta from Sicily.

The Ottomans carried out several weeks of probing actions until in early June, with the arrival of their commander, Admiral Dragut Reis, they made a determined attempt on Fort Saint Elmo on the tip of the Sciberras promontory. The fort, though stoutly built, had been weakened by a long bombardment from the sea. The Turks went in by night, capturing the fort's seaward side and moving round to the landward tower that was soon reduced to rubble. De la Valette hoped vainly that Toledo would send 600 experienced soldiers to Malta, as he had promised. On 23 June Dragut launched what he hoped would be the decisive hammer blow, but Saint Elmo still held, though its defenders suffered seventy-five per cent casualties while about 5,000 Turks perished, including Dragut Reis himself, hit by a cannonball. The next morning a fresh attack by the new Ottoman commander, Mustafa Pasha, captured the fort. The bodies of dead Knights were tied to crosses and thrown into the harbour. In retaliation, and not to be outdone in savagery, de la Valette beheaded his Ottoman prisoners and used their heads as ammunition for his cannon.[17]

Mere hours after Fort Saint Elmo fell, a small but welcome reinforcement of 600 men under Melchior de Robles made it to Malta. They had been held up by Ottoman intercepts, but successfully entered Birgu on 29 June under cover of a foggy night, and probably thanks to a gap in the Ottoman siege lines connecting the fort with the harbour. Mustafa renewed the attacks on

Birgu in mid-July, but the Knights' artillery in the Castel Sant'Angelo (not to be confused with Rome's famous castle of the same name) smashed a seaborne assault; stakes planted underwater in the harbour accounted for many Ottoman vessels. After a couple of weeks' fruitless bombardment Mustafa Pasha hurled his choice units against San Michele Castle at Senglea, and he may very well have carried the position had not a squadron of Saint John horsemen struck at the Ottoman rear, forcing him to call off the advance.

At the beginning of September Mustafa must have begun to worry that his overall strategic plan had gone wrong. First, the Hospitaller resistance had lasted longer than he or anyone else had expected; he, the supreme admiral of the mighty Ottoman Empire, was still thwarted by this piddling excuse for an island. Second, all armies and navies, going back to ancient times, needed the good weather of late spring, summer and early autumn for fighting. A campaign still not over by, say, October was in serious danger of being aborted as winter quarters had to be sought. Navies powered by sail and oar were almost completely at the mercy of the whims of the weather, which in most parts of the Mediterranean in the autumn is unpredictable. Third, the Ottoman supply line to Constantinople was dangerously long, and as the weeks passed would be increasingly vulnerable to the weather. Mustafa knew he had to carry Malta by the end of September or return to pay the price of defeat with his own head. The issue was in the balance when Don Garcia de Toledo's 16,000 men finally arrived, over a month behind schedule. The night crossing from Sicily had been made in total silence. Toledo landed most of his force before the Ottomans realized what was afoot. A stream of Turkish ships full of demoralized Ottoman soldiers fled into the open sea, ignoring Mustafa's anguished appeals. Malta was free.

The importance of the defence of Malta in 1565 can hardly be overstated. Its capture would have given the Muslim powers a foothold from which to surge into Italy and Western Europe. Already they were in control of Greece and the Balkans, and had advanced almost as far as Vienna. The Knights of Saint John, like the Byzantines and the Spanish monarchs before them, were 'the shield of Christian Europe'.[18] Throughout Europe, pope and prince alike rejoiced. The Knights themselves were flooded with funds which de la Valette used to rebuild Birgu and give it his name by which it is now known – Valletta. Pius IV would have had every reason to be glad that Clement VII's plan to turn the Knights of Saint John into a mere ornamental papal guard had been turned down.

In the year following the siege Pius IV died and was replaced by a former shepherd who had become a professor of theology and had risen to the office of Perpetual Supreme Inquisitor. Michele Ghisleri, who took the name Pius V as a sign that he wished to stay in the favour of the cardinals who had supported his predecessor, was known for his honesty and ascetic way of life. He strongly believed in keeping the Papal States under personal papal control and put more teeth into the Inquisition, drove out Rome's bevies of prostitutes and taxed the nobles' luxuries. Believing that Protestantism should not be handled with kid gloves, Pius V excommunicated England's Queen Elizabeth I (which, however, caused serious problems for England's Catholics). On the constructive side, he cemented a holy alliance with Spain and Venice, which came just in time for Catholic Europe to take the fight against the Ottomans into their own territory.

Chapter 8

The Pope's Navy

In 1570 Spain under Philip II had passed the peak of its power. Though plenty of gold flowed in from the New World, his predecessor Charles V had spent huge sums maintaining an aggressive foreign policy, forcing Philip to raise taxes on his people, strangling potential trade which went instead to the enterprising English and Dutch. But as Europe's strongest Catholic monarchy, Philip's court and state maintained the outward appearance of substantial power. In this he was abetted by popes Paul IV, Pius IV and Pius V, who saw him as the single most important guarantor of the power of the papacy, especially at sea. In the year after the siege of Malta Süleyman had died, but the Ottoman navy was as aggressive as ever; their galleys could often be seen cruising off Italy's east and west coasts. Italians often wondered whether and when the Turks would attack.[1]

The state that stood most to lose from Muslim sea power was Venice, one of two Italian city-states (the other was Genoa) whose very existence and prosperity was bound up with Mediterranean-wide sea trade. For at least a hundred or so years the Venetians had fought to retain their commercial outposts in the Adriatic, the Aegean and as far into the East Mediterranean as they could penetrate. The conflict had expanded into the Balkans, where the Ottomans forced Venice out of most of its Greek possessions. A respite for Venice had come at the start of the sixteenth century when a serious challenge from the Persian Safavi dynasty engaged the sultans' attentions. The Safavis were Shia Muslims who had managed to influence much of the sultan's soldiery. The initial efforts of Sultan Bayezid II to contain the crisis ended in disaster, forcing him to abdicate in favour of his son Selim I.

Of much tougher material than his father, Selim the Grim (*Yavuz*) brought his massed artillery and *Yeni Cheri* (Janissary) units armed with hand-held guns against the Shia Safavis at Chaldiran in August 1514, smashing them to bits. Selim had not stopped there; in a whirlwind campaign he seized Syria and Egypt, handing his son Süleyman the Magnificent a huge basin of grain, timber and other resources which he would use to invade the West. At the same time Venice lost much of its trading capacity to the Ottomans (although the Venetians were allowed to maintain a trading colony in Constantinople). By the 1559 Treaty of Cateau-Cambrésis between France and the Habsburgs, Ottoman ships were banned from using French ports in their forays into the West Mediterranean. More importantly for the Papal States, the treaty bound them into a strategic but rather loose alliance in which the Habsburgs and Spain would have the main say. The line-up against Ottoman expansionism was forming, and destined to meet it was Sultan Selim II, a weak and unhealthy man with a passion for the good things in life, especially alcohol. 'Ugly ... miserly, sordid, lecherous, unrestrained and reckless', according to the Venetian ambassador, Selim the Drunkard seemed to be a poor substitute for his father the Magnificent. Yet his advisers would make up for the judgement he himself lacked.

In Rome Pope Pius V had been busy cleaning the papal house, insisting on higher moral standards for the clergy and performing conspicuous deeds of charity. He was, says one modern writer, 'a giant in an age of giants'.[2] Of course he could by no means ignore the Ottoman menace, and planned ways of meeting it. Most of Europe seemed indifferent: the French actually had an alliance going with the sultan, while the Venetians were reluctant to enter into hostilities, fearing that their Levantine trade, already curtailed, might collapse altogether. This left Spain as Pius' most obvious partner; Philip II promised to contribute to a thrust into Ottoman-held waters as long as he could put together the requisite army and fleet. He made use of his right, granted by the papacy, of taxing the ecclesiastical establishments of Castile and Aragon for five years at a stretch; this tax, the *quinquennio*, raised the funds for forty Spanish and sixty papal galleys. Philip, however, seems to have had his doubts about the prospects of success of a campaign against the Turks. In the late 1560s he was preoccupied with a serious revolt in Flanders which the Duke of Alva put down with great brutality – and which cost the king a lot of money.

Philip found a way of meeting the pope's wishes by enrolling his vassal, Duke Cosimo I de'Medici of Florence and Siena, who was under obligation to bring his 4,000 infantry and four hundred horsemen to help whenever the Spanish holdings of Milan and Naples were threatened. The Florentines were beginning to experiment with naval operations; in early clashes with

Muslim corsairs off the Algerian coast they came off badly, but in 1569 four Florentine galleys with crews belonging to the newly-established Order of Saint Stephen smashed an Ottoman squadron under Kara Ali, freeing two hundred and twenty Christian slaves from the chains of their oar-benches. Pius at first didn't quite trust the Florentines, but he won them over by promoting Cosimo de'Medici to Grand Duke of Tuscany. The problem was that Tuscany was not one of the Papal States; Philip II considered the pope's action completely unlawful and threatened to intervene in Siena. Neither was Emperor Maximilian II very pleased, as Tuscany was Holy Roman Empire territory. All possible cooperation with Pius appeared to have been scuttled.

This disunity among the Christian states of Europe was doubtless good news to the Ottomans. In 1568 the Turks attacked their rebellious vassal in Tunis, taking the city and reducing the Spanish presence in North Africa to a few weak outposts. The Venetians at the time had a peace treaty in effect with the Turks, but the treaty was never very secure. Selim II had his eye on Cyprus, which as a major Venetian trading outpost stuck in the Ottoman craw. Ever since crusading times Cyprus had been a prime way-station for western merchants and armies on their way to the Levant; no Ottoman ruler could feel secure as long as this large island, geographically close to Asia Minor, remained in Christian hands. There was always the problem of leaving enough ships and men behind to guard Cyprus whenever a major sea campaign, such as the attempt on Malta, was planned. Several skirmishes between Turkish and Venetian ships occurred in Cypriot waters, forcing Venice to declare war in the spring of 1570.

A concerned Pius decided that now might be an opportune time for a rapprochement between Venice and Philip II. The Spanish king never had much confidence in the Venetians, who he believed were just out for themselves and would quit an alliance whenever it suited them. In April the pope sent a special Vatican emissary, Monsignor Luis de Torres, to Philip, who after some negotiation agreed to send sixty galleys to Sicily 'to please the Pope and provide always for Christendom's needs'.[3] This clever diplomatic phrase masked Philip's real intention, which was to get the pope and the Venetians to contribute to his planned attacks on North Africa as well as – eventually – the Protestant English. Philip also wanted the papacy to help pay for his own galleys' upkeep. Several months of bickering followed as

Rome, Venice and Spain angled for advantage in the budding alliance. It was agreed fairly quickly that as Philip would be putting up most of the money, his half-brother Don John of Austria would command the fleet that would carry the war into Ottoman seas.

The pope appointed Marcantonio Colonna, a mediocre commander, to lead the papal flotilla of twelve galleys that would form a part of Don John's expeditionary force. But distrusting Colonna's abilities, he added a redoubtable Knight of Saint John, Mathurin Lescaut Romegas, to be Colonna's executive officer. Pius would have been hard put to find anyone better qualified than the forty-three-year-old Romegas to campaign in the Mediterranean. He knew intimately every island, inlet, cove and depth, and had the committed faith to use that knowledge to fight any adversary, Protestant or Muslim. Though he was afflicted with a nervous disorder after a harrowing experience trapped in the hull of a galley sunk by a storm, he overcame it by sheer force of will which, however, made him harsh with his men at times. Many papal subjects also served on board the Tuscan galleys, with about a hundred officers belonging to the Order of Saint Stephen. The pope himself preferred grown men for his forces, banning the recruitment of 'any beardless boy' of the kind who in all ages have tried to get into wars without being old enough – in fact, many underage volunteers were sent home.

Colonna started at Civitavecchia on 21 June and sailed to Naples, picking up his crews on the way. There was not much love lost between the papal troops and the local Spaniards, who brawled bloodily. Colonna's original plan was to wait in Naples for Don John, but Pius sent him new orders to sail on to Messina at the north-east tip of Sicily, where Italians and Spaniards again bloodied each other until Colonna had to hang some men and send others below decks to the oar-benches. Some Venetian squadrons arrived in due course, while Don John himself did not turn up until September, after taking many weeks to make the trip from Spain with its many ceremonial stopovers. Much of the time was also taken up with the tedious process of securing victuals and other supplies for the fleet. But the delay fired the suspicions of the Venetians, who feared that Philip II was none too enthusiastic in committing a large force against the Ottomans and was playing for time to get out of his obligation. In fact, while at Barcelona Don John had received explicit royal instructions not to engage in hostilities unless expressly authorized to do so; Don John, eager for a showdown, bristled at this order but dared not overtly disobey his royal half-brother in Madrid.

Finally, on 23 August, Don John sailed into Messina and called a war council for the following day. Some galleys, mostly Venetian, were still expected to arrive, and Don John felt that it would be better to wait for the Spanish squadrons under the Marquis of Santa Cruz and Giovanni Andrea Doria before he began his strategic planning. Yet distrust still permeated the allied ranks. The Spanish approached Colonna and tried to talk him into lining up his papal ships with theirs instead of the Venetians. Uncertain about what to do, Colonna dithered and even considered resigning his command until Don John, who was impatient to get going and valued the papal flotilla, kept him in place. D-day was set for 16 September: Don John assembled his fleet of 208 Holy League galleys, including squadrons from the Papal States, Spain, Savoy, Florence, Parma, Lucca, Urbino, Genoa and Venice, carrying 50,000 seamen and 29,000 soldiers. Every mast was topped by a crucifix; every flag and banner was blessed by the Jesuit and Capuchin chaplains, and thousands of voices addressed their prayers heavenward. 'Christ is your general', Don John intoned. 'You fight the battle of the Cross!'[4]

The Ottomans, meanwhile, were by no means inactive. One reason for the Venetian jitters was Selim's aggressive probes in the Adriatic and against Crete. It was quite conceivable that the Turks could strike straight across the Adriatic at Venice itself. There was also Cyprus which had to be cleared of its Venetian colonists. Venice, finding itself on the defensive in other theatres, was unable to save Cyprus. Selim's soldiers overran the island, slaughtering 20,000 inhabitants of Nicosia. The last Cypriot outpost to fall was Famagusta; in August, as Don John's fleet was slowly assembling in Messina, the commander of the Venetian defenders, Marcantonio Bragadin, was flayed alive; his skin was stuffed with straw, clad in a red robe, carried about by scoffing Turks and finally sent to the sultan as a present. Don John's men heard of the atrocity after they had set sail from Messina and arrived at Corfu (or, by some accounts, Kephalonia). Their fighting ardour was fired to a white heat. In one stroke the bitter and sometimes murderous rivalry between Italian and Spaniard evaporated. '*Vittoria! Vittoria!* ' the crews yelled as the ships sailed down the north-west coast of Greece and into the Gulf of Patras where the Ottomans lay in wait.

The Holy League fleet sailed in a very loose formation; the scout ships were placed ten miles ahead of the main force, which was not too great a distance to close up in case they encountered the enemy. In the lead was Colonna's papal flagship, a large galley with up to two hundred soldiers on board; right behind sailed Don John's even bigger flagship, the *Real*, flying the standard of Christ crucified, while behind it sailed the flagship of the Venetians under their admiral Sebastiano Venier. Don John had reserved the centre, the strongest part of the fleet, for himself and sixty-three galleys; these included the three galleys of the Maltese Knights of Saint John, eager to avenge the siege of Malta six years before. The Venetian deputy commander, Agostino Barbarigo, took up the left of the line with sixty-three more ships. The right was given to the mostly mixed division of Philip II's Italian admiral, Giovanni Andrea Doria, while Santa Cruz remained in the rear with a large thirty-ship reserve.

The twelve papal warships under Marcantonio Colonna, flaunting the Medici coat of arms and accounting for a total of sixty guns, were distributed along the line at various points and in the reserve in the rear. The typical papal galley was of the *ponentina* type, around forty metres long and some six metres in the beam, with two sails and displacing some two hundred tons. It was pretty much the same type as that used by Genoa, Malta and Spain, powered by up to twenty-four banks of oars. The Venetian-type galley, the *levantina*, stood higher in the water and was consequently faster – some could attain ten knots – but the *ponentina* had larger sails and hence could make better use of the wind. Combat tactics had not changed much since classical times, the object being to disable or board an enemy vessel, and there were limited ways of doing this as long as ships were made of wood and hence vulnerable to ramming or gunfire. On the Ottoman side, the *levantina*-type galleys were generally of poorer construction, often having been put together in haste when the wood was still green. But the Ottomans' fighting men had a more hands-on approach and relied more on their deck-to-deck fighting abilities than on their artillery.[5]

Don John didn't have to look very far for the enemy. Blocking his route off the Greek town of Navpaktos, called Lepanto by the Italians, was a somewhat larger Turkish force commanded by Müezzinzâde Ali Pasha, whose flagship bore a banner with the name of Allah embroidered 29,800 times in gold. He had 222 galleys and 60 smaller ships bristling with cannon and manned by 12,900 sailors (plus 43,000 rower-slaves) and 34,000 soldiers. In the morning of 7 October, when the Holy League fleet was off the West Greek islet of Koutsilaris, it caught sight of the Ottomans.[6] Marcantonio Colonna, for one, had been expecting it; one of his scouts had returned with disquieting reports of enemy strength, and not wishing to be overheard, had whispered to the papal admiral that he had better prepare himself for a stiff fight that same day. When the first sightings were called down from the crow's nests, Don John halted his ship to get the whole fleet into battle order; when it was, he hoisted a green banner on his mainmast and fired one gun to signal a state of battle-readiness.

For all his cool demeanour, Don John was nervous. The observed strength of the enemy was greater than he had thought. As the Holy League crews poised for action he called a meeting of division commanders to ask for their opinions. Some of the Spaniards urged caution, noting that the fleet was now in Ottoman waters and would have nowhere to take refuge in case of defeat; besides, they still had not received any further instructions from Philip II, who they all knew wished to avoid unnecessary hostilities. Others, however, dismissed such talk as defeatist nonsense. Romegas, the doughty Knight of Saint John, appealed to the memory of John's father Charles V who, he said, would never have hesitated and would have surged on 'to Constantinople with ease'.[7] Colonna, too, voted for joining battle, though more out of fatalistic resignation than any fighting ardour. Doria's division tacked to the right, towards the open sea, to allow the fleet to spread out; the necessary manoeuvres took some time in the brisk wind, and a nervously excited Don John had to resort to 'unholy curses' to get everyone in a proper position.

On the other side, Müezzinzâde Ali spread out his own fleet in a crescent formation designed to outflank the Holy League; his original tactical plan, in fact, was envelop the Christian flanks while aiming the main thrust at the enemy centre, hopefully to breach the line in several places to enable his galleys to mop up the disconnected pieces of the Holy League fleet. Müezzinzâde Ali must have been aware that the quality of his fighting men, many if not most of them drawn from subject nations, was inferior to that of the Christians. But he hoped that by sheer weight of ship timber, and by employing it in a mighty blow at the centre while keeping the flanks occupied, he might overcome that handicap. Don John saw what was happening and extended his own lines accordingly. Doria extended his division a little too far, opening up a gap between him and the centre; he was not too concerned, however, as he was confident that if the enemy did break through, Santa Cruz's reserve would be able to deal with it.

Don John donned a suit of glittering armour, picked up a crucifix and stepped into a frigate to check his sector's vessels and where necessary give a little pep talk or two. Colonna did the same for his sector. Back on board the *Real*, Don John heard mass; crews all over the fleet bowed their heads in prayer, and in case anyone had forgotten, the chaplains read Pius V's decree of absolution for anyone who would die fighting the infidel. Just before noon a blank cannon shot sounded from the Ottoman fleet – Müezzinzâde's formal announcement that battle would commence. Don John replied with an actual cannonball. A second blank shot from the Ottomans was answered in a similar manner; Don John was able to gauge his cannons' range from the water columns thrown up by the solid shot. At the sound of trumpets the great Holy League standard of the crucified Christ was hoisted on the *Real*, alongside the banners of the pope, the king of Spain and Venice. Cries of *'Vittoria! Viva Cristo!'* echoed over the waves.

The wind was against the Holy League fleet and aided the Ottomans as they surged forward in an array that would have chilled the blood of even the bravest soldier facing them. The din raised by trumpets, horns and drums echoed across the Gulf of Patras from coast to coast. After the Ottoman fleet had advanced some way the wind – reminiscent of the sudden, almost miraculous midmorning breeze that blew in favour of the Athenians in the 480 BC battle of Salamis – unexpectedly changed; the Turkish ships' momentum evaporated and Don John, watching from the poop deck, must have smiled grimly as he called for his musicians and launched into a sprightly Italian dance designed to breathe new courage into the men watching him.

Four large galleasses – larger and slower versions of the ordinary galleys – stood out as a kind of skirmish line in the sea. They were well-armed with cannon, and when the Turkish ships were about half a mile distant the commander of the galleasses, Francesco Duodo, gave the order for his gunners to fire. The salvoes, likened to 'all one flame', hit the Ottoman fleet like a multiple thunderbolt: chunks of timber and body parts flew through the air. Müezzinzâde Ali was shaken to his core, wondering how he could get out alive. In one case the impact of a Venetian shot lifted a galley out of the water, its oars waving helplessly like the legs of a wounded centipede, before sending it to the bottom with all hands.[8]

This devastating blow threw the Ottoman fleet into chaos. Some crews courageously continued to advance on the galleasses, firing as they went, but the majority backed water in confusion. In short order Müezzinzâde Ali lost a third of his entire force.

At this point the Holy League ships began their advance, but cohesion appears to have been lost as some captains sped ahead impetuously, endangering the whole formation. One Ottoman commander, Suluç Mehmet Pasha, tried to exploit the momentary confusion by swinging around the Christian left, and he might well have turned the flank had not Barbarigo, the Venetian deputy commander, on the *Santa Maria Maddalena* placed himself directly in the Turks' path, defying murderous fire from eight Ottoman galleys at once. Thanks to Barbarigo's heroism the Ottoman attempt to turn the northern flank was halted, buying time for the rest of Don John's fleet. Barbarigo's command included several papal galleys that did their bit in pouring shot into the Turkish hulls. Within a short time the Ottoman right wing was totally shattered, and the victorious Venetians were in no mood to take prisoners (though indications are that the mostly Tuscan papal crews were rather more merciful).

Meanwhile Müezzinzâde Ali himself had recovered from his initial shock and was aiming his flagship, the *Sultana*, straight for the *Real*, at the head of his entire centre division. The clash with the Holy League centre was severe. A Venetian skipper, Giovanni Contarini, described the scene:

Many Turks and Christians had boarded their opponents' galleys fighting at close quarters with short weapons, few being left alive. And death came endlessly from the two-handed swords, scimitars, iron maces, daggers, axes, swords, arrows, harquebuses and fire weapons. [Those] escaping from the weapons would drown by throwing themselves into the sea, thick and red with blood.[9]

With great difficulty the contingent on the *Sultana* managed to board the *Real*. During the vicious hand-to-hand combat Colonna steered his papal ship towards the *Real* to help, but on the way it was struck by an Ottoman vessel that caused it to lurch leftwards and hit in turn the *Sultana*, whereupon

Colonna's ship was hit from behind by another Turkish ship. In the middle of the deadly fight over the *Real* the Venetian commander Venier made for the *Sultana* but found his way blocked by more Ottoman ships; the captains of two Venetian galleys speeding to help him were killed. With the Ottomans now clearly trying to break the Holy League line, Santa Cruz deployed his reserve.

Colonna was still engaged in trying to extricate his galley from the meleé surrounding it when another papal ship, the *Grifona*, leased to the pope by Cosimo de'Medici and skippered by Alessandro Negroni, resolutely fought off an attack by two Ottoman galleys until relieved by a galley from the reserve. When the immediate pressure on Colonna was off, he was faced with the choice of hastening to the aid of the *Real* or finishing off another enemy galley. His deputy Romegas was all for attacking another ship but Colonna thought it better to help his commander and steered towards the beleaguered *Real*. On board his flagship, Müezzinzâde Ali fought valiantly to the last; he is believed to have perished in one of three ways: killed by a harquebus ball in the head, beheaded by a Spanish soldier or slitting his own throat in despair. What is certain is that his head was stuck on a spike and raised aloft to cries of '*Vittoria! Vittoria!*' from the survivors of the Holy League crews. But the battle was not yet over by a long shot.

The fight had not been going so well on the Holy League right, where Doria found he had to extend his line farther to the south and the open sea; the commander on the Ottoman left, Uluç Ali, had manoeuvred to get out of the way of the galleasses' fire and in the process attempted to outflank Doria's line. In this way a mile of sea opened between Doria and the rest of the fleet, but inexplicably, Uluç Ali made no apparent attempt to take advantage of the widening gap; perhaps his crews were unnerved by the constant gunfire from the stationary galleasses. But neither did Doria make any aggressive move, being content to block what seemed to be the Ottoman admiral's attempt to outflank him. Uluç Ali's unexpected moment came when he saw that a mere handful of Venetian galleys had become detached from Doria's main force and were thinly strung out over the mile-wide gap.

Masked by billows of thick smoke, the Ottoman headed straight for this flimsy screen; Doria saw what was happening and led a dozen fast galleys in chase, but too late – Uluç Ali's hardened Algerian pirates smacked into the Venetian line. The carnage was horrifying. Captain and crewman alike fell under the Ottomans' assault, the decks of the disabled Venetian vessels filled with piles of bloody bodies. Next to be attacked was the flagship of the Knights of Saint John, captained by Pietro Giustiniani. Uluç Ali had a personal score to settle here, as he had played a part in the siege of Malta and still burned with humiliation at the Ottoman defeat. The hand-to-hand combat on the Knight's ship was merciless until Giustiniani bought off the Algerian attackers with money and silver. Giustiniani's Muslim slave rowers had meanwhile mutinied, and the sale was the only way he and what remained of his crew could survive.

Uluç Ali now swung round behind the Holy League centre with at least fifty galleys, mopping up isolated League ships. But his turned out to be the only Ottoman success in a battle that elsewhere had gone against them. As Doria sped up from the right, the rest of the Christian fleet turned in on Uluç Ali. The fighting was intense, with severe casualties on both sides, but in the end the Ottoman commander, outnumbered and outgunned, was forced towards the Koutsilaris islets. He himself escaped through a narrow channel, leaving many of his men to either surrender, continue to fight stubbornly in pockets, to drown in the sea or be shot as they floundered in it. By late afternoon it was clear that Don John had won. The weather was closing in, and the Holy League fleet retired to safe havens just before a thunderstorm hit. Marcantonio Colonna received Don John's hearty gratitude on board the *Real* that evening, though many of the officers and men fervently believed that the Almighty was really the one to thank.

In the Battle of Lepanto some 20,000 Holy league soldiers and sailors were killed and wounded, against at least 35,000 Ottomans – the discrepancy is probably attributed to the Christian troops' wearing bulletproof armour.[10] About 800 papal troops died and 1,000 were wounded. At least 12,000 Christian slaves labouring on Ottoman vessels were freed from their shackles. To the surviving participants, the battle was the experience of a lifetime. One of them was Miguel de Cervantes, who received a wound in the left hand which, as he later quipped, would free his right hand to pen *Don Quixote* in later years. He remembered the encounter as 'the most memorable occasion that either past or present ages have beheld, and which perhaps the future will never parallel'.[11] As the fleet sailed back to Corfu, Colonna had to settle the inevitable spats between the Venetians and Spaniards, this time exacerbated by conflicting claims over the spoils. On 27 October Don John left for Sicily on the instructions of Philip II.

Don John of Austria leaves behind a glittering reputation as one of those men, in the company of Roland and Byzantine emperor Leo III the Isaurian, who halted what could have turned out to be Muslim conquests of Europe. Field Marshal Montgomery of Alamein salutes Don John as both a fearless and clever commander and an able diplomat who could keep order and discipline in a notoriously fractious allied fleet.[12] The victory, though, did not improve the strategic position of Catholic Europe in the Mediterranean; its value was less strategic than moral – it proved that nations loyal to the pope could stop the aggressive Turk in his tracks without the help of Protestant Northern Europe that to all appearances had taken no part in the momentous showdown.

When news of Lepanto reached Rome by fast courier from the papal nuncio in Venice on 21 October, Pius V must have smiled knowingly; two weeks before, on the very evening of 7 October, long before anything could be known about what was happening at that hour far away in the Gulf of Patras, he had been conducting business with his treasurer when on an impulse he walked over to his window and gazed over the rooftops of Rome bathed in the setting sun. There he may have prayed, as he had done for several weeks, agonizing over the Muslim menace. When he turned away, he somehow knew what had occurred, and smiling contentedly told the treasurer to put away his documents and instead join with him in thanking God, as 'this very moment our fleet has defeated the Turks'.[13]

He at first told no-one else; despite his metaphysical certainty, he wisely waited for the official news to arrive to let Rome know. When it did, the city erupted in joy. Don John was the hero of the hour. Of the 117 Turkish galleys that he had captured, 10 went to the pope, who likened the admiral to John the Baptist as described in John 1:6: 'There was a man sent from God …'.[14] The churches echoed to celebratory masses, cannon shots boomed over the rooftops (though Pius grumbled at the waste of powder) and bonfires lit up the streets. The seventh day of June, echoing past Byzantine Orthodox practice, was consecrated to Our Lady of Victory. (In 626 the Byzantines had beat back an assault on Constantinople by the heathen Avars, a victory attributed to the Virgin Mary, whose icon was held up on the walls and in a timeless hymn hailed as the 'Champion General' of the Greeks.)

Marcantonio Colonna, the commander of the papal squadron, received his due praise from the pope, who insisted on awarding him a grand processional entry into Rome in the manner of the ancient consuls. On 4 December the parade entered Rome from the south and wound its way up past ecstatic crowds to Saint Peter's, accompanied by the thunder of cannon from Sant'Angelo Castle. The procession included several Ottoman prisoners in chains; the pope had scotched a foolish and barbarous Venetian resolution that all enemy prisoners should be massacred. The whole Colonna clan was there to greet Marcantonio who brought up the rear riding a white horse and clad in a black robe. But even here a sour note injected itself, as rival noble families, jealous of the fame of the Colonna, snubbed the whole thing.

Pius knew that the victory of Lepanto, though brilliant, was only partial. The Ottomans had merely been halted, not pushed back. The Muslims were still in iron control of the whole East Mediterranean. But, Pius thought, might not another resolute attack recover some of the subject Christian lands such as Greece? He threw himself into plans for a grand crusade to finish what Lepanto had left unfinished. But the French put their spanner in the works – they needed their alliance with the sultan against both Philip II of Spain and the Holy Roman Empire. Philip himself was preoccupied with rivalry with England and Venice, and had no desire to see the latter monopolize Mediterranean trade. The Holy League thus barely outlasted its greatest victory and died altogether with Pius himself in May 1572.

The new pope, Gregory XIII, was more cautious than his predecessor. In this he took his cue from Philip II, who was now quite absorbed with problems in Flanders and the Netherlands and feared an imminent war with France. He could not afford to keep large numbers of men afloat in the East Mediterranean, and wrote to Don John, who was languishing inactive in Messina, ordering him to use any stratagem to delay another expedition. Don John, eager for a second round and 'feeling more and more lonely each day', was disappointed.[15] With Pius dead he had lost his most fervent champion. But when word leaked that Philip intended to go after the Barbary pirates in North Africa, and the news broke that a new Ottoman fleet was making aggressive moves, the Venetians agitated for a new expedition to the East. Don John in fact had already taken some of his force to Palermo to prepare for a descent on the Barbary pirates' bases when he received orders to turn about and proceed with all speed to Corfu. Also heading east was Colonna with fifty-seven galleys with which he joined Santa Cruz and other Venetian units.

Don John signalled Colonna and the other commanders to wait for him in Corfu. But Colonna and the Venetians were eager to attack the Ottomans before they could build up their forces, and went on the offensive in defiance of orders. The opposing fleets collided off the Greek island of Kythera on the south-east tip of the Peloponnese. There was a brief but confused encounter, in which Colonna in the centre failed to bring the elusive enemy to heel and in the end broke off the action, returning to Corfu at the end of August. A furious Don John tore a strip off his disobedient commanders and planned a new drive south. On 16 September his fleet arrived off Navarino (ancient Pylos) to find the Ottomans unapproachable in a safe anchorage. Discouraged, he sailed back to Messina towards the end of October.

None of this would have mattered much to Gregory XIII, safe behind the bulwark of the king of Spain. But the Venetians were another matter; their ruling mercantile class saw nothing but a loss of trade in the constant clashes with the Turks, and sought to reverse the trend. After a string of secret negotiations, on 7 March 1573 Venice and the Ottoman Empire signed a treaty of peace that gave the Venetians trading posts on the East Adriatic coast, plus the Greek island of Zakynthos. The pope's reaction was explosive. When the Venetian ambassador to Rome informed him of the treaty, Gregory sprang from his chair and ordered the diplomat from the room, roaring excommunication threats which the Venetians by now knew would be ineffectual anyway. Colonna himself remained under a cloud until given a job by Philip as viceroy of Sicily. There he was accused of mismanagement and arrogance; he died in 1584 while travelling to Madrid to answer the charges.

The sixteenth century was a time of progress in naval technology and tactics. England under Henry VII, being on the edge of the Atlantic and poised to exploit the New World, had made great strides in building sailing ships. Henry VIII's ship designers made a breakthrough in firepower by placing cannon on the cargo decks rather than in the bow or stern, and cutting holes in the bulwarks for the guns to shoot through, thus enabling broadsides to be fired. By about 1580 both England and Spain developed the galleon out of the older galleass, some displacing as much as 1,000 tons. It would be some time, however, before the Mediterranean-friendly galley was fully superseded, and in the meantime one Mediterranean power, with the pope's backing, almost single-handedly defended Christian seas against the ubiquitous Muslim pirates. This was the Malta-based Knights Hospitaller Order of Saint John.

From the outset of their career in late-eleventh-century Jerusalem, the Knights Hospitaller had considered themselves a fighting force in the service of the pope. But just what 'service to the pope' meant was always rather ambiguous. Though Pope Paschal II had formally named the Hospitallers an official military order, the upper channel of command from pope downwards was never really defined. Every knight, of course, owed formal allegiance to the pope as a basic requirement of membership, but taking direct orders from the pope was another matter. Jerusalem and Palestine were far away from Rome, and naturally the Knights Hospitaller found it easier to coordinate their actions with the Frankish rulers of Outremer, and where these were weak, to take action on their own. The successful defence of Malta in 1565 boosted the order with a new pride that, as we have seen, enabled it to acquit itself well in the Battle of Lepanto. Those three galleys of Saint John were subsequently parlayed into a formidable Maltese navy that became known in Catholic Europe as the Navy of the Religion.

It could be argued that the Maltese navy was an arm of the Spanish navy, as their aims were identical: to keep the Mediterranean seaways free of Muslim corsairs. Its professionalism, by all accounts, may well have been superior to the Spanish. Every knight of Saint John was required to serve three 'caravans,' or terms of six months, on board a galley to gain experience in the *corso*, a general term for naval campaigning. To be sure, many if not most of these campaigns degenerated into little more than piracy, itself a useful adjunct to the Spanish operations. Fighting the wily Muslims required being wily oneself, and few cared to analyse tactics from a purely moral point of view. Thus English and Dutch merchantmen trading with the Ottoman Empire sometimes found themselves under attack. The more successful a Hospitaller galley captain was, by either fair means or foul, the more chances he had of becoming a Grand Master of the order. The point to be made here is that the Navy of the Religion, though maintaining its aggressive independence, rarely hesitated to join the papal naval forces whenever called upon to do so in the following two centuries.[16]

Chapter 9

Digging In

T he Rome of the end of the sixteenth century was a city that had settled into a comfortable existence under a series of popes who had lavished extensive care on its upkeep. In 1580 it had about 100,000 inhabitants, a good number of them 'criminals and prostitutes'.[1] New wealthy families had arisen to elbow the old Colonna and Orsini aside and forge power links with the papacy, such as the Aldobrandini, Barberini, Farnese and Rospigliosi. Gregory XIII, aged seventy when he was elected, was a competent pontiff who gave the world today's Gregorian calendar but otherwise concerned himself little with the world's affairs. However, he approved of the butchery of French Protestants in the Saint Bartholomew massacre of 1572, an attitude not calculated to improve ties with the rising Protestant North, especially as he nursed a plot to depose England's Elizabeth I. The Holy Year of 1575 brought another cascade of pilgrims and their money into Rome – which issued its very first tourist maps and brochures for the occasion – but eventually he was unable to solve chronic problems of tax evasion and brigandage in his realm.

The next pope, Sixtus V, took office in 1585. Born near Ancona in such poor circumstances that he would later joke that he came from an 'illustrious house' – that is, a cottage whose roof was so full of holes that it let the light in – he rose in the clergy by his own abilities until at the age of sixty-four he was picked as the man who could make the Vatican solvent and strong again. Contemporaries described Sixtus as 'broad, strongly built … [with] piercing eyes that could silence opposition without a word'.[2] Such a strong character, it seems, had to have its tempestuous side, which spent itself in a workaholic routine. He showed what stuff he was made of on the day before his coronation when he sentenced four youths found to have been carrying prohibited weapons to be hanged. Deaf to the heart-rending pleas of the youths' families, he had the boys strung up; their swinging bodies were visible on the Sant'Angelo bridge during the nearby coronation celebrations.

No social class was immune from Sixtus' crackdown on crime; families of known bandits were threatened with mass execution if they refused to bring them in; the countryside around Rome was studded with corpses suspended from gallows – high-born miscreants were punished along with the humbler sort, and not even a crooked priest or two was exempt. Those who were beheaded had their heads nailed to the Sant'Angelo bridge as a deterrent. A priest and a youth who were found having a homosexual relationship were both burned; a mother who sold her daughter into prostitution was hanged, and the daughter forced to watch. Adultery became a capital crime. There were naturally protests against this severity. The pope's detractors claimed he was unbalanced, even insane. A wry saying made the rounds that 'Pope Sixtus would not even pardon Christ'.[3] But travellers such as diplomats and merchants marvelled at the sudden peace and security they found on the roads.

Sixtus was able to impose his extreme views of the papal office because the climate of the papacy at the time seemed to require it. Protestantism had now consumed all of Northern Europe, and in strategic terms posed a threat equal to the Muslims at the opposite side of the continent. In 1588 Philip II sent his Armada to hopefully neutralize England's Protestant monarchy, but got his nose bloodied, and Spain's prestige took a severe blow. A year later King Henry IV of France (Henry of Navarre) was crowned in a compromise with France's own Protestants after decades of civil conflict; though officially a Catholic, the French king in 1598 issued the Edict of Nantes that established religious toleration. The message for the Papal States was that henceforth France would not automatically be a papal ally.

With such troubled horizons, it was understandable that Sixtus' strong-armed policies were his remedy for the general insecurity of his domains. The pope was the unquestioned absolute ruler of Rome and the Papal States, protected by an army and navy and Rome's first proper police force. Apart from the Curia and the cardinals – and pliable noble houses – there was no-one and nothing to limit that personal power. Many intimidated cardinals stayed in their dioceses, eroding their influence in Rome. Anyone now calling on the pope had to kiss his foot (though his knee was allowed for bishops). Any letter to him had to end with the ritual phrase: 'I kiss your holiness's holiest feet.' It was common for sycophants to call him 'Patriarch of the Whole World.' Gregory XIII even went so far as to accept the title of 'Vice-God'.[4]

There was no parliament or any kind of consultative body that could, however incompletely, represent the mass of people or redress grievances. Yet there is scant evidence of any major complaints. The great majority of papal subjects, knowing nothing and caring less about democratic theory, wanted to practise their Catholicism in peace and go about their daily lives with some modicum of security. If they caught a rare glimpse of the pontiff in his magnificent robes, playing the part of the Almighty's deputy on earth, they probably felt a sense of security rather than resentment. Moreover, even if a pope proved to be cruel or otherwise manifestly ungodlike, it was the papal office that was revered rather than the individual occupying it, and therefore there could be no cause for disrespect.

The other side of the security coin was, of course, intolerance. Sixtus maintained the rigours and cruelties of the Inquisition. When he died in 1590 after a mere five years on the throne, he was followed by three short-lived popes in the space of sixteen months: Urban VII, Gregory XIV and Innocent IX, who were merely place-holders. In 1592 a member of Rome's powerful Aldobrandini family became Pope Clement VIII, who was an even crustier and more austere pontiff than Sixtus. A true figure of the Counter-reformation with its emphasis on a thoroughgoing spiritual reform of the Catholic Church as a response to the Protestant wave, Clement spent much of his day in prayer and meditation. In the administrative sphere he decreed severe penalties for anyone throwing rubbish in the streets and organized the Holy Year of 1600 to showcase the capital of Catholicism, providing food and shelter for the many thousands of visitors; a few dozen Protestants were sufficiently impressed, it was said, to return to the mother Church. But that same year saw the burning at the stake of the freewheeling philosopher Giordano Bruno and two other convicted heretics in the centre of Rome.

In the foreign policy sphere Sixtus had eagerly seconded Philip II's despatch of the Spanish Armada to bring back England to the Catholic heel, but had wisely made any practical help contingent on an actual landing, which thanks to the efforts of Lord Howard of Effingham never took place. When Henry of Navarre, a Protestant Huguenot, seemed poised to seize Paris, Sixtus allowed it to happen on condition that Henry become a Catholic, which he did. Clement VIII at first helped Spain and Austria in the Thirty Years' War which embroiled the Holy Roman Empire in conflict with Protestant states. But when the Austrians made threatening moves on Mantua the pope changed sides and encouraged the pressures on the empire by the French and the Protestant king of Sweden, Gustavus Adolphus. Proving himself to be a political realist, Clement seized the finances of Urbino to bankroll a papal campaign against Spanish-controlled Parma. The campaign, besides being an utter failure, seriously depleted the papal reserves of money and morale.

The Jesuits, meanwhile, were flourishing. The Counter-reformation had triggered a surge of new piety in the average European Catholic, rich or poor. Jesuit schools, besides being free, strove to inculcate knowledge, devotion and nobility into their students; even for Protestants they were the only serious sources of education in the classics and religion. The early Jesuit insistence on military-style physical and mental discipline paid off well; by 1615 the order operated 372 colleges around the world. The fourth Jesuit general, Claudio Acquaviva, wanted to keep his members away from politics and the lures of frequenting the halls of power. But one Jesuit became the spiritual mentor of France's Henry IV; it was by then agreed that 'the best way to mould a nation is to mould its king'.[5]

In 1610 Henry IV, while riding through the streets of Paris, was felled by an assassin. As his son and heir, Louis XIII, was just eight years old, Henry's widow Marie de' Medici took over as regent. She proved to be woefully inadequate for the task, spending recklessly, favouring the nobility and in short, undoing almost every one of her late husband's reforms. Marie reversed Henry's anti-Habsburg policies and sought a marriage alliance with Spain. Louis, meanwhile, was all but neglected; chronically ill and sickly, he tried to make up for it by training himself to endure hardship with the army. His character, however, was stouter than his body. When he was still sixteen he plotted to do away with his mother's latest court favourite, and when she protested he had her banished from the court. In April 1621, at the urging of Pope Paul V, he launched a campaign against the Huguenots that ended inconclusively. On the dynastic side, however, there was a problem; Louis was openly gay, and it wasn't until he was thirty-seven that he could be persuaded to father a son by his official wife, Anne of Austria. Until then, however, a strong hand was required at the administrative helm of France, and Louis found one in the person of a cardinal who, it seems, was intent on promoting the model of a strong centralized Catholic state like the papacy in Rome.

Armand Jean de Plessis de Richelieu was just twenty-one when Henry IV nominated him for bishop of Luçon. For confirmation he had to go to Rome, but being actually two years too young for the post he lied about his age. After hearing the young Frenchman deliver a speech in flawless Latin, Paul V had no hesitation in awarding him the Luçon see, whereupon Jean admitted his lying, forcing an admiring pope to remark: 'This youth will be a great knave.'[6] Richelieu still had not reached forty when Louis XIII made him a cardinal and then prime minister of France. His resolute character became evident in 1627 when he supervised the blockade of the Huguenot-held port of La Rochelle and forced its starved inhabitants, surviving on stray cats, to surrender. His treatment of the defeated Protestants was lenient, contrary to the wishes of many French Catholics; he had the canny good sense to recognize that the commercial and business talents of the Huguenots could be put to good use in helping build up the French state as Europe's most formidable power.

Richelieu was one of the first European statesmen to base all his actions on the basis of *raison d'état* – the principle that all political action should be judged as good or bad according to whether it benefited the state and its security. The good of the state was the supreme good, higher than any principles of individual good. This was, in fact, precisely the stance of the Counter-reformation popes; the Catholic faith, properly and morally practised, outweighed in importance any personal political or religious belief. It was no accident that Richelieu was a cardinal. He recognized – though it's quite unfashionable to hold such views in our 'democratic' age – that state morality was different from personal private morality. The state contained millions of people whose general interest had to be looked after, and therefore, in the interests of the many, much of what in private life we would consider evil – killing, theft, torture, lying – was not only allowable but sometimes very necessary on the state level for the nation as a whole to survive. And if it could be done with God's blessing, all the better. Not for nothing has Richelieu been called 'the father of the modern state system'.[7] Durant, more cynically, avers that he knew 'he could not afford to be good'.

Though Richelieu was hugely important to the history of France in the seventeenth century, followed by another cardinal, the Italian Guilio

Mazzarino (better known as Mazarin), who continued his policies, the effect on the papacy in Rome was mixed. The city itself was in the full flower of a wave of baroque artistic brilliance, where military affairs took second place to art and culture. Popes moved into ever-grander quarters; one of them was a new palace on the Quirinal Hill (now the residence of Italy's presidents) that was first occupied by Paul V, supplemented later by a sprawling villa at Castel Gandolfo south of Rome that still serves as papal summer quarters. The ceremonial surrounding the papacy became ever more elaborate, symbolized by the flamboyantly-attired sentinels of the Swiss Guard. It all may have served as compensation for a papacy that feared a resurgent France and cannot have looked kindly on Richelieu's full absorption of the French clergy into the state mechanism.

In was in the last years of Paul V's pontificate that the storm clouds of a general European war, which had been building for years blown up by the rivalry of Catholic and Protestant, broke over the uneasy continent. The newly-powerful France of Cardinal Richelieu, the problems of the Habsburgs in controlling their far-flung possessions, and rebellious tendencies among the Protestant princelings of Germany all fused to explode in 1618. Triggering the Thirty Years' War was a revolt in Bohemia by its Calvinist Protestants, who threw the representatives of the Holy Roman Empire out of the windows of a palace in Prague. The new emperor, Ferdinand II, a fanatical Catholic, mobilized the Catholic League including Spain and the papacy to punish the revolt. An attempt by the Bohemian rebels to enlist outside support fizzled, and they were crushed in battle near Prague in late 1520. The victorious Catholics then embarked on a campaign of revenge. The leading rebels were executed; 'for ten years twelve severed skulls grinned from the tower of the Charles Bridge over the Moldau.'[8] This and other severities prompted King Christian IV of Denmark to invade North Germany in support of the beleaguered Protestants in 1625.

At this stage Ferdinand turned to a remarkably able military adventurer named Albrecht von Wallenstein, a former Protestant who had recently converted to Catholicism more out of opportunism than any genuine promptings of faith. Wallenstein turned his genius for making money and winning influence into competent generalship. His almost limitless wealth enabled him to recruit some 50,000 mercenaries from all over Europe, regardless of which creed they professed. With this army he drove out the

Danes at Lutter and proceeded to establish himself along the Baltic coast in a kind of military dictatorship to serve the interests of the empire. Ferdinand, suspicious of this, urged Wallenstein to employ his superior abilities in the cause of the Catholic League rather than himself. The general in his turn was becoming alienated by the emperor's insistence on Catholic vengeance and made his peace with Christian of Denmark; the growing rift ended with Wallenstein's dismissal in 1620 (and murder four years later).

Wallenstein had been prescient; for some time he had been aware that Sweden would enter the war in the person of King Gustavus Adolphus, who saw in the turmoil a chance to carve out some extra territory in Northern Europe as a territorial buffer for Swedish security. In fact, he wanted the Baltic Sea to be essentially a Swedish lake. Gustavus Adolphus had been battling continuously to this end for nearly twenty years, against Denmark, Russia and Poland, to earn the sobriquet 'Lion of the North'. The Swedish Protestant king, aided by funds from France, swept across Germany to besiege Berlin, smash the imperial army at Breitenfeld in September 1631 and again at Lützen in November 1632. The most shocking incident of this phase of the war was the destruction of Magdeburg by pro-Catholic forces under the Count of Tilly. For four days, according to a contemporary writer:

> There was naught but beating and burning, plundering, torture and murder ... [Magdeburg was] given over to the flames, and thousands of innocent men, women and children, in the midst of a horrific din of heart-rending shrieks and cries, were tortured and put to death in so cruel and shameful a manner that no words would suffice to describe, nor tears to bewail it.[9]

The elderly Tilly himself, unable to stop the butchery, feared correctly that it would add fire to the Protestant cause. And sure enough Gustavus Adolphus, leading what has been called 'the most formidable military machine in Europe', became master of the field, only to perish at Lützen, where the wind suddenly went out of the Swedish sails.[10] In 1634 the Swedes were worsted at Nördlingen, and the two exhausted sides signed the Peace of Prague the following year.

And there the issue might have rested had not Richelieu taken fright at the resurgence of Habsburg power; his concern was for a defensive position along France's eastern frontiers, especially on the Rhine – a concern that still applies, albeit lurking beneath the thin mantle of European 'unity.' After securing alliances with Sweden, the Netherlands and the Duchy of Savoy on the Italian frontier, the French attacked Austria and Spain simultaneously. For thirteen dreary and bloodstained years the French hacked away at the Habsburgs, trouncing the Spaniards at Rocroi in 1643. Cardinal Mazarin carried on Richelieu's war policy, gradually eroding Habsburg power with the help of the Swedes in the north.

The Thirty Years' War sputtered out when the Habsburgs threw in the towel and agreed to the Peace of Westphalia of 1648. France grabbed Alsace, Sweden came away with territory on the North German and Polish coast, and most of Germany was confirmed under Protestant princelings. Ferdinand III had to make do with an emasculated Holy Roman Empire centring on Austria, the heartland of the Habsburgs. The structure of what was to become modern Europe, with large nation-states assuming the role of principal actors in international politics, began to take shape.

We have gone into this admittedly gross oversimplification of the Thirty Years' War because it was the last, longest and worst of Europe's religious wars, and by that fact was of vital importance to the Papal States. It had been some time since papal troops had fought in any of Italy's territorial wars – the era of the *condottieri* had long since passed – and we don't know whether any papal subjects were among those who volunteered to join Wallenstein's Catholic League army. But the wider implications of the Protestant ascendancy and the humiliation of the Habsburgs surely were not lost on the Vatican. The French monarchy might still be technically Catholic, but any potential advantage from that quarter was effectively ruled out by the *Realpolitik* of Richelieu and Mazarin, who threw their weight behind the Protestant cause even though they themselves were cardinals of the Church! Nationalism had finally overridden religion as the determinant of a nation's policies.

It is legitimate to wonder whether any pope or cardinal or senior papal official living the good life in Rome realized the immense tectonic shift in European history that had just taken place at Westphalia. Had it or had it not become apparent that from now on religion would not be a prime cause of European war? The entire military policy of the papacy, from its earliest years, had been predicated on fighting for the Catholic faith and specifically safeguarding the Papal States from aggression or civil unrest. The popes had no interest in expanding into non-papal or foreign lands (with the possible exception of the Crusades or Orthodox Byzantium before the fifteenth century), no imperialist impulse to seize raw materials or expand trade at the expense of others. The military policy of the Papal States was basically a defensive one against potential aggression, from other Italians as well as Protestants and Muslims. The domain of Christ, centred on the domes and church bells of Rome, must not be aggressive but preservative. It had been just a hundred or so years since the ferocious German '*Lanzichenecchi*' had wrought their fearful horrors on Rome, and the collective memory of that event was still relatively fresh. With Germany now largely in Protestant hands, who could be sure that the Germans might not carry their war to the Catholic heartland? We may imagine that these issues were earnestly debated in the Vatican, but with no definite outcome. Thus the papacy entered the new world of secular European nation-states unaware that the consequences of the Peace of Westphalia would eventually determine its political fate.

Paul V's successor Gregory XV lasted just two years, to be followed by Urban VIII, a member of the wealthy Barberini clan, whose dubious contribution to Vatican defence was taking the bronze destined for eighty cannon in Sant'Angelo Castle and using it to forge the magnificent *baldacchino* in Saint Peter's – supplemented by nearly 10,000 metal spikes pulled from the Pantheon in central Rome. Caustic messages appeared on the Pasquino statue playing on the pope's surname; one read: 'What the barbarians failed to do, the Barberini did.'[11] Urban needed even more precious metal to fund the 1625 Holy Year, and had to resort to hiking taxes, which did nothing for his popularity. Another stain on his reputation was his condemnation of Galileo to imprisonment for astronomical heresy, later commuted to house arrest.

As a Barberini, Urban seems to have inherited the tendency to clan conflict endemic in Italian political life. When in 1641, following bad advice from his self-seeking relatives, he attempted to seize the duchy of Castro and Ronciglione from the Farnese family, the head of the family, Odoardo Farnese, defied him. Brushing off the excommunication thrown at him, Farnese gathered troops and marched on Rome. As the pope quit his favourite Quirinal Palace for the better security of the Vatican, he recruited a militia of sorts to stem Farnese's advance. He was unable to find allies, as the acquisitiveness of the Barberini was well known. Farnese, on the other hand, received the eager backing of France (ever eager to fish in troubled Italian waters) and a league of North Italian states (ever eager to see the papal wings clipped). Three years of intermittent clashes with the untrained papal forces ended with the latter's decisive defeat north of Rome.[12] By the 1644 Treaty of Venice the pope faced bankruptcy, which he could stave off only by raising taxes further and losing whatever public respect had remained to him. By the time of his death in 1644, four years before the end of the Thirty Years' War, Urban had left his state in a dangerous state of diplomatic isolation.

What was called the War of Castro revealed the weakened military condition of the papacy after decades of spending huge sums of money on personal, family and urban luxuries. It was as if the spirit of the Counter-reformation, with its inward-looking emphasis on preserving the Catholic status quo, had all but given up thoughts of projecting the Papal States' power. Pope Innocent X continued this timidity, buttressed by untrammelled nepotism designed to secure his own personal power base. As a member of the influential Pamphili family, he too was steeped in the tradition of looking out for one's own and thwarting the ambitions, real and imagined, of rival families. He was, in fact, under the almost complete domination of his sister-in-law Olimpia Pamphili, a cunning and autocratic social climber who revelled in intrigue, theft, and all the other dark arts of the backstage of power. Furtive notes on the Pasquino statue claimed that Donna Olimpia was the pope's mistress; that cannot be corroborated, but without doubt she was an unofficial *papessa*, wielding her considerable influence without scruple and personally organizing the Holy Year of 1650. Her clout, however, did not outlive Innocent, who died in 1655, and she herself succumbed to plague two years later.[13]

The immediate problem facing Innocent's successor, Alexander VII, was a cold war with France, which had backed the campaign against Urban VIII and was now asserting the total independence of the French clergy from the popes. On the French throne sat Louis XIV, just sixteen and still a long way from his fabled 'Sun-King' years. Alexander's involvement in the complex negotiations leading to the Treaty of Westphalia had given him an intense dislike of the French, including the originally-Italian Cardinal Mazarin, the king's first minister. In the conclave following Urban's death Mazarin had tried to veto Alexander's election. The young Louis, moreover, ordered his ambassador in Rome to create as many petty difficulties for the pope as possible. Alexander, for his part, could not see how officially-Catholic France could in good conscience ally itself with powers such as Protestant Sweden. The tensions erupted in August 1662, when a brawl between the pope's Corsican Guard and the French ambassador's security men resulted in the death of an ambassadorial servant. Louis XIV responded by severing diplomatic ties with the Papal States and sending troops to seize Avignon, the old papal domain in France. There was little Alexander could do but accept humiliating terms that included giving the French king the right to nominate Catholic bishops.

To one faction in the College of Cardinals, this new phase of French domination was not to be tolerated. But as the papacy was weak and France was strong, a policy of inner reform was seen to point to a way out, like the Counter-reformation after the emergence of the Protestant powers. For too long, too many cardinals had served the interests of powers such as France or the Holy Roman Empire or Spain, often putting those interests ahead of their allegiance to the pope. This ingrained practice had seriously threatened the independence of a papacy that after 1648 had turned inwards on itself, as if somehow it could shut out the noise of the new, emergent nation-state system. A part of this defence mechanism had been a resurgence of nepotism – never fully absent even under the sternest pontiffs – and a comfortable sense that in order to become pope, an ambitious cardinal need only belong to the right clique.

Eleven cardinals led by Pietro Ottoboni got together in a movement to abolish secrecy in cardinals' conclaves and bias in papal diplomacy; all secular powers were to be treated equally, with no single one allowed to exert undue influence in Vatican affairs. The same should apply, they said, in the seventy-strong College of Cardinals, which was no place for partisanship and group machinations. From the nickname bestowed on it by a Spanish diplomat – the Flying Squadron (*Squadrone Volante*) – the group's purpose and influence appear to have been clear: to act as a moral riot squad engaged in cleaning up the papal administration to make it less susceptible to criticism from secular Europeans and lend it some ethical clout, which was always useful at times when the papacy was called upon to fight, either diplomatically or militarily.[14] Accordingly, from this point the proportion of Italian cardinals in the college began to rise.

Alexander VII was the first pope elevated by the Flying Squadron in defiance of France and Spain, which had long been used to engineering papal elections by ordering the cardinals of their respective nationalities to support or boycott anyone they did not favour. One surprising champion of the Flying Squadron was the former Queen Christina of Sweden who had abdicated in 1654, moved to Rome and become a Catholic. But her subsequent record of intrigue and cruelty, including angling to become the ruler of Naples by expelling the Spanish, soured her image in the eyes of many. Yet she is believed to have influenced the election of Clement IX, a saintly cleric and accomplished librettist. A member of the Rospigliosi family, Clement appointed his brother Camillo as general of the Church and his nephew Tommaso as governor of Sant'Angelo Castle. The pope's gentle diplomacy impressed even the distrustful Louis XIV, who decreed a coin struck in memory of 're-establishing unity in the Church'.[15] Clement succumbed to a stroke in 1669, to be succeeded by a relatively new cardinal (even though he was pushing eighty) who took the name Clement X. This Clement was not so lucky in diplomacy, but one bright spot was the election of Jan Sobieski as Catholic king of Poland, the recipient of considerable Vatican funding as the north-east bulwark of Catholicism against the ever-present threat of Ottoman aggression in Eastern Europe.

In the latter half of the seventeenth century one figure cast his lengthening shadow over the length and breadth of Europe, and that was Louis XIV. His France had become the greatest power on the European continent; Spain was in decline, the Habsburgs squeezed into Austria and preoccupied with Ottoman advances up the Danube, Germany in tatters after the Thirty Years' War and England in the throes of the Cromwellian revolution and troublesome restoration. The whole period from about 1660 to 1715 has been justifiably described as the Age of Louis XIV. It was a period of relative peace and growing prosperity in Europe as the nations took a breather from the previous century of brutal religious wars and convulsions. Louis and other monarchs considered themselves rulers by divine right, and philosophers such as Thomas Hobbes wrote that people needed not only God but also a 'mortal God': that is, a powerful state, to ensure peace and security on earth.

The philosophy was fully in accord with that of the papacy at the time. The popes indeed considered themselves absolute rulers by the grace of God, with somewhat more of a direct connection to heaven than the strongest monarch had. With the end of the religious wars the Vatican must have experienced some relief; it had been obliged to support the Catholic powers even when they were responsible for atrocities such as the sack of Magdeburg. But as long as France was flexing muscle there could be no complacency in Saint Peter's. The Papal States were as they had been for several centuries: an uneven strip of territory from the Po river in the north to the border with Naples in the south, vulnerable at many points. At their narrowest point they were hemmed in by Naples (part of the kingdom of the Two Sicilies) that accounted for almost all the southern half of Italy, and by independent Florence to the north-west, squeezing the Papal States like a pincers. To the north lay Venice and farther west was Milan under Spanish Habsburg control. Like the content of a sandwich, the Papal States seemed under perpetual threat of being swallowed.

Popes Innocent XI, Alexander VIII and Innocent XII were reformers who did much to raise the prestige of the papacy. Excessive spending and nepotism were reined in, while the Holy Year of 1675 saw more than 1.4 million visitors pour into Rome with their spending money. The epochal repulse of the Ottoman Turks before Vienna in 1683 owed something to papal support of the Christian powers. The captured Turkish banners and trophies were taken to Rome and put on display in the newly-built church of Santa Maria della Vittoria (Our Lady of Victory). Three years later the Ottomans were evicted from Budapest, and a year after that the Austrians trounced them at Mohács, the same battlefield on which Suleiman the Magnificent had prevailed a century-and-a-half before. In 1688 Max Emanuel of Bavaria wrested Belgrade from the Ottomans, and it seemed as if the way was open to chase the retreating Turks all the way to Constantinople and liberate that ancient Christian city.

But not if the Sun King could help it. Louis saw in the Turkish defeats a resurgence of France's long-time opponents, the Habsburgs and other Central European powers. He seemed concerned less with fighting the Muslims than defending himself against fellow-Christians. Some of the fabled French cynicism and political opportunism also came into play. But the Turks proved unable to recover from their defeats and their sultan, Süleyman II, signed the 1699 Treaty of Karlowitz, ceding Hungary and West Ukraine. It was the last time that the Ottomans would directly threaten the heart of Europe.

It's not certain whether Louis XIV ever uttered the famous phrase attributed to him: '*L'état, c'est moi*'. But he might equally well have said '*le pape c'est moi*', as he considered himself the proper head of the French church. In fact, it was no longer called the Roman church but the Gallican church, as if to emphasize its freedom from 'Italian' papal control. The famous (or infamous) Four Articles promulgated by Louis in March 1682 left no doubt about his intentions:

1. The pope has jurisdiction in spiritual concerns, and has no authority to depose princes or release their subjects from obedience.
2. Ecumenical councils are above the pope in authority.
3. The traditional liberties of the French Church are inviolable.
4. The pope is infallible only when in accord with the council of bishops.[16]

The last article of the four is a sure clue as to what really stuck in the craw of the French (and, for that matter, of the Greek Orthodox and Protestants as well) – the doctrine of papal infallibility. In the emerging system of nation-states, where the civil religion of monarch and flag was supplanting allegiance to the institutions of God, such a doctrine could not really survive. Even in Rome it was paid mere lip-service to. Of course Innocent had little choice but to declare the Four Articles null and void, but the Gallican church remained adamant. Only eleven years later did Louis mellow enough to disavow the Four Articles, with the result that Pope Innocent XII (1691–1700) accepted the king's right to nominate bishops. With the holy quarrel patched up, Louis could again legitimately call himself the Most Christian King (*Rex Christianissimus*). Playing a part in Louis' better mood was the Glorious Revolution in England, when the Dutch William of Orange was called in to avert the prospect of a Catholic monarchy – eliminating the danger of a potential Protestant enemy on France's north-east frontier.

But the Vatican was put on the spot in 1700 when called on to decide which side to support in the War of the Spanish Succession. The cause of the war was the long-expected demise of the weak and sickly King Charles II of Spain. On his deathbed Charles had named Philip of Anjou, a grandson of Louis XIV, as his successor. Europe was thrown into a panic, as it was apparent that the Bourbon Philip would bring Spain into the French camp against the Habsburgs. Louis relished the prospect of war with an array of foes that included Austria, England, the Netherlands and a new rising Protestant power in North Germany, Brandenburg-Prussia. Where would the papacy stand – with the untrustworthy French, or with the Protestants? In part it depended on the preferences of the individual popes. When the War of the Spanish Succession erupted in 1700, the papacy had just devolved on Clement XI, who was widely suspected to be pro-French.

The Austrian Habsburgs sent an army into the northern Papal States and another to seize Naples, with the object of dissuading Clement from any pro-French moves. The pope instead declared war on Austria. Some 20,000 papal troops suffered a resounding defeat by a Habsburg force at Ferrara in November 1708. As the Austrians moved threateningly on Rome – sinister echoes of the *Landsknechte* irruption of 1527 – Clement gave in and agreed to demilitarize the Papal States. His submission to the Habsburgs enraged the Spanish church, which had backed Philip the Bourbon and now cut formal ties with Rome.

That was not the sole example of the diplomatic and military tightrope a pope was often compelled to walk in a turbulent Europe. Clement XI had to deal with the Jansenists, a sect that tried to reconcile Protestant themes with Catholicism and had gained some influence in the Gallican church. The Jansenists had no use for the Jesuits, whom they regarded as something close to a religious mafia. Louis XIV agreed with the pope that the Jansenists should be suppressed. The pope attempted to impose doctrinal discipline through his bull *Unigenitus*, but all it accomplished was to open up a couple of minor schisms in the Church. Meanwhile, thanks largely to the Duke of Marlborough, the French were driven out of Germany and the Netherlands, and out of Italy by Prince Eugene of Savoy. By the 1714 Peace of Utrecht Philip Bourbon (Philip V) remained on the Spanish throne but pledged never to unite with France; more importantly for Italy, King Eugene of Savoy (as he now was) was awarded Sicily. A year later an exhausted and disillusioned Sun King died after the longest reign in French history, after advising his great-grandson not to 'imitate my love of war but ... make peace with your neighbours'. The boy, who became Louis XV, apparently took little notice.

Clement XI also had a curious run-in with the Chinese. The Jesuits had been active in China since at least 1582, and in the following hundred or so years had agreed to accept certain Confucian rites in order to maintain good relations with the Chinese and make the Roman Catholic faith more palatable to them. The tactic worked, but in Rome the Congregation for the Propagation of the Faith, which oversaw all missionary activity, frowned on such instances of 'going native'. To the hardliners Confucius was a false god and thus had no place in Catholic worship. The issue of the 'Chinese Rites' boiled to the surface in 1702 when Clement sent an envoy to Chinese Emperor Kangxi asking for approval to establish a papal diplomatic mission in Beijing – the mission's real purpose being to monitor Jesuit activity.

Kangxi, who valued the Jesuits' contributions to his people's education and medical welfare but didn't take their doctrines terribly seriously, was amused by the papal envoy, 'a biased and unreliable person, who muddled right with wrong'. The emperor turned down flat the envoy's request for a diplomatic mission with the arch comment that China 'had no common concerns with the West'. He also had some knowledge of the destructive politico-religious quarrels of Europe and marvelled that even in the Catholic Church various groups were always snapping at one another. Yet it appears that Kangxi was able to recognize Christian virtue. He wanted to keep the genuine missionaries in his country. But Clement was adamant in banning the 'Chinese Rites', and Kangxi in retaliation restricted the Jesuits' activities; in 1707 the emperor jailed the papal envoy in Macao and kept him there for the rest of his life. The Jesuit mission in China entered terminal decline as a result.[17]

Influential men of the papacy in the first decades of the eighteenth century looked outwards with foreboding. Absolutist France and parliamentary England (Great Britain after the 1707 Act of Union), with diametrically-opposed philosophies of government, dominated the stage of nation-states. The remnant of the Holy Roman Empire under the Habsburgs held on to its base in Austria while eyeing expansion possibilities in North Italy. Spain remained reliably Catholic, but also was a potential threat to the papacy as it held the Two Sicilies – Sicily and Naples. By contrast, the Papal States appeared dormant, their leadership unsure about how to handle the new political challenges springing up around the continent. Several Italian writers commented acidly on the Papal States' lack of progress in commerce and farming, for example; in 1723 Lione Pascoli wrote in a political tract that the pontifical realm was 'the most miserable of all' in Europe; in Rome, he charged, the rich preferred to gather bank interest rather than invest their money and the citizens spent and consumed without producing – a classic recipe for economic collapse.[18]

Militarily the Papal States were all but powerless; Habsburg and Bourbon armies marched and fought at will over the pope's territory. In 1763 the depredations would be so severe as to trigger a famine that forced the papal administration to import wheat and almost double its price. Innocent XIII (1721–24) had attempted to deregulate the price of grain, but a knowledge of economics was probably not very high on the list of papal attainments. The Holy Year of 1725 saw the elaborate Roman wedding of France's Louis XV with Maria Leszczynska of Poland, a good Catholic subject, and the inauguration of the Spanish Steps in the Piazza di Spagna that have been so far iconized as to be buried under today's heaps of lounging tourists. Yet that's as far as Rome itself went – it served as a mere ceremonial fountainhead for Catholic Europe without any real political clout; it was the only role allowed for the papacy by the powerful states of Europe. A sense of decline pervaded the Vatican. The German historian Ludwig von Pastor, perhaps the best-known chronicler of the popes, wrote that Innocent XIII installed a special funeral parlour in the Vatican for senior clergy, a striking sign of the dark mood of the time.[19]

Partly because of the economic defects of the Papal States, the papal treasury was always in a parlous condition. A chief culprit, according to most authorities, was Cardinal Niccolò Coscia, whom Benedict XIII had installed as controller of finances, and whose corrupt and venal practices almost bankrupted the papacy. Pope Clement XII (1730–40), who had served as papal treasurer and governor of Sant'Angelo Castle, excommunicated Coscia and eventually had him jailed for ten years. With the corrupt cardinal out of the way, expenses and revenues were rationalized in order to beautify Rome yet more with gems such as the Trevi Fountain; but the eighty-year-old pope's encroaching blindness and debility prevented him from completing the financial reforms he had planned.

Succeeding him in 1740 was Benedict XIV, who took the holy part of his office seriously enough to state, on his consecration, 'I am a pope before I am a sovereign.' He was as good as his word, mingling with the poorer people of Rome to learn at firsthand how hard life was for them. He slashed the number of Vatican servants and lackeys and cut the salaries of papal officials and troops. A convinced pacifist, Benedict wondered aloud whether it might be better for the papacy to divest itself of all temporal and political power and remain a shining example to the warring nations of a purely spiritual institution devoted to the welfare of mankind and not a part of the deadly chess-game of power. In a way it was a recognition of the declining status of a holy state in a system of aggressive secular states; Benedict knew that no papal army could now play any meaningful part in the continental power game, and that it would be futile to even try. He is best known for consecrating the Colosseum of Rome as a place of Christian martyrdom during the 1750 Holy Year celebrations.

The mid-eighteenth century was the beginning of the 'Enlightenment,' when advances in science and new ways of political thinking threatened to push the Catholic Church into irrelevancy. The French *philosophes* were especially active in this sphere, concentrating some of their fire against the Jesuits. The order was gradually being forced out of France, the Bourbon lands of Spain and Naples, and Portugal. King Charles III of Spain blamed them, unfairly, for stirring up riots in Madrid against a requirement for Spaniards to wear French dress, confiscated their property and decreed their expulsion in February 1767. The Bourbon Charles had a bone to pick with Clement XIII, pope at the time, as the papacy had consistently opposed Charles' legitimacy as King of the Two Sicilies.

The king's decree also applied to Spain's South American colonies, and the prospect arose of up to 20,000 persecuted Jesuits sailing back across the Atlantic and crowding into the Papal States, the only place on the globe where they would be welcome. Clement, refusing to recognize Charles' order, had the first arriving Jesuits turned back at the ports of Civitavecchia; the refugees sailed on to Genoese-held Corsica, where they were also barred from landing. For five wretched months these remnants of the noble order of Saint Ignatius Loyola languished at sea until they were allowed to set foot on Corsican dry land; but in May 1768 the Genoese handed Corsica over to France, sending the Jesuits on their travels and travails again, first to Genoa and then down to the Papal States, which they reached in a pitiable condition. The strength of the popular prejudice against the Jesuits can be gauged from Naples and Sicily, from where they were booted out on the convenient excuse that by some mystic skulduggery they had caused an eruption of Mount Vesuvius.[20]

Clement XIII (1758–69) had no intention of abandoning the Jesuits without a fight. He threatened to excommunicate the monarchs of those lands persecuting members of the order, but they responded with military measures; France took over papal Avignon and Naples marched into Benevento. More chips were hacked off the Papal States. Three months later, in January 1769, the Bourbon ambassadors called on the pope with a demand that he dissolve the Jesuits forthwith. The strain was too much for the seventy-eight-year-old pontiff, who suffered a fatal cerebral haemorrhage. Sir Horace Mann, the British minister to Florence, wrote to London that he hoped Clement's demise might prove beneficial to the Papal States in that it 'could produce a new system in [the papal] court conformable to the times' and preserve those states from destruction.[21] Mann's letter appears to signal an emerging British concern that either the Bourbons or the Habsburgs might swallow the Papal States, strengthening their European holdings and hence British security, and a hope that the pope's domains could continue to exist as a counterweight to the designs of France above all.

Many in Europe were prepared to write off the Papal States, believing their last hour had come before Bourbon or Habsburg made a strike for Rome. Some statesmen wondered whether the conclave following Clement XIII's death would end up electing 'the last pope'. They need not have worried. It fell to Clement XIV (1769–74), a youngster at sixty-four, to try and negotiate some compromise with the courts of France, Savoy, Prussia and Russia. The Bourbons, however, continued to press for a flat-out ban on the Jesuits; Clement, outgunned, very reluctantly signed the document titled *Dominus ac Redemptor Noster* (Our Lord and Redeemer) on 21 July 1773, finally suppressing the order. The Jesuit general, Lorenzo Ricci, was jailed in Sant'Angelo Castle solely on the basis of a (false) rumour that he considered Clement an illegal pontiff; and evidence was supposedly uncovered indicating Jesuit involvement in the London Gunpowder Plot of 1605. Interestingly, only Catherine II of Orthodox Russia and Frederick William II of Protestant Prussia did not enforce the resolution. As for Clement XIV, he followed his predecessor to the grave within a year; for some time a variety of ailments had been plaguing him. A persistent rumour, that cannot be either corroborated or proved false, was put about that the Jesuits had poisoned 'the Protestant pope' by spiking his drinking chocolate.[22]

During the conclave that would elect Pius VI (1774–1799), a Venetian humorist noted that while the English were known for 'fighting everybody' and the Dutch for 'buying everything,' the popes were known for being 'afraid of everything.'[23] They had reason to be. Pius ascended the throne of Saint Peter as the American Revolution was about to break out across the Atlantic, the effect of Protestant ideas of political liberty and popular representation having now taken firm root in the prosperous and expanding Anglo-Saxon world. The same flames were roiling France, which was heading pell-mell towards its own revolution of 1789. In the decaying shell of the Holy Roman Empire – now more accurately described as Austria – the autocratic emperor Joseph II arrogated ecclesiastical affairs to himself, decreeing religious toleration in 1781; influencing Joseph were the writings of a German bishop, Nikolaus von Hontheim, who argued (under the pen name Justinus Febronius) that popes had no business in secular and political affairs. This principle, known as Josephism, was the Enlightenment's encroachment on traditional notions of papal authority and infallibility. Enforced in the Habsburg-ruled areas of North Italy, it gained ground among clerics of all levels. Veneration of the saints was discouraged, and in these areas the Church became Protestant in all but name.

Pius VI, elected after five months of wrangling among the cardinals, was well aware that Europe's rulers had all but discounted the pope as one of their number. He learned it the hard way when he took the highly unusual step of crossing the Alps to Vienna in 1782 to try and talk Joseph II into softening his stand against the Church. It was the first time a pope had set foot on German-speaking soil in well over three hundred years, and the public reception was tumultuous; an estimated 60,000 people mobbed him as he blessed them from a palace balcony. Buoyed up by such a demonstration of popular adulation, Pius took new strength. His warning to Joseph pulled no punches:

> If you persevere in your projects, destructive of the faith and the laws of the Church, the hand of the Lord will fall heavily upon you; it will check you in the course of your career, it will dig under you an abyss where you will be engulfed in the flower of your life, and will put an end to the reign which you could have made glorious.[24]

The emperor took not the slightest notice; indeed, his chancellor deliberately insulted the pope by declining the usual custom of kissing the papal hand, preferring to shake it instead, and boasting afterwards that he had given Pius 'a black eye'.[25]

Before the year was out Joseph II had reason to regret his defiance of the pope. In December 1782 we find him scurrying to Rome and professing allegiance to Pius. What had happened? In a diplomatic spat over the confirmation of the archbishop of Milan the emperor backed down, fearing a complete break with the Vatican. Happy at the reconciliation, the emperor threw fistfuls of coins to the Roman mob which howled his praises to the skies. His contentment was not to last for long. Hungary, long subject to the empty shell of the Holy Roman Empire, agitated for independence and was mollified only when Joseph sent the crown of Saint Stephen back to Budapest. Then came the Austrian Netherlands, which declared their independence of the empire in 1788, defeated punitive forces sent against them, and proclaimed the Republic of the United States of Belgium. At home, Austria's Catholic populace was turning against the monarch who had so high-handedly swept aside its religious customs and plunged it into war with Turks and Belgians and Italians. Despite drastically worsening health, Joseph Habsburg became a workaholic; he was still only forty-eight years old when he could carry on no longer, and died on 20 February 1790. One wonders, when he received the last rites of the Catholic faith, whether he recalled what the stern Pius VI had told him eight years before.

In Rome Pius made a favourable impression on foreign diplomats as a relatively open-minded pontiff, though seemingly addicted to a certain level of pomp and decoration, and quite as nepotistic as his predecessors. But this does not mean he was at all influenced by the so-called 'Age of Reason' that involved only a small minority of intellectuals; most devout Catholics wanted little or no change in the ancient rites and precepts, and approved when new saints were canonized and new rituals adopted. Elaborate rococo and neoclassical churches and other buildings continued to go up in Rome, and in July 1785 a Catholic newspaper, the *Giornale ecclesiastico di Roma* (Church Newspaper of Rome) began its career as a standard-bearer of the old faith and the popes' authority.

Events in France, however, soon placed the pope's jurisdictional problems in the shade. One of the first acts of the French revolutionary regime in

1789 was to confiscate all the property of the Gallican church, which was about equal to the national debt. The clergy, stripped of all they had, were then turned into state employees (which meant being paid from taxes on the middle class and peasantry), and required to swear fealty to the Civil Constitution of the Clergy if they wished to keep their jobs. They would be no longer subject to the pope but elected by the people. Pius declared the requirement illegal and threatened with suspension any French priests who complied; a Parisian mob publicly burned the papal document in the Place Royale. A French revolutionary diplomat in Naples, Nicolas-Jean-Hugon de Bassville, was slashed to death while handing out Jacobin cockades in Rome, of all places. Diplomatic ties between Rome and Paris were ruptured; the French kept their now-permanent grip on Avignon, and French royalists found refuge in the Papal States. Pius' stand was a brave one, but in the end hopeless. Revolutionaries or not, the French saw their chance to seize Rome and eliminate what the fire-eaters saw as the last remaining bastion of reactionary Catholicism in Europe.

The man whom fate picked to do this was one Napoleon Bonaparte, a young Corsican artillery officer who had thrown in his lot with the Revolution but had soon come to see through its violent idealism to conclude that only the army could restore stability to France. He made his first mark on 5 October 1795 when he helped put down a populist revolt in Paris 'with a whiff of grapeshot'. The following year saw the installation of the Directory, whose main interest seems to have been in enriching its members at the expense of the starving masses; Napoleon was given the job of invading Italy to eliminate any threat from that quarter as well as to avenge the recent slights to revolutionary France from the Papal States. As Pius VI could only watch helplessly, Napoleon marched into the Church lands with 35,000 ragged French troops in 1796, seizing Bologna, Ferrara and Ancona in short order; the turmoil interrupted the grain harvest in those regions, triggering bread riots in Rome. The Austrian and Sardinian resistance was crushed (though the Austrians outnumbered the French two to one), and in February 1797 Napoleon seized Mantua. The Austrians sued for peace; by the Treaty of Campo Formio they gave Napoleon his Italian conquests, which he organized into the Cisalpine and Ligurian republics, both under the control of *la France*.

The road to Rome was now open. The city trembled with insecurity. It was reported that three dozen images of the Virgin Mary in public places were seen to move their eyes as if alive; the phenomenon was supposedly observed over a period of months, and attested even by sober witnesses. Into this climate of trepidation came French General Leonard Duphot, whose assignment was to stir up a Roman popular revolt against the pope. He achieved some success, as on 28 December he was leading a mob shouting 'Long live the republic! Death to the tyrants!' Those words were Duphot's last, as that same day he was killed in a shootout with papal troops. Napoleon thus had the revolutionary martyr his cause needed: on 10 February 1798 General Louis Alexandre Berthier occupied Rome. Five days later he proclaimed the Roman Republic in the name of the French Directory, deposed Pius VI as head of the Papal States and proceeded to loot the Vatican treasures for the greater glory of France. On 20 February Pius was taken to Siena and then to Florence. The only one to pay homage to him was King Carlo Emanuele of Sardinia; fearing plots to free the pope, the French took him to Briançon and then to Grenoble. Soon afterwards, the shattered Pius passed away. Napoleon saw to it that he was buried in Valence, and three years later he allowed the papal body to be returned to Rome. Was this the end of the papacy as Europe and the Catholic faithful had known it for eighteen centuries?

Chapter 10

The Humiliation of Pius VII

The eighteen-month French occupation of Rome was a cold and callous business. All the Gallic prejudice against Italians and Catholics poured out in many ways. To be sure, there were poor and underprivileged Romans who applauded the French Revolution and its principles and wished to see the same apply in their ancient city. On 20 March 1798 the constitution of the Roman Republic was presented to the public in Saint Peter's Square, adorned by a so-called 'Liberty Tree' (which according to Jacobin philosophy needed to be 'watered occasionally by the blood of tyrants') and three statues depicting the new trinity of France, Rome and *Égalité*. Rome was to be run by a bicameral legislature and five consuls under the authority of the French military governor, and the former Papal States divided into eight French-style *départements*. The calendar was purged of all its old and venerated saints' days, and all religious holidays abolished. On 14 July, Bastille Day, a great pile of Catholic literature and Holy Office files went up in a bonfire in the Piazza di Spagna.

Such callous excesses did little to endear the average Roman to the haughty Frenchman. Many who at first supported the new rulers quickly turned against them, calling the new regime 'the laughable republic (*la repubblica per ridere*)'. One voice that could not be stilled was that of Pasquino, whose role as social media network had never been dimmed. The statue's marble surface bristled with anonymous scorn. Ran one verse:

> Trees without roots?
> Caps without a feather?
> Rome a republic?
> It cannot last, no, never.[1]

Words turned to action. French soldiers were knifed in the streets. Cries of 'Long live Mary! Long live the pope!' echoed in the alleyways. One group burst into an arsenal in the Trastevere district, a focal point of opposition, and used the weapons they seized to shoot any Roman Jacobins they came across. The French authorities reacted swiftly, ordering the arrest of anyone found bearing arms; twenty-two men of Trastevere were publicly shot in Piazza del Popolo. The revolt spread to the countryside, where Cardinal Fabrizio Ruffo raised mercenary forces to harass the French; one of the leaders was a fiery Neapolitan named Michele Pezza who joined a pro-papal force called the Reggimento de Messapi as a sergeant. As a boy Pezza had been bumptious and mischievous, earning the nickname Diavolo, or devil. It was as Fra Diavolo (Brother Devil), and now a colonel, that he harassed the French in Neapolitan territory wherever he could find them, slaughtering those he captured. His efforts, however, proved in vain, and the French hanged him in 1806.

Rome groaned under the exactions of the French and their commander, General Jean-Étienne Championnet, who sucked the city and its environs dry to pay for his soldiers' occupation. Many churches were deconsecrated and used as billets for French troops, and church bells were melted down for currency. Those cardinals remaining in Rome had their horses and carriages requisitioned, and the images of the Virgin Mary that had supposedly moved their eyes before the French invasion were removed from public view. The secular French, it seemed, weren't taking any chances.

Napoleon, meanwhile, had other anti-Catholic fish to fry. We have seen that in 1530 the Knights Hospitaller of Saint John had settled in Malta, ending a decade of wanderings after the Ottomans expelled them from Rhodes. Finding that to survive they had to become a naval power, they had built up the so-called Navy of the Religion to fight Muslim piracy in the Mediterranean and help Christian powers fight the Ottoman Turks wherever necessary, as at Lepanto in 1571. The Ottoman failure before Vienna in 1683 encouraged the Maltese Navy of the Religion to sweep the Turks from Greek seas, in alliance with the Papal States and Venice. Between 1684 and 1694 the Knights' galleys, which included some of the biggest ever seen until that time, drove the Ottomans from several strongholds off the west Greek coast. Buoyed by these successes, Hospitaller Grand Master Antonio Manoel de Vilhena proclaimed the Knights of Saint John to be a sovereign entity, which they still are.

The Hospitallers continued their naval strikes against the Ottomans through the eighteenth century, forcing the Turks to a truce in 1723. The naval Knights could then direct their attentions to the noisome Barbary pirates operating off the North African coast and preying on Christian shipping. It is often alleged that the Hospitallers were little better than pirates themselves, and there is some truth to that; but in the circumstances, it was felt, the only way to defeat a ruthless foe was by adopting his tactics. Arguably, the Navy of the Religion was the most powerful navy in the West Mediterranean and Malta proved to be a good training college for Italian naval officers from a variety of states.

The French Revolution of 1789 threw this comfortable state of affairs into disarray. The suppression of the French clergy made a very bad impression on the Order of Saint John, whose grand master, Emmanuel de Rohan-Polduc, attempted to mollify the revolutionaries by disavowing any connection with the French nobility (to which he in fact belonged) and insisted on the Order's untouchability as the 'Sovereign Order of Malta'. But in 1792 an ill-judged attempt by the Hospitallers' man in Paris to help Louis XVI escape his confinement backfired. The revolutionists confiscated all the Hospitallers' considerable assets in France, almost bankrupting the order in one blow. Thus weakened, the Knights of Malta were in a poor position to resist Napoleon when on 10 June 1798 he launched a three-pronged naval attack on Malta. The Knights' resistance was brave but hopeless; after barely a day of fighting Napoleon marched proudly into Valletta, the Maltese capital, as what was left of the Hospitallers fled to wherever a Christian government would welcome them.[2]

When he decided to eliminate Malta, Napoleon was in his way to Egypt, where within weeks he came to grief at the hands of Lord Horatio Nelson in the Battle of the Nile. Nelson sailed to Naples, where he received a hero's welcome. At the instigation of Naples, Austria sent three columns of troops that penetrated to Rome and made a show of force outside the city. Championnet, his own 15,000-strong force outnumbered, wisely evacuated Rome, leaving a garrison in Sant'Angelo Castle. The Austrians entered Rome on 29 November 1798 to a great and joyful pealing of church bells; the hated 'Liberty Trees' were felled and the king of Naples, Ferdinand IV (who was also, confusingly, Ferdinand III of Sicily), installed himself in the Palazzo Farnese as a Roman ruler of sorts. The newcomers may have been a bit too complacent, as within a matter of hours the French had defeated an Austro-Neapolitan force at Civita Castellana and surged back into Rome. Ferdinand scurried back to Naples, but too late to avert the proclamation of a pro-French republic in that city. Rome was plunged back into despair. French repression was tighter than ever – there was this time no talk of a constitution – and was aggravated by famine. Ferdinand, ousted from Naples, again marched on Rome with the aid of a small Russian contingent. But the French didn't have the resources to govern a sullen and hostile city, and on 30 November 1799 the pressure from Ferdinand forced them out of Rome and onto ships at Civitavecchia.

Ferdinand's first care was to restore the papacy, but who would be pope? The hapless Pius VI had died in exile in France three months before, and so far the discouraged cardinals, scattered over various territories, had hardly been in a position to hold a conclave. On 1 December, partly thanks to the efforts of Austrian emperor Franz II, the College of Cardinals met in Austrian-controlled Venice but refused to elect Franz's nominee and the conclave broke up without result. The cardinals themselves were split into three factions: one traditionalist, one favouring the Habsburgs and one toying with reforming ideals. The cardinals met again in Venice in March and after much wheeling and dealing elected Cardinal Barnaba Chiaramonti, Pius VI's confessor, who took the name Pius VII to stress a continuity with his ill-fated predecessor.

The new Pius, a man so diminutive that he had to have special pontifical vestments and slippers made, leaned towards the liberals. But he firmly rejected a plea by Franz II not to make the hazardous journey to Rome; the emperor may have feared that once in the traditional seat of the papacy, Pius might slip out of Habsburg control. After an uncomfortable sea voyage from Venice to Pesaro he crossed overland through territory devastated by war to reach Rome on 3 July 1800. A squad of Neapolitan troops saw him safely to the Quirinal Palace. Rome itself, according to the pope's secretary of state, Cardinal Ercole Consalvi, languished in 'general disorder, desolation, ruin, robbery, murder and crime of every sort'.[3] The French occupation had bled the Romans of all they had. By 2 September Pius VII had managed to put the city back on a shaky economic footing (though the Jews, whom the French had freed from their ghetto, were shoved back into it).

Security, naturally, was one of Pius' prime concerns. On 11 May 1801 he set up the Noble Guard (*Guardia Nobile*) to replace the special corps known as the 'Broken Lances' (*Lance Spezzate*) that had served as a papal protection unit in the later decades of the eighteenth century and had been dissolved by the French when they had set up Rome's Jacobin republic. The Noble Guard, the forerunner of today's Vatican *Gendarmeria* Corps, was made up of younger members of the Roman nobility. Its task was to protect not only the pope but also the cardinals, and to provide an honour guard to escort senior Church figures and legates. The ceremonial uniform, inspired by that of Napoleon's dragoons, consisted of a scarlet tunic, a dark blue collar and cuffs, plenty of gold braid on the epaulettes, tight white pantaloons and black leather riding boots reaching to above the knee; white plumes topped the dragoon-style helmet. The guardsman's weaponry consisted of a sabre and two pistols. Pius created a new standard for the Guard featuring the papal crest on a white background bordered in gold. The Guard was probably never intended for much more than ceremonial duties, but it developed an impressive 'salute to the pope' routine which involved a coordinated kneeling and simultaneous striking of the ground with the sabres in a single crash of steel.[4]

But the papal reprieve did not last long, and again the cause was Napoleon Bonaparte. Towards the end of 1799 he had seized power in a coup in France, setting himself up as First Consul. The following year he moved against Austria, which was proving implacably hostile. His first targets were the Austrian possessions in North Italy; defeating an Austrian army at Marengo in May 1800, he humbled the empire with the Treaty of Lunéville which essentially gave him Naples, Genoa (the Ligurian Republic) and the so-called Cisalpine Republic, which included Milan and all Lombardy plus Venice. But Napoleon was also cannily aware that most ordinary French people remained Catholic and that if he wished to preserve his popularity he needed to come to some accommodation with the papacy. The papacy itself was hardly in a position to argue the point, but Napoleon was generous: by the Concordat of 1801 he agreed to recognize the Roman Catholic faith as the prevalent one in France and restore the positions and rights of consecrated priests hounded by the excesses of the recent revolution. In return Pius VII conceded the right of the French government (i.e. Napoleon) to appoint clergy and abandoned previous claims of church property seized by the revolutionaries. The Vatican's relations with the Gallican church were thus restored.

However, if the pope thought that the Concordat could restore his temporal power in addition to his spiritual status, he was in for a rude shock. The Treaty of Lunéville handed Napoleon great swaths of Papal States territory. In essence, the Papal States were now history. Rome was but a tiny enclave in an expanding French European empire. This uncomfortable hemmed-in feeling was one reason behind Pius' creation of the Noble Guard as well as another body, the Palatine Guard of Honour (*Guardia Palatina d'Onore*) that had been created by Pius VI for purely ceremonial purposes but, like the former, dissolved by the Jacobin regime. Unlike the Noble Guard, whose membership was restricted to the nobility, the Palatine Guard recruited Roman men of the middle class as a kind of civil guard; especially sought after were those who practised 'scientific and liberal professions' as well as 'public servants on a fixed salary and master artisans owning their own business'. The Palatine Guard's uniform consisted of a dark blue tunic, light blue trousers with a red stripe down the outside leg and scarlet beret. Like the Noble Guard, the Palatine Guard turned out almost exclusively for ceremonial occasions where a certain level of pomp was deemed necessary. The Swiss Guard was also reconstituted after having been abolished by the French.

Pius VII's submission to Napoleon – in contrast to his predecessor's combative spirit – earned him some criticism. A trenchant verse appeared on Pasquino:

One Pius loses his seat to preserve the faith / One Pius loses the faith to preserve his seat.[5]

To mollify the Romans, Napoleon allowed the body of Pius VI to be transported to Rome, where it arrived on 16 February 1802 to be entombed in Saint Peter's. It was no mere polite gesture. Napoleon never did anything without an agenda, and in this case it was to pretend to be kind to the papacy because he had rather grand plans for himself. His so-called 'Constitution of the Year X' (1802) made him Consul for life. He then spent two years preparing the groundwork for turning himself into Emperor of the French. An emperor, of course, needed a coronation, and in a Catholic country who better to do it than the pope? Against the advice of a majority of his cardinals, Pius dutifully travelled to Paris for the ceremony in Notre Dame cathedral that took place on 2 December 1804. His consternation can be imagined when, expecting to crown Napoleon in the time-honoured ritual, he could only stand by as the new emperor grabbed the crown and set it on his own head. The message was plain for all to see: Emperor Napoleon I had no intention of being morally or spiritually bound by the Church.

To drive that message home, Napoleon kept Pius as a virtual prisoner in Paris for four months; the pope was a mere stage prop, to be used to bolster the prestige of the new French Empire and its head: a mere gaudily-dressed extra to be trotted out for a bit of pomp and circumstance. When Pius was finally allowed back to Rome in June 1805 he was little more than Napoleon's vassal; in a haughty note of February 1806 Napoleon proclaimed himself 'Emperor of Rome' and ordered the pope to deny entry to Rome to 'foreign enemies', especially the British. The pope should be told in no uncertain terms, Napoleon said, that 'I am Charlemagne, the sword of the church, and must be treated as such.' In case of papal defiance, he warned, 'I shall reduce the papacy to the state that it occupied before Charlemagne.'[6] Momentarily Pius protested, but was forced to replace his secretary of state, Cardinal Consalvi, who was believed to be anti-French. In a spasm of timidity Pius also removed several other cardinals, but Napoleon could not tolerate any protest by any pope. On 2 February 1808 French General Sextius-Alexandre François Miollis entered Rome through the Porta del Popolo, swept aside a handful of papal troops that tried to stop him and occupied Sant'Angelo Castle, turning the guns onto the Quirinal Palace where the pope lived.

Once more the Romans endured the harshness and dullness of a French occupation. Priceless works of art were looted. The religious festivals so dear to the Italian Catholic heart were again done away with; Miollis' unsuccessful attempts to replace them with secular holidays met with sullen resistance. Rome itself, along with what remained of the Papal States, was subsumed into the French Empire. Napoleon himself visited the stubborn city on 17 May 1810, giving himself an imperial-style entry; he remained for several weeks, during which he put a formal end to the pope's temporal rule. The administration was turned over to General Miollis. The diminutive pontiff now finally got together the nerve to make the ultimate move and excommunicate Napoleon. The printed bulls of excommunication appeared on churches all over the city. But conditions had changed hugely since the time when excommunication had been the popes' 'nuclear option', able to terrify rulers with metaphysical penalties. Too many times it had been weakened from overuse, and the latest papal 'nuclear' blast had the same effect as a popgun.

Napoleon, raging at the pope as 'a dangerous madman', ordered Miollis to arrest him. In the early hours of 6 June General Étienne Radet took a cavalry squadron and three columns of infantry, accompanied by about sixty pro-French civilians, to hammer on the doors of the Quirinal Palace. Getting no response, Radet and a squad managed to scale a wall and enter the building through a window. Beating down doors with axes, the invaders reached the papal apartments, surprising a squad of the Swiss Guard, which promptly surrendered, acting on prior instructions by the pope who must have expected such an eventuality. Bursting through more doors, Radet found Pius seated calmly with his secretary of state, Cardinal Bartolomeo Pacca. The pope jumped up in alarm as Radet informed him that 'in the name of His Majesty the Emperor', he was obliged to accompany Radet to Miollis who would 'tell him his next destination'. Pius asked only that Pacca accompany him, and Radet agreed.

Fifteen minutes later, resplendent in red cape and cap, and carrying only his breviary and rosary, Pius was led through the shattered interior doorways along with Pacca. At the foot of the palace steps a closed carriage stood waiting. The pope and cardinal were bundled inside; the blind on the pope's side was nailed shut. Escorted by a cavalry unit, the carriage trundled through the sleeping city, exiting at the Porta del Popolo, where additional horses waited for the long journey ahead. Radet sent a message to Miollis informing him that his mission had been carried out; looking into the carriage he tried to reassure the pope that two more carriages bearing his relatives would soon join him. Pius protested that he had been told he would be taken before General Miollis and not kidnapped. The protest might as well have been addressed to the dark night. Getting no response, the pope 'fell silent and resumed his usual serenity'.[7] There has been some doubt about whether Napoleon actually ordered Pius' arrest, which has been attributed instead to the emperor's viceroy in Italy, Marshal Joachim Murat, who could have taken his boss's ire too seriously.[8]

The road to exile was long and arduous. Pius and Cardinal Pacca were driven first to Venice and then to Grenoble in France. There Pacca was moved to Fenestrelle, while Pius on 20 August was carted back to Italy, to be confined in the Episcopal palace at Savona. The Noble Guard and Palatine Guard were disbanded. In Rome a French official, Camille Tournon, acted as mayor, introducing one of the more baleful instruments of French justice, the guillotine. A decree of conscription into the French army was widely defied, leading to disturbances and desertions; between 1810 and 1813 a total of fifty-six people were guillotined. Religious institutions and monasteries were closed, throwing thousands of people on the streets where they begged for bread. Many men fled to the countryside to become brigands, some in the name of the dethroned pope. A number of opportunist nobles, on the other hand, were happy to seize lucrative (and largely decorative) high positions in the French-run administration. But the ordinary people could never be reconciled to the suppression of their Catholic culture. Writes one Italian historian: 'They could accept the blessing or the curse, but not atheism.'[9]

Late at night on 23 March 1811 the cannon of Sant'Angelo Castle thundered the news of the birth of Napoleon's first-born son Napoleon II, who even before his entry into the world had been destined for the title of King of Rome. The impressions the tidings made on the average Roman ranged from 'indifference to hostility, and resentment to coldness'.[10] A month later posters began appearing on walls praising Britain and Spain, Napoleon's enemies, and proclaiming 'Death to the tyrant!' A rigged municipal election on 10 January 1812 triggered another mass flight of young men to the brigand bands in the hills south of Rome. Napoleon persisted in his hard line. The Paris police claimed to have uncovered evidence of a papist plot for an uprising; on the basis of the claim a commission of French bishops was ordered to supplant the pope's authority, but it refused to go that far. After another explosion of rage from Napoleon the commission reconsidered its stand and ruled that the pope no longer had the power of excommunication over secular rulers.

For some time, however, efforts had been underway to revise the Concordat of 1801. Pius was willing enough to negotiate, and his health was failing, but he balked at Napoleon's more extreme demands. The emperor in exasperation would seize little Pius by the shoulders and shake him violently, and the pope, in poor health much of the time, caved in. Pius agreed that the

Papal States be dissolved, in return for which he could live out the rest of his years at Avignon. The Papal States' many monasteries and convents were closed, throwing thousands of monks and nuns onto the streets. In 1812, for fear that the British might free him, the pope was taken from his lodgings at Savona to the palace of Fontainebleau near Paris. Then the world began to crumble for Napoleon. Hardly had Pius settled in to his new abode than Napoleon made the well-known fatal decision to invade Russia; the 1812 catastrophe cost him a quarter of a million men as well as his own reputation for invincibility. At Leipzig in October 1813 an army of Prussians, Austrians and Russians smashed what was left of the *Grande Armeé*; on 31 March 1814 Napoleon agreed to abdicate, and was exiled to Elba. The Bourbon royal line was restored, with Louis XVI's brother Louis XVIII as king.

The effects of Napoleon's fall in Italy were rapid. General Murat, who by now had become King of Naples, had been in disagreement with Napoleon for some time and saw the chance to make a grab for Rome, whose French administration was crumbling. Murat's advance columns under General Michele Carascosa entered Rome on 25 November 1813. A coup two months later installed another general, Paul de la Vaugoyon, as 'governor-general of the Roman states' while Prince Agostino Chigi, of an old Roman noble family, was appointed mayor. Miollis was holed up in Sant'Angelo Castle with a contingent attempting some sort of resistance. One of Napoleon's last acts before his exile was to free Pius. In part the move was designed to thwart Murat's ambitions in Italy. It seemed to work, as Murat agreed to Pius' return to Rome without argument and pulled his forces out of the city. The pope returned to the Quirinal Palace, from where he had been so abruptly kidnapped four years before, on 24 May 1814. (Little Napoleon II never saw the city of which he was supposed to be king; after his father's fall he was taken under the wing of Austrian emperor Franz II. He succumbed to tuberculosis in 1832, aged twenty-one.)

The Napoleonic rules were promptly taken off the books, to be replaced by the old papal structure. Though severe punishments were meted out to leading 'collaborators' of the French occupation, Pius issued a general amnesty in July and re-formed the Jesuits. Then Napoleon slipped out of Elba and began his famous Hundred Days attempt to claw back power. The situation in Rome was serious enough for Pius to up stakes yet again and flee to Genoa on 22 March 1815, to place himself under the protection of

King Vittorio Emanuele I of Sardinia. Napoleon met his final nemesis at the hands of the Duke of Wellington at Waterloo on 18 June; but by that time Pius had been back in Rome for a week. The Congress of Vienna that same year vindicated Pius; the Papal States were reconstituted from the Po river in the north to the border with Naples, to include all the old regions of the Romagna, Benevento and Pontecorvo. The pope's sovereign authority over the States was reaffirmed, and many in the Church hoped no doubt that they could reconstruct the old comfortable pre-Napoleonic order.

Considering the formidable shocks the papacy had undergone in the past twenty or so years, when even the most devout papal subject feared that the institution had finally been dashed on the rocks, and somehow, incredibly, it had survived the Napoleonic juggernaut, it would have been surprising if Pius VII and his immediate successors had not made sure to anchor their old authority as firmly into the ground as possible. The Rome of the first half of the nineteenth century has often been termed 'reactionary Rome,' where the papacy set its face against new trends in political liberalism and reaffirmed the absolutist character of the Papal State (which we can now refer to in the singular, as it was revived as a single government entity). Nothing, if the popes could help it, would be allowed to upset the venerable Patrimony of Saint Peter again, no matter where the rest of Europe might be going.

But the French occupation of much of Italy had left its mark on Italian society; many Romans and Italians had internalized the libertarian principles of republican France, and the poorer regions began to simmer with discontent. The papacy's deliberate non-involvement with social issues allowed social sores to fester. Though Pius – over the objections of conservative cardinals – installed street lighting in Rome and created a municipal fire service, he could not satisfy those of the merchant classes and old aristocracy who resented being kept in what they considered a near-mediaeval political condition. The Papal State was arguably Europe's least representative government. Anti-clericalism, fuelled by decades of French republican propaganda, was on a sharp rise. Freemasonry raised its anti-clerical head, as did secret societies of all kinds. The best-known of these were the Carbonari (charcoal-burners) whose aim was to drive the French from Naples but also the pope from power. The secret societies in Sicily eventually would develop into the Mafia.

The famine of 1817 was the trigger for an uprising in Bologna, Ferrara and Ancona, where several papal civil and police officials were assaulted. A riot in Macerata in June resulted in eleven of those arrested being condemned to death. Cardinal Consalvi, in charge of internal affairs, judged it prudent to avoid excessive harshness and commuted the sentences to life imprisonment. There were, however, some executions in the Romagna. Brigandage continued to be a problem in the environs of Rome. On 18 July 1819 the pope ordered the small town of Sonnino, that had served as a bandit headquarters, razed to the ground; the destruction had already begun when a public outcry forced Pius to revoke the decree. Instead, the communities of the Papal State were encouraged to use their own means to suppress the brigands, backed up by pledges of financial rewards for each brigand killed or captured. The tactic appeared to work; in 1821 papal troops killed a bandit chieftain, Alessandro Massaroni, in a shootout. Other brigands were sent to the guillotine, gallows or chopping block, whichever method was the handiest.

A public execution in early-eighteenth-century papal Rome must have been a remarkable spectacle. The acknowledged master of the task was Giambattista Bugatti, who had worked in an umbrella factory but had somehow been appointed as the state executioner, probably thanks to his nervelessness. When the guillotine was introduced, Bugatti marvelled at 'the new structure for removing the head', that promised to make his job a lot easier. He quickly earned the sobriquet of 'Mastro', which was given to respected leading craftsmen. When his services were required he would mount the scaffold, resplendent in a scarlet robe from which he would produce holy water and religious symbols in case the condemned man wanted them. Flanking the scaffold would be a group of chanting priests and a square of papal troops to keep the hushed crowd at a distance. During an extraordinarily long career, starting from when he was seventeen and ending when he retired at eighty-five, the umbrella-maker Bugatti and his assistants despatched five hundred and sixteen convicted criminals, meticulously listing them all in a notebook.[11]

In the belief that the Carbonari and other secret societies were undermining the Church and inciting violence, on 21 September 1821 Pius issued a blanket ban on them all. Rome itself appeared little bothered by the autocracy. It was becoming a long-desired destination of the 'Grand Tour' of young British aristocrats, and was attracting writers and artists from all over Europe. Gioacchino Rossini was there writing his brilliant operas. But the tired pope was failing fast. Eighty years old and worn out by nearly a quarter-century of tribulations, for some time he had withdrawn into a cocoon of depression. 'He would occupy himself with nothing', wrote an Italian nineteenth century chronicler. 'He never even performed his solemn duties.'[12] He left everything to Cardinal Consalvi, whom some Romans considered a despot. Pius suffered two falls, the second breaking his leg. On 15 July a metalworker labouring on repairs to the Basilica of San Paolo Fuori le Mura in the south of Rome forgot to put out a flame he had been using when he stopped work for the day. That night the whole church burned down. Pius, in pain and debilitated, was in no shape to be told the news. Five days later he died.

The conclave to elect a new pope was held in the Quirinal Palace on 2 September 1823 and by all accounts was an acrimonious affair. The more conservative cardinals had never been quite happy with Pius VII or Cardinal Consalvi, believing them to have been infected with liberal ideals. The Austrian ambassador reported that the atmosphere in the conclave was one of 'passions, hate and revenge ... the price of the papacy would be to humiliate Consalvi and destroy his works'.[13] After the usual horse-trading, the reactionaries triumphed in the person of Cardinal Annibale della Genga, who at age sixty-three became Pope Leo XII – despite his ill-health and his own warning that he was already virtually 'a corpse'. Leo had ample diplomatic experience, having served as a secretary to Pius VI and attended the Diet of Regensburg which officially buried the Holy Roman Empire and replaced it with a German confederation. Elegant and a ladies' man, he was familiar with firearms and liked to shoot birds. The Roman rumour mill claimed he was having an affair with the wife of the commander of the Swiss Guard. Soon this verse appeared on Pasquino:

> As della Genga passed by, a woodsman
> Asked, 'Is this the Holy Father, my goodman?'
> But the captain of the Swiss, standing by,
> Responded: 'Holy nay, but father aye'.[14]

One of Leo's first acts was to move the seat of the papacy from the Quirinal Palace back to the Vatican – after sacking his supposedly liberal rival, secretary of state Consalvi. Public festivities and the heavy layouts required for them were severely curtailed. The new pope continued his predecessor's muscular policy against brigandage (giving executioner Bugatti plenty to do) and issued a strong condemnation of freemasonry which he sensed, with some justice, would grow into a major foe of the papacy in Italy. For six years Leo ruled along strict lines of papal infallibility, going strictly against the grain of the prevailing political tendencies in Europe; memories of Jacobin rule were still relatively fresh and he didn't want to risk a repeat. The Holy Year of 1825, with the usual huge influx of pilgrims, was designed to reinforce that message. But the visitors provoked security concerns, as almost certainly members of the Carbonari and other subversive groups used the event to filter into Rome. Two Carbonari (one of them the son of the pope's chef) were arrested in June, accused of murdering an informer, and delivered to 'Mastro' Bugatti, who on 23 November guillotined them with due ceremony in Piazza del Popolo.

After Leo's death in 1829, his successor Pius VIII relaxed the stern regime; he was seconded by the influential Austrian chancellor, Prince Klemens von Metternich, who feared that an excessively reactionary papal regime might provoke unrest and revolt. Metternich, however, was a classic conservative himself and in Pius VIII believed he had found the ideal combination of traditionalism and a willingness to reform. But this eighth Pius lasted just twenty months. On his death in November 1830, and before a new pope could be elected, an insurrection broke out, triggered by a Carbonari gunsmith and apparently involving officers of the papal army. The real leaders, however, were two of Napoleon's nephews, Louis Napoleon and Louis Charles Napoleon, who had chosen to live in Rome and had good relations with the nobility. Both men, still in their twenties, dreamed of abolishing the papal regime and placing young Napoleon II at the head of a new 'Kingdom of Italy' with Rome as its capital. Security, however, was poor, and the police got wind of the plot. A few papal officers were confined in Sant'Angelo Castle; about sixty hopeful rebels had gathered in Saint Peter's Square, but dispersed on the personal appeal of the Napoleonic siblings, who were expelled from Rome.

The year 1830 saw a fresh revolution in France, where Charles X was toppled and replaced by the more liberal king Louis-Philippe ('dearest son in Christ'), and the splitting of the Catholic southern Netherlands to form independent Belgium. Against this backdrop, and that of the abortive revolt, the conclave got underway on 14 December. Pius' secretary of state, Cardinal Giuseppe Andrea Albani, wanted to keep his job, and so delayed the election of a new pontiff as long as he could until a favourable candidate could present himself. Albani was pro-Austrian, but he overplayed his hand and Metternich was irritated at the delay. In the end, on 2 February 1831, Cardinal Bartolomeo Alberto Cappellari, sixty-five and a dark horse candidate, was picked as Pope Gregory XVI. Two days after the election a revolt broke out in Bologna, where the papal insignia on public buildings were pulled down and the green, red and white nationalist Italian colours raised.

The revolt cast the papacy again into the cauldron of European politics. Napoleonic influences had remained in Rome despite the reaction, and were stronger in the provinces. Among these influences were the idea of popular nationalism, already well advanced in countries such as Britain and France, which provided an alternative narrative to that of older monarchies, of which the papacy was one. Popular nationalism preached that the ultimate value of a people was its inclusion in a distinct nation-state, with its own flag and sovereignty, and that the supreme task of the citizen was to serve the nation-state. The philosophy was the direct opposite of that of the papacy, which based its authority on the timeless values of the Church, and by extension, the brotherhood of mankind. In past centuries the papacy had been forced to become a state precisely in order to defend its lands; but it had never worshipped statehood as an end in itself, and always asserted the superiority of the spiritual over the temporal world. Flag-waving chauvinism was never the Church's style. In papal eyes nationalism was a civil pseudo-religion, creating turmoil where the Church would pray for peace.

Peace would continue to elude the papacy. Six days after Gregory's consecration some of Rome's Carbonari took advantage of a carnival parade to stage a riot in Piazza Colonna. Some shots were fired, but the vast majority of Romans stood fast against the malcontents, who nine days later attacked the pope's carriage. To the rescue came the papal militia, beefed up by volunteers from the Trastevere district, who unhitched the horses from the carriage and bore it along by hand with the pope inside. 'Don't worry, Holy Father, we're here', one of the helpers was heard to say.[15] Cardinal Tommaso Bernetti, the Vatican secretary of state, issued a ringing call for Catholic solidarity in the face of the secret societies; in case any other attempt should be made on the pope's life or security, he said, church bells would be rung and 'all those registered in the military units … [should be] ready to run to the colours at once, in generous defence of the Religion, the Country and the Throne'.[16]

As Bernetti's announcement shows, the need to militarily defend the Papal State remained, and Gregory XVI came to the reluctant conclusion that, as so often in the past, the papacy would have to place its fortunes under the protection of a European great power. In 1830 this was Habsburg Austria, which already controlled Lombardy (including Milan) and Venice. Cardinal Bernetti tried to infuse fresh blood into the indifferently-led papal militia by recruiting devout peasants; but the result was nowhere near enough to be able to put down the spreading nationalist revolts. In March 1831 an Austrian army entered papal territory to suppress the risings there. Yet the Austrians themselves had misgivings about papal-style rule, which even to conservatives appeared to be at odds with the rising tide of sentiment for popular representational government surging through Europe.

Austria, now joined by France under its 'citizen-king' Louis-Philippe, pressured Gregory to allow constitutional reform in the Papal State. The pope flatly refused, triggering more social unrest that was put down harshly with plenty of help from that experienced executioner, 'Mastro' Bugatti. Exasperated, the French and Austrians marched into the Romagna and the Marches, which were technically papal territory, where they stayed for seven years. Only Rome and its province of Lazio (Latium) remained independent. All this left Gregory quite unmoved; in fact, he hardened his political and theological stand, condemning the supremely fashionable ideas of freedom of conscience which instead of promoting human happiness, 'spread ruin'. In his view, secular nationalist states based on the popular will were prone to making war for the worst of reasons – territorial and economic gain. To him it beggared belief that countries ostentatiously touting human rights such as the United States and Britain should engage in disgraces such as the slave trade; in a thunderous encyclical Gregory fulminated against that 'inhuman traffic' by which:

[T]he Blacks, as if they were not men but rather animals, having been brought into servitude, in no matter what way, are, without any distinction, in contempt of the rights of justice and humanity, bought, sold, and devoted sometimes to the hardest labour.[17]

These words show that behind Gregory's hard-shelled intransigence against what the West considered social progress lay a deep-hearted humanitarian spirit. Where other nations saw popular liberties as freeing people from the shackles of tyranny, the pope saw those same people as tragically deluded and falling under satanic rule. His encyclical of August 1832, *Mirari vos*, condemned freedom of the press and conscience as nothing better than 'civic wickedness and shameful licence'. Papal finances, however, were deteriorating. Like his predecessors, he never could eradicate the plague of self-enrichment afflicting some of his senior people. There was only so much tax that could be wrung out of Rome's 170,000 inhabitants and the Lazio area. To stave off collapse, the Papal State resorted to securing five loans from the Rothschild house in Paris between 1831 and 1846.

It was in this spirit that Gregory opposed the construction of a railway between Rome and Spoleto, not so much because he thought that trains were instruments of the devil but for fear that a railway network would facilitate the spread of liberal ideas. But not all the senior clergy agreed with him. Thanks to the archbishop of Spoleto, Giovanni Maria Mastai Ferretti, the line was built. Liberal notions were penetrating to the clergy. In 1837 three Augustinian friars were found to have joined a young nationalist organization, but because they were monks their punishment was mild. The following year Rome was hit by a severe cholera epidemic, which the pope attributed to 'divine justice for our sins'. More than 7,500 Romans perished. Rome's medical services, believed to be among the best in Italy, could do little to alleviate the suffering. The epidemic did nothing to improve the morale of the Romans, and even the Church was beginning to be swayed by the arguments of the Italian nationalists. Especially influential was a thick tome called *The Moral and Civil Primacy of the Italians*, written by a Piedmontese priest, Vincenzo Gioberti. In it Gioberti argued persuasively for a federation of Italian states under the pope's leadership – a kind of admixture of the two hitherto diametrically opposed practices of nationalism and clericalism. One senior cleric who read it carefully was the former archbishop of Spoleto,

Mastai Ferretti, who had done so much to give the town a railway link. That was in 1845, when Mastai Ferretti was a cardinal. The following year, when Gregory XVI died of cancer, Mastai Ferretti was in a position to change things as Pope Pius IX.

Chapter 11

St Patrick's Crusaders

W hat history has come to call the 'unification of Italy' in the late-nineteenth century had in fact a long period of germination, going back at least to Dante. The Italians had always considered themselves a single ethnic group, with their own culture and language, even though for many centuries the various Italian city-states, much like their ancient Greek counterparts, were more often than not at each others' throats, and hence easy marks for domination by stronger powers. Early in the sixteenth century Machiavelli concluded his masterpiece *The Prince* with an impassioned appeal to Cesare Borgia, the son of Pope Alexander VI, to assume the reins of all Italy and throw out the foreigner:

> There is nothing now [Italy] can hope for but that your illustrious house may place itself at the head of this redemption... This barbarous domination stinks in the nostrils of everyone. May your illustrious house therefore assume this task with that courage and those hopes ... so that under its banner our fatherland may be raised up.

Machiavelli ended by quoting the poet Petrarch, who sang of 'the ancient worth that in Italians stirs the heart' and 'is not yet dead'.[1] Italy had to wait at least three more centuries until the visions of Dante and Machiavelli could begin to harden into reality, and the event that hastened the process was the series of revolutions that roiled Europe in 1848.

The shaky status quo preserved by Europe's conservative powers after 1830 never really had a chance. In France, always the epicentre of political games, five factions vied for power, from those who wanted a restored strong Bourbon monarchy to the radical socialists; somewhere in the middle was the clerical party, backed by much of the Catholic peasantry, which resented the loss of the Church's influence. To the clericals, King Louis-Philippe was little more than a tool in the hands of godless liberals. A poor harvest in 1846 and rising unemployment helped trigger an uprising in Paris on 22 February 1848 that grew so serious as to force Louis-Philippe off his throne. A temporary and quite incompetent interim government of republicans and socialists was ousted in a national election two months later; this, however, drove the Parisian radicals to a new insurrection which was put down with some severity, including generous use of the guillotine.

In the neighbouring German states, the intellectual classes were inspired by events in France to try and crack the set-in-concrete conservative system of the Austrian Metternich. Riots in Berlin and other cities moved King Friedrich Wilhelm IV of Prussia to call a representative assembly at Frankfurt. Though it convened with much promise, the assembly wrecked itself on the rocks of a dispute over whether a united Germany should be a monarchy or a republic. Austria also feared a united Germany overshadowing it, as did Russia. In a clumsy compromise, Friedrich Wilhelm gave the Prussians a constitution, though he consented to remain in a German confederation that would not make Austria feel too insecure.

But neither was Metternich's arch-conservative Austria immune to the waves of idealistic unrest emanating from France. A popular uprising in Vienna in March toppled the presumably all-powerful chancellor and squeezed a promise of a constitution out of Emperor Ferdinand I. The spirit of revolt spread to two of Austria's subject peoples, the Czechs and the Hungarians, while the South Slavs set up their own Serbo-Croat state. But dissent among the various rebel factions and nationalities enabled the imperial government to rebound and restore order in Vienna and the outlying districts. Ferdinand I was forced to abdicate in favour of his nephew Franz Josef I, who buried all popular and ethnic agitation under a new layer of authoritarian concrete. One of the imperial army's signal successes was scored by Marshal Josef Radetzky, who effectively put down revolts in Lombardy and Venice. As usual, it was divided Italy that paid much of the price for the problems of Europe's great powers.

Throughout the first half of the nineteenth century nationalist sentiment in Italy was growing. The seed had been planted by Napoleon's influence and nourished, as we have seen, by ill-judged authoritarian crackdowns, including those by popes Leo XII, Pius VIII and Gregory XVI. It seemed natural that secular nationalist sentiment would grow more quickly in those areas most distant from the papacy and geographically closer to France and

Austria, that is, North Italy. The most cohesive of the Italian powers was the kingdom of Piedmont and Sardinia, which had been going through a series of convulsions dating back to the 1820s and now was headed by King Carlo Alberto. This monarch placed himself at the head of the nationalist movement, planning to boot Radetzky's white-coated Austrians off Italian soil. He found an ally in the popular new pope, Pius IX.

On his accession two years before, Pius had made sincere efforts to lighten the more severe laws and taxes that had oppressed the Romans, and his popularity had rocketed sky-high as a result. The 'liberating and renewing pope', backed up by an administration of liberal cardinals, appeared to have an auspicious future ahead of him. On 12 March 1847 he decreed press freedom. Protestants and Jews were reported to be converting to the Roman Catholic Church in admiration.[2] Banners and posters went up all over Rome, lauding the pope as 'consolation of his subjects and marvel of the world'. The unassuming Pius himself was embarrassed, even alarmed, by all this, and felt compelled to issue an edict banning the showier manifestations of adulation. Pius appointed a cousin, Cardinal Gabriele Ferretti, as secretary of state. Ferretti dissolved the old papal contingents of the Papal State, replacing them with a loyal citizens' militia.

When Pius added his voice to the call for Italian freedom against Austrian occupation, Romans and others flocked to the white and gold papal banner. 'May the Almighty God bless Italy!' he intoned in a speech on 10 February 1848, at about the time when Louis-Philippe was swept away by public discontent in France. Later that year Ferretti resigned as papal secretary of state and was replaced by Cardinal Giacomo Antonelli, an experienced administrator of liberal leanings. Antonelli engineered a constitution for the papal state, but those who hoped that Pius would be relegated to a mere figurehead role, confined to 'praying and blessing', would be disappointed. The reality was that he had to walk a tightrope, maintaining his popularity among Italians on the one hand, but reluctant to overly antagonize Austria on the other. Austria, he knew, could snuff out the Papal State whenever it had a mind to do so. On 17 March a revolt broke out in Milan – supported by the clergy among others – forcing Radetzky to withdraw his troops to the city fortress. After five days of street fighting a provisional government asked for Carlo Alberto's protection. The Sardinian king then declared war on Austria; troops from Naples marched north, as well as a column of papal troops under General Giacomo Durando.

Durando's participation was short-lived. No sooner had he arrived in Lombardy than Pius had a change of heart; Austria was a Catholic state, and the pope did not want to begin a precedent of one Catholic power marching against another. Durando was accused of exceeding his orders and called back, though many of his men supported the anti-Austrian cause. Pius most likely changed his mind because he saw that the political wind was not blowing in the Sardinian king's favour. His words on 29 April were clear: 'He Who is the author of peace' embraces 'all peoples with equal care and paternal love.' In fact he considered the Sardinian king to be the aggressor and in case anyone did not get the message, set his face against the idea of a united Italy with himself at the ceremonial head.[3] Confirming the pope's concerns, Carlo Alberto was trounced at Custozza in July.

Many contrasted Pius' new attitude with his earlier 'God bless Italy'. But there was no contradiction. Asking for divine benediction on one's own people did not necessarily mean demonizing others, as some naive souls had hoped. Pius was not a chauvinist: quite the opposite – he was quite prepared to bless every nation on earth if they pursued the path of peace. Nevertheless, his motives were inevitably misunderstood; phrases such as 'traitor pope' began to be bandied about. To placate fickle public sentiment Pius toyed with the idea of further liberalizing his administration. But something in him rebelled at the idea of being a powerless constitutional monarch, so he brought in an Italian who until then had been Louis-Philippe's ambassador to the Papal State, Count Pellegrino Rossi, as prime minister. Rossi satisfied no-one, with the result that on 15 November 1848, while entering the Chancellery Palace, he was stabbed to death by a group of discontented former papal troops.

The assassination was the signal for a liberal-led demonstration in front of the Quirinal Palace. The crowd demanded a democratic government from the pope and, as a concession to the nationalists, war with Austria, the oppressor of North Italy. When the pope flatly refused to countenance those demands – he would not declare war on a Catholic power – the mob brought in a cannon to point at the papal residence. A few armed hotheads fired at the building, killing a monsignor standing at a window. On 17 November Pius acceded to the demands, though making clear that he was acting under duress and hence his decision could have no real validity. Now he felt real danger approaching. Leaving the papal government under the control of Monsignor Carlo Emanuele Muzzarelli, he slipped out of the Quirinal Palace on the night of 24 November disguised as an ordinary priest and accompanied only by his personal valet. He was met by the Bavarian ambassador, Karl Spaur, who took the fleeing pope into his own carriage and trundled him out of papal territory to Gaeta, over the Neapolitan border. At Gaeta to meet him was Cardinal Antonelli, who had left Rome in disguise a few days earlier. Ferdinand II, the king of Naples and Sicily, made the fugitive pope feel at home as he issued a call to Europe's Catholic powers to help him regain the throne of Saint Peter.

Muzzarelli's administration in Rome merely marked time, limiting itself to issuing messages to the people of the Papal State to keep calm. On 3 December Pius, still at Gaeta, nominated a commission to govern Rome in his absence. But such was the uncertainty that permeated the entire state that the nominees refused to serve. Muzzarelli sent envoys to the pope to discuss the conditions under which he might return, but the Neapolitan authorities refused them access. Impatient at the delays, on 12 December the liberals in Rome took over the running of the city by a coup d'état that installed a three-man junta as the ruling body. However much Pius protested this 'usurpation of [his] sovereign powers', two weeks later the junta dissolved the moribund papal parliament and announced elections for 21 January 1849.

Pius' response was to threaten excommunication against anyone voting in that election, which he considered thoroughly illegal. Yet the election went ahead anyway, electing as representatives some of the leading figures of Italian nationalism and liberalism, such as Giuseppe Garibaldi and Giuseppe Mazzini (neither of them Romans, it might be added). The resulting Constituent Assembly met on 5 February in the Campidiglio (the old Roman Capitol), and after a curious religious ceremony of sorts elected an old papal associate, Giuseppe Galletti, as president. Three days later the Assembly took the revolutionary step of proclaiming a new Roman republic. Article 1 of the new constitution declared: 'The papacy is defunct in fact, and by order of the temporal government of the Roman State.' Article 2 went on to add, however, that the pope would continue to be granted the right to exercise his spiritual functions. The constitution was voted into law on 3 July.[4]

None of this went down well with Europe's leaders, especially the man who after 1848 took over the reins in France. That year's excesses in Paris had alarmed the French middle classes and Catholic peasantry enough to vote for stability in the form of the Second French Republic, and the late Napoleon I's nephew (there is some doubt about whether he was legitimate), Louis Napoleon Bonaparte, emerged as president of France. Basically an adventurer, this man had already staged two abortive attempts to seize power that had earned him a term in jail. He had escaped to England, where he spent a number of years, returning to France in 1848 to take advantage of the turmoil. He had little but the name Napoleon to recommend him, but the name itself acted like a magnet on French people of all classes, and barely forty years old, he was elected president of France by a landslide. To traditionalists he also had the advantage of belonging to the Napoleonic royal family; he used this connection to the full, presenting himself as a new Napoleon who would restore greatness to *la France*.

Italy had always loomed large in French geopolitical calculations. Louis Napoleon, alarmed at the rising power of Austria and its control over large swaths of North Italy, and disinclined to alienate his loyal French Catholics by allowing the papacy to be swept away, decided to become the pope's saviour. In December 1848 a French flotilla with 3,500 soldiers under General Nicolas-Charles-Victor Oudinot anchored off Civitavecchia ready to march on Rome if necessary. In March 1849 the ardent nationalist Mazzini put himself at the head of a Roman triumvirate protected by about 20,000 soldiers under Garibaldi. On 28 April Oudinot, now reinforced to about 6,000 men, disembarked and moved on Rome to restore the pope – the exact opposite of what French armies had done forty years before. Curiously, Oudinot had neither artillery nor any sort of siege apparatus, and appeared to be under the comforting impression that the Romans would gratefully throw open the gates at his mere appearance.

He could not have been more wrong. About 10,000 of Garibaldi's men waited in Rome to repel the French; these were organized into four brigades, each one guarding a sector of the city. On 30 April Oudinot ordered an assault on the Porta San Pancrazio at the southern end of Gianicolo Hill in order to penetrate the Trastevere district. The attack smashed itself against determined resistance, and fell back in tatters at the cost of 1,000 Frenchmen dead, wounded and captured, against a loss of about 200 for the Romans.

Oudinot appealed to Paris for reinforcements; Louis Napoleon consented, but also sent an envoy, Ferdinand-Marie de Lesseps (later to earn fame as the digger of the Suez Canal), who patched up a temporary truce with Mazzini. Oudinot protested strongly; after receiving his requested reinforcements he was eager to resume the offensive.

While de Lesseps and Mazzini were negotiating, however, Austrian forces had taken Bologna in the Papal States, followed in short order by Imola, Forlì, Cesena and Rimini with hardly a shot fired. At the end of May an Austrian fleet in the Adriatic Sea landed troops at Ancona after a four-day siege. A Neapolitan force moved into Lazio, but was repulsed by Garibaldi. In the early hours of 3 June – a day earlier than he had let on – Oudinot, now in command of 35,000 troops in three brigades and seventy-five field guns, unleashed his force against Rome's western suburbs. A fierce firefight raged around the elegant Casino dei Quattro Venti and other patrician villas and grounds. By 6 July the French had reached the Milvian Bridge where, 1,500 years before, the Roman emperor Constantine I had defeated his pagan foes and inaugurated a new era in Roman history. In like manner Oudinot, similarly out to defeat a new secular paganism, tried to secure a footing on the left bank of Tiber to get into the heavily-defended heart of Rome. Constant artillery barrages smashed the resistance on the ridge of Gianicolo Hill. The defenders fought valiantly, but dissention between Garibaldi and other senior commandeers weakened their efforts.

The Battle for Rome reached its climax on 30 June when Garibaldi, whose pregnant Brazilian-born wife Anita fought at his side, defended the Aurelian Walls almost single-handedly, but the sheer force of French numbers broke the republic's morale. Against the will of Mazzini, the two-hundred-member Constituent Assembly voted to break off hostilities 'in the name of God and the People'. A new triumvirate was elected to confirm the capitulation. In the morning of 3 July French troops paraded along the Via del Corso, amid catcalls and insults from republican bystanders. At some points the troops had to disperse hostile crowds; Oudinot personally tore down a green, white and red nationalist flag from a café window. The following morning Oudinot declared the Roman republic dissolved, muzzled the press and appointed General Louis de Rostolan as military governor of Rome. Garibaldi had already left the city with 4,000 men in the hope of somewhere carrying on the fight. He eventually retired to Venice; on the way his wife Anita died of malaria. On 15 July 1849 a hundred cannon shots from Sant'Angelo castle announced the imminent return of Pius IX.[5]

The pope waited at Gaeta until some semblance of normality could return to French-occupied Rome; in the meantime three cardinals were appointed to run the papal administration in his absence. This cardinalate promptly nullified all laws enacted under republican regimes and launched a witch-hunt against all unreconstructed republicans and liberals. Clergy who had collaborated with the republic were put on trial and strict allegiance to the papacy was demanded of all public servants. Only when all dissent was suppressed (though some cardinals protested at the severity of the cardinalate's measures) did Pius return to Rome on 12 April 1850.

It is the custom among liberal historians (especially in Protestant countries) to bewail the restoration of the papacy as a political step backward in the history of modern Europe. The terms 'reactionary,' 'despotic' and 'a return to the past' are usually and liberally employed, as if that was all there was to the story. True, repressive measures were restored, dissent was hounded and some unpopular taxes reinstated and raised in an effort to balance the state budget. True, also, the Inquisition was restored and the Papal State took on some of the characteristics of a police state. The poor of Rome remained poor, and to outsiders the Papal State seemed to be a throwback to the Middle Ages. So far, that has been the politically fashionable view to take. But one must remember that Pius, on his return to Rome in 1850, was a badly rattled man. His earlier liberal idealism, based on a genuine humble concern for human welfare, had evaporated after seeing what evils could come from notions of popular sovereignty taken to extreme lengths. He now would have fully agreed with Gregory XVI that the ideas of democracy and nationalism that had taken over Europe and America were actually arrant and dangerous nonsense. Mankind was deluding itself if its intellectuals thought that peoples could rationally rule themselves. So far this principle had brought nothing but war, death, destruction and ethnic hatreds to millions of people. Pius wished to make the Papal State a refuge from all this, a small example of a state based on the rule of God rather than Mammon. And if it took strong-arm methods, so be it.

The pope had a powerful European ally in the person of Louis Napoleon, who on 2 December 1851 gave himself a new job as Emperor Napoleon III. From the first, he aimed to be the arbiter of Europe's destiny and needed papal support, not because he was particularly devout himself, but because he knew it would keep the French Catholic masses happy. He had already secured their support by placing French schools under clerical supervision which most law-abiding French people, still remembering the recent socialist agitation, applauded. While Napoleon III beautified Paris, turning it into the charming metropolis it is today, he coddled the army and hoped to use it to realize dreams of foreign conquest.

In Italy, however, the nationalist cause was gathering steam. Its standard-bearer was the king of Sardinia and Piedmont, Vittorio Emanuele II of the house of Savoy, who was determined to unite all Italy, including the Papal State, under his rule (Carlo Alberto had abdicated after proving unable to defeat the Austrians). The Kingdom of Sardinia, which included Piedmont, boasted a competent army and a hard-working population supporting a healthy economy; but alone it could not kick out the Austrians. Mazzini, though expelled from Rome after the pope's return, as a left-leaning liberal distrusted the house of Savoy. But one man in Vittorio Emanuele's cabinet saw the European kaleidoscope for what it was, and felt he could manipulate it. This was the minister of trade and agriculture, Camillo Benso di Cavour, who had been waiting patiently to put in motion a plan he had been nurturing for a long time. This was nothing less than to give Italy a unified parliamentary government on the British model. Just forty, but greatly experienced and highly successful in business, he had a razor-sharp as well as a cool mind that instinctively understood the intricacies of European politics and knew how to harness them for Italy. His plan for Italy can be summarized in his slogan: 'A free church in a free state'.

This suggestion for a separation of church and state in a unified Italy was flatly rejected by Pius, who responded by excommunicating the Piedmontese. His argument reflected the unchanging philosophy of the papacy over the centuries: that 'temporal power is necessary to this Holy See, so that for the good of religion it can exercise spiritual power without any hindrance'.[6] In short, the pope had always needed a state set-up and an associated armed force to protect the faith from its worldly enemies. The chief enemy here had become Vittorio Emanuele II, with the impulsively anti-clerical Garibaldi running a close second – not to mention Cavour, the cleverest and most patient of them all. Cavour had been assiduously cultivating his contacts with the European powers; he enlisted the kingdom of Sardinia on the side of Britain and France in the Crimean War, which he saw as a chance to bring his country to the notice of Napoleon III in the peace settlement. In 1849 Cavour and Napoleon signed the Pact of Plombières, in which Cavour gave France the region of Savoy (for which some Italians still haven't forgiven him) in return for French help in establishing the house of Savoy as the royal family of Italy. The state was thus set for the final showdown of nationalist Italy with the Papal State.

In that state Cardinal Antonelli had been responsible for suppressing brigandage; the most notorious bandit, an ex-ferryman called Stefano Pelloni, was killed in a shootout with papal gendarmes. The trial for the 1848 murder of papal finance minister Rossi ended with death sentences for those convicted. An opposition movement of monarchists and republicans in Rome, the National Roman Committee (*Comitato Nazionale Romano*), backed by Mazzini, was accused of plotting to assassinate the pope. Five of those tried were sentenced to death and fifty-three others to long terms in jail. Pius himself, however, mitigated the sentences, so no-one had to climb the scaffold. Austrian general Radetzky in Ferrara had three liberal conspirators shot. On 12 June 1855 a disgruntled priest attacked Cardinal Antonelli with a pitchfork and ended up on Bugatti's guillotine.[7]

In 1859 Pope Pius IX was sixty-seven years old. His silver hair and kindly expression were reassuringly familiar to Romans. He had been born into a well-to-do family in Senigallia in papal territory. A serious fall when he was an infant had left him with epilepsy that became severe enough to interrupt his studies when he was sixteen. But the young Giovanni Mastai Ferretti had a sociable and outgoing character, and was good in sports, including horsemanship and fencing. He was also a lusty youth, scoring considerable success with women, including married ones. A messy affair with a local actress resulted in Giovanni being packed off to Rome to be under the guardianship of an uncle who was a canon of Saint Peter's. Once there he tried to join Pius VII's Noble Guard, but failed the medical because of his record of epilepsy. In 1815, while on a pilgrimage to the Catholic holy site of Loreto in north-central Italy, he was cured of his epilepsy, an event which fortified his already growing faith. In Rome he resumed his studies in theology and philosophy in the Collegio Romano. He was already a seminarian when he obtained his university degree and made a name for himself helping homeless children in the Tata Giovanni hospice.[8]

Giovanni Mastai Ferretti appears (despite the claims of detractors) to have been sincere in renouncing his privileged upbringing and dissolute youth habits. He returned to Senigallia as a Franciscan monk and preached in the main square, drawing large crowds (which cynics claimed included his ex-lovers). In 1823 he was sent to the papal mission in Chile, where for two years he experienced at first hand life under a violently anticlerical government. Two years after his return Pope Leo XII named him archbishop of Spoleto, where, as we have seen, he helped start up one of Italy's first railways. Thanks to his eagerness to help families in need, his reputation survived the upheavals of 1830; when papal forces were about to fire on protesters, he talked the commanders out of it while getting the rebels to lay down their own arms. He allowed several Carbonari sympathizers to escape to France – one of whom was the future Napoleon III.

Hostilities between Sardinia and Austria broke out in 1859, thanks to Cavour's manoeuvrings. His deal with Napoleon III, he believed, had freed his hands for what he and many Italians considered a war of liberation. Austrian forces were pulled out of the Papal State to defend Lombardy and Venice. At once revolutionary committees sprang up in Bologna and other cities declaring that they were throwing off papal rule and wished to unite with Piedmont-Sardinia. Pius could only renew his excommunication on the kingdom, which was long past taking such moves seriously. Fierce and bloody battles between the French and Austrians were fought on Italian soil at Magenta and Solferino. In both those encounters the French worsted their opponents, and the Austrians appeared to be on the run, but without warning Napoleon about-faced. First, the carnage at Magenta and Solferino had shocked him; second, Prussia was making threatening noises; third, he was suddenly suspicious of the strength of Italian national feeling and feared it might turn against him. He wanted to control Italy, plus Rome, as that way he could also control the pope and with him the sentiments of his French Catholic subjects. It was a devious game, but the mid-nineteenth century was a time of very devious diplomatic games played by all the European powers in the struggle for mastery of the continent. In the words of A.J.P. Taylor, 'the world of diplomacy was much like the world of business, in which respect for the sanctity of contract does not prevent the most startling reversals of fortune.'[9]

Pius was neither a businessman nor a wily diplomat but a sincere prelate who measured the European scene by the yardstick of whether it conformed to Christian ideals and found that it decidedly did not, hence he wanted as little as possible to do with the diplomatic machinations of his time. It's not clear whether he realized he was being used by Napoleon, but as for Cavour, he was devastated by French duplicity and resigned his office. In solidarity with Cavour the people of the Romagna in the Papal State voted to join Vittorio Emanuele's kingdom of Sardinia. Copycat revolts broke out elsewhere, including Bologna, where the pope sent 1,700 papal troops, mainly Swiss, under Colonel Antonio Schmidt d'Altdorf to restore order. On 20 June 1859 Schmidt d'Altdorf approached the city, defended by less than a thousand poorly-armed civilians. In the ensuing clash at the appropriately-named Porta San Pietro ten troops were killed and thirty-five wounded, at a cost of twenty-seven rebels killed and more than a hundred wounded. Having driven the rebel administration from Perugia, the papal troops went on a rampage described by *The New York Times* as a series of 'shocking murders and other barbarities on defenceless men, women and children'.[10] It was the worst possible publicity for Pius.

By the 1860 Treaty of Turin, Sardinia annexed the Romagna as well as Lombardy and Tuscany, taking a few more bites out of Pius' domain. The settlement encouraged Cavour to return to office, but meanwhile the joker in the Italian pack, Garibaldi, had emerged to create fresh trouble. After his ejection from Rome Garibaldi had languished in exile until the events of 1859 drew him back to Italy. He recruited a company of volunteers to fight the Austrians; he was good at fighting, but lacked the character and political maturity to appreciate what Cavour was trying to do. He was a sort of naive far-left firebrand who had no use for aristocracy or royalty of any sort, and particularly popes. In 1860 Cavour needed time to organize Sardinia's new territorial gains at the expense of the papacy before attempting any more military moves.

But Garibaldi, the man of action, was impatient; he could not rest until all Italy was free. On 5 May 1860 he sailed from Genoa with 1,088 red-shirted enthusiasts (later romanticized into 'The Thousand') to attack the kingdom of Naples and Sicily (the 'two Sicilies'). Though the Sicilian people were not exactly revolt-minded, Garibaldi defeated the vastly superior forces of the weak Neapolitan King Francesco II (nicknamed 'Lasagna' because of his pliability) in a series of battles in the Sicilian mountains. That same month he sent Colonel Callimaco Zambianchi, known as a chicken thief, and sixty men to Perugia to divert papal attention away from the threat from the south. The largely hostile inhabitants of Lazio soon tipped off Rome; on 19 May eighty mounted papal gendarmes under Colonel Georges de Pimodan surprised Zambianchi's men at Grotte di San Lorenzo as they were sitting around the village square drinking. After a brief and unequal exchange, nine redshirts lay dead among the café tables and the rest had fled in disorder. (Among the former was the brother of the man who had tried to assassinate Napoleon III in Paris two years before.) De Pimodan, a former officer under the Austrian Radetzky, was promoted to brigadier, while the Roman press sang the praises of a company commander, Luigi Evangelisti, who had led the attack.

Garibaldi occupied Naples on 7 September, driving out the Bourbons. By now, however, Pius had finally been gathering a military defence force worthy of the name. He had the good sense to appoint a Belgian nobleman and ex-soldier who had taken holy orders, François-Xavier de Mérode, a former chaplain of the papal army, to take charge of the army itself and reorganize it. De Mérode's first move was to call on a distant relative, General Christophe-Léon de La Moricière, to command the army. A French former war minister who had fallen out of Napoleon's favour and had been exiled to Brussels, La Moricière had meanwhile found solace in the Catholic faith and was delighted to be offered command of the pope's forces. Arriving in Rome, he found a weak and demoralized military establishment of eleven under-strength battalions totalling some 7,000 men with very few senior officers; fortifications were crumbling, cannon dismantled, munitions stocks low, and medical and hygienic equipment scarce. With the cloud of invasion always hanging over Rome, La Moricière proposed a kind of European crusade to save the state and reputation of the papacy, and the pope agreed.[11]

Garibaldi, meanwhile, was widely and correctly believed to be plotting to seize Rome. In such a case, the fate of the papacy would be sealed. Not even in 410, when Alaric's Goths had sacked the city, and in 1527, when the German *Landsknechte* in 1527 perpetrated an even worse outrage, had the papacy been in such direct danger. The tsunami of the new European civil religion of liberalism and nationalism, it seemed, was about to sweep it away for ever. But at this juncture Pius, still holding out for his ideal of what a Christian state should be, received a welcome response from the most unexpected of quarters. For devout Catholics all over Europe, and even in America, had become angry enough to flock to the papal banner and finally give the Pius the army he needed. The last of the crusades was on.

As the threat to Rome gained press publicity all over Europe and North America, recruiting centres for a new pope's army began to spring up. Austrian and German volunteers flocked to the centres in Vienna and Ancona, Belgians to Ancona and Marseilles, French to Civitavecchia, and Irish to Ancona. All were baptized on presentation but only bachelors and widowers with no dependants were accepted for service, with the additional requirement that the volunteer be between eighteen and fifty years old (fifty-five for those with previous military experience), and at least 1.53 metres tall (1.55 metres for a horseman). On enlistment each soldier was entitled to a bounty of twelve *scudi* (about 900 euros in today's European money) and a guarantee of a pension after thirty years' service.

La Moricière organized the volunteers into ethnic battalions to preserve unit morale; the Franco-Belgians specialized as snipers, the Germans as riflemen and the Irish – now the proud 'Saint Patrick's Crusaders' – as front-line shock troops. The first unit to take shape was a sharpshooters' platoon of seven Frenchmen and four Belgians who had travelled to Rome, plus four volunteers from the Swiss Guard. They were placed under the command of Captain Athanase de Charette de la Contrie, who brought his three younger brothers with him. By June this unit had grown to battalion strength, to be led by Count Louis de Becdelièvre, a decorated Crimean War veteran, who inspected it daily at its training base at Terni.

The most dedicated of Pius' volunteers were the 'Saint Patrick's Crusaders'. Refusing to fraternize with the French or Belgians, they retained a fanatic Irish identity of their own. The reasons were partly political; many Irishmen joined up to strike a blow, however indirect, against an England which was looking kindly on Cavour's efforts to unite Italy. A recruiting centre was set up in Dublin, but Lord Palmerston's British government banned Irishmen – still British subjects – from fighting for a foreign potentate, so the centre had to masquerade as an overseas employment agency. When the number of Irish recruits – some of them veterans of British Army campaigns in India – reached about a thousand they were placed under the command of a charismatic ex-journalist, Major Myles William O'Reilly.

A rigid disciplinarian known as 'Mad Eye', O'Reilly was often flanked by Irish priests in Rome. He had under his wing his nineteen-year-old cousin Albert O'Reilly, the youngest Irish volunteer. Typical of the attitude is what one man wrote in a letter home: 'We came to Italy with the sole thought of defending our religion! We all knew that we would earn nothing but danger and death.'

Members of the Catholic nobilities of Europe also flocked to the papal colours. Many had no problem at all with being given non-commissioned rank or even none. Counts, barons, counts and viscounts, used to giving orders to servants at home, willingly consented to serve as sergeants, corporals and even privates in Pius' army. When it came to fighting for the faith, social distinctions were sloughed off. The pope himself, moved by the response, wrote to the army chaplain, Monsignor Gilbert Talbot: 'In our extreme anxiety we are truly inspired to see with what alacrity and concern illustrious men and youths, even of noble lineage, flock daily to the courageous defence of the Apostolic See.' Would Garibaldi's 'Thousand' finally meet their match?

The South Italian realm of the Bourbons was no more; thanks partly to the help of Naples' infamous Camorra, Garibaldi had put paid to it in an amazingly short time. But Cavour had become alarmed; Garibaldi's impetuousness might bring a French army to the pope's rescue, and that was the last thing he wanted. He persuaded Europe's powers that 'continental stability would be promoted' if Vittorio Emanuele annexed Umbria and the Marches while allowing the redshirts to infiltrate into papal territory from the south, thus enclosing the Papal State in a vice. On 8 September Colonel Luigi Masi of Garibaldi's force invaded the Papal State while nationalist Piedmontese (a term that can now be safely used instead of Sardinian) forces under General Enrico Cialdini pressed on the northern frontier; the small Piedmontese navy under Admiral Carlo Pellion di Persano sailed from Naples around the boot of Italy and up the Adriatic to Ancona, to prepare to support the nationalist campaign.

To avoid the impression of being the aggressors, Vittorio Emanuele and Cavour protested to the pope about his use of foreign mercenaries to fight Italians, giving themselves a kind of moral cause. An ultimatum was delivered to La Moricière, who rejected it, and the Piedmontese had the excuse they needed. Cialdini told his troops they were about to move against 'a gang of inebriates [who] have no country and seek to lord it' over the people. La Moricière could not yet bring himself to believe that Vittorio Emanuele, a Catholic monarch, would actually move against the Vicar of Christ. But numbers showed otherwise. The Piedmontese king had 28,000 disciplined troops under arms and modern rifled cannon. Against this La Moricière could field just 8,000 infantry, 1,000 cavalry and about thirty obsolete field guns. The papal front-line force consisted of four brigades along the Foligno-Terni-Macerata line: the 1st Brigade under Schmidt, the 2nd Brigade under de Pimodan, and the 3rd Brigade under Rapahel de Courten; the 4th Brigade under Colonel Cropt was held in reserve at Spoleto. Some 5,000 more papal troops defended Ancona and 8,000 were assigned to the defence of Rome.

Nationalist forces occupied Urbino on 11 September and moved on Pesaro, defended by Colonel Giovanni Battista Zappi, eight hundred gendarmes and three antiquated cannon. Zappi was prepared to resist to the last but was dissuaded by the papal legate, who wished to avoid bloodshed and harm to civilians. The following day Fano fell, and Senigallia, Pius' birthplace, the day after. Pius sent a rising star of his officer corps, Colonel Hermann Kanzler, to Ancona with two columns totalling 1,200 men; on the approaches to the city he fought off three nationalist cavalry charges and secured the port. Meanwhile, the Garibaldian General Zambianchi and Colonel Masi made a joint move on Perugia, defended by Schmidt and an assortment of Swiss, Italian and Irish papal troops. Schmidt, however, appears to have lost his nerve and offered to surrender on 14 September. But his Irish contingent remained defiant and about a score of them escaped to join Major O'Reilly's men at Spoleto.

It wasn't long before Piedmontese advances left O'Reilly in an untenable position. He had six hundred men, half of them Irish and the rest a mixture of French, Belgians, Swiss, Austrians and Italians, plus an old howitzer. A message from de Mérode in Rome told him he could not expect reinforcements. The Piedmontese opened up with a cannonade from four batteries, followed by a bayonet charge that O'Reilly, hanging on among ruined walls, successfully resisted. In Spoleto itself, the battle raged as the Irish stayed put like a stone wall, beating off successive attacks that continued into the night. O'Reilly had a problem maintaining the flow of supplies and manpower among sectors, and as the night wore on he felt himself failing. After a solid fifteen-hour fight, and to save the lives of his men, he offered to surrender on condition that he and his contingent, including the wounded, be allowed to evacuate Spoleto. The Piedmontese commander, General Filippo Brignone, shaken by the casualties his attacking division had sustained, agreed.

La Moricière sent the brigades of Cropt and de Pimodan to reinforce Kanzler in Ancona, but the mood in the Vatican was grim. Vittorio Emanuele's forces, cheered on by Europe's leaders (as well as Protestants everywhere) seemed unstoppable. At this point Napoleon III stepped in to see if he could earn a bit of prestige by halting the scrap. There was a spark of hope in the Vatican that French forces might come to the rescue of the papacy, but Napoleon's move, like everything else he did, was duplicitous; he had no intention of aiding Rome militarily, and Cialdini knew it. On 15 September La Moricière entered Macerata and Loreto the next day, scattering a squadron of Piedmontese dragoons, coming within sight of Cialdini's camp at Castelfidardo that lay in his path to Ancona. That night a papal patrol stumbled on a Piedmontese outpost; in the exchange of fire patrol leader Mizael de Pas, who was the first Frenchman to enlist in the pope's army, was also the first to die in the pope's service.

The 4,600 papal infantrymen and four hundred horsemen spent the following day in prayer and confession, knowing they would soon be tested in battle. De Pimodan's brigade flew Don John of Austria's standard of the Battle of Lepanto. What happened next is disputed. La Moricière's eight battalions had to descend from high ground at Loreto, cross the Musone river and climb again to Castelfidardo. Arrayed against them in the front line were Cialdini's *bersaglieri* under the cover of trees and a line of cannon. De Pimodan, in front, knew that his paltry four cannon would do little if anything, and ordered a bayonet charge. In the lead was a Swiss gendarme detachment under Colonel Joseph-Eugène Allet and de Becdelièvre's marksmen. The mostly-green papal troops fell back under a hail of fire from the *bersaglieri* and Cialdini's artillery; but de Becdelièvre's bayonets cut through the first Piedmontese position, taking more than a hundred prisoners. At that point two papal cannon, dragged by hand by the Irish, arrived to pour some fire into the Piedmontese positions. Cialdini responded with a counterattack; de Charette was wounded in the hand and groin, but the papals stood fast.

By sheer numbers, however, the Piedmontese began to push the papals back; in response, de Pimodan spurred his horse forward, shouting 'God is with us!' Prodigies of valour were performed by Viscount Couëssin de Broiriou who served as a mere corporal. Henri Wyart, a former Cistercian monk, his forearm shattered by a ball and with a bayonet wound in his neck, fought on until losing consciousness. A ball smashed de Pimodan's jaw. La Moricière was on the point of riding up with reinforcements when the Piedmontese howitzers opened up, cutting large swaths in his Austrian units. The papal troops had to fall back; a volley of bullets hit de Pimodan, who fell from his horse and died after being taken to Loreto. De Becdelièvre tried to resist the enemy advance with the one-third of a battalion left to him; a ball hit Gaultier de Kermoal between the shoulder blades and exited from his chest – miraculously, he survived. Couëssin was captured, but treated kindly, thanks to a sympathetic Piedmontese captain.

No more than 2,000 papal troops – about half the number that had set out for Ancona – straggled into Loreto. Irish and French–Belgian units lost half their effectives. Many of the wounded were to die in the next few days. One of them was Joseph-Louis Guérin, an ex-seminarian, who before expiring got a friend to help him write a last letter home:

> A long time ago I offered God and the Church the sacrifice of my life. Envy me my happiness and comfort my poor mother. Long live Pius IX, Pontiff and King!

La Moricière was criticized for assaulting numerically superior, better-trained and well-equipped troops holding a strong position. But at least his conduct was nobler than that of Cialdini, whom a modern Italian historian has called 'one of the worst generals of our sad military history'.[12] After his victory at Castelfidardo, without any attempt to follow it up, Cialdini boasted that he had overcome a papal army 'three times the strength' of his own and captured noble names that in the view of one of his officers were like 'a list for a ball in Louis XIV's court'.

While La Moricière and a few hundred men fled towards Ancona, the rest of the papal army at Loreto still had some fight left in it. De Becdelièvre and other commanders argued for a fight to the last, but others had had enough of suicidal tactics. The senior commander present, Colonel Gudenhoven, decided to err on the side of caution and approached Cialdini with an offer of surrender. Cialdini accepted, allowing the papal soldiers to go home after a brief detention. La Moricière, however, was determined to fight on; leaving three hundred infantrymen to block the Piedmontese pursuit, he and eighty others reached Ancona on the evening of 18 September. The port, meanwhile, was being bombarded by Persano's Neapolitan flotilla of six frigates offshore. Over the next three days the Piedmontese artillery joined in the bombardment. On 23 September someone patrolling the defences seems to have fired at La Moricière and missed; one man was arrested and tried, but the real identity of the shooter remains a mystery.

The Piedmontese-Neapolitan attack on Ancona began in earnest on the night of 25 September. An attempt to break the chain across the harbour mouth came to nought. The mass of Piedmontese under General Manfredo Fanti hammered at the outer defences of Ancona, while the Irish and Austrian defenders fiercely contested every inch. On two occasions Saint Patrick's Crusaders staged counterattacks, halting the nationalists. On 27 September Cialdini sent Brigadier-General Raffaele Cadorna (the father of Luigi Cadorna who would command Italy's forces in World War One) to break through the Porta Pia; five times he managed it and five times he was driven back by the head of the defence, Captain Fortunato Rivalta. Five thousand papal troops in Ancona were holding back ten times the number of Piedmontese, so Fanti appealed to Persano to step up his bombardment by sea. The Neapolitan admiral concentrated his fire on the twelve papal guns on the seafront, as only by knocking them out could he snap the harbour chain. The papal artillery commander, Austrian Lieutenant Westminthal, never had a chance. Only three of his pieces were able to fire before one of Persano's ships, the *Vittorio Emanuele*, took care of them; Westminthal himself fell dead over his last gun.

La Moricière raised the white flag in the afternoon of 28 September. As he considered that his defeat was caused by the fire from the ships rather than by any action by the Piedmontese land forces, he offered to surrender to Persano. Conscious that he was not the senior commander in the campaign, the Neapolitan admiral rejected the offer but is understood to have suggested a cease-fire while the offer went through the proper channels. However Cadorna, seeing victory within his grasp, ordered a furious bombardment that ended only when an envoy from La Moricière signed the papal capitulation. The terms were as generous as those agreed at Loreto: all the papal troops would be allowed to go free after a brief detention period. La

Moricière spent some days as a guest of Persano on his flagship, the *Maria Adelaide*, but was excoriated in the Roman press as incompetent.[13]

Oddly enough, the fall of Ancona came as a relief of sorts to the papacy. The city's exposed position in the far north of the Papal State had made it a liability. The criticism aimed at La Moricière thus may not have been quite fair, as in strategic terms he may have been ordered to do something for which the papal forces were ill-equipped, both in numbers and weapons. Napoleon III ordered his military chief in Rome, General Charles-Marie-Augustin Goyon, to brace for the protection of the pope and the Church; it was clear, however, that Goyon's orders applied only to Rome and its environs and not the rest of the Papal State, which was seen as virtually finished. Napoleon himself, however, was now in agreement with most of Europe that the time for a papal state was over, and that a pope must from now on be a spiritual figure only.

All this was grist to the mill of Garibaldi and what the pope regarded as his rabble of atheists and freemasons, but the grizzled guerrilla leader would soon be outmanoeuvred by the Piedmontese king. On 26 October Garibaldi defeated the Bourbon forces at Volturno, and on the same day met up with the king, asking for the right to run the South by decree for a year; the king refused and the grizzled old guerrilla retired in high dudgeon to his home at Caprera, a small island off Sardinia, still vowing to take Rome by storm someday. But before leaving he organized plebiscites in Sicily and South Italy which overwhelmingly voted for Vittorio Emanuele as king of a united Italy. Similar one-sided results were obtained in Umbria and the Marches. Now confident that he had the great bulk of the Italian peninsula under his control, Vittorio Emanuele – still under formal sentence of excommunication, but encouraged by Great Britain above all – took the momentous step of proclaiming the Kingdom of Italy on 17 March 1861. Italy had joined the European concert of powers. Just as the Greeks, for example, had made the ancient city of Athens the capital of their own modern kingdom in the 1830s, so it appeared natural that Rome should be the capital of the new Italy. On 27 March the parliament in Turin decreed that very thing. The only task left now was to solve what had become known as the 'Roman question', or what to do with Pius IX if he continued to insist on independence.

Chapter 12

Pius IX versus Italy

The Italian term for Pius the Ninth is *Pio Nono*, and that's how the Italians – whether supporters or detractors – remember him to this day. Inevitably, in Italian as well as English, he became known as Pius No-no, which may aptly describe the pope's attitude to the outside world that was crushing the papacy in on itself. When it appeared a foregone conclusion that it was only a matter of time before the new Kingdom of Italy swallowed Rome, Pius refused to give an inch. After all, the new Italian state had grabbed two-thirds of the Church's land. He would go down fighting for the Church and its liberty if he had to.

Italy was now in the full grip of what became known as the Risorgimento, or 'resurgence' of Italian national aspirations that had lain dormant at least since the time of Dante. It has been well said that Pius' reaction to the Risorgimento was a determination to 'save the Kingdom of God from the Kingdom of Italy'. His reaction to the decree of the Turin parliament was immediate and severe: a mass excommunication of Vittorio Emanuele's entire Italian government. Legally, Pius was within his rights; he was still a legitimate head of state, and hence any outside attempt to wrest his capital from him was quite illegal. Cavour had not moved from his original aim of a 'free church in a free state', but Pius was dead set against any dilution of his authority, which he claimed derived directly from God and not from any assembly of fallible human beings. Cardinal Antonelli, the Vatican secretary of state, staunchly supported his boss. There was a grim last-stand atmosphere about Antonelli's proclamation *Non possumus* ('We cannot'):

> In the event that we are finished, it is better that we perish as who we are, along with the grand ideals and all the powers of our great past.[1]

At this juncture Garibaldi, fresh from a rest at Caprera, decided to settle the Roman question in person. He had been doing a slow burn over the fact that Vittorio Emanuele had snubbed the redshirts who had contributed to the unification of Italy, but his bitter complaints had been ignored. His main opponent, the right-winger Cavour, died of malaria in June 1861. Early the following year Garibaldi set up a Society for the Emancipation of Italy. He may have been influenced by U.S. President Abraham Lincoln, who that year issued his Emancipation Proclamation – and had offered Garibaldi command of the Union army in the Civil War, only to withdraw the offer after Catholic Irishmen and Poles in the Union ranks protested.[2]

In the summer of 1862 Garibaldi toured Sicily where he had triumphed two years before. He stopped at Marsala to deliver a speech. Someone in the admiring crowd shouted, 'Either Rome or death!' (*'O Roma o morte!* '), a battle-cry which he took up as his own. Hoping to repeat his previous stunt with 'The Thousand', on 1 August he gathered together between 2,000 and 3,000 volunteers (the accounts differ) in a field outside Palermo and took ship with them to the toe of Italy from where the march to Rome would begin. The move shook the courts of both Napoleon and Vittorio Emanuele; the last thing they needed was this naive adventurer upsetting their plans for diplomatically regularizing the Roman question. Though Garibaldi enjoyed some sympathy in the Italian government of Prime Minister Urbano Rattazzi, the king ordered General Cialdini south post-haste to stop the old guerrilla in his tracks. He did so on 29 August at Aspromonte, where twelve of Garibaldi's men were killed and forty wounded, one of whom was Garibaldi himself. He was arrested and packed off back to Caprera, and his men pardoned; but Rattazzi was forced to resign, and another direct threat to the pope was averted.

The Italian government fretted at having to be based in Turin, a long way from Rome. Negotiations between the new prime minister, Marco Minghetti, and Napoleon III in September 1864 ended with a French agreement to evacuate Rome in two years in return for the Italian government moving to Florence, much nearer its goal. Napoleon thought the Italians had given up their claim on Rome, which was hardly the case; but many Italians believed it, and two dozen people died in riots in Turin and Minghetti was sacked. Next on Vittorio Emanuele's list was Venice, held by the Austrians. A large Italian army moved on the numerically inferior Austrians, but in late June 1866 it was trounced in the (second) Battle of Custozza. Fortunately, Italy had brought Prussia to its support; the Prussian victory over the Austrians at Sadowa on 3 June forced Austria to hand over Venice to France, which promptly passed it to Italy. A plebiscite in Venice approved the transfer by an unreal proportion of nearly 99.9 per cent.[3]

Pius, meanwhile, had not been inactive. Antonelli had been supervising a series of secret meetings with Italian envoys who appear to have genuinely wanted to avoid a final rift with the papacy. But the pope had his own agenda. Going over to the offensive, on 8 December he published his *Syllabus of Errors*, condemning all the fashionable 'isms' of the day, such as socialism, liberalism and rationalism, as delusional traps for the unwary. All of what popular liberation armies had been fighting for, in the name of flags and peoples, simply did not correspond to God's transcendental truths. (It was a stance shared by the Constantinople-based Orthodox Church, which also fretted at turbulent national liberation movements in Greece and the Balkans.) Moreover, the Roman Catholic Church insisted on overseeing education, including culture and science, and for that the papacy needed to be a temporal as well as a spiritual power. The *Syllabus* disappointed those clergy, especially in the kingdom of Italy, who had hoped that Pius might be more amenable to a compromise.

Meanwhile, duly embellished stories of the papal forces' heroism at Spoleto and Castelfidardo had circulated throughout Europe and America and brought a fresh wave of volunteers to Pius' aid. As before, counts, viscounts and barons flocked to Rome to take up the muskets and if necessary accept low rank. There was the case of Mexican Prince Iturbide, who enrolled as a private, as did at least one nobly-born former officer in the Austrian army. Yet another willing common soldier was a Polish duke, Ladislas de Dabrowa Garwanowicz. The motives, of course, were mixed; many simply wished to get back at nationalist governments that had taken away their ancient privileges, and others were in it for the money, but most appear to have been moved by genuine Catholic faith. One of them was Randolph Gabriel Wiseman, a nephew of the Catholic archbishop of Westminster. Another was the first American to cross the Atlantic to fight for the pope, one Richard Hopkins of New Orleans, a former Confederate soldier. A Canadian, Benjamin Testard de Montigny, followed, as did one Hugh Murray from Illinois. Hopkins, who appears to have had problems with discipline, joined the pope's army simply because most of American public opinion seemed to be in love with Garibaldi – as Lincoln's offer appears to attest.

The survivors of Castelfidardo had been organized into the Zouaves battalion as of 1 January 1863 under Lieutenant-Colonel de Becdelièvre, who had designed their baggy-pantalooned uniform that was becoming fashionable in France and had caught on in some units of the Union Army in the American Civil War.[4] Ten days later (after being reassured by the Catholic hierarchy that the uniforms did not suggest anything Islamic), the Zouaves in their new light blue outfits paraded in the Piazza del Laterano to swear fealty to the pope. They had scored some initial success against the Piedmontese, but de Becdelièvre's wish to stay on the offensive came up against Antonelli's caution. De Becdelièvre resigned, to be replaced by the popular Swiss Colonel Joseph-Eugène Allet, who put to flight a band of *bersaglieri* at Ceprano.

Since then, however, morale in the papal ranks had declined. Many of the Zouaves who had signed on for a year's service left when their term was up, and by 1863 the battalion strength had been halved, to three hundred. The Romans became familiar with the sight of Dutch and German papal troops filling the taverns (and brothels), and young papal officers sitting in noble drawing rooms being assessed as possible husbands for high-born damsels. Romances blossomed, and inevitably the high ideal of fighting for the pope gradually gave way to the delights of Rome for their own sake; thanks to the influx of soldiers' money, market and property prices soared, banks and smart restaurants flourished, and we are told that many an ordinarily respectable family woman was not above selling her sexual favours to the troops to secure a bit more family income.[5] In the barracks, however, the troops reverted to good behaviour: daily rosters were compiled for who would recite the rosary or conduct morning Mass.

The common people of Rome, however, were divided. Though instinctively loyal to the pope, they looked askance on the good relations between the papal officers and the upper class, while they stayed poor and bankers and traders and restaurant-owners got rich, all thanks to the Vatican. Not surprisingly, a large pro-nationalist faction was active in the city, but then again, its romantic plans for popular insurrection came up against the canny realism of the Roman people.

A new wave of volunteers for the papal force – some of who considered they were on a 'Ninth Crusade' – after 1864 re-galvanized it into action. General Raphael de Courten, who had been with the papals from the beginning, sent Colonel Achille Azzanesi to stamp out a nest of brigands outside Rome; Azzanesi enrolled locals familiar with the terrain who were not inclined to take any prisoners, and those brigands who were captured were promptly sentenced to death. The Zouaves were also brought into the clean-up campaign and scored considerable success, though some men were lost to malaria, pneumonia and desertion. Then, in April 1866, there arose the curious case of John Watson.

Watson was an American who had crossed the Atlantic to fight for the pope. It was while he was in camp at Sezze, on a campaign to put down brigands, that a Canadian Zouave, Henri Sainte-Marie, thought there was something familiar about the American's face. He became quite sure, in fact, that 'John Watson' was in reality John Surratt, wanted by the American government for complicity in the assassination of President Lincoln. Sainte-Marie, who had been a schoolteacher in Maryland, had known the Surratt family since before the Civil War; having fought on the Union side, after the war he had run into Surratt as a fugitive in Montreal and fingered him to the authorities. To escape arrest, Surratt had fled to Britain and then to Rome, hoping to hide his identity in the pope's army. By the purest chance he and Sainte-Marie had found themselves in close proximity again.

The United States consul at the Holy See, Rufus King, tried for months to establish the accuracy of Saint-Marie's charges; Surratt, the Canadian said, had confided to him his complicity in the assassination. In mid-July, King, having obtained a sworn statement from Sainte-Marie, was convinced that the charges were true and revealed the case to the Vatican authorities. But because of the slowness of communications between Rome and Washington, some time passed before the United States government asked King to obtain a photograph of 'John Watson' and send it to Washington. Sainte-Marie, meanwhile, seemed to lose interest; his term of service was almost up and he was impatient to migrate to the Far East to seek his fortune. Cardinal Antonelli ordered 'Watson's' arrest; as the American was being taken under escort to Rome, he surprised his gendarme escort by leaping over a precipice and escaping among the wooded ravines. Still in his Zouave uniform, he turned up at Naples, where he avoided arrest by claiming to be a deserter from the papal army. Not knowing his real identity, the Neapolitans let him sail for Alexandria. But the State Department telegraph wires hummed, and when he docked at Alexandria he found himself under arrest. Taken to

Washington, Surratt was put on trial but acquitted for lack of evidence of complicity in the Lincoln assassination. He was last heard of somewhere in the American South.[6]

The second Battle of Custozza dented the reputation of the Kingdom of Italy; it was reported that Cialdini's army entered the fray without maps and boots for the soldiers. Hard on the heels of that defeat for Vittorio Emanuele came another: ever since his forces took Ancona his navy had remained offshore. Now an Austrian fleet under Admiral Wilhelm von Tegetthoff was descending on Ancona, to secure the offshore islet of Lissa to prevent Persano from exiting. Against an Italian fleet twice the size of his own, von Tegetthoff opened the action on 20 July. Like Cialdini, Persano totally lacked a battle plan. Early in the action the powder magazine of the Italian *Palestro* blew up; von Tegetthoff's flagship, the *Ferdinand Max*, rammed and sank Persano's, the *Re d'Italia*. The battle was short and technically a draw, but the Austrian commander had succeeded in keeping the Italian fleet bottled up.

It was at this point that Napoleon III, keeping a close watch on European developments, decided that Prussia, the victor in the Austro-Prussian War in that year, was now the greater danger to France. He was jittery about keeping valuable French troops tied up in Rome protecting the pope, and in December 1866 the last of the French garrison pulled out of the city. Papal detachments that so far had been busy in South Italy fighting brigands were ordered to return to Rome. In a festive atmosphere Generals de Courten and Giovanni Battista Zappi paraded through the Porta San Giovanni in the south of Rome, lining up their units for an inspection by Pius in his carriage, flanked by his dragoons and Noble Guard. On 11 December the papal banner replaced the French flag on Sant'Angelo Castle. But the pope was uneasy. The French troops had given him a measure of protection which was now being stripped away. 'Do not delude yourselves', he had told French officers in November. 'The revolution will come here.'

By now de Mérode, the defence chief of the papal realm, had been replaced by General Hermann Kanzler, the ex-Swiss Guard officer who had joined the papal army as a lieutenant and had led the initial march on Ancona. He had also shared Pius' temporary exile at Gaeta in 1849. Volunteers from France, Germany and the Netherlands continued to pour off the ships at Civitavecchia. Kanzler organized his growing army into two brigades,

240 The Pope's Army

commanded by de Courten and Zappi; Colonel Cesare Caimi was put in charge of the artillery and Colonel Giovanni Lepri di Rota commanded the dragoons. Colonel Evangelisti, who as a captain had routed a detachment of Garibaldi's redshirts at Grotte di San Lorenzo seven years before, commanded the 3,000-strong corps of gendarmes. Colonel Azzanesi headed an ethnic Italian regiment of 1,700 men. Kanzler's spearhead were the 1,500 Zouaves under Colonel Allet, with Lieutenant-Colonel de Charette as his second-in-command.

The pope also had a navy of sorts. Colonel Alessandro Cialdi was an experienced sailor who in 1842 had taken three steamers from Britain to Rome and sailed them up the Tiber. Now Cialdi had at his disposal the steam corvette *Immacolata Concezione* (Immaculate Conception) and a handful of other steam vessels under seven officers and one hundred and fifty seamen. These ships were tasked with controlling the mouth of the Tiber and keeping a watch over the port of Civitavecchia, where an Austrian warship was also stationed in case the pope needed evacuating in a hurry. It was a genuine concern, as by now the Papal State had been reduced to a mere slab of territory barely a hundred kilometres long and one-third as wide, with Rome as its centre, and pressed on all sides by nationalist Italian forces. The forces were there ostensibly to 'protect' the papacy, but few in Rome believed that fiction – especially as Vittorio Emanuele would privately refer to Pius as 'that poor devil of a Holy Father'.

In the summer of 1867 a cholera epidemic hit Lazio, with most of the victims in the town of Albano, south of Rome. Forty-two Zouaves of the Sixth Company were sent to help, and found the public square full of corpses. Only a few priests and monks had remained to do what they could; Cardinal Lodovico Altieri caught the disease and died. The scene was similar in nearby Velletri, where the commander of the Sixth Company, Lieutenant de Resimont, and Sergeant Major de Morin had to carry the first corpses to the cemetery; the rest of the Zouaves spent all night burying the victims by torchlight. Three members of the family of Neapolitan ex-king Francesco II living in the area also succumbed. The cholera crisis earned the Sixth Company – which itself lost six men to it – praises all round; Kanzler attended the funeral of the six and showered decorations on the eighty Zouaves of the Sixth Company.

At about that time a young Irishman from Limerick, Patrick Keyes O'Clery, arrived in Rome to join his countryman Major O'Reilly in the pope's army. He was just in time to meet a sudden new threat by Garibaldi, who after the French withdrawal from Rome saw his chance to capture the Eternal City. Garibaldi formed three attack columns to converge on Rome from three directions. He naively told his men that Rome would fall with barely a shot being fired and that the men would be hailed as liberators. He could not have been more wrong. Moreover, he found no support in the Italian king, who harboured the gravest distrust of the grizzled old radical. The fear in Rome was that Garibaldi's move might prompt Vittorio Emanuele to forestall him by taking Rome himself.

In Paris Napoleon III called for the 'dangerous revolutionary' to be stopped. But already in September Garibaldi's columns, totalling 13,000 men, were on the move. One, under Giovanni Acerbi, stood at the Tuscan border ready to strike south; the second, under Giovanni Nicotera, was in readiness in the east. Their orders were to engage Kanzler's attention while the third column, under Garibaldi's son Menotti, made a strike for Rome. The plan looked good on paper, but it was carried out quite sloppily, and thus Kanzler had plenty of time to avoid the trap that had been set for him. He had organized the Papal State into four defence zones: Viterbo in the north (under Azzanesi), Civitavecchia on the coast (Colonel Serra), Tivoli in the east (de Charette) and Velletri-Frosinone in the south (Lieutenant-Colonel Giorgi). Kanzler himself was installed in a command post in constant telegraphic communication with his units; he also had the advantage of being able to switch forces along internal lines by rail. It was arguably the first time after the American Civil War that railways were used as a vital strategic tool in wartime.

Acerbi made some probes into papal territory, to be repulsed by Azzanesi. The redshirts, finding none of the popular support their leader had led them to expect, fell back in disorder. They had rather more success at Bagnorea, where Lieutenant Wyart's Seventh Company of Zouaves was pushed back; O'Clery, in the company, reported that the enemy robbed homes and profaned churches. Twenty-seven Zouaves were taken prisoner. On 5 October Azzanesi struck back, sending Olivier de Gonidec's battalion, comprising Wyart's company as well as two others, to retake Bagnorea. De Gonidec was a flamboyant figure who refused to carry either pistol or sword, being content to go into battle armed with a mere officer's baton; his explanation was that a commanding officer should be busy organizing tactics rather than actually fighting. In any case, he drove the redshirts out of Bagnorea, killing forty-five of them and capturing one hundred and ten, at a cost of just one man killed, the Dutchman Nicolas Heykamp (the first Zouave to die in combat).

Operations against the encroaching redshirts continued through October. De Charette repulsed a Garibaldian attack at the summit of Mount Carpignano, and was about to pursue the enemy across the frontier, but Kanzler held him back; now was the time for defence, not offence, and resources had to be saved. At sunset on 13 October Guillemin's Fifth Company of Zouaves charged a redshirt outpost on the height of Montelibretti. Shouting in French '*Vive Pie neuf!*' ('Long live Pius the Ninth!'), Guillemin led half of the Fifth up one side of the vine-terraced hill, sending his second-in-command, the Viscount Urbain de Quélen, up the other side with the other half of the company. They may have been the last words Guillemin ever uttered; a stray ball wounded him, and as he was being helped to the rear another, fatal, ball hit him in the head. As night fell, the fighting became confused; after De Quélen had fallen the battle petered out with no clear victor. The Fifth Company suffered fifty per cent casualties. (The redshirt general Menotti Garibaldi nobly sent back Guillemin's wristwatch with a note paying tribute to the Frenchman's courage.)

The redshirts on Montelibretti retired when Azzanesi turned up with papal reinforcements. On 18 October one hundred and thirty-four redshirts surrendered and De Charette chafed at the bit to resume the offensive, but Kanzler ordered him back to Rome to defend the city proper. On the following day a new Garibaldian offensive threatened the papal position at Farnese; O'Clery, at the scene, recalled Lieutenant Emmanuel Dufournel (whose elder brother, a captain, had just been killed) as telling his men to prepare themselves for death 'in the name of the Father, Son and Holy Spirit'. The Fourth Company of Zouaves, under Captain de Couëssin, however, put their opponents to flight.

Garibaldi himself, directing operations from his island hideaway on Caprera, had set the date of 22 October for a popular uprising in Rome that would hopefully fling wide the gates for the advancing redshirts. But he had woefully miscalculated the mood of the 230,000 Romans, nobles and commoners alike, who depended on the papal administration both for their livelihoods and their faith. Besides, on the day set for the rising, torrential rain in Rome dampened any tendency to take to the streets. Kanzler's efficient intelligence service, meanwhile, had become aware of the rebel plan, which was why he had recalled de Charette. He and his chief of staff, Major Giacomo Ungarelli, had planned for three lines of defence around Rome. The outer line, commanded by Allet, lay along the Aniene, a tributary of the Tiber in the northern suburbs of Rome; Zouaves and foreign gendarme volunteers would line the banks of the Aniene while armed gunboats would patrol the waterway. The middle line, commanded by Colonel Charles d'Argy, covered the twenty-five-mile circumference of the old wall of Rome, with cannon placed at six of the thirteen gates and earthworks raised behind the rest. The inner line, commanded by Colonel Jeannerat, formed a triangle enclosing the Vatican and Sant'Angelo Castle, with the apex at Monte Mario in the north.

In the evening of 22 October a terrific explosion blew up the Zouave barracks in Via di Borgo Vecchio. Twenty-men were killed, mostly members of the Zouave military band, as well as a family of three that happened to be walking by. It was the signal for a series of dissident attacks on arsenals and jails, which were put down without too much trouble. A handful of papal artillerymen were reportedly involved in a plot to torch sixteen tons of gunpowder in Sant'Angelo Castle; the plot was betrayed from the inside and thus the ancient edifice – and half of Rome – remained standing. That same evening someone tossed a grenade at the army offices in Piazza Colonna; the grenade, ending up at the feet of Colonel Evangelisti, failed to explode. A volley of gunfire dispersed the perpetrators.

Hearing of the destruction in Via di Borgo Vecchio, Kanzler sent a detachment of Zouaves and gendarmes to secure an ammunition cache discovered in a nearby villa. Soon about forty insurgent prisoners were being led back to Rome, plus two hundred rifles that would come in very handy for the city's defence. In the early hours of 23 October, near the San Paolo basilica, General Zappi dispersed a redshirt band and seized a store of gunpowder. At about that hour two brothers who were officers in the Italian nationalist army, Enrico and Giovanni Cairoli, attempted a rising with seventy followers. The group had been secretly receiving arms for some time. But as usually happened with visionary romantics, their hopes were at variance with reality. Boating down the Tiber, the Cairoli brothers expected to find supporters at Ponte Milvio, but found no-one and retired to Villa Glori in the Parioli district where the Tiber forms a loop. There they were attacked by the Fifth Company of Zouaves under Captain Julius Meyer; he and Enrico Cairoli engaged in a furious hand-to-hand fight which ended with Cairoli's death and Meyer staggering back with eight wounds. Giovanni Cairoli was seriously wounded and captured.

Kanzler's agents suggested that he check out a building in the Trastevere district that housed a weaving establishment but was suspected of being a redshirt cell. Twenty Zouaves and six gendarmes were sent to the building in question, where about eighty conspirators were meeting. A lookout on the roof warned of the approach of the papal patrol which, after knocking on the door, received an explosive device in reply, wounding a few men. Rifles appeared in windows and doorways and bullets began to fly. The gunfire attracted two companies of Zouaves, who surrounded the building and took up position on the adjacent rooftops, pouring fire into the windows. As those inside retired to the upper floors, the papal troops burst through the front door. The first one to enter, Sergeant Ruiz de Torralba, fell dead. Floor to floor, room to room, the fighting was brutal. When the insurgents ran out of ammunition they used broken wine bottles instead. The papal troops seem to have had no hesitation in killing the couple who owned the building and their young son in a back room. At the end of the fight one Zouave was dead and four wounded, to sixteen insurgents dead and five wounded. In another incident, Dufournel was killed while storming another insurgent house in which his men did not hesitate to employ their bayonets.

By 25 October the insurrectionists of Rome had been suppressed; two of the main plotters were guillotined – the last time anyone was executed in the Papal State. Yet Garibaldi, against all the evidence, still seems to have been convinced that the Romans were awaiting him as a liberator. Though his forces had been reduced in numbers to some 7,000, they moved on the small town of Monterotondo that controlled the Via Salaria and Via Nomentana leading into Rome from the north-east. In charge of the papal garrison at Monterotondo was Captain Costes with about three hundred and seventy men and a battery of artillery. While an urgent message was sent to Kanzler, Costes' men came under fierce attack from some 4,000 of Menotti Garibaldi's redshirts. Though the papal artillery crews suffered grave casualties, three redshirt assaults were hurled back. The fourth redshirt attack, by Major Marziano Ciotti, burst into Monterotondo; half the papal force surrendered, but the other half, with Costes, held out until his opponents threatened to blow up the building he occupied. Garibaldi himself, now in the field with his force, graciously complimented Costes and his men on their valour while decrying the lack of it among some of his own men. Colonel Allet had been on his way to Monterotondo with 1,500 Zouaves and gendarmes, a cavalry squadron and a battery of guns, but on learning of Costes' debacle, ordered them back.

Continuous redshirt probes in the northern sector forced Kanzler and Azzanesi to try and halt them with the most economical use of force possible. Acerbi, the redshirt commander in the Viterbo district, began to push steadily forward. Now Napoleon III became alarmed; neither he nor Vittorio Emanuele wished to see redshirts running Rome and providing inspiration to other European radicals. The Italian government was in fact in a quandary – while despising Garibaldi, it did not want to give the French an excuse for invading Italy for the umpteenth time in history. But while the government dithered, the French moved in to save the pope. After less than a year's absence, French troops again strolled through Rome; a week after their arrival, on 3 November 1867, Napoleon's troops joined the papals to confront the redshirts at Mentana.

The Fifth and Sixth Companies of Zouaves under de Charette launched a bayonet charge that drove back the *bersaglieri* on their front. Kanzler wanted to take a strategic spot known as the Santucci vineyard, where the fighting was intense. Captain Arthur de Veaux, who led the Sixth Company, was fatally hit by a bullet that drove a medal he had been awarded at Castelfidardo into his heart. De Charette had a horse shot from under him. Kanzler's artillery blasted the last redshirt defenders out of the Santucci vineyard. After an afternoon of see-sawing fortunes a final assault was launched at the redshirts' stronghold in Mentana castle; during this attack the sole English volunteer in the Zouaves, Julian Watts-Russell, was killed. By nightfall the issue was decided: the Garibaldians were finished. At least 2,400 redshirts were taken prisoner; one hundred and fifty others were killed and two hundred and forty wounded. Papal casualties were thirty dead and one hundred and seven wounded, mostly Zouaves. The French troops suffered a mere two dead and thirty-six wounded. Garibaldi, a prisoner, found himself confined in the same quarters as the papal prisoners of Castelfidardo had been.

It has become customary to attribute the French-papal victory at Mentana to the use of the new French breech-loading *chassepot* rifles that could fire up to twelve rounds a minute. In fact, most histories credit the French with winning the battle, with little or no mention of the papal force which, as the casualty figures attest, bore the brunt of the fighting. In fact, the *chassepots* often jammed, were prone to overheating, were inaccurate at longer ranges and sometimes served better as bayonet platforms. But all that was forgotten as the papal troops re-entered Rome in triumph, showing off captured rebel berets. Seven French generals doffed their hats in respect as the Zouaves paraded in the Stazione Termini square. Pius chanted a hymn as he greeted Kanzler. Along with the pope's army, the French were the heroes of the hour in Rome. But Paris was jittery. The French emperor was now in poor health and obsessed by the rise of Prussia as France's main European rival power. By intervening to save the papacy he had weakened himself elsewhere, as he would soon find out the hard way.[7]

Pius, once more handed a reprieve, was inclined to be generous to his foes. He rejected a suggestion by one of his generals that the redshirt prisoners in Sant'Angelo Castle be shot out of hand on the grounds that as guerrillas they were not entitled to protection under the laws of war. Photos of him blessing some prisoners were issued to the press. On 11 March 1868 more than one hundred and thirty French-Canadian volunteers from Quebec arrived in Rome to join Kanzler's force. In fact by now men from twenty-seven countries, a true international brigade, had joined the pope's army that now totalled 15,000: volunteers came from such diverse places as China, Peru and the Ottoman Empire. Cardinal Antonelli, meanwhile, had boosted papal revenues to be able to buy modern American-made Remington rifles to replace the obsolete German-made muzzle-loading Schützen carbines that had been in use so far.

Pius, meanwhile, sought to prop up the spiritual leg of his domain by forming the Circle of Saint Peter, designed in part to raise the Church's social profile and provide an alternative to left-wing radicalism for the discontented. To rally the hierarchy and assert papal infallibility, he issued his encyclical *Aeterni Patris* (Of the Eternal Father) and called the first-ever Vatican Council for 8 December 1869. Once more, as in the Holy Years of old, pilgrims and tourists flocked to Rome, and the city regained some of its glitter. Some writers have suggested that reasserting papal infallibility was an aim not so much of Pius himself as of the rank and file clergy who needed something to hold on to in the face of the constant political threats to the papacy.[8] Certainly it triggered controversy in Catholic communities around the globe, not to mention outright rejection by the Orthodox and Protestant churches. As a diplomatic move by the Vatican, the council decrees earned it less international support than might otherwise have been the case.

Napoleon, meanwhile, after having played intricate diplomatic games over nearly twenty years, finally overplayed his hand. His main nemesis now was Prussia, against which he light-heartedly declared war in mid-July 1870. A mere six weeks later, the French had been trounced at Sedan, Napoleon was a prisoner, and France became a republic. In the meantime, French troops had been withdrawn from Rome for service at the front, leaving the city wide open for the Italian nationalists to seize. Barely had the guns at Sedan fallen silent than the Italian government notified the European powers that it intended to make Rome the capital of the Italian kingdom while maintaining the pope's independence as a spiritual rather than a political leader. The government sent an envoy, Count Gustavo Ponza di San Martino, to negotiate with Cardinal Antonelli; the count handed the cardinal a letter from Vittorio Emanuele to the pope that claimed in treacly terms that as Pius was (supposedly) in danger from revolutionaries, the king felt it was his duty to occupy Rome 'to guarantee the pope's security'. Pius, seeing through that flimsy excuse, flatly turned down the offer. 'I am neither a prophet nor the son of a prophet', he icily informed San Martino. 'But I assure you that you will not enter Rome.' To the king he wrote a caustic reply:

> I thank God that He has allowed Your Majesty to refill the last days of my life with the most bitter pain. For the rest, I cannot be in agreement with certain requests or accept certain principles contained in Your letter. Again I invoke God and place my cause, which is completely His, in His hands. I pray that the Lord concede much grace to Your Majesty, free you from dangers and render to You the mercy of which You are in need.[9]

That same day, 10 September, General Cadorna received orders to move on Rome with 50,000 troops. Nine days later the city was surrounded, defended by General Kanzler and a mere 15,000 men plus 150 ageing artillery pieces. Earlier in the year Kanzler had told the French ambassador: 'We know we're going to be annihilated, but we'll do our duty to the end.' Neither he nor Antonelli nor the pope himself had any confidence that the Italian takeover would be a peaceful affair, and correctly believed the king's pious assurances to be hollow. Prussia, meanwhile, had assured Vittorio Emanuele of its backing for a move on Rome and a settlement of the pesky 'Roman Question' that was complicating European politics. The new republic in France was also turning many minds against monarchical regimes such as the pope's. The cards were stacking up against Pius.

From his base at Orte, Cadorna with the Italian army IV Corps set off slowly on the seventy-five-kilometre road to Rome down the Via Flaminia. With him was a bevy of foreign correspondents, as by now public relations had become a vital component of military operations – a big international news story was unfolding, and there was a fast-growing newspaper-reading public out there that had to be kept satisfied. Cadorna appears to have hoped that the papal government *in extremis* might reconsider its intransigent stand, which is why he took his time. Partly for the benefit of the domestic and foreign press he issued a proclamation repeating the king's assurance that he was coming not to conquer but to 'restore order' – a favourite excuse of aggressors since time immemorial – 'in our common country'. Meanwhile, political machinations in Florence, the provisional capital, had forced him to accept two ex-redshirt commanders, Nino Bixio and Enrico Cosenz, on his staff. He also fretted that the nosy correspondents with him might reveal his operational plans to the wider world and scupper his chances of success.

Kanzler on 12 September declared a state of emergency in the Papal State, suppressing several fifth-column activities that were known to be underway in the city. His 13,600 troops – a mere one-fifth of what Cadorna was leading against him – consisted of 3,040 Zouaves in four battalions, 1,860 Italian gendarmes, 1,020 special troops, 1,170 rangers (*cacciatori*), 1,700 line infantry in two battalions, 1,090 Roman legionnaires, 1,190 foreign gendarmes, 560 dragoons, 999 artillerymen and about 800 garrison troops and auxiliaries. The force included some 3,000 Frenchmen, 3,000 Italians, 1,000 Swiss, 900 Dutchmen, 600 Germans, 600 Austrians, 300 Canadians and a mixed bag of 100 or so Irish, English, Spanish, Portuguese, Russian, American, Turkish, Tunisian, Syrian, Brazilian and Swedish volunteers; among them were one

Moroccan, one Mexican and one New Zealander. Allet was placed in charge of the Zouaves, Azzanesi of the rest of the infantry, Evangelisti of the special troops, Caimi the artillery, Jeanneret the gendarmes and Lepri the dragoons. Also on hand in case of need were the Noble Guard, seven companies of the Swiss Guard under Colonel Alfred von Sonnenberg, and several hundred of the Palatine Guard plus the Rome police force.

Cadorna pressed on steadily. Bixio's 2 Division overcame a small Zouave squad at Bagnorea and took Montefiascone, vacated by de Saisy's Zouaves. Emilio Ferrero's 13 Division, the IV Corps vanguard, moved on Viterbo, which had been evacuated by de Charette. As 12 Division under Gustavo Mazè de la Roche approached Civita Castellana he found it defended by about 200 papal troops under de Resimont, the officer who had distinguished himself in the cholera epidemic at Albano. As 12 Division encircled the town, de Resimont organized the defence in a fifteenth-century castle that served as a prison, with the convicts still inside. The nationalist artillery, observed by Cadorna in person, pounded the castle until some of de Resimont's troops advised surrender. Their commander would not hear of it. But the prison warden warned him that if the whole castle were to collapse, the inmates would perish, and so de Resimont agreed to raise the white flag.

On 14 September Cosenz's division reached Monterosi to join up with Ferrero. But Cadorna was unhappy with the progress, as his army's supply situation was parlous; he could expect little help or provisioning from the uncooperative papal subjects in the countryside who refused to billet the troops. Bixio pursued de Charette but the latter, along with some of de Saisy's Zouaves, managed to reach Civitavecchia over mountain paths. Bixio, however, soon formed a ring around the port that was defended by about 1,000 papal troops under the Spanish Colonel Serra. The garrison was willing enough to fight, but Bixio was coordinating his moves with a nationalist naval squadron offshore; Kanzler therefore ordered de Charette and his men to get on the next train to Rome. Serra remained in Civitavecchia to face a two-front attack by land and sea. He quickly realized the hopelessness of his position and agreed to capitulate; his men were promised a safe-conduct and entitled to keep their ranks and seniority if they chose to serve in the Italian royal army. No sooner had Serra given his assent than Major Numa d'Abiousse of the Zouaves protested that Kanzler had ordered that they at least put up some kind of fight rather than surrender without a shot. But

Serra had the safety of the terrified civilians of Civitavecchia to worry about, and on the evening of 16 September he affirmed his decision. D'Abiousse's subordinate, one Captain Saballs, snapped his sabre in two in his fury and stormed out.

Seaborne troops from the royal ironclad *Terribile* occupied Civitavecchia, most of whose inhabitants welcomed the landing; Kanzler was right to pull out most of his men while he could. Early on 16 September Diego Angioletti's 9 Division moved on Velletri in the south; Azzanesi wanted to stay and fight, but again Kanzler – backed by Antonelli and the pope – preferred to pull his outnumbered defences back to Rome proper. Cadorna meanwhile had arrived at Giustiniana, from where he could see the roofs and classic domes of Rome. There he waited impatiently for the divisions of Bixio and Angioletti to join him from the other sectors. A nationalist scouting party of cavalry on misty Monte Mario was surprised by a couple of companies of Zouaves who captured the squad leader, Lieutenant Carlo Crotti. The lieutenant's father, however, was a Piedmontese parliamentary deputy who had opposed the use of force against the Papal State. The pope ordered Crotti freed; Kanzler treated him to dinner before sending him under escort back to Cadorna's lines.

As Kanzler was pulling back units for a defence of Rome proper, Cadorna wrote to him appealing for an avoidance of bloodshed – it would be better for everyone concerned, the commander of the IV Corps said, just to let his troops occupy Rome peacefully and all would be well. Kanzler's reply was uncompromising:

> His Holiness desires to see Rome occupied by his own troops and not those of a foreign sovereign. I thus have the honour to reply to You that I am determined to resist by all the means at my disposal, as honour and duty demand of me.

Technically, Kanzler was quite right. Rome already had a legitimate sovereign, the pope, and Cadorna's campaign was aggression, pure and simple, designed to impose an alien (albeit Italian) ruler on the independent papal domain. The Italian nationalists could allow no-one else to exercise any rival authority, especially in the city they already considered their capital. Hence the pope was duty-bound to resist, like any legitimate ruler would. He knew it was a lost cause, but that made his resistance all the more determined.

Antonelli convened the diplomatic corps in Rome with the news that the city was surrounded, and indeed the first detachments of *bersaglieri* had occupied the left bank of the Tiber in the north. At this point the Prussian ambassador, Count von Arnim, took it upon himself to act as mediator. He arranged a meeting with Cadorna to plead for some time in which the pope might hopefully abandon his 'insane' tough stand. Cadorna agreed, but only in order to give himself time to consolidate his positions: Bixio's division now stood before Trastevere and Gianicolo Hill, Anglioletti's occupied the southern approaches before the Porta San Giovanni and the rest of IV Corps stood poised at Giustiniana.

One last hope remained to Pius: that the world would see who was the real aggressor and who the victim. He found it hard to believe that Vittorio Emanuele, despite the three excommunications over his head, would actually commit the crime of extinguishing the Roman state by force. He also nursed a faint hope that Austria might dissuade the Italian king from the move with the threat of force. In Rome itself, wherever he went, Pius was acclaimed and cheered by the mass of people. The Roman nobility, however, were jittery. Foreign flags began to appear on balconies in the hope that Cardorna's troops might respect those homes. Exchanges of fire between the nationalist advance units and the Zouaves echoed distantly over the rooftops. Deserters from Cadorna's force warned of an imminent final assault.

Kanzler installed a council of war in the Piazza Colonna headquarters. The first act was to cut the telegraph lines to hinder enemy communications. The operational plan was to isolate Bixio from Cadorna's other divisions by sending a column of 8,000 Zouaves and gendarmes through the Porta Angelica by night to burst through the nationalist line at that point. The attack never took place. Pius delivered a message to Kanzler imploring him to avoid shedding needless blood and conduct a resistance consistent with his sense of duty only. The message, though deploring the 'gross injustice and sacrilege' of a 'Catholic king, with no cause whatsoever, besieging the centre of the Catholic world', thanked Kanzler for what he had done so far:

> As regards the duration of the defence, it is my duty to order that it must consist solely of a protest as a contrast to violence and nothing more,

252 The Pope's Army

that is, to open negotiations for a surrender at the first cannon shots. At a time when all Europe deplores the many victims of a war between two great countries [the Franco-Prussian War], it should never be said that the Vicar of Jesus Christ, though unjustly assailed, consented to any bloodletting … From the heart I bless you, General, and all our troops.

Kanzler read the message with a sinking heart.

From his headquarters in the north of Rome, Cadorna planned a quick thrust down Via Nomentana to the Porta Pia which was the entrance to central Rome. By way of diversion he would order Bixio to advance in the Gianicolo-Trastevere sector while Ferrero and Angioletti moved in from the east. The drive down Nomentana was entrusted to Cosenz and Mazè de la Roche – though Cardorna wanted to ensure that the latter would receive the honour of penetrating to the centre rather than the ex-redshirt Cosenz. The contest would be most unequal: 40,000 nationalists against 13,000 papal troops and a strong preponderance of nationalist artillery.

Before dawn on 20 September Cadorna's guns opened up with a bombardment of Rome – though the gunners were given strict orders to avoid hitting, if possible, any church or building known to house the papal administration. The waiting foot soldiers were told not to violate the Vatican or Sant'Angelo Castle. Among the defenders, some men took communion. As the day dawned, Kanzler prepared his one hundred and seven cannon to face Bixio's 2 Division on the right bank of Tiber, saving forty-three other guns to face the main nationalist advance from the north. At 4 a.m. papal sentries at the Porta Pia reported that the enemy was on the move. Mazè de la Roche had placed his batteries and Major Luigi Pelloux's brigade of three companies in position ready to effect the breach at Porta Pia. To the right of the gate, at Villa Patrizi, the Zouaves of Lieutenant Johannes Baptiste von der Kerckhove opened fire on the nationalist gunners, who after taking some losses rained shot and shell on the houses of Rome, where terrified civilians sat huddled in cellars.

Yet there was no order from Kanzler to 'surrender at the first cannon shots', as the pope had solemnly urged. Kanzler appears to have taken matters into his own hands, deliberately countermanding the pope simply because he was not the type to give up without a fight. Of course he knew the game was up, but he wanted to be sure the enemy got a few black eyes before it won the fight. In the Vatican a tired and unshaven Pius pored over table maps. He had not slept; his valet had heard him moving about restlessly all night, and at dawn he had dressed in his finest robes to meet the day of doom. An artillery battle developed on Bixio's front, within clear sight of Saint Peter's. Kanzler's guns hammered Bixio's 2 Division mercilessly; Bixio's own gunners were none too careful in their aim, blasting apartment buildings, convents and a hospital.

At 7:15 a.m., as the thunder of cannon fire rent the air, the pope celebrated a special Mass in his private chapel. Attending was the Rome diplomatic corps, whose members surely were wondering when Kanzler would call a halt to the battle. Moreover, none of the papal troops manning the various defences had been told what to do in case they were overrun – should they raise the white flag, or fight to the last? As far as Azzanesi was concerned, there wasn't much choice; to him, Bixio and other ex-redshirts were little better than devils incarnate, and he didn't believe in taking prisoners. Azzanesi's fierce resistance halted Bixio in his tracks.

In the south-east sector, at San Giovanni, de Charette with a few old artillery pieces fired on Angioletti's 9 Division as it drew near. The nationalist artillery retaliated with a rain of shells that exploded around the venerable San Giovanni basilica. De Charette had the papal forces' sole machine gun, an American-made Claxton that had been used by the Union army in the American Civil War and somehow had found its way to Rome. It remains a matter of dispute, however, whether the Claxton was actually used. De Charette's lack of artillery hindered him from inflicting much damage on the nationalists, but Kanzler appears to have kept him in position to be as much of a nuisance as possible.

After the morning Mass, Pius gathered the diplomats in his study. Von Arnim, the Prussian ambassador, had procured a large pair of binoculars and was constantly running from window to balcony to roof to provide a running commentary on what the nationalists were doing. Three kilometres away, the Porta Pia was coming under heavy bombardment from Mazè de la Roche's artillery; some three hundred rounds had seriously damaged the old fortified gate, and a breach seemed imminent. Major Ferdinand de Troussures, a viscount who was among the earliest volunteers for the pope's army, messaged Kanzler that the Porta Pia would withstand no more than two more hours of pounding. At about the same time Kanzler received a panicky message from General Zappi that the Porta Pia had already been overrun; two minutes later a contradictory despatch arrived saying that the gate was still intact, but only just.

Kanzler and Rivalta, his number two, called together a council of war to decide what to do. It wasn't often that Kanzler, the man of steel, sought anyone's advice, but now he was at a dead end. Present was the pope's own military aide, the elderly Colonel Gustavo di Carpegna, sent to press for a cease-fire. The council almost unanimously recommended surrender. As Carpegna left to inform the pope, Kanzler seems to have toyed with the idea of further token resistance and sent Rivalta to the Porta Pia to assess the situation. But Zappi's false report had done its damage. Colonel Jeannerat and his men, including Major O'Reilly, had fallen back to the Stazione Termini in the mistaken belief that they had been outflanked. A vigorous counterattack by the papal Zouaves under de Troussures, who used their new Remington rifles to good effect, regained some lost ground. Cadorna, observing the action from a balcony of the Villa Albani half a kilometre north of the Porta Pia, had to seek cover from the bullets.

The shellfire from Bixio's division, meanwhile, was creeping dangerously close to the Vatican. Captain Luigi Salimei, the papal battery commander at Sant'Angelo Castle, resisted the temptation to fire back; the sixteen tons of powder that had been destined to blow up the castle and its environs three years before were still in the vaults, and any direct hit would be calamitous. Salimei messaged his immediate superior, Caimi, for instructions, but Cardinal Antonelli replied instead, with an order to cease hostilities. Colonel Carpegna had returned to the Vatican with the news of the crisis at Porta Pia, and the pope, his eyes brimming with tears, decided that the game was up.[10] At about that time, Rivalta had arrived at Porta Pia, decided that the situation was hopeless, and had ridden back to Kanzler to tell him so. And Kanzler by now had no choice but to agree. He sent a mounted dragoon to Major de Troussures at Porta Pia with orders to raise the white flag. De Troussures, full of fight, initially declined but then demanded that the order be delivered by a soldier of equal rank to himself, and sent van der Kerckhove back with the dragoon for confirmation.

At about 10 a.m. the Italian *tricolore* of the 39th Regiment appeared over the Villa Patrizi, a stone's throw from Porta Pia. It was the signal to advance: as Cadorna's guns fell silent, three battalions of infantry and three of *bersaglieri* surged out from the gardens of the Villa Patrizi. Watching the nationalists advance, the Zouaves began singing crusader songs. Their first burst of return fire stopped the attackers in their tracks; the feather-plumed *bersaglieri* of the 34th Battalion of the 39th Regiment found it hard going. The firefight had begun to intensify when Captain François de France rode up at a gallop bearing a white sheet for a surrender flag. At that moment Cadorna's 40th Regiment rushed out of the grounds of the Villa Torlonia to join the attack. Among the defenders, Lieutenant Augusto Valentani, a former republican who had joined the pope's service as a private secretary, fell dead. In the confusion de France dropped the sheet, which was picked up by Captain Bertrand Ferron, but the melée around Porta Pia was now so intense that no-one had time to raise it.

The first man through the breach was *bersaglieri* Lieutenant Federico Cocito, at 10:10 a.m. A writer who was present remembered hearing the cry '*Savoia!*' (Savoy, after the royal house), and moments later: 'They're through!'[11] The papal troops continued to fire into the confused mass of men surging over the rubble through the gap, killing at least one major and several soldiers. There seemed nothing to do but keep firing, even though their cause was now irretrievably lost. De Couëssin's company was surrounded and disarmed, though de Couëssin himself continued brandishing his sabre until tackled by a *bersagliere*. At Porta San Giovanni de Charette received the order to surrender, and had to comply, but not before tearing up the message in fury. In the Gianicolo sector Bixio's 20th and 33rd Battalions of *bersaglieri* advanced steadily, fighting hard against fanatic papal resistance. At about the time the nationalists broke through at Porta Pia, Lieutenant Guilio Cesare Carletti of the pope's staff found a white tablecloth from somewhere and climbed up to the top of Saint Peter's cupola to hoist it. A breathless dragoon rode to where Captain Enrico Roversi was holding on fanatically to Porta San Pancrazio with the order to find a white flag and use it; Roversi was about to pull down a white shop awning in the vicinity when a shell fragment wounded him. There was some uncertainty about what to do after that; some papal troops headed back to the Vatican to defend the pope, leaving behind nineteen dead and sixty-eight wounded (to forty-nine dead and one hundred and forty-one wounded in Bixio's division). The rest were captured.

The firing from both sides petered out as Cadorna's men fanned out into Rome, admiring the monuments they had so often read and heard about, but put off by the dirty streets and alleys. To this day, however, their reception by the Roman public is disputed; the official national line is that most Romans welcomed the nationalists as heroes and that the Italian flag fluttered from almost every balcony, while papal apologists insist that the prevailing atmosphere was one of sullen indifference. Accompanying the national army were opportunists of various kinds, including past opponents of the papal regime who now wished to get their own back; O'Clery witnessed some of their alleged acts of violence against papal troops and officials, including the destruction of sacred symbols and Church property.

Kanzler asked Carpegna, Rivalta and de Maistre to go to Cadorna's headquarters at the Villa Albani to conduct surrender negotiations. They were received coldly, and somewhat surprised to see Prussian ambassador von Arnim already there and acting as the envoy of a Protestant great power backing Italian unification. Other ambassadors were present, and Cadorna assured them that any of their nationals who had fought for the pope would be pardoned and allowed to go home. Cadorna frostily told Carpegna that he would treat only with his equivalent in rank, Kanzler. The papal commander sent a letter confirming the authority of his three negotiators, but Cadorna was adamant – Kanzler must come in person. Rivalta, meanwhile, had been using the long wait in an ante-room to engage in friendly conversation with nationalist officers – a preliminary to his eventually joining the Italian army he had so recently fought against.

Cadorna was irritable for other reasons as well. The enthusiastic ex-redshirt Bixio had already cabled the king and government that Rome was in his hands – a task that should have fallen to the army commander. Angioletti had gone further and installed himself in the Campidoglio – the ancient Capitol – and on his own initiative had proclaimed a united Italy with Rome as its capital. Kanzler finally turned up at the Villa Albani to spend an hour wrangling with Cadorna over the wording of the official communiqué; Kanzler wanted to stress that the nationalists had entered Rome 'with violence', but eventually he was talked into dropping that accurate (but politically incorrect at the time) phrase. The final document of capitulation was signed at 5:30 p.m. by Cadorna, Kanzler, the IV Corps chief of staff Lieutenant Colonel Domenico Primerano and Rivalta.

Cardinal Antonelli messaged Cadorna imploring him to restore normality as soon as possible, authorizing him even to occupy the Vatican and its environs if he thought it necessary. That evening, as Cadorna hastily put together a temporary junta to run the city before a more permanent authority could be formed, what remained of the pope's army gathered in Saint Peter's Square. By midnight the square was full of weary soldiers grouped around campfires wondering what would come next and keeping their weapons at hand just in case. At one point someone began to sing Charles Gounod's *Hymn to Pius IX*, and soon Saint Peter's Square echoed to a massive chorus. Kanzler, meanwhile, received a despatch from Cadorna instructing him to parade his troops in two brigades for the formal surrender of arms.

At 10 a.m. on 21 September Rivalta read to the assembled brigades, resplendent in dress uniform, a touching farewell from Kanzler, who had been unable to bring himself to be present at the humiliation, delegating the duty to de Courten and Zappi. There had been unrest in the ranks earlier that morning, with many soldiers preferring to smash their weapons rather than surrender them. Pius himself briefly appeared at a Vatican window to bless his troops as they marched off for the last time. At noon at Porta San Pancrazio, Cadorna, Bixio and Mazè de la Roche formally took the surrender from de Courten and Zappi. Someone shouted, 'Long live Pius IX!', bringing a frown to Cadorna's face. Bixio, the ex-redshirt, asked a noble papal officer, Don Alfonso Carlos de Bourbon of Austria-Este, if they could exchange sabres. Don Alfonso coolly declined on the grounds that the sabre he held had been his grandfather's, and hence a family heirloom. Bixio did not press the point.

About 2,500 weaponless Zouaves marched past Cardorna; some of them muttered a sarcastic '*au revoir*' to him as they passed. Captain de Fumel hid under his tunic the papal standard he had carried at Mentana. The largest Zouave contingent was the Dutch, with 1,172 men; next came the French with 760, the Belgians with 573, the Canadians, English and Irish with 297, the Italians with 242 and the Germans with 113. Fifteen other nationalities accounted for the rest. Every papal soldier had received a gratuity from the pope to tide him over until he could find employment. The pope's foreign volunteers were transported to Civitavecchia where they could take ship for home; the Italians were taken to prison camps in the South. Cadorna urged many to join the Italian Army, where rank and seniority would be preserved, and some took up the offer.

On 2 October Italians overwhelmingly voted in a plebiscite to annex Rome as Italy's capital. Of Rome's 45,000 eligible voters, a mere forty-six (about one-tenth of one per cent) voted no. This fantastically lopsided result, not even equalled by dictatorships, cannot be credited as genuine, and can be explained only by massive ballot-stuffing and voter intimidation. On the last day of 1870 Vittorio Emanuele II, the King of all Italy, arrived in Rome to grandly take up residence in the Quirinal Palace. The papal state was no more.

Chapter 13

Farewell to Arms

The Italian papal prisoners spent long weeks languishing in the camps, where they were often abused, waiting for the grindingly slow bureaucracy to let them go home. The French, on the other hand, were enlisted in the French Army as soon as they landed at Toulon. Three weeks before, France had suffered its devastating defeat at Prussian hands at Sedan, but there were still plenty of Frenchmen determined to fight on. Many French ex-Zouaves, including de Charette and Allet, enlisted in the 'Legion of Western Volunteers' – part of the Army of the Loire – wearing their papal uniforms. Even though Napoleon III was gone and France was now a republic, their banner read: 'Heart of Jesus, save France'. In their hearts, however they were still fighting for the pope in Rome.

The unit, commanded by de Gonidec, received its baptism of fire at Cercottes on 11 October; a second battalion under de Mocuit was formed soon afterwards. On 2 December, at Loigny north of Orléans, the Legion mounted a furious bayonet charge against Grand Duke Mecklenburg's Prussians, yelling: '*Vive la France! Vive Pie neuf!*' It was the last time a battlefield would resound with that cry. The Legion was mown down; fully two-thirds of the attackers were killed – eighteen officers and nearly two hundred enlisted men. Many able papal veterans fell that day, including Major de Troussures and Captain de Gastebois. De Charette, wounded and taken prisoner, managed to elude his captors and regain the French lines. Promoted to general, he was about to take the field against the Prussians again when Emperor Wilhelm I, monarch of a united Germany, strutted in triumph in the Hall of Mirrors at Versailles in January 1871, signalling the formal end of the Franco-Prussian war five months later. Even then, the papal veterans preferred to stay loyal to the papacy rather than join the regular French Army, and held annual reunions for years afterwards. (At the 1910 reunion in Montmartre de Charette and the surviving French papal soldiers and their descendants were served dishes named after their battles, such as *Croustades Castelfidardo* and *Glacées à la Mentana*).[1]

Pius IX considered himself a prisoner in the Vatican, and he was not far wrong. There was no way he could bring himself to recognize the new Rome-based Italian government, which he considered the child of outright and blatant aggression. Hence he could not legally negotiate with Italian government ministers and officials, or even members of the Rome local government. Faithful Catholics, he said, had no business voting in national or local elections. On 1 November, a month after the nationalist victory, he issued the stinging encyclical *Respicientes*, in which he lambasted the 'illegal, violent, null and void' occupation of the papal domains and excommunicated all who took part or acquiesced in it.[2] He stayed behind the wall of papal infallibility decreed in the Vatican Council of 1869, available to the world's Catholic faithful but staying away from the wielders of worldly power. On 13 May 1871 the administration of Prime Minister Giovanni Lanza attempted a reconciliation with the Vatican by its Law of Guarantees, which offered extraterritoriality to the Vatican, freedom for the pope to exercise his spiritual office and a generous financial settlement to enable the Holy See to go on functioning. Pius turned down the entire package, as acceptance would imply his recognition of the Italian government, and renewed his excommunication of the king for good measure.

Pius IX, still embittered, died on the evening of 7 February 1878 in his private quarters in the Apostolic Palace. King Vittorio Emanuele had preceded him to the grave a month earlier, to be succeeded by Umberto I. Large crowds filed past Pius' body as it lay in state in the Sistine Chapel. Pius had reigned for thirty-two years, the longest ever in the history of the pontificate, and the mourning was genuine. One modern historian rates Pius IX as 'the first really popular pope in history'.[3] The body was taken for burial in the church of Santa Maria Maggiore. Three years later, in accordance with his last wish, his body was transferred by night to the basilica of San Lorenzo fuori le mura (the entrance to the Campo Verano cemetery). While the torch-lit cortege was crossing Sant'Angelo bridge a group of about thirty liberal and anarchist students shouting 'Into the river with the pope!' and 'Death to priests!' stormed it with the intention of throwing the casket into the Tiber. Some of the faithful hit back with their flaming torches, dispersing the students. Similar scenes unfolded when the procession reached Via Nazionale after midnight, when the police finally decided to intervene.[4] It was rumoured that Pius was buried in a secret vault at San Lorenzo to thwart other attempts at desecration.

The conclave to elect Pius' successor met in the Sistine Chapel; though the anti-clerical Prime Minister Francesco Crispi guaranteed that the cardinals would not be disturbed, the latter didn't trust the assurance and obtained rather more solid guarantees from the French and Austro-Hungarian governments. In a mere two days – the choice of a pope did not now seem so world-shaking a process as before – the cardinals agreed on one of their number, sixty-eight-year-old Gioacchino Pecci, to become Pope Leo XIII. Leo regarded the Italian government in the same way as his predecessor, as 'an illegal usurper'. To offset this hostility, however, Leo made an effort to reach out to the world's Catholics as a purely religious leader rather than a political one. He was, in effect, the precursor of the modern papacy, with its emphasis on social and moral welfare, though he set his face firmly against socialism and all theories of re-engineering society without religious faith.

Leo made General Hermann Kanzler into a baron; the former commander of the pope's army lived quietly in Rome until his death in 1888. General Raphael de Courten, after a brief period in Switzerland, returned to Italy to live in Florence. Colonel Achille Azzanesi retired from public view and continued to live sadly in Rome 'like a stranger in his own land'. The Spanish noble Alfonso Carlos de Bourbon of Austria-Este, who had refused to hand his sabre over to Bixio, became involved in Catholic charity work until the 1930s, when he joined the forces of General Francisco Franco in the Spanish Civil War. Other veterans, such as Colonel Carpegna, Colonel Evangelisti, Salimei and Lepri di Rota, among others, refused offers to join the Italian Army.

Leo tried genuinely to raise the Vatican's prestige in the wider world, but most of Europe was still under anti-papal influence, and Protestant countries cared little for 'popery'. Hopes for a reconciliation with the Anglican Church were raised briefly in 1896, but the talks foundered on the three-hundred-year-old Edwardian Prayer Book, which the Vatican deemed uncanonical. Leo had more success with the Greek Orthodox Church, which in the nineteenth century had found itself in a situation more or less identical to the papacy, challenged by the new doctrines of nationalism and liberalism in the Balkans, including Greece, that were seen as setting eastern Christians at one another's throats. By 1888 relations between the two churches were at their most respectful since the bitter schism of 1054.

The last decades of the nineteenth century were a time of dizzying economic and social change, which Leo realized had to be dealt with by the

Church. In particular, the troubled relations between capital and labour were tackled in the famous 1891 encyclical *Rerum novarum* (Of New Things), which noted the imbalance in worker-employer relationships and decried 'the enormous fortunes of some individuals' at the expense of 'the utter poverty of the masses'. However, he was no socialist, and saw the Church in the potential role of playing a part in easing class and wealth differences according to Christian principles. Anarchist strikes and riots were beginning to disturb Rome, as in other European cities. A major banking scandal gave ammunition to the radicals. Leo also had definite ideas on politics, strongly criticizing American notions of the freedom of the individual and where it could lead – 'Americanism' looked like becoming the new heresy.[5] While maintaining the policy of non-recognition of the Italian kingdom, Leo secretly continued paying the water bill for the Quirinal Palace, which he considered papal property even though the Italian royal family was living in it.[6]

The pontificates of Leo and his successor, Pius X (1903–1914) were attempts to keep the papacy relevant in a rapidly industrializing and militarizing world while itself excluded from military affairs and power politics. The Swiss Guard, Noble Guard and Palatine Guard were there to give a ceremonial military-style flourish to the Church, but none of their members were ever expected to fire a shot or wield a sword in anger. The new pope 'would above all be a father and a shepherd', and actually allowed people to sit, rather than stand, in his presence.[7] But the state could not afford to alienate the Vatican entirely, as in the Holy Year of 1900 more than half a million pilgrims poured into Rome with their spending money, giving a healthy shot in the arm to the national economy. Then on 29 July, in the middle of the jubilee year, an anarchist assassinated King Umberto I in Monza. Though Umberto had gone on record as saying that 'all clergy should be castrated',[8] the Church authorized special prayers for the king's soul, another sign of a growing reconciliation.[9]

In 1901 French President Émile Loubet paid an official visit to Rome, in part to repair French-Italian relations that had remained shaky after the turmoil of Napoleon III's machinations. The visit, however, upset Pius X, as the French republic was seen as radically anti-clerical; moreover, the new Italian king, Vittorio Emanuele III, was still under excommunication as a member of the Savoy royal family. He was fully as anti-Church as his father, threatening to abdicate if his government ever began negotiations with the Vatican. As the anti-clerical campaign progressed in France, the Vatican severed diplomatic ties on 30 July 1904. That same month, Pius finally lifted a thirty-year boycott of national and local elections urged by Pius IX, on the grounds that Catholic votes were needed to prevent 'subversives' from being elected to office. Blocking the way for socialists to take power was now the prime political aim of the papacy. The old Colonna family found its way back to prominence in the person of the mayor of Rome, Prospero Colonna, who did much to rebuild the city and ease social tensions.

Colonna was elected mayor for a third time in July 1914, defeating an anti-clerical incumbent. The result gave impetus to a pact signed the previous year between Catholic and Liberal politicians to join forces against the left. Pius had given his blessing to the pact, called the Gentiloni Pact after Vincenzo Ottorino Gentiloni, the leader of the Catholic Electoral Union that opposed divorce and supported religious instruction in the schools. Three months later, as Europe plunged into World War One, Pius X died, to be succeeded by Benedict XV. Italy at once proclaimed its neutrality, despite agitation in nationalist circles to join the Entente powers in order to seize ethnically-Italian regions ruled by Austria-Hungary. World War One, in fact, found the papacy in a curious position. The Vatican could not, of course, offer support to either side. But it was the subject of some weird theorizing on the part of the warring governments. Some in Britain, for example, fretted that the pope could be plotting to turn the war into a crusade against the Protestant British and Orthodox Russians; Italian military intelligence believed the pope was being run by a shadowy Swiss-based clique that included the Jesuit leadership; the Germans, for their part, wooed the papacy hoping for some sign of favour.[10]

None of this could be proven. But what was obvious was the growing sentiment among the Italian public to join the war in order to gain some territorial aggrandizement in the north. Giovanni Giolitti, the veteran prime minister who wanted to keep Italy neutral, resigned under pressure. Giolitti himself was for a time in danger of his life as crowds in Rome's *piazze* clamoured for war. As Vittorio Emanuele III himself was rattling his sabre, any voices of moderation were drowned out. The Entente were willing to let Italy have anything it wanted as long as it joined them; the Treaty of London, signed on 26 April 1915, sealed the deal. On 24 May an overwhelming majority of the Parliament voted to declare war on Austria-Hungary.

Whatever his personal convictions, Benedict XV of course could not endorse any act by the Italian government, which he still considered illegal. That is what most likely triggered dark suspicions in London and other capitals that he might secretly be backing the Germans. But the unprecedented bloodshed appalled him, and in 1917 he saw a chance to enhance the papacy's standing by urging an end to the war; Europe's socialists had been agitating in the same direction, and he didn't want his own peace impulses to be upstaged. When the papal nuncio in Berlin informed Wilhelm II of the pope's sentiments, the kaiser replied that he expected that 'peace should be introduced by the pope, not the Social Democrats'. It was a lukewarm response, but the pope went ahead on 10 August by proposing peace to all the belligerent powers on the basis of a return to the pre-1914 status quo. The only foreign statesman to reply was the British foreign secretary, Arthur Balfour, who suggested politely that the pope's proposal might be a tad unrealistic. But merely by replying to the pope, Balfour earned the ire of the Italians and French and was forced to admit that his communication had been 'a mistake'.[11]

Undaunted, the pope pressed his peace proposal. One of his unstated aims was to discourage Italy from laying claim to Tyrol in the north. The claim reminded him too much of the Italian state's chauvinist swallowing of the Papal State thirty-seven years before, and besides, would become a cause of chronic instability, as all irredentist campaigns tend to be.[12] In Benedict's thinking, if Germany could be induced to drop its annexation of Belgium, and France to give up Alsace-Lorraine, Italy might be shamed into dropping its own Tyrol claim, and hence the way could be open for a European peace. But nobody would play ball: Germany made polite noises but essentially brushed aside the attempt at papal mediation, while France and Britain ignored it altogether.[13]

The reaction from official Italy was frigid. The foreign minister, George Sidney Sonnino, accused the pope of being a tool of Germany and Austria-Hungary. The idea of the pope being an active enemy agent at a time when Italy was at war is hard to credit. But a good many Italians were prepared to believe something of the sort; rumours abounded, for example, that the kaiser planned to restore the Papal State. This rumour was apparently based on a 1915 plan to engineer an Italian annexation of Tyrol with the help of Austria–Hungary, for which Italy would reward the papacy by restoring its independence and giving it a corridor to the sea.[14] Nothing had come of this complicated scheme, and by the war's end the Vatican had little if anything to show for its peacemaking bid.

One foreign leader did wish to know the pope's thoughts after the Armistice of 1918, and that was U.S. President Woodrow Wilson, who visited Rome to sound out the Italians about his ambitious Fourteen Points, designed to remove the focal points of European war. Point 9 read: 'A readjustment of the frontiers of Italy should be effected along clearly recognizable lines of nationality.' It was a faultless idea on paper, but as any student of European history could have told Wilson (and many did tell him), 'clearly recognizable' boundaries of nationality were a rarity in Central and Eastern Europe. The issue, moreover, was precisely that which had led to the Italian state's aggression on papal territory in 1870. Wilson sided with the pope against irredentist claims in the north and gave Sonnino to understand that the United States was opposed to the victorious states of Europe carving out their own spheres. Benedict would have seen the American view as vindicating his own on the perils of great-power chauvinism. As Woodrow Wilson returned to America ill, exhausted and disillusioned, his Fourteen Points in tatters, Italy seized most of Tyrol and cast covetous eyes on Fiume, a coastal area in what is now Slovenia but which then had a large Italian-speaking population.

In the meantime, the Bolsheviks had seized power in Russia, upending the traditional European power equation. The creation of the communist Soviet Union alarmed the pope enough to begin considering the Italian state as less of a foe than the spread of communism. Benedict XV died in February 1922, to be succeeded by Cardinal Achille Ratti as Pope Pius XI. In his previous post as papal nuncio in Warsaw, the new Pius had witnessed how the Soviets crushed Polish resistance, and realized that the papacy could not remain indifferent to the spread of communism and radical socialism. Pius was not a politician by nature, and thus had no axes to grind. However, he was conscious of how a public image would play a key role in maintaining the papacy's status; on his election he appeared in public to bless the crowds in Saint Peter's – the first time a pontiff had so appeared in more than fifty years. He also negotiated concordats (papal treaties) with several European countries.

By these, the Vatican regained its right to appoint bishops in Catholic and non-Catholic countries alike. Since by now this once-contentious issue had lost most of its emotional baggage, the countries involved gave no trouble over it.[15]

Barely had Pius XI taken up his sceptre than a radical organization called the Fascist Party marched on Rome under its leader, the firebrand Benito Mussolini, to take over the weak parliamentary government by force. Mussolini, an ex-socialist revolutionary, had tapped into widespread public discontent with economic problems, political instability, riots and left-right gang warfare, plus the yearning for a strong and even dictatorial leader who would put everything in its place. Mussolini had been born into a radical left-wing family that had no use for the clergy or religion. He grew up sharing that sentiment, lambasting priests as 'black microbes' and slaves of capitalism. In fact, in his early years as a journalist he kept a portrait of Karl Marx in his office.[16] By 1919, however, his thinking had evolved to become what he termed 'fascist,' that is, an amalgam of radical socialism with uncompromising nationalism and anti-clericalism thrown in. It was through the newly-formed Fascist Party – a development of the *Fasci di Combattimento* (Combat Leagues) that he gained enough adherents to be a national force in his own right.

As Mussolini marched on Rome, King Vittorio Emanuele III mulled over using martial law to stop him, but decided against it. The king appeared to share the public mood, fanned by massive pro-fascist rallies in Rome in what foreign journalists reported as 'a fever of delight' that someone was finally coming to put an end years of misgovernment. The Vatican (or most of the people in it) almost certainly shared this view. Yet there were some who must have remembered some of Mussolini's past aggressive anti-papal statements; as recently as 1920 he had gone on record as calling Christianity 'detestable' and calling on the pope to leave Rome for good.[17] When in power, however, he called a different tune. First, he could not afford to alienate the mass of Catholic citizenry; second, he needed to cultivate the Catholic *popolari* party, the second biggest in the Parliament. In sharp contrast to his earlier pronouncements, he now declared himself 'deeply a Catholic' and 'profoundly religious'. Whether these statements could be taken at face value is still debatable, but they had the effect of raising his popularity and easing the Vatican's concerns.

Relations between the papacy and Italy's new ruler were put to an unexpected test when in late 1924 a socialist deputy, Giacomo Matteotti, was kidnapped and murdered in Rome, almost certainly at the instigation of the Fascist Party. The Catholic *popolari* walked out of the Parliament in protest, but Pius did not support the move; though he was fairly sure that Mussolini was implicated in the murder of Matteotti, he was more afraid of a return to 'liberal agnostic governments' than the possibility of a fascist dictatorship. With the Catholic party thus restrained, Mussolini proceeded to a full dictatorship via a political coup on 3 January 1925. It was a masterstroke for Mussolini, who for some weeks had been in danger of losing power in the national revulsion over Matteotti's murder. Had the Vatican reacted more vigorously, could it have stopped Mussolini in his tracks?

The question became academic, as 1925 was a Holy Year and 600,000 pilgrims, caring little for politics, flooded into Rome. Pius tirelessly supervised all aspects of what had become an increasingly complex project, meeting diplomats and discussing world affairs. Mussolini held his own prestige events in Piazza Colonna (surviving four assassination attempts between November 1925 and October 1926). He knew, however, that to stay in the public's goodwill he needed to cultivate (or pretend to cultivate) good relations with the Vatican. Churches in Italy regularly echoed to *Te Deums* in thanks for Mussolini's deliverance from the attempts on his life. The Duce himself took advantage of the Holy Year by honouring Saint Francis of Assisi, 'the most Italian of saints', with a large statue in the Lateran square.[18] Yet a state of mutual non-recognition, the half-century-old legacy of Pius IX, continued to exist between the Italian state and the Vatican. The psychological groundwork for an improvement in relations had been laid in Mussolini's early years in power; now it was time to regularize the relationship, and settle the lingering Roman Question once and for all.

Popes since Leo XIII had never been quite happy with the Vatican's political isolation, and Pius XI hoped to end it in some way. So did Mussolini, for different reasons. The historical evidence points to the Duce never really abandoning his dislike of the clergy but he saw an opportunity to enlist it on his side. 'History taught him that he would hardly emerge unscathed from a head-on struggle with the papacy.'[19] Mussolini's fascist system elevated the state as the supreme good in national life, to which everything else had to be subordinated, even the Church. Pius, of course, strongly disagreed. But he had to mask this distaste as Mussolini cultivated the clergy by exempting them from paying tax and saving Catholic banks from collapse. He also used Roman Catholic missions abroad to further Italian foreign policy and flattered conservative clergy by pushing family values in a big way.

Above all, both Duce and pope wanted to go down in history as the ones who stanched the running sore of the Roman Question. There were several secret contacts, and Mussolini tapped the Vatican's telephone lines to keep abreast of what the Church was thinking. A major issue was how much the Vatican should receive in compensation for the forced seizures of 1870; a sum was eventually agreed that was less than half of what was originally demanded – and far less than what Pius IX had been offered and had turned down. In return, Mussolini's government agreed to restore clerical authority over marriage and family matters – though it would be honoured more in the breach than in the observance. Pius agreed to exercise sovereignty over the one hundred and eight acres of Roman real estate that now constitute the independent Vatican City, including the Lateran basilica, the papal summer retreat at Castel Gandolfo south of Rome, and the city's Gregorian University.

The result was the concordat known as the Lateran Treaty, signed in the Lateran basilica on 11 February 1929 by the Duce and the papal secretary of state, Cardinal Pietro Gasparri. The vexatious Roman Question was no more. The papal state was revived, though under another name. Church and state were reconciled. Italy's Catholic population could rest in the knowledge that the Duce was taking care of their spiritual as well as material welfare. Ironically, it was the biggest success of Mussolini's career; the man who had begun that career as Church-hating as any of Garibaldi's 'priest-eaters' had saved the Vatican from lasting irrelevance and possible extinction. Pius justifiably extolled Mussolini as 'a man sent by Providence', but privately fretted that the Duce's already considerable ego would inflate even more, and warned him that he must not deem himself 'a demi-god half-way between heaven and earth'.[20] There was some grumbling in the Curia about the paucity of the compensation received, but Pius scotched it by sheer force of personality. In fact, the pope could be thought of as a clerical Duce of sorts, impatient of criticism and determined to impose his will though his 'terrifying rages' if necessary. 'He tolerated nothing less than total obedience.'[21] The euphoria of the Lateran Treaty wore off quickly. Fascist Party attacks on Catholic organizations triggered a sternly-worded encyclical from the pope, *Non abbiambo bisogno* ('We have no need'), protesting the 'inventions, falsehoods and real calumnies' featured in the controlled national press. The Duce stepped back, allowing the Catholic organizations to function as long as they stuck to religious affairs.

In foreign policy the papacy had to face the growing political tensions and totalitarian movements of the 1930s, all of which threatened the Church's traditional teachings. In France an extreme Catholic group called *Action Française* was suppressed and excommunicated by Pius for being anti-Semitic. A year after the signing of the Lateran Treaty, Cardinal Eugenio Pacelli was named papal secretary of state; a talented diplomat, he had spent time as papal nuncio in Germany and had got to know the country quite well. In 1933 Adolf Hitler came to power in Germany, and one of Pacelli's first tasks was to negotiate a concordat with Hitler's government which involved some very delicate diplomatic manoeuvring in order to secure freedom for the Catholic Church in Germany – on condition that German clergy take an oath of loyalty to the German state and avoid involvement in politics of any kind. Pius considered this a fair deal and ratified it on 20 July 1933. Responding to later criticism of his accommodation with the Nazi regime, Pacelli defended it on the grounds that he 'had to choose between an agreement and the virtual elimination of the Catholic Church in the Reich'.[22]

As the thirties progressed, however, the Vatican became much less certain of being able to live with totalitarian regimes of any stripe. In the Soviet Union the Russian Orthodox Church had submitted to Joseph Stalin to become a clear tool of the communist state, and the Vatican hoped to avoid that fate. It was whispered behind the walls of the Vatican that the Duce could be slightly mad; when it became obvious in 1935 that Mussolini was about to invade Ethiopia, Pius privately condemned the idea of 'a civilized nation setting out to grab another country'. It was all too reminiscent of the militant Italian nationalism of the 1860s. Three years later, when Mussolini enacted new racial laws against the Jews, Pius issued a strong protest which the newspapers were forbidden to publish. The Duce reacted with a fresh burst of anti-clericalism, hoping privately that the pope would leave this world soon and confessing himself now a disbeliever in God. The papacy, he said, echoing Garibaldi, was a malignancy and had to be 'rooted out once and for all'.[23]

In 1937 Pius issued his encyclical *Mit brennender Sorge* ('With burning anxiety'). Couched in German so that there could be no mistake about its intended recipient, it contained a definite note of regret that Nazi Germany was blatantly breaking its concordat with the Vatican. By now Pius' health was failing, but he planned another encyclical that would lambast all forms of 'mechanical-totalitarianism' as contrary to human nature as intended by God. It would be a direct development of papal themes of the nineteenth century, when aggressive liberalism and nationalism threatened to sweep away the old faith. Now, human individuality and dignity were being eroded by political 'systems' that were turning people into state-controlled robots. Pius never got to issue this document, as he died on 10 February 1939, as the political skies over Europe were darkening.

At the time all the Italian cardinals were in Rome to mark the tenth anniversary of the Lateran Treaty and the conclave for the succession was convened quickly. As it was apparent that war in Europe would soon erupt, few, if any, cardinals were in the mood for innovation or adventurism. Foreign issues would be paramount for the new pontiff, and therefore on the very first day of the conclave Pacelli, the experienced diplomat and 'a very gentle, cultured, shy, prayerful lonely young man', was elected Pope Pius XII. The day after his election, on 3 March, he issued a radio call for global peace. Hitler and Mussolini paid little heed, but he did receive backing from General Francisco Franco, who had emerged from the Spanish Civil war as head of the Spanish state; Pius actually sent Franco a telegram of thanks for having saved Spain and its Church from socialism.[24] On 24 August, a day after the signing of the Hitler-Stalin pact, Pius took to the airwaves again with the warning that 'nothing is lost with peace [but] everything can be lost in war'. But as for his predecessor's planned encyclical, he chose not to issue it; he apparently decided that now was not the time to fan more flames. Instead, he issued one of his own, the *Summi Pontificatus* ('Of the Supreme Pontificate') which blamed the war which had just broken out on 'religious and moral agnosticism'. On a spiritual rather than a political level, the encyclical said that war was caused by 'the abandonment of that Christian teaching of which the Chair of Peter is the depository and exponent'.[25] The embattled pontiffs of the nineteenth century could not have expressed it better.

Mussolini was in no mood to listen to the pope's broadcasts because he was preparing for war himself. He joined Hitler's offensive in the West on 10 May 1940, announcing the event with great fanfare from his usual balcony of the Palazzo Venezia. As young Italians went off to war, many of them not to return, a German army intelligence officer in Rome began secret contacts with Vatican clergy to sound out what the Allied reaction was likely to be if the Fuehrer was assassinated, as some German officers were plotting. Captain Josef Müller met in the basement of Saint Peter's with a German cleric, Monsignor Ludwig Kaas, under cover of an archaeological project to find Saint Peter's bones. The Vatican informed the British, who suspected a trap to lure Allied agents to destruction, and declined to get involved. When war erupted in earnest on the Western front, the contacts were broken off.[26]

As the war dragged on, and Mussolini's forces lost ground to the Allies in North Africa and Albania, Italian public opinion began to turn against the Duce. Pius, who all the time maintained a strict neutrality in the conflict, tried to revive public morale – and faith in the Church – by a special jubilee on 13 May 1942 to mark the quarter-century since his consecration as bishop. But though neutral, he still feared a German victory and knew that Hitler planned to eliminate the Vatican. Pius had ready a resignation letter to use if the Nazis occupied Rome and jailed him, and a successor had to be picked. He kept packed suitcases in case he had to flee in a hurry. In such an eventuality, he told the commander of the Swiss Guard, the Germans should be allowed to seize the Vatican without resistance.[27] The pope was right to worry, as the Germans knew he was protecting Roman Jews and escaped Allied servicemen and considered it a breach of neutrality. If he had been captured, his fate would not have been pleasant. Meanwhile, Romans were beginning to go hungry. The Mussolini regime had appointed Major-General Domenico Chirieleison, the commander of the 4th Livorno Division that had fought by the side of the Germans in the Sicilian campaign, as military commander of the Rome area. The pope prevailed upon Chirieleison to ensure that the Romans had enough to eat. The general appears to have done his job satisfactorily, enabling him to escape a charge of committing atrocities during the war.[28]

In early 1943 most of the Italian public had definitely turned against the Duce. The army had suffered embarrassing reverses in North Africa and Albania, the casualty lists were lengthening, and economic problems at home were mounting. His outward reaction was to blame the Jews and (of course) the Vatican for the decline in Italy's fortunes. Inwardly, he was looking at ways to get out of the war. Hitler browbeat him into keeping up his flagging war effort, but as an Allied invasion of Italy crept ever closer, the Duce sank more and more into listless depression. Pius perceived the danger of a leaderless Italy threatened by a communist revolution and attempted a half-hearted mediation with the Allies. To prepare the atmosphere, the *Osservatore Romano*, the official Vatican daily, correctly reported that the British were treating Italian prisoners-of-war quite well, earning the Duce's ire. But the mediation attempt foundered on the rock of Allied insistence that Mussolini must go before anything could be discussed. On 18 July Allied aircraft bombed Rome. The shock was profound. Less than a week later the Fascist Grand Council appealed to the king to find another national leader. On 25 July Vittorio Emanuele personally placed the unprotesting Duce under arrest, replacing him with Marshal Pietro Badoglio with instructions to arrange an armistice with the Allies.

Barely had World War Two closed than Pius XII braced himself to face down a threat he considered worse than fascism – the global rise of communism, fomented by the Soviet Union. Not only was communism a sworn enemy of religion, but it preached the ideology of class warfare as a substitute for the Christian ideal of social harmony. Almost as bad, in his view, were the tendencies towards socialism in Western Europe, a trend which could, and often did, unwittingly aid Soviet subversion in that region. From the Soviet point of view, of course, the Vatican was an archaic and useless speck in the new map of the world that Stalin wished to create. Yet a small papal shadow did intrude in the Yalta conference of February 1945, where Stalin hosted Winston Churchill and Franklin Roosevelt to see what that new map might look like. According to one account – albeit unconfirmed – American Democratic politician Ed Flynn asked Stalin if he was prepared to admit the pope to his world scheme. Stalin is reported to have replied with an ironic smile, 'How many divisions has the pope?'[29] It was the classic attitude of power-worship, in which the only things that counted in the world were 'divisions' and number of gun barrels.

Closer to home, at the close of the war Italy was a shambles, politically and militarily. It was now a republic, a referendum in June 1946 having abolished the monarchy. What was left of the Italian Air Force's aircraft, for example, were scattered around the country in various stages of damage. After a purge of officers tainted by loyalty to the Duce, the air force leadership looked to the Allies to help reorganize the *Aeronautica Militare* along modern lines. But what the Allies delivered was a slap in the face – the Allied Control Commission in Italy demanded that all surviving warplanes be handed over for demolition. No self-respecting country could swallow such a peremptory demand, and the Italian government found itself in a quandary; it was particularly unwilling to give up thirty-six three-engined Savoia-Marchetti SM82 bomber transports that were the pride of the air fleet. The deputy chief of the Italian Air Force staff, General Alberto Briganti, happened to be a Knight of the Hospitaller Order of Saint John, the nine-hundred-year-old military organization that had fought innumerable times for the popes. Thanks to the approval of Pius, he had the eight-pointed Hospitaller cross painted on the aircraft. As the Hospitallers were, and remain, a sovereign order, they were technically not Italian and hence outside the Allies' remit. The planes were saved to be able to carry out relief and pilgrimage work for the next thirteen years.[30]

The pope no longer had an army, but he had the weapons of words, and in the post-war years Pius employed them often. He used the Holy Year of 1950 to reach the faithful of five continents by radio. In the following eight years he averaged about three encyclicals a year warning of the spread of atheism through communism; walls in every Italian parish featured Vatican posters with dire warnings:

1. *IT IS NOT LAWFUL* to enrol in communist parties or give them help.
2. *IT IS NOT LAWFUL* to publish, distribute or read books, magazines, newspapers or flyers which assert the doctrine or practice of communism, or collaborate with such through writings.
3. *THEY WILL NOT BE ADMITTED TO THE SACRAMENTS*, those faithful who knowledgeably or willingly commit the above acts.
4. *THEY ARE EXCOMMUNICATED AS APOSTATES*, those faithful who profess the doctrine of materialist and anti-Christian communism, as well as those who defend them and act as their propagandists.

EXCOMMUNICATION is a medicinal penalty by which one is excluded from the Communion of the faithful with the effects sanctioned by Canon Law.

APOSTASY is the abandonment of the Catholic faith.[31]

Pius practised a more hands-on approach to the papacy than was usual, leaving the post of secretary of state mostly vacant. He seems to have left internal Vatican administration to essentially take care of itself while he occupied himself with weighty issues of foreign and spiritual policy. Between 1953 and 1958 he appointed no new cardinals. His lingering last illness, covered by the mass media, ended in October 1958 at the papal retreat at Castel Gandolfo.

The election of Pius' successor, Pope John XXIII, set a new trend in that it was the first papal election to receive televised coverage; millions of viewers around the world became familiar with the iconic elements of papal elections – the black smoke and then the white smoke, the titillating secrecy surrounding the proceedings in the Sistine Chapel, the great bells of Saint Peter's tolling in triumph, the surging crowds, the white-hatted newcomer emerging onto the balcony for the world to see – in a single bound, the papacy had entered the media age. A process that was once quietly serious had morphed into a form of global entertainment. John himself, with his kindly face and pleasant demeanour, became a star almost at once. At the height of the Cold War he cast his blessings on East and West alike. His humanitarianism was in keeping with the spirit of the age, but his comforting exterior masked the mind of a keen and experienced diplomat. He had high hopes of reconciling eastern and western Christendom, but as he was already seventy-seven when he became pope, many felt he would not have enough time for his ambition, and they were right; with only days to go before the opening of a modernizing Church council, John was diagnosed with stomach cancer and died on 3 June 1963. (He was beatified on 3 September 2000.)

Cardinal Giovanni Battista Montini, a liberal, was elected Pope Paul VI to succeed John XXIII. Outwardly he appeared to be the antithesis of his predecessor, austere-faced where John had never been without a benevolent grin, a man of few words. Paul nonetheless was determined to mend the long breach between liberals and conservatives in the Curia. He also shared

John's concern with bringing the churches together, and for the first time in hundreds of years a pope received an archbishop of Canterbury. In 1965 he flew to Istanbul (formerly Constantinople, as the Greeks still call it) for an epochal meeting with Greek Orthodox Patriarch Athenagoras and at one stroke healed the 911-year-old breach between the two churches. The trip was the start of another new trend for the papacy – flying around the globe to enable the faithful to see and hear a pope in person. Paul was not one to revel in the showy side of the papacy; he sold the papal tiara for charity and replaced it with the humbler *pallium* as a symbol of authority.[32] The sternly censorious attitude of Pius XII to subversive literature and works of art was abandoned in an Italy that since 1957 had been a member of the fledgling European Economic Community (the precursor of the European Union).

It was Paul VI who on 14 September 1970 abolished two of the last vestiges of what had in past ages been the pope's army – the Noble Guard and the papal police, or Palatine Guard. Both bodies had come to be seen as having outlived their usefulness and hence had become a drain on papal finances. Nobles of the former, in compensation, were named 'Gentlemen of His Holiness' but no longer wore uniform or had a banner. The Swiss Guard, however, was too much of a tourist attraction to tamper with; its colourful Renaissance ceremonial attire had become a vital part of the iconic image of the Vatican, and therefore it remains in its original form. It might also be argued that by the late 1960s militarism was getting a bad press around the world, highlighted by the American plight in Vietnam and the rise of the hippie 'make-love-not-war' movement. For Paul it was a chance to get rid of the showier items that he felt he did not need.

Between 1968 and 1978 Paul VI issued no encyclicals. He was saddened by the intense controversy that erupted over the Church's strict teachings against birth control, a controversy that split Catholic faithful around the world. Nevertheless, the Holy Year of 1975 was heralded as 'the opening of a new phase of theological, spiritual and pastoral teaching', and as usual it drew hundreds of thousands of visitors. But the political atmosphere in Italy was darkening, with the emergence of far-left violence by the 'Red Brigades', who kidnapped and murdered a former prime minister, Aldo Moro, in the spring of 1978. It was nasty blow for the ailing pope, who died at Castel Gandolfo on 6 August that same year. By now the cardinals' conclaves, held under the pitiless glare of the impatient media, had become fairly short affairs, and after just four ballots Cardinal Albino Luciani, the patriarch of Venice, was elected to take the unusual name of John Paul, signalling that he would continue the work of his two predecessors.

But unbeknownst to the world (and to the Curia), Pope John Paul I suffered from a heart ailment that killed him less than a month into his pontificate, the briefest in more than three-and-a-half centuries. His successor was a novelty in more ways than one; Cardinal Karol Wojtyla was a Pole, the first-ever (and so far only one) of that nationality to occupy the throne of Saint Peter, and almost at once he was transformed into the papacy's second media star after John XXIII. Wojtyla's choice of the name John Paul II was designed to ease the public shock of the first John Paul's untimely demise as well as pay tribute to his conciliatory character. As a cardinal the new pope had a well-publicized history of standing up to the communist regime in his native Poland, endearing him to the West. His election as pope signalled that the Vatican had aligned itself ideologically with the Western powers, in a way abandoning its previous neutral and apolitical stance in world affairs. John Paul's election prefigured the rise to leadership within the next two years of Prime Minister Margaret Thatcher in Britain and President Ronald Reagan in the United States, both of them firm cold warriors who backed the new pope to the hilt.

A failed attempt on the pope's life in Saint Peter's Square in 1981 permanently harmed his health, but gained him greater public adulation than ever before. In the 1980s he embarked on an unprecedented number of travels that were sure-fire media fodder and turned him into the best-known pontiff of all time. The Curia was not always happy about his absences, especially the prolonged ones,[33] and the conservatives always feared that his global fame might corrupt his essential holiness. In doctrine he was staunchly conservative – given his bitter experience of communism – relying on Cardinal Josef Ratzinger of Germany to enforce it through the Congregation of the Doctrine of the Faith (formerly the Inquisition). Though some recent critics have accused him of having 'a clerical mind-set reminiscent of the Middle Ages',[34] it was precisely that mind-set which touched the hearts of millions of believers and turned him into an icon. Even the ill-health and suffering of John Paul II's final years were minutely covered by the global media. The transformation of pope into personality cult was apparently complete.

When on 19 April 2005 Cardinal Ratzinger was elected pope as Benedict XVI, the paradigm shifted. The soft-spoken, scholarly German was the anti-celebrity, avoiding when he could the television cameras and the headlines. Media stardom was not for him. In this he gained the warm approval of the conservative elements in the Church but disappointed many media-wise Catholics who had wanted someone to showcase the Holy See like John Paul II had done. Benedict's achievements were more internal; he had the good sense to confront, and not hide from, a messy paedophilia scandal in which the Catholic clergy of several countries had become involved. He largely successfully avoided the traps of populism and cut down the number of papal trips abroad, preferring to concentrate on the Church's moral and spiritual regeneration from within, rather than intervene in the outward organization.

But foreign issues continued to press in on the papacy in the first years of the twenty-first century. The communism which had so worried Pius XII and Paul VI had gone, to be replaced by what many considered to be a more direct threat – terrorism inspired by Islamist extremism. Events of the 2000s convinced him that European Christendom was coming under its biggest threat from aggressive Islam since the Turkish siege of Vienna in 1683. By expressing this fear he earned himself a burst of media coverage, not all of it favourable. But it clearly expressed his long-term strategic thinking and helped to bring security back to the forefront of Vatican concerns. Yet even Benedict could not finally withstand the merciless demands of the media industry for more exposure; in fact, as early as 2005 *The Times* of London considered downgrading its Rome bureau on the grounds that 'with John Paul gone, the papacy is no longer interesting enough for our readers'.[35] On 28 February 2013, believing at age eighty-six that he could 'no longer physically, mentally and spiritually accomplish the mission of his ministry', (as he put it in a 2010 interview) he bowed out by abdication.

Globalization had a hand in electing the next pope, Archbishop Jorge Mario Bergoglio of Buenos Aires, as Pope Francis. His election was another fresh departure from Vatican tradition: first, he was the first-ever Latin American pope (though of Italian descent) and thus was familiar with the burning issues of poverty and violence among the disadvantaged of Latin America; and second, breaking all manner of precedents, he took for himself the name Francis, which had never before been used by a pope, hence the unusual lack of a Roman numeral after it. It was a tribute, he said, to Saint Francis of Assisi, with whose gentleness and holiness he wished to identify. The world media have portrayed Francis as something of an admixture of centrist politician and social worker at the expense of his function as leader and head of a state. Like John Paul II before him he has been criticized on those grounds by the more conservative elements of the Curia; but as long as the world media promote what has inevitably emerged as a Francis personality cult, with the Argentine pontiff seemingly pressing most of the right liberal buttons, the opposition is likely to remain muted.

There is, of course, the question of how much attention a pope who concentrates on social welfare issues can give to security and even military affairs. Francis is not unacquainted with the propensity for human violence and ways of dealing with it – he did, after all, work as a nightclub bouncer as a young man, surely the only pope to include such a job on his employment record – and has not hesitated to pronounce on world security issues. Nuclear weapons and their proliferation have always been of concern to the Vatican, but it was Francis who in November 2017 hardened the Church's stance on them, condemning even their stockpiling as a deterrent. Previous popes, he said, had tolerated nuclear weapons as long as they served as a deterrent to general warfare, but in his view there was no need even for that in the twenty-first century.[36] Two months later he gave the diplomatic corps accredited to the Holy See his ideas of war and security on the centenary of the end of World War One.

A defining feature of twenty-first century conflict is what the pope described as 'a third world war fought piecemeal'. Well knowing 'war's perverse logic', Francis nevertheless argued that 'it no longer makes sense to maintain that war is a fit instrument with which to repair the violation of justice' and that 'love, not fear, must dominate the relationships between individuals and nations'. More to the point, when wars had to occur, he said, 'victory never means humiliating a defeated foe'.[37] Yet some quarters of the Church fear that he could be too mild on militant Islam. He has been urged to take a tougher line to the point of issuing a full encyclical in the manner of Pius XI's warnings against Nazism and Pius XII's strong injunctions against communism. Wrote one commentator in June 2016: 'He might review the decisions of former pontiffs who once organized resistance against existential threats to Judeo–Christian Civilization', citing the precedents of Leo I, Urban II, Pius V and Pius XII, 'The Good Shepherd must now protect his sheep.'[38]

So far, however, Francis prefers to employ the essentially Wilsonian paradigm that human goodness can be expected to eventually win out against the baser human instincts. To be sure, there are plenty of security and military experts around the world who might disagree. Yet Francis has shown that he can have a core of steel on some issues. One is freemasonry, a bugbear of the papacy since the eighteenth century and a movement which the nineteenth century popes deemed partly responsible for the Italian nationalist and redshirt war on the papacy. The official Roman Catholic view of freemasonry is that, as a fruit of the Enlightenment, it 'believes that Christ and his teachings, as taught by the Church, are an impediment to human freedom and self-fulfilment', and hence to be condemned out of hand.[39]

Francis' implacable opposition to any signs of freemasonry within the ranks of the Church had an unexpected casualty. On 24 January 2017 the pope called into his office the Grand Master of the Order of the Hospitallers of Saint John, Matthew Festing, and asked him to resign his office. For a pope it was an unprecedented move; though the Order of Saint John had been founded in the twelfth century by a pope, and ever since had acknowledged the pope as its spiritual – though not its military – commander-in-chief, it had always insisted on a certain independence of the Vatican. Its grand masters had either held office for life or had been replaced by internal processes. Technically, a pope cannot sack a Hospitaller grand master, but such is the prestige of the papal chair that it would take a very rash grand master to resist a papal call to step down. A shock ran through the order. 'The most astonishing feature', reported London's *Catholic Herald*, was that the pope installed an 'apostolic delegate' to run the order until a new grand master could take office. 'In effect,' the newspaper wrote, 'this abolishes the Order as a sovereign entity … what we are seeing is effectively the annexation of one country by another.'[40]

What had really happened? News reports indicated that worrisome signs of freemasonry among the Knights of Saint John forced Francis to act. Yet sources inside the order have played down that issue; the real problem, they say, is that senior figures in the Hospitallers consented to the use of condoms as birth control measures in missions in Africa, and if there is any one issue which every pontiff to this day has firmly upheld, it is that birth control of any kind is a sin, no matter what the extenuating circumstances might be.[41] Of course, freemasonry and birth control are moral and social rather than security issues. Papal security is in the hands of the Vatican Security Gendarmerie Corps (*Corpo della Gendarmeria dello Stato Città del Vaticano*) with its military-status personnel and range of services, commanded at this writing by Domenico Giani and paid entirely by the Vatican with no Italian state contribution. The Swiss Guard also have security duties, and often their men, still attired in Michelangelo's pantaloons and Spanish helmets, can be seen sliding mirrors under cars entering the Vatican confines to check for explosives.

The papacy at this writing has to confront a dilemma that in a way is common also to the Orthodox and Protestant churches: should the Church 'change with the times' (in the time-worn phrase) or stick to the solid tenets of its apostolic tradition? For the Vatican in particular, since for centuries it was a state with a government and an army, will security considerations, and the threat of Islamic jihadism in particular, bring a time when the popes will need a real army again? It may not be wise to rule it out.

The Popes

(Anti-popes not included)
Source: Vatican *Annuario Pontificio*, cited in Rendina 711–15)

St Peter (Simon of Bethsaida)	30–67
Linus of Volterra	67–76
Anacletus of Rome	76–88
Clement I of Rome	88–97
Evaristus of Bethlehem	97–105
Alexander I of Rome	105–115
Sixtus I of Rome	115–125
Telesphorus of Terranuova	125–136
Hyginus of Athens	136–140
Pius I of Aquileia	140–155
Anicetus of Syria	155–166
Soterus of Fondi	166–175
Eleutherius of Nikopolis	175–189
Victor I of Africa	189–199
Zephyrinus of Rome	199–217
Calixtus I of Rome	217–222
Urban I of Rome	222–230
Pontian of Rome	230–235
Anteros of Greece	235–236
Fabian of Rome	236–250
Cornelius of Rome	251–253
Lucius I of Rome	253–254
Stephen I of Rome	254–257
Sixtus II of Greece	257–258
Dionysius (origin unknown)	259–268
Felix I of Rome	269–274

Benedict I (Bonosio) of Rome	575–579
Pelagius II of Rome	579–590
Gregory I (the Great) of Rome	590–604
Sabinian of Blera	604–606
Boniface III of Rome	607
Boniface IV of Marsica	608–615
Adeodatus I of Rome	615–618
Boniface V of Naples	619–625
Honorius I of Campania	625–638
Severinus of Rome	640
John IV of Dalmatia	640–642
Theodore I of Greece	642–649
Martin I of Todi	649–653
Eugenius I of Rome	654–657
Vitalian of Segni	657–672
Adeodatus II of Rome	672–676
Donus of Rome	676–678
Agatho of Palermo	678–681
Leo II of Sicily	682–683
Benedict II of Rome	684–685
John V of Antioch	685–686
Conon (origin unknown)	686–687
Sergius I of Palermo	687–701
John VI of Greece	701–705
John VII of Greece	705–707
Sisinnius of Syria	708
Constantine of Syria	708–715
Gregory II of Rome	715–731
Gregory III of Syria	731–741
Zacharias of Santa Severina	741–752
Stephen II of Rome	752–757
Paul I of Rome	757–767
Stephen III of Sicily	768–772
Hadrian I of Rome	772–795
Leo III of Rome	795–816
Stephen IV of Rome	816–817

Paschal I of Rome	817–824
Eugenius II of Rome	824–827
Valentine of Rome	827
Gregory IV of Rome	827–844
Sergius II of Rome	844–847
Leo IV of Rome	847–855
Benedict III of Rome	855–858
Nicholas I (the Great) of Rome	858–867
Hadrian II of Rome	867–872
John VIII of Rome	872–882
Marinus I of Gaul	882–884
Hadrian III of Rome	884–885
Stephen V of Rome	885–891
Formosus of Rome	891–896
Boniface VI of Rome	896
Stephen VI of Rome	896–897
Romanus of Gaul	897
Theodore II of Rome	897
John IX of Tivoli	898–900
Benedict IV of Rome	900–903
Leo V of Ardea	903
Sergius III of Rome	904–911
Anastasius III of Rome	911–913
Lando of Sabina	913–914
John X of Tossignano	914–928
Leo VI of Rome	928
Stephen VII of Rome	928–931
John XI of Rome	931–935
Leo VII of Rome	936–939
Stephen VIII of Rome	939–942
Marinus II of Rome	942–946
Agapitus II of Rome	946–955
John XII (Octavian, Count of Tusculum)	955–964
Leo VIII of Rome	963–965
Benedict V of Rome	964–966
John XIII of Rome	965–972

Benedict VI of Rome	973–974
Benedict VII of Rome	974–983
John XIV of Pavia	983–984
John XV of Rome	985–996
Gregory V (Bruno of Saxony)	996–999
Sylvester II (Gerbert of Belliac)	999–1003
John XVII of Rome	1003
John XVIII of Rome	1004–1009
Sergius IV of Rome	1009–1012
Benedict VIII (Theophylact, Count of Tusculum)	1012–1024
John XIX (Romanus, Count of Tusculum)	1024–1032
Benedict IX (Count of Tusculum)	1032–1044, 1045, 1047–1048
Sylvester III of Rome	1045
Gregory VI of Rome	1045–1046
Clement II (Suitger of Saxony)	1046–1047
Damasus II of Bavaria	1048
Leo IX (Bruno of Alsace)	1049–1054
Victor II (Gebhard of Dollnstein-Hirschberg)	1055–1057
Stephen IX (Frederick of Lorraine)	1057–1058
Nicholas II (Gerard of Savoy)	1059–1061
Alexander II (Anselm of Milan)	1061–1073
Gregory VII (Hildebrand of Soana)	1073–1085
Victor III (Desiderio of Benevento)	1086–1087
Urban II (Eudes de Lagery)	1088–1099
Paschal II (Ranier of Blera)	1099–1118
Gelasius II (Giovanni Caetani)	1118–1119
Calixtus II (Guy de Bourgogne)	1119–1124
Honorius II (Lambert of Fiagnano)	1124–1130
Innocent II (Gregorio Papareschi)	1130–1143
Celestine II, (Guido of Castello)	1143–1144
Lucius II (Gerardo Caccianemici)	1144–1145
Eugenius III (Bernard of Montemagno)	1145–1153
Anastasius IV of Rome	1153–1154
Hadrian IV (Nicholas Breakspear)	1154–1159
Alexander III (Rolando Bandinelli)	1159–1181

Lucius III (Ubaldo Allocingoli)	1181–1185
Urban III (Uberto Crivelli)	1185–1187
Gregory VIII (Alberto de Morra)	1187
Clement III (Paolo Scolari)	1187–1191
Celestine III (Giacinto Bobone)	1191–1198
Innocent III (Lotario dei Conti di Segni)	1198–1216
Honorius III (Cencio Savelli)	1216–1227
Gregory IX (Ugolino dei Conti di Segni)	1227–1241
Celestine IV (Goffredo Castligioni)	1241
Innocent IV (Sinibaldo Fieschi)	1243–1254
Alexander IV (Rinaldo dei Conti di Segni)	1254–1261
Urban IV (Jacques Pantaléon)	1261–1264
Clement IV (Guy Foulques)	1265–1268
Gregory X (Tebaldo Visconti)	1272–1276
Innocent V (Pierre de Taranteise)	1276
Hadrian V (Ottobono Fieschi)	1276
John XXI (Pietro Juliani)	1276–1277
Nicholas III (Giovanni Gaetano Orsini)	1277–1280
Martin IV (Simone de Brion)	1281–1285
Honorius IV (Giacomo Savelli)	1285–1287
Nicholas IV (Girolamo Masci)	1288–1292
Celestine V (Pietro Angeleri)	1294
Boniface VIII (Benedetto Caetani)	1294–1303
Benedict XI (Niccolò Boccassini)	1303–1304
Clement V (Bertrand de Got)	1305–1314
John XXII (Jacques-Armand d'Euse)	1316–1334
Benedict XII (Jacques Fournier)	1335–1342
Clement VI (Pierre Roger)	1342–1352
Innocent VI (Etienne Aubert)	1352–1362
Urban V (Guillaume de Grimoard)	1362–1370
Gregory XI (Pierre Roger de Beaufort)	1371–1378
Urban VI (Bartolomeo Prignano)	1378–1389
Boniface IX (Pietro Tomacelli)	1389–1404
Innocent VII (Cosma Migliorati)	1404–1406
Gregory XII (Angelo Correr)	1406–1415
Martin V (Oddone Colonna)	1417–1431

Eugenius IV (Gabriele Condulmer)	1431–1447
Nicholas V (Tommaso Parentucelli)	1447–1455
Calixtus III (Alonso de Borja)	1455–1458
Pius II (Aeneas Silvius Piccolomini)	1458–1464
Paul II (Petro Barbo)	1464–1471
Sixtus IV (Francesco Della Rovere)	1471–1484
Innocent VIII (Giovanni Battista Cybo)	1484–1492
Alexander VI (Rodrigo de Borgia)	1492–1503
Pius III (Francesco Todeschini Piccolomini)	1503
Julius II (Guilano Della Rovere)	1503–1513
Leo X (Giovanni de'Medici)	1513–1521
Hadrian VI (Adriaan Florensz)	1522–1523
Clement VII (Giulio de'Medici)	1523–1534
Paul III (Alessandro Farnese)	1534–1549
Julius III (Giovanni Maria Ciocchi del Monte)	1550–1555
Marcellus II (Marcello Cervini)	1555
Paul IV (Gian Pietro Carafa)	1555–1559
Pius IV (Giovan Angelo de'Medici)	1560–1565
Pius V (Michele Ghisleri)	1566–1572
Gregory XIII (Ugo Boncompagni)	1572–1585
Sixtus V (Felice Peretti)	1585–1590
Urban VII (Giovanni Battista Castagna)	1590
Gregory XIV (Niccolò Sfondrati)	1590–1591
Innocent IX (Giovanni Antonio Facchinetti)	1591
Clement VIII (Ippolito Aldobrandini)	1592–1605
Leo XI (Alessandro de'Medici)	1605
Paul V (Camillo Borghese)	1605–1621
Gregory XV (Alessandro Ludovisi)	1621–1623
Urban VIII (Maffeo Barberini)	1623–1644
Innocent X (Giovanni Battista Pamphilj)	1644–1655
Alexander VII (Fabio Chigi)	1655–1667
Clement IX (Giulio Rospigliosi)	1667–1669
Clement X (Emilio Altieri)	1670–1676
Innocent XI (Benedetto Odescalchi)	1676–1689
Alexander VIII (Pietro Ottoboni)	1689–1691
Innocent XII (Antonio Pignatelli)	1691–1700

Clement XI (Giovanni Francesco Albani)	1700–1721
Innocent XIII (Michelangelo Conti)	1721–1724
Benedict XIII (Pier Francesco Orsini)`	1724–1730
Clement XII (Lorenzo Corsini)	1730–1740
Benedict XIV (Prospero Lambertini)	1740–1758
Clement XIII (Carlo Rezzonico)	1758–1769
Clement XIV (Gian Vincenzo Antonio Ganganelli)	1769–1774
Pius VI (Giovanni Angelo Braschi)	1775–1799
Pius VII (Barnaba Chiaramonti)	1800–1823
Leo XII (Annibale Sermattei della Genga)	1823–1829
Pius VIII (Francesco Saverio Castiglioni)	1829–1830
Gregory XVI (Bartolomeo Mauro Cappellari)	1831–1846
Pius IX (Giovanni Maria Mastai Ferretti)	1846–1878
Leo XIII (Gioacchino Pecci)	1878–1903
Pius X (Giuseppe Sarto)	1903–1914
Benedict XV (Giacomo della Chiesa)	1914–1922
Pius XI (Achille Ratti)	1922–1939
Pius XII (Eugenio Pacelli)	1939–1958
John XXIII (Angelo Giuseppe Roncalli)	1958–1963
Paul VI (Giovanni Battista Montini)	1963–1978
John Paul I (Albino Luciani)	1978
John Paul II (Karol Wojtyla)	1978–2005
Benedict XVI (Josef Ratzinger)	2005–2013
Francis (Jorge Mario Bergoglio)	2013–

Notes

(Roman numerals after the works by Durant, Ferguson and Bruun, and Runciman denote the relevant volume.)

Prologue
1. Monsignor Charles Burns to author.

Chapter 1
1. Rendina 121.
2. Durant III, 618.
3. Msgr. Burns to author.
4. Rendina 160–1.
5. Durant III, 619.
6. *City of God*, London: Penguin 1984 (tr. Henry Bettenson), 6–7.
7. Rendina 165, citing Ferdinand Gregorovius.
8. *Ibid.* 169.
9. Durant IV, 41.
10. *Ibid.*

Chapter 2
1. Norwich, J.J, *Byzantium I*, 179.
2. In Feruguson and Bruun I, 112.
3. In Durant IV, 519–20.
4. Rendina 184.
5. Gregorovius, quoted in Rendina 189.
6. Collins 109.
7. Norwich, *op. cit.* 318–20.
8. Rendina 194.
9. In Gibbon/Trevor Roper, *The Decline and Fall of the Roman Empire*, London: Phoenix 2005, p. 505.
10. *Ibid.* 488.
11. Six centuries later Dante would suggest that the Church was all along driven by greed: '*Gold and silver are the gods you adore ... Ah, Constantine, what evil marked the hour / not of your conversion but of the fee / the first rich father* [Sylvester] *took from you in dower!*' (*Inferno* XIX, 105–11).
12. Durant IV, 530.

13. Collins 119.
14. *Ibid.* 134.
15. So-called 'Constantine II' is recorded as an anti-pope, and hence not on the official roster of popes.
16. The source of this story is the *Liber Pontificalis*, a chronicle of the papacy that was regularly updated over the centuries but in the view of most authorities seriously lacks historical reliability.
17. Collins 142–4.
18. Sherrard 10.
19. Durant IV, 290; Rendina 222.
20. Rendina 223.
21. Quoted in *ibid.* 230.
22. The story first took written form with the fourteenth-century pen of Giovanni Boccaccio, to be repeated by others including Lawrence Durrell (1919–1990).
23. Rendina 233.

Chapter 3
 1. Ferguson and Bruun I, 168.
 2. Quoted in Rendina 238.
 3. Durant IV, 538.
 4. In Rendina 243; author's translation.
 5. Collins 181–2.
 6. In Rendina 242.
 7. *Ibid.* 243; author's translation.
 8. Norwich II, *op. cit.* 220.
 9. Rendina 245–6.
10. Norwich II, *op. cit.* 254.
11. The hill was subsequently called Mons Malus (Evil Hill), which mutated into Monte Mario, the name it bears today, graced by an upscale suburb. See Rendina 248.
12. Durant IV, 513; German writers, however, cast doubt on the story.
13. Collins 199.
14. Rendina 258.
15. Durant IV, 540.
16. Collins 201.
17. Durant IV, 543.
18. Nicolle EMT 36.
19. Rendina 260.
20. The mutual excommunications were lifted in 1965.
21. Named after Simon Magus who tried to buy the gift of the Holy Spirit from the Apostle Peter (Acts 8:18–24).
22. The origin of the name is obscure. At the time it was believed to derive from *Hellbrand*, or pure flame. See Durant IV, 545.

23. *Ibid.*
24. *Ibid.* 547–8.
25. Quoted in Rendina 263; author's translation.
26. Quoted in Durant IV, 549–50.

Chapter 4
1. Quoted in Durant IV, 586.
2. *Ibid.* 585; the term crusade derives from the Spanish *cruzada*, meaning marked with the cross.
3. The phrase is Durant's, IV, 588.
4. Runciman I, 112.
5. *Ibid.* 115.
6. For a fuller account, see Carr, *op. cit.*
7. Durant IV, 760; Anacletus was probably the origin of the fourteenth-century legend of 'Andreas, the Jewish pope'.
8. Rendina 276–7.
9. Durant IV, 594–5.
10. Collins 230.
11. Gregorovius, cited in Rendina 280–2.
12. Runciman III, 108.
13. Ferguson and Bruun I, 193.
14. Durant IV, 761.
15. Quoted in *ibid.* 762.
16. *Ibid.* 603.
17. Niketas Choniates, cited in Runciman III, 123.
18. *Ibid.* 130.
19. *Ibid.* 137.
20. *Ibid.* 146.
21. *Ibid.* 160.
22. *Ibid.* 170.
23. *Ibid.* 175.
24. Durant IV, 607.
25. Runciman III, 190.
26. *Ibid.* 191–2.

Chapter 5
1. Durant IV, 725.
2. Norwich III, *op. cit.* 225.
3. *Ibid.* 339.
4. *Ibid.* 340.
5. Durant IV, 726.
6. Runciman III, 421.

7. The abdication has entered Church lore as 'the Great Refusal' (*il Gran Rifiuto*). Dante consigned Celestine to a tortured afterlife in the *Inferno*, as having grievously sinned in declining an office that God had offered him.
8. Durant IV, 811.
9. *Ibid.* 753.
10. In Rendina 299; Collins 77–97.
11. Durant IV, 815.
12. Ferguson and Bruun I, 303.
13. Durant V, 51.
14. Rendina 307.
15. Gregorovius, quoted in *ibid.* 308.
16. Durant V, 363.
17. See the concise account in Nicolle, IMA, 3.
18. *Ibid.* 7.
19. *Ibid.* 8.
20. *Ibid.* 13.

Chapter 6

1. Collins 311–12.
2. In Rendina 327; author's (loose) translation.
3. Hollingsworth 35.
4. In Durant V, 390.
5. In Hollingsworth 60.
6. See Carr 120–6.
7. In Hollingsworth 97.
8. Collins 332.
9. Durant V, 395–402.
10. *Ibid.* 407.
11. Machiavelli 89.
12. *Ibid.* 69.
13. This account is based on Nicolle, IMA, 31–3.
14. Hollingsworth 168–9.
15. Durant V, 413.
16. *Ibid.* 414.
17. *Ibid.* 424.
18. *Ibid.* 427; Hollingsworth 228–9.
19. Durant V, 433.
20. William Roscoe, *Life and Pontificate of Leo X* (1853), quoted in *ibid.* 435.
21. The priest was found murdered in Ferrara two years later; Hollingsworth 275.
22. Durant V, 444.
23. *Ibid.* 447.
24. In Collins 341–2.
25. Durant V, 447.

Chapter 7

1. Durant V, 481.
2. In Rendina 348.
3. Durant V, 623.
4. *Ibid.* 624.
5. *Ibid.* 628.
6. *Ibid.* 629–30.
7. *Ibid.*
8. *Ibid.* 632.
9. Collins 345.
10. Rendina 355.
11. Durant VI, 906.
12. In *The Outline of History* (London: Cassell 1951) Wells curiously likens the Society to Britain's Salvation Army.
13. Ferguson and Bruun I, 403.
14. Collins 356; Rendina 359.
15. Durant VI, 922.
16. Rendina 359.
17. For a fuller account of the siege of Malta, see Carr 146–52.
18. Henry Sire, a Hospitaller Knight, in *ibid.* 152.

Chapter 8

1. Capponi 8.
2. *Ibid.* 104.
3. *Ibid.* 130.
4. Durant VII, 284.
5. Capponi 179–88.
6. Koutsolaris has long since been silted up and is now part of the mainland; it and a few other islets are usually referred to as the Curzolaris. See Capponi 253–4.
7. *Ibid.*
8. *Ibid.* 266.
9. Quoted in *bid.* 273.
10. Figures by Capponi 288–9.
11. Quoted in Durant VII, 523.
12. Montgomery of Alamein, *A History of Warfare* (London: Collins) 1968, 260.
13. Capponi 5; the experience was later cited as evidence for Pius' canonization.
14. Durant VII, 524.
15. Capponi 306.
16. For more on the Navy of the Religion, see Carr 160–9 and Sire 74–92.

Chapter 9

1. Durant VII, 238.
2. *Ibid.* 240.

3. Rendina 374.

4. Collins 372.

5. Durant VII, 245.

6. *Ibid.* 380.

7. Henry Kissinger, *Diplomacy* (London: Simon & Schuster) 1994, 58.

8. Durant VII, 557.

9. In *ibid.* 563.

10. The quote is from Ferguson and Bruun I, 447.

11. *'Quod non fecerunt barbari, fecerunt Barberini'*; Rendina 338.

12. Collins 381.

13. Rendina 394–5; Collins 376.

14. Collins 389.

15. Rendina 402.

16. Cited in Durant VIII, 49.

17. Collins 398–401.

18. Rendina 414–16.

19. In *ibid.* 420.

20. Collins 409.

21. In *ibid.* 411.

22. Rendina 428; Collins 413.

23. Collins 413.

24. Quoted in Durant X, 359.

25. Collins 417.

Chapter 10

1. In Rendina 438; author's translation.

2. Carr 170–80.

3. In Rendina 444.

4. *Ibid.* 447.

5. In *ibid.* 448; author's translation.

6. Collins 425.

7. Rendina 453.

8. Collins 426.

9. Rendina 452.

10. Diego Angeli, quoted in *ibid.* 454.

11. *Ibid.* 461.

12. Davide Silvagni, quoted in *ibid.* 465–6.

13. *Ibid.* 466.

14. In *ibid.*; author's translation.

15. *Ibid.* 476.

16. *Ibid.* 477.

17. Collins 435–6.

Chapter 11

1. Machiavelli 125–7.
2. Rendina 488.
3. Collier 39–40.
4. Rendina 492–7.
5. *Ibid.* 496–502.
6. In Collins 439.
7. Rendina 508.
8. Caruso 9–10.
9. Taylor xxii.
10. Caruso 45–6.
11. *Ibid.* 50–1; most of this chapter and the next draws heavily on Caruso's work.
12. *Ibid.* 75.
13. La Moricière returned to France and died at Amiens in 1865.

Chapter 12

1. In Rendina 514.
2. The story, long denied in America, was revived in 2000 when scholars going through a Turin archive found a postcard written by Garibaldi confirming the president's offer. Caruso 95; *The Guardian*, 8 February 2000.
3. Collier 80–1.
4. The term Zouave derives from the Arabic *zwawa*, the name of a flamboyantly-attired Algerian unit in the French army.
5. Caruso 120–1.
6. *Ibid.* 140–2.
7. Taylor 187.
8. Collins 444.
9. Rendina 520; Caruso 244; author's translation.
10. Rendina 521.
11. *Ibid.*

Chapter 13

1. Caruso 289–90.
2. Rendina 525–6.
3. Collins 449.
4. *Ibid.* 446; Rendina 559.
5. Collins 454–6.
6. *Ibid.* 464.
7. *Ibid.* 456.
8. *Ibid.* 464.
9. Rendina 563.
10. Collins 465.
11. Taylor 564–5.

12. The term irredentism derives from the phrase *Italia irredenta*, or 'unredeemed Italy,' which were the Italian-speaking districts in Austria, Switzerland and Slovenia.
13. Taylor 564–5.
14. Collins 465.
15. *Ibid.* 467–8.
16. Mack Smith 15.
17. *Ibid.* 44.
18. Rendina 594.
19. Mack Smith 159.
20. *Ibid.* 162.
21. Collins 468.
22. *Ibid.* 472.
23. Mack Smith 222.
24. Rendina 610.
25. Collins 475–6.
26. *Ibid.*
27. *Ibid.* 477.
28. Rendina 624; the uncommon surname is actually the Italian spelling of the Greek liturgical phrase *kyrie eleison*, or 'Lord have mercy.'
29. Quoted in Adam Ulam, *Expansion and Coexistence* (New York: Praeger) 1968, 377*n*.
30. See John Carr, 'St. John's Air Force' in *Aeroplane*, May 2018.
31. In Rendina 637; author's translation.
32. Collins 485–6.
33. *Ibid.* 493.
34. *Ibid.*
35. Personal communication from the newspaper's correspondent in Rome to the author.
36. *Daily Mail*, 11 November 2017.
37. Address to the Vatican diplomatic corps in the Regia Hall, 8 January 2018.
38. Lawrence A. Franklin, the Gatehouse Institute, 27 June 2016 (www.gatehouseinstitute.org).
39. Letter No. 4 from the Journal of Robert Moynihan, 25 January 2017 (www.insidethevatican.com).
40. Cited in *Ibid.*
41. Knights of St John to the author, November 2017.

Bibliography

It has been said that in order to objectively understand European history, one needs to turn to American historians (and vice versa). In order to fill out the general historical background to the story of the popes, their wars and their diplomacy, I thus have had recourse to two major American works on European history that are at least half a century old but in my view remain among the best in the field. They are Will Durant's multi-volume *Story of Civilization*, on which I have drawn heavily for the penetrating insights and vignettes that I hope have enlivened my narrative. and the two-volume *A Survey of European Civilization* by Wallace K. Ferguson and Geoffrey Bruun (Third Edition, Boston: Houghton Mifflin 1964). The *Survey* by now may be hard to find, but the search would be well worth the effort. The quality of writing in both is first-class. Durant brings a wryly philosophical flavour to his history, while the calmly objective and understanding approach of Ferguson and Bruun – aided perhaps by the transatlantic distance between them and their subject – have helped me put papal history into proper perspective. The other sources I have used are:

Atiya, S. *The Crusade of Nicopolis* (London: Methuen) 1934.

Capponi, N. *Victory of the West* (London: Macmillan) 2006.

Carr, J. *The Knights Hospitaller: A Military History of the Knights of St John* (Barnsley: Pen & Sword) 2016.

Caruso, S. *Con l'Italia Mai!* (Milan: Longanesi) 2015.

Collier, M. *Italian Unification 1820–71* (Oxford: Heinemann) 2003.

Collins, R. *Keepers of the Keys of Heaven: A History of the Papacy* (London: Phoenix) 2009.

Dante, *The Paradiso* (tr. M. Musa) (London: Penguin) 1986.

Esposito, G. *Armies of the Italian War of Reunification* (Oxford: Osprey) 2017.

Eusebius of Caesaria, *Life of Constantine* (tr. A. Cameron & S.G Hall) (Oxford: Clarendon Press) 1999.

Hollingsworth, M. *The Borgias* (London: Quercus) 2011.

Machiavelli *The Prince* (tr. L. Ricci and E.R.P. Vincent) (New York: New American Library) 1952.

Mack Smith, D. *Mussolini: A Biography* (New York: Vintage) 1983.

Nicolle, D. *European Medieval Tactics (1)* (Oxford: Osprey) 2011.

Nicolle, D. *Italian Medieval Armies 1300–1500* (Oxford: Osprey) 1983.

Rendina, C. *Storia Insolita di Roma* (Rome: Newton & Compton) 2001.

Runciman, S. *The Crusades* (3 vols.) (London: Penguin) 1991.

Sherrard, P. *Church, Papacy and Schism* (Limni, Evia: Denise Harvey) 1996.

Stephenson, P. *Constantine: Roman Emperor, Christian Victor* (New York: Overlook Press) 2009.

Taylor, A.J.P. *The Struggle for Mastery in Europe* (London: OUP) 1954.

Trevelyan, G. *Garibaldi and the Thousand* (London: Thos. Nelson & Sons) 1921.

Index